THE AUTHOR

Dr Charles Doyle is a director of global marketing with Accenture. With 20 years of experience with major international companies throughout the world, Dr Doyle has specialized in strategic marketing and international business development for a range of high technology and professional service firms. Dr Doyle has also held marketing positions with British Telecom, where he developed marketing strategies and programmes as part of BT's overall global market expansion strategy. Before British Telecom, he was European Director of Marketing for Fujitsu. Earlier in his career, he held the post of corporate business strategist at the UK Atomic Energy Authority, helping to reposition the nuclear research resources of the UK following the privatization of the UK electricity supply industry. A former university lecturer, he holds the degree of D.Phil. from Oxford University and an MA from the University of Glasgow. He is an author of several publications for think tanks and business journals and is a regular conference speaker.

Marketing

DICTIONARY

HarperCollins *Publishers*

HarperCollins*Publishers*
Westerhill Road, Glasgow G64 2QT

The HarperCollins website is www.collins.co.uk

First published 2003

© Charles Doyle 2003

Reprint 10 9 8 7 6 5 4 3 2 1 0

ISBN 0 00 713136 4

A catalogue record for this book is available from the British Library.

Typeset by Davidson Pre-Press Graphics Ltd, Glasgow

Printed and bound in Great Britain by Clays Ltd, St Ives plc.

For Katherine, Alexander and Caroline.

INTRODUCTION

Marketing is a constantly developing professional discipline, which grew in influence throughout the 20th century. It has become pervasive in business and society. It is ubiquitous in our everyday lives. All indications are that marketing will have an even more powerful effect on many aspects of our lives in the 21st century.

Although there is evidence of advertising in the very earliest societies, in its modern form, as a professional business discipline, marketing is around 100 years old. The first known academic courses in marketing were taught in the American midwest at the beginning of the 20th century. Now, at the start of the 21st century, marketing is taught as part of the core curriculum in business courses all over the world. All major businesses practise marketing. Marketing has expanded exponentially, and is no longer confined solely to the business world. Today it is a vital element in the work of charities, hospitals, the arts, the armed services, public services, social and environmental causes, countries, cities, regions, political parties, sports teams, and individuals, such as actors, entertainers and top sportspeople. Even secretive organizations have succumbed to marketing: for example, the CIA, the FBI, the British monarchy and the Vatican all have their own promotional websites. They feel it necessary to explain themselves, and what they stand for, to the public, their followers and their supporters.

The universe of marketing

There are many sophisticated definitions and complex models of marketing. Fundamentally, however, the practice of marketing still goes to the heart of that most perennial form of human interactions: that people make and exchange resources, goods and services that are needed or desired, and that they will want to obtain these goods and services at the right time, place and price, and by means of a convenient method of purchase.

Worldwide spending on marketing activities in 2001 reached around 1 trillion dollars. The universe in which marketing has grown has become one of abundant information and proliferating media channels. In our time, marketing is compulsory. Companies and organizations no longer have any choice, because in order to thrive (and in some cases, to survive) organizations and individuals simply must be proficient and accomplished in the practice of marketing. Robert Louis Stevenson's famous phrase that 'everybody lives by selling something' could now, with some justice, equally be applied to marketing.

Marketing remains most powerful in consumer goods industries within the advanced economies. However, it has also grown in power in industrial and in services markets. Industrial companies tend to focus on product marketing, expressing their identity through their products and related services. Services companies focus on image, reputation building and direct customer relationships, expressing themselves through the expertise of their people. Countries and cultures have individually different approaches to marketing. The USA, where modern marketing techniques were pioneered, has the most sophisticated approach to marketing. There, marketing is treated as a profession; it enjoys much higher esteem and is better understood as a central factor in economic development than in other countries. The UK has capability in media, communications, consumer goods and creative advertising, but has always been weak in industrial product marketing and in commercial exploitation of its innovations. Germany, with its strong engineering roots, has majored on product marketing, but is weaker in services marketing, creative advertising and in its general marketing culture. Japan is skilled in advertising, market research and product marketing, but does not accord any distinction to marketing as a profession. Eastern Europe, Russia and China, always strong on the uses of state-controlled propaganda within their own countries, are now coming to appreciate the necessity of marketing as they start to compete in the global economy. All countries, of whatever size, or stage of development, have come to realize the power of the Internet as a marketing tool.

Marketing under fire

Power attracts criticism and breeds suspicion. The practice of marketing has become controversial. At the time of compiling this first edition of the *Collins Dictionary of Marketing*, marketing stands accused of having become too powerful, too pervasive and too insidious. Marketing is criticized more than it is praised: whether for its role in the creation of global brands that invade many aspects of public and mental space, or for the intensive hyping that creates artificial economic booms. Marketers are often blamed for being, in fact, successful. Marketers are trained to listen, analyse and act upon what they hear from the marketplace and from customers, rather than tell the market what they actually think that customers want. For a range of reasons, this has often given marketing a somewhat sinister reputation, suspected of everything from the brainwashing of consumers to the subversion of the democratic process. Frequently, supporters of political parties or campaigns complain that the competing party, campaign or cause has won because of expensive or well-orchestrated marketing. Political parties and governments can help to win elections, and to propagate messages about their policies and actions, by employing superior marketing techniques. This has led to accusations that marketing has fuelled an art of public relations deception (often called 'spinning'). The net effect of spinning has been to diminish the public's trust in public institutions and politicians and often corporations.

Public space and culture is perceived as being invaded and colonized by marketing sponsorships and brands. Every major sporting event and sportsman is a major advertising platform. Places like Times Square in New York assault the senses with marketing messages and billboards. Advertising and branding have been quick to invade the World Wide Web. The few remaining public service broadcasting channels are always under constant pressure to become more commercial and to use advertising as a revenue source.

In private life, parents tend not to celebrate the creation of global brands, but they do feel the consequences of the persuasive power of those brands through the demands of their children for branded goods. Parents feel that marketers manipulate the young. Fashionable clothes have become wearable billboards for youth-centred brands. For the individual consumer, marketing is held responsible for junk mail, intrusive telemarketing and aggressive selling of certain products and services to the detriment of consumers and private investors.

Marketing in the new millennium

Despite the criticism, marketing is essentially a discipline that studies and looks to exploit changes. These can range from changes in consumer taste to changes in demographics, society, technology, business structure and income distribution. As the world changes, so must marketing. Although an agent of change in business and society, marketing itself, as a professional discipline, has been much slower to change its range of approaches and techniques. In the past decade, there have been dramatic changes. Marketing is adapting and developing new thinking for a new age and new market forces.

Since the end of World War II, two major trends have been affecting the practice of marketing: customer power and self-service. Customers are smarter, better informed, better protected and have a much greater range of choices. Greater choice and information have increased customer sophistication and buying power. This new power often manifests itself in customers being able to negotiate better deals across a vast range of producers. The ways in which customers want to buy goods and services are also changing. Self-service, where companies enable customers to do things for themselves in the name of greater convenience, has been a powerful factor in the rise of consumer empowerment, particularly in services. We now pour our own petrol, become our own bank teller, pick and pack our own groceries, arrange our own holidays, review books, publish ourselves, analyse markets, buy and sell our own investments directly, and electronically deliver our own mail – activities that previously required a skilled assistant.

The consequence of these changes is that many of the 'classic' functions of marketing – such as mass advertising – are under scrutiny, and their effectiveness is questioned. In the industrial past, the mass market was served by a few mass media that could grab general attention and create demand for mass-produced products. The mass market was characterized by a common culture, a single geographical location and served by few but familiar types of media. No longer. The apparent decline in effectiveness of many of the classic marketing techniques is partly attributable to the changes in the market and to the vast range of media now available. Multi-media outlets and channels are proliferating. There simply is no one medium that can any longer reach a mass audience on a continuous basis in the way that the press, radio or public broadcaster could have done in the past. For example, in addition to mass media that boomed in the 20th century (such as radio, cinema, telephone, video, satellite and cable television, billboards, the popular printed press and magazines) there is now the Internet, multi-media, interactive television, and personal mobile communications devices with imaging capability. Moreover, digitalization of content enables marketers to use media channels in different ways. Digital content can be distributed faster and wider than its physical counterpart. It can also be updated more rapidly and can be replicated endlessly. Not only are media and content proliferating, markets are simultaneously fragmenting and globalizing. This fragmentation of markets into smaller and smaller segments, but with wider and wider geographical reach, has caused the inexorable decline of what used to be known as the mass audience, or mass market.

The fundamentals of 'classic' marketing in the 20th century – that it served the producer interest and that marketers could, through various 'mixes', control the market – are now of questionable validity. In the early 21st century we have entered a time when marketing has moved from the 'production' or 'sales' era to that of the 'customer' era. Customers can no longer be *talked at*, or sold to, or be told what is good for them, which was the essential marketing characteristic of the heroic industrial production era.

Today, it is the retailers and the customers, and not the producers, who control the market. Consequentially, the old ways of classifying and segmenting the market into producers and buyers are now strained and inadequate to the task of focusing and allocating market resources to a cornucopia of fragmented niches and customer groupings. Philip Kotler, one of the leading thinkers in marketing since the 1960s, summed up very succinctly the two most important changes in marketing in the last 30 years. 'First, marketers have moved from thinking their job is to sell whatever the company makes to thinking that their job is to influence what the company makes. Second, marketers now have tools to focus their efforts on reaching and satisfying niches and individuals'.

Marketing is now the religion that instructs on how to worship at the altar of the glorified customer. It has helped to extend the concept of customer service beyond the simply commercial; now governments talks of citizens as customers, hospitals call patients customers, employees call each other customers of internal services. All enterprises and organizations are expected to adopt a *marketing orientation* in order to understand, then to serve, customers more efficiently, effectively, and even, in some cases, to delight them. What is this much sought-after marketing orientation? In simplest terms, it means that companies now have to develop a much deeper *insight* into their customers' wants, needs and desires and seek to deliver satisfaction beyond their expectations in effective ways. Insight is more than analysing market data or conducting individual and group customer research. It is a deep desire to serve, and willingness to listen to, the marketplace, then, to enable customers to define the products and services that they want and need, and then to let them determine how they wish to interact with the company. The customer is at the centre of everything the company does and makes.

The Marketing Paradox

Aside from the contemporary polemics and the gradual changes of approach, marketing's longer-term problem has always been its perceived lack of financial accountability. These are the hard results that accountants and chief financial officers can understand. Marketing, with its vague emotional appeal, its intangible benefits, and even its artistic elements, is still viewed as more of an art than a science. Yet, the ethos of our times demands tangible numerical measurement for everything. The standard measures for a set of marketing programmes – customer awareness and satisfaction, product and sales growth, and market share increases – are not the most important to the Chief Executive and his chief financial officer. They tend to be squarely focused on profit and loss, shareholder value, market capitalization, share price and share dividend, return on assets and return on investment. This makes marketing a continuous battleground for both belief systems and for everyday investment allocation.

For, as long as it remains difficult for marketers to quantify their results in terms that the CFO can understand, they will face an uphill struggle to gain investment for marketing programmes. This problem, perceived or real, has not yet been solved. No-one is quite sure if marketing is a necessary operating expense (or, worse, an overhead expense) or a strategic investment. Marketers, particularly of intangible services, are everywhere compelled to produce detailed measurements of their added value. There are some models that claim to be able to quantify accurately brand value and equity, but these are not yet *accountable* in the classic sense of the word as defined by accounting standards bodies and accepted worldwide.

Consequently, the value and the professional status of the marketer continue to be a paradox. The discrepancy between the manifest power of marketing in practice, and the relative powerlessness of marketers within companies and organizations, is everywhere observable and, for practising marketers, a constant frustration. Marketing does not have the status of a profession, in the absence of standardized professional qualifications that distinguish law, medicine and accountancy as professions. In most companies, marketing is not a board-level function, such as finance. It would seem that, despite the success of the practice of marketing, marketers have forgotten to market themselves and their role within their own spheres of influence. Perhaps all professions undergo a 100-year period of scepticism from their inauguration before they are fully established and accepted? Nevertheless, I confidently predict that marketing will be a full profession within the next 30 years, with established professional qualifications and perceived status. It is a good time for students to be thinking of marketing as a profession.

I have tried, in compiling this *Collins Dictionary of Marketing*, to reflect the crossroads that marketing has reached, and the tensions within it, as well as its substantial achievements, influence and possibilities. I have given much space to the new techniques of marketing in the Internet, information rich age, without neglecting the tried and tested techniques, models and assumptions of classic marketing which have served many generations well. I have also adopted a wide view of marketing as an all-encompassing business discipline. By this I mean a multi-dimensional function which involves, and has impact upon, every part of the modern enterprise. I have not confined marketing to the activities of a single function discipline or department. As the management guru Peter Drucker said, 'Marketing is so basic that it can't be considered as a separate function on a par with others such as manufacturing or personnel. It is a central dimension of the business. It is the whole business seen from the customer's point of view'.

I have also taken a practitioner's viewpoint in compiling this dictionary, rather than the academic's. Much of the academic theory of marketing is based upon what academics think that professional marketers ought to do, rather than what they really do each day. Readers will not find many theoretical marketing models in this dictionary. I have rarely seen complex marketing models and theories used purposefully in operational practice for the 20 years that I have been a marketing practitioner, with several international companies. However, I have had many opportunities to observe the interplay between marketing theory and marketing reality. Both have value, but are better working in combination than studied as separate disciplines. I have tried to do justice to both the practical and to the conceptual aspects of marketing when working in combination. I have used many case studies to illustrate theory turned into reality and the resulting consequences. I have also been struck by how often marketing touches so many other disciplines – economics, finance, sociology, psychology, statistics, and the creative arts. It is not possible to develop each of these areas in the depth that they deserve. I have, therefore, defined all related areas which have influence and bearing on the subject and context of marketing, rather than as absolute definitions in their own right.

The format of the dictionary is by subject-based alphabetical entries, with the exception of major subjects in the field of marketing. These major subject categories have been highlighted and the various subentries have been grouped under these major subjects, allowing a more in-depth analysis with practical guidance on how they might be used. These mini essays on the subject, supported by related entries, will enable the reader to take a thematic as well as an alphabetical approach to the subject matter. As with markets, some segments merit more attention than others.

Charles Doyle

ACKNOWLEDGEMENTS

I am grateful to Edwin Moore of HarperCollins for having presented me with the opportunity to work on this dictionary and for his support and advice throughout, and to Mike Munro for his editing skills. I have drawn on my experience working in various marketing roles in my years with Fujitsu, British Telecom and, currently, Accenture, and continue to learn from and be inspired by the people with whom I have worked in the past, and work with today, in these companies. Much of what I have learned 'the hard way' during my time in these companies has been reflected in this dictionary.

My special thanks go to Julia Wu of Accenture, who provided additional research for some parts of this dictionary, to Chris Goodman of Young and Rubican who commented from a practitioner's perspective on the sections on advertising, and to Joy Palmer, for her insights on the effects of public relations on society.

This book is dedicated to my wife Katherine and to my children, Alexander and Caroline, who have all been very curious and enquiring as I worked on this dictionary. Caroline, my ten-year-old daughter, in particular, constantly asks me 'what is marketing? What is it... you actually do?' so that she might better explain to her friends at school what her father's somewhat vague job really is. My struggle to answer her questions, in a clear and comprehensible way, was a major motivation, and constant test, in compiling this dictionary for HarperCollins.

Charles Doyle

A

above-the-line refers to marketing activities for which an agency is paid a commission, as opposed to those for which no agency commission is paid (BELOW-THE-LINE). Originally a financial term, it has now come to mean highly visible 'mass' advertising, for example, a campaign that is targeted at everyone in certain countries simultaneously in print and broadcast media.

This type of promotional activity tends to be more expensive and less targeted than below-the-line activities. Recent trends and new techniques in marketing have tended to question the impact and measurable value of above-the-line advertising on target audiences. Over the past decade it has declined relative to below-the-line promotions, with a greater percentage of spending annually dedicated to below-the-line. See also BELOW THE LINE ADVERTISING.

acceptance a positive act by a person accepting an offer so as to bring a contract into effect. It can also mean the acceptance of a new idea or concept that was not previously understood or known about. Acceptance is the stage beyond attention and awareness. Market acceptance, which is a high volume of sales to a defined market place on a consistent and recurring basis, is the desired outcome of much marketing and sales activity. The opposite of market acceptance is market rejection. See also ADOPTION.

account in marketing, advertising, and sales, an existing client and their associated revenues and profits. Can also be known as **client account**.

account activity discussions of accounts won and lost, and re-assignments of existing accounts among the representatives of a marketing agency.

account director a senior person in an advertising or marketing services agency, usually focused on a single or small group of clients. The Account Director's main role is to ensure client satisfaction and to ensure the maximum amount of billings from the client with the agency. The Account Director is normally the main point of contact between the agency and the client. See also ADVERTISING.

account management the individuals involved in, as well as the processes and techniques of, managing clients, advising on, and developing their creative briefs, as well as the execution of campaigns on their behalf. See also ADVERTISING.

account planning the process of market and client research, development of a strategy that is specific to the client's needs, and the programmes and creative briefs that address them. The function was developed in UK agencies in the 1960s but is now also used widely in the US. The Account Planning process uses research from potential consumers in the marketplace to inform advertising and message development. The account planner acts as the 'conscience' of the market, and brings to bear the mindset of the end consumer and target audience to the development of advertising messages prior to testing with the actual clients themselves. See also ADVERTISING.

account review the process of evaluating and selecting an advertising agency or selecting a new agency. This process usually culminates in a pitch to the potential client from the pre-selected, short-listed agencies. These can be among the most stressful preparations in advertising activity.

ACORN a classifications system (also known as a geodemographic system) based upon the segmentation of consumers in various types of residential neighbourhoods. It was first developed in the 1970s by CACI using data from the census. Its primary purpose is for direct marketing. See also GEODEMOGRAPHICS, DIRECT MARKETING (under MARKETING SPECIALIZATIONS).

ADOPTION

Adoption refers to the processes through which an individual passes, from first hearing about an innovation to final adoption, via the intermediate psychological stages of awareness and interest, to the final stages of evaluation and trial. The usual purpose of the adoption model is to determine the process for buying either a new or previously unknown product or service. The rate and speed of adoption varies from product to product and depends upon the different types of consumer. These consumers are divided into the categories described below which indicate the extent to which people are prepared to innovate and try out new products. See also BUYER AND BUYING BEHAVIOUR, HIERARCHY OF EFFECTS, AIDA.

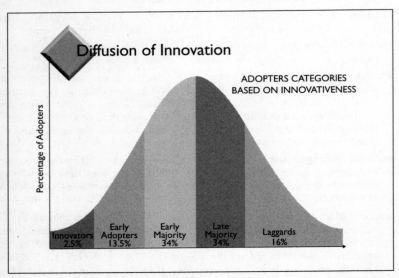

The Adoption Curve (For Innovation)
E. M. Rogers (1962)

The adoption curve for innovation, developed by Everett M. Rogers in 1962, provides a stage-by-stage analysis to show how new products and services spread through markets. The original diffusion research was done as early as 1903 by the French sociologist Gabriel Tarde who plotted the original S-shaped diffusion curve. In Tarde's model some innovations diffuse rapidly, creating a steep S-curve; other innovations have a slower rate of adoption, creating a more gradual slope of the S-curve. As Tarde says in *The Laws of Imitation*, 'A slow advance in the beginning, followed by rapid and uniformly accelerated progress, followed again by progress that continues to slacken until it finally stops: These are the three ages of ... invention ... if taken as a guide by the statistician and by the sociologists, (they) would save many illusions'. These observations are as valid today as they were 100 years ago.

In the 1940s, the sociologists Bryce Ryan and Neal Gross published their 'seminal' study of the 'diffusion of hybrid seed among Iowa farmers' renewing interest in the diffusion of innovation S-curve. This now infamous hybrid-corn study resulted in a renewed wave of research. The rate of adoption curve was similar to the S-shaped diffusion curve graphed by Tarde forty years earlier. As the technological advances of the late 19th and early 20th centuries became commercial realities in the everyday lives of consumers, the rate at which technology turned into marketable goods was a compelling subject. The rate of adoption, or diffusion rate, has become an important area of research to sociologists, and more specifically, to advertisers and marketers of new products.

In his book *Diffusion of Innovations* (1983) Everett Rogers defines diffusion as the process by which an innovation is communicated through certain channels over time among the members of a social system.

The stages through which a technological innovation passes are:

- **Knowledge** (including exposure to the existence of the innovation, leading to an understanding of its functionality and uses);
- **Persuasion** (involving the formation of a favourable attitude towards the innovation by potential consumers);
- **Decision** (where the consumer becomes committed to its adoption);
- **Implementation** (where the consumer puts the innovation to use and starts to feel its effects in their everyday lives);
- **Confirmation** (the reinforcement of the decision to have purchased the innovation based on the positive outcomes from it).

Early adopters are generally are more highly educated, have higher social status, are more open to both mass media and interpersonal channels of communication, and have more contact with change agents. Mass media channels are relatively more important at the knowledge stage, whereas interpersonal channels are relatively more important at the persuasion stage.

Innovation decisions may be optional (where the person or organization has a real opportunity to adopt or reject the idea), collective (where a decision is reached by consensus among the members of a system), or authority-based (where a decision is imposed by another person or organization possessing requisite power, status or technical expertise).

Important characteristics of an innovation include:

- **Relative advantage** (the degree to which it is perceived to be better than what it supersedes or replaces; for example, the telephone was perceived to be an improvement both on the postal system and the telegraph);
- **Compatibility** (meaning a consistency with existing values, past experiences and needs);
- **Complexity** (difficulty of understanding and use, which is one of the major inhibitors to early uptake);
- **Trial** (the degree to which the innovation can be experimented with, or tried and tested, on a limited basis and for a defined time period);
- **Observability** (the visibility and tangibility of its results. All innovations thrive and become adopted by a critical mass of consumers when they can be shown, whatever their complexity, to have practical and useful purposes. An example is the PC, which became a mass product only when it had practical uses such as word processing, spreadsheets, design, databases and entertainment).

The different adopter categories are identified as:

- **Innovators** (who are bold, risk-taking and venturesome);
- **Early adopters** (who are socially respectable);
- **Early majority** (who are cautious and deliberate);
- **Late majority** (who are sceptical and difficult to convince);
- **Laggards** (who are traditional).

See detailed descriptions below.

The adoption of innovation process is characterized by important **roles** that include:

- **Opinion leaders** (who have relatively frequent informal influence over the behaviour of others);
- **Change agents** (who positively influence innovation decisions, by mediating between the change agency and the relevant social system);
- **Change aides** (who complement the change agent, by having more intensive contact with clients, and who have less competence credibility but more safety or trustworthiness credibility).

The **change agent's roles are**:

- to develop a need for change on the part of the client;
- to establish an information-exchange relationship;
- to diagnose the client problems;
- to create intent to change in the client's culture;
- to translate this intent into action;
- to stabilize adoption and prevent discontinuity; and
- to shift the client from reliance on the change agent to self-reliance, and to adopt the innovation themselves.

Rogers' definition contains four crucial elements that are present in the diffusion of innovation process. The four main elements are:

1. Innovation – an idea, practice, technique, method or object that is perceived as new by an individual or other group.

2. Communication channels, or the means by which messages get transmitted from one individual to another about the innovation and its benefits.

3. Time, of which the major parts are (a) the Innovation-decision process itself (b) the relative time with which an innovation is adopted by an individual or group in a market or society and (c) the innovation's rate of adoption in the marketplace.

4. Social system – which is an important set of interrelated groups that are engaged in joint problem solving to accomplish a common goal.

Also, Rogers categorized the type of people who constitute the various segments of the market who make up the overall curve: although additional names and titles for the adopters of an innovation have been used in other research studies, Rogers' original labels for the five adopter categories are now standard for the industry.

Why is the Adoption Process of any relevance to marketers and advertisers? A primary purpose of marketing and advertising is to increase sales. It is through analysing and understanding the adoption process that marketers and advertisers are able to develop fully integrated marketing and communication plans against each stage of the adoption process to ensure an appropriate return on the original product investment. Moreover, the specific characteristics that Rogers identifies for each adopter category is of significance to advertisers and marketers interested in creating an integrated marketing plan targeting a specific audience at defined stages in the process.

Innovators are active early in the adoption process and tend to be a small (typically less than 5% of the market) risk-taking group. They are characterized by their zeal for new ideas and new products. They tend to have higher disposable incomes. They are anxious to be in the lead and to avoid being followers. Therefore, they tend to gain their information from expert sources rather than from peers and social group.

Rogers identifies the following characteristics dominant in the innovator type:

1. venturesomeness, desire for the rash, the daring, and the risky;

2. control of substantial financial resources to absorb possible loss from an unprofitable innovation;

3. ability to understand and apply complex technical knowledge;

4. ability to cope with a high degree of uncertainty about an innovation.

Early adopters buy the product or service early in its lifecycle. They represent a slightly larger part of the market (typically around 12–15%). Not as zealous for newness as the Innovators, they will seek information and approval from their peers and group. Earlier adopting individuals tend not to be different in age, but to have more years of education, higher social status and upward social mobility, or are working in larger organizations, have greater empathy, less dogmatism, and a greater ability to deal with abstractions than the later majority adopters. They have greater rationality, intelligence, ability to cope with uncertainty and risk, higher aspirations, more contact with other people, greater exposure to both mass media and interpersonal communications channels and engage in more active information seeking. The Early adopters are likely to be more socially integrated and conscious than the Innovators: they are also likely to be able to influence larger groups. However, taken together, the Innovators and Early adopters are the minority when it comes to the marketing stakes – a starter gunner in the race that leads to the mass market. They are often regarded as crucial to the launch of the new product or service, because of their ability to influence the next, and potentially much larger, segment of the market, which is known as the Early and Late majority.

The **Early majority** is one of the larger segments of the market (typically 30–35%). They are characterized by their cautious and thoughtful approach to new products and services. They will tend to analyse the product or service by collecting more information and making comparative evaluation of existing, competing or alternative brands than will the Early adopters. The Early majority have frequent interactions with their social peers, which helps in the communications process. Although they seldom lead opinions, they do tend to influence others in moving towards a decision. Reaching this segment of the market will take longer; the process of adoption is slower. However, this is a critical part of the market as they perform two vital roles: they vastly increase the take-up of the product or service (that is usually marked by a price reduction) and they also form a bridge between the early and later adopters.

Late majority (typically 35–40%) tend to adopt only after their Early majority peer group has already done so. The reasons for this range from economic (they were waiting for the price to come down) to scepticism (they remained unconvinced about the benefits for a longer period of time than the other groups) to lack of confidence and caution (they tend to conform to peer and group pressure in decision making). Typically, this group is older with lower disposable income. Often they will buy the innovation out of economic necessity – for example they may have purchased an early television because it was cheaper than going to the cinema or theatre. This group tends to receive information by word of mouth rather than from expert sources.

Laggards (typically 15–20%) are usually the last people in the marketplace to adopt a new product or service. They bear some resemblance to the Innovator type because peer and group pressure do not sway them. However, while the Innovator is fixed upon the future, the laggard tends to consider the past and tradition before making decisions. They are suspicious of the future and of innovation. Usually with a low disposable income, the product or service is no longer an innovation by the time they adopt it. They have no opinion leadership and are often quite isolated from their peers, for example older people living on their own.

ADVERTISING

The main purpose of advertising is the promotion of ideas, goods or services, or any combination of these, that are paid for by an identifiable sponsor. Advertising is among the most visible, most expensive and most controversial of the elements and techniques of marketing communications. Bruce Barton, the legendary advertising executive who helped develop the image of General Motors in the 1920s, said that 'the role of advertising is to help corporations to find their soul'. The media philosopher, Marshal McLuhan, called it the art form of the 20th century. Advertising has attracted artists, intellectuals, movie directors, politicians, poets, hard-headed businessmen ... and controversy.

The first known advertisement in English 1477.

> If it plese ony man spirituel or temporel to bye ony pyes of two and thre comemoracios of Salisburi use enpryntid after the forme of this preset lettre whiche ben wel and truly correct, late hym come to Westmonester in to the almonestrype at the reed pale and he shal have them good chepe .˙.˙
>
>   Supplico stet cedula.

One of the dominant techniques of persuasion and selling in the last century, advertising is now changing in nature, purpose and form. Advertising content was historically directed through mass media to achieve agreed marketing objectives. The relationship between media channels and advertising is a symbiotic one in which the nature of the media channel has always been a major determining factor in the development and diffusion of advertising content. The economics of media channels are dependent upon revenues from advertising. The proliferation of new media channels is the greatest force of change that is bearing down on the advertising industry. Nowadays, there is a greater multiplicity and fragmentation of media channels that can be used for advertising. Traditional media channels have now been challenged by new media channels. This gives a significantly different advertising media mix, including radio, the press, magazines, posters, brochures and catalogues, telephone, the World Wide Web, broadcast satellite and cable channels, physical objects, apparel and interactive digital television. New media, such as the World Wide Web have started a revolution in creative advertising development, distribution and audience feedback and interaction. New media have also vastly increased consumer choice and consumers' ability to select and customize in receiving information and images. Consequently, this affects the ability of advertising to gain attention then to persuade audiences to act.

Although advertising can be traced back to the earliest times (see above), making use of all media and visual aids available to it at the time, it has always been a much-debated topic. The role of early 20th-century advertising was to shift products in an age of mass production; later, it became a way of changing public opinion, lifestyles and consumer habit. In more recent times it has fuelled the 'personality' of brands and become something of an art form in its own right. One of the more enduring criticisms of advertising, both as a marketing discipline and as an industry, is its lack of financial accountability and uneven effectiveness. Great minds have been consumed in developing incontrovertible formulas that will one day show exactly how many sales emerge from each advertising campaign. In an age that likes to have measurable results and analyses for every type of business investment, advertising remains difficult to assess and quantify with agreed metrics. It is both emotional and rational, both an entertainment and a way of conveying information.

Few doubt that advertising is crucial to economic development, market competition and dynamism. It is most prevalent in economies with the highest standards of living (for example the United States spends roughly three times as much on advertising as the next largest spender, Japan, the second largest economy in the world). The chart below shows the vastness of expenditure on this one discipline of marketing:

Spending on advertising by major geography, year 2000 in US $ bn

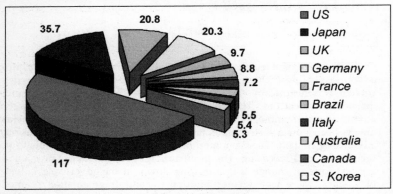

Source: www.adage.com

It has also been argued that advertising helps to promote and diffuse innovation throughout society and to give stimulus to new product development. Many of the great modern inventions – such as cars, telephones, cameras, record players, air travel, electrical appliances, and computers – were initially promoted through advertising. Because advertising is essentially the consequence of market competition, it can also contribute to lower prices and the prevention of monopoly. Beyond that, advertising also provides a means by which information on products and issues of interest to society are diffused. It can be an entertainment in its own right (some directors and actors have started their careers in advertising) and it can be used in the promotion of cities, countries, regions, charities, causes, political manifestos and environmental issues.

TYPES OF ADVERTISING

1. **Institutional or corporate advertising**, also known as Image advertising, which promotes an organization's brand, image, people, capabilities, employment opportunities, ideas or political issues or anything that the advertiser wants to publicize.

2. **Product and services advertising** promotes specific goods and services to target audiences.

3. **Location advertising** is advertising by communities, states, cities or destinations; for example, the 'I Love New York' or 'Glasgow Smiles Better' campaigns designed to attract tourists and businesses and to revitalize the images of these once maligned cities.

4. **Classified advertising** is for the sale of goods, services, jobs between individuals, usually smaller centres, without display, in newspapers. It is a $50bn global market.

PURPOSES OF ADVERTISING

Advertising is used for different purposes, among which are:

1. Promotion of the value of products and services, which has tended to be dominated by advertising of consumer products.

2. Promotion of ideas, organizations, and causes. These techniques have also been used in one-party states for political and social purposes, or to 'enlighten' captive populations.

3. Increasing the use of existing products and services. This can also be referred to as category brand advertising, especially when a product or service is already well known and repeat purchase is the goal.

4. Reinforcement or extension of existing brand recognition, awareness, value and esteem. For example, this is often used when a brand has become 'tired', or subject to declining awareness, or needs to be repositioned in the minds of target audiences, or positioned for the first time in the minds of new audiences.

5. Building a new brand from zero, in which case the goal of advertising is rapid recognition and awareness building for the new brand.

6. Acceleration of revenue, sales growth or number of buyers – in which case advertising can be more directly measured as a contributor to sales. For example, BT could instantly measure the effect of its television advertising by the number of additional calls over and above the norm that were made during and immediately after its famous advertising campaigns.

7. Increasing total market share – in which case advertising supports other elements of the marketing mix in order to increase share relative to competition.

8. Reaching new markets and buyers – particularly important when entering a new market or country or in expanding the market for an existing product or service.

9. Influencing buying decisions – in which case advertising works on the practicalities of moving buyers to make favourable buying decisions for the

product or service that is being advertised. This type of advertising is usually characterized by practical information copy rather than advanced concepts.

10. Increasing sales and supporting sales functions.

11. Developing customer loyalty. This is related to 4 above, but may also used when customer loyalty is threatened by a competing product or service.

12. Announcing a new offer or sales promotion. This is related to 5 above, but may also provide a 'kicker' to a well-established product range.

13. Announcing a product price or service change.

14. Announcing a company vision, mission or values, or a new company. This is related to 4 above.

15. Announcing a merger of two or more companies. This includes practical information, but usually starts to announce the purpose and values of the new entity.

16. Educating existing customers or new customers and audiences.

17. Attacking or counteracting competition or competitor advertising. This type of advertising used to be banned and even today is used in limited doses. Examples are the battle for the British business traveller waged between Virgin Atlantic and British Airways, or for the Cola drinker between Coke and Pepsi.

18. Making a formal statement or supplying direct information to the public. This is where advertising and public relations merge.

19. Recruiting people for a company, organization or institution.

20. Correction of an advertised claim that has been found by a regulatory body to be deceptive.

21. Promotion of a product or service under the guise of a learned detached copy or programme: known as advertorial in print or infomercials on broadcast media.

ELEMENTS AND DISCIPLINES OF ADVERTISING

Research: Advertising research is done in several stages.

Qualitative and Quantitative Research is the creative development research in which the advertising concept's appropriateness for the market and its target audience is researched. This is usually conducted prior to a full-blown advertising campaign.

Pre-production Research Testing: this involves pre-testing the concept and creative work with representative audience samples and panels. This is usually done before and during a campaign.

Post-production research testing: this studies overall reactions after the advertising campaign has run, which contributes to the effectiveness measure.

See also MARKET RESEARCH.

MEDIA CHANNELS

A huge variety of media channels is used for the display of advertising, usually in the form of combination or 'mix'. The most recent addition to these channels is interactive, involving a two-way exchange between the presentation of advertising and the target audience. Below is a brief survey of the range of media available to advertisers. See also MEDIA.

1. **Printed media**: the prolific and traditional medium for advertising is newspapers, journals and magazines. These can operate locally, nationally, regionally or globally. As well as product and service advertising, this can also take the form of *classified advertising*. Advertising in this medium can either be directly on the page or take the form of insertions. The economics of newspapers and magazines are entirely dependent on advertising revenues.

2. **Broadcast media**: mainly radio and television, where the message consists of packages pushed out to the audience over the airwaves. This is the most expensive form of advertising, often with the promise of the largest audience.

3. **Film**: advertising can appear either before a film or, more subtly, as indirect advertising within a film, in which the sponsor pays for their product to be used in a particular film. This type of advertising can also be adapted to the local cinema audience.

4. **Ambient media** is advertising in unusual objects or places, such as light projected into the skies or imposed on any non-traditional physical object, for example roofs, pavements and floors, petrol pumps, wastepaper bins, seat covers and cushions, papier-mâché animals on streets and on peoples' bodies.

5. Advertising on **merchandise goods** such as pens, hats, bags, badges, apparel, sports equipment.

6. **Moving objects**: advertising is widely used on transport such as buses, trains, taxis (the majority of London taxis now carry advertising), aeroplanes (usually to promote the carrier's brand) and, to a lesser extent, airships.

7. **Direct mail** including catalogues, brochures, free samples, newsletters, fly sheets or special offers sent directly through the physical mail to the potential buyer from the producer or sales point. In this case the recipient is given contact and payment details by the advertiser. This is often considered a much lower-cost advertising medium that can also result in direct sales or contact. Direct mail can either be personalized or it can be general. In more recent times, direct mailing can also be done by electronic mail, either on a targeted or untargeted basis (see also E-MAIL SPAM). See also BELOW-THE-LINE, DIRECT MARKETING under MARKETING SPECIALIZATIONS, DATABASE MARKETING under MARKETING SPECIALIZATIONS.

8. **Brochures**: along with catalogues, the most everyday form of advertising, usually portable, either mailed directly or handed over in person. This medium is very dominant for physical product, professional services and tourist holiday sales.

9. **Posters and billboards** are the most popular medium for outdoors advertising. It is also one of the oldest forms of advertising. It is targeted at the general and casual audience who happen to pass the poster. This medium tends to be placed near where there are lots of travelling audiences, such as

at the sides of busy or congested roads, high-density pedestrian areas, at airports or other transport centres. Billboards can also be placed at the side of buildings on a near-permanent basis. They are often used in conjunction with other media. There is no standard international poster size.

10. **Displays** are any form of merchandising combined with the use of posters, billboards or other similar formats at trade shows and exhibitions or retail outlets.

11. **Directories** are either printed or electronic listings, usually in alphabetic order, usually of businesses in a local area. Typically, a business directory or 'yellow pages' is an important form of local classified advertising. Increasingly, business service and product directories are moving to electronic database and can be used interactively. Electronic directories can achieve far greater reach and coverage than the printed versions.

12. **Websites** have become a very important part of the business advertising mix over the past few years. Their format is very different from broadcast or print media advertising. The website is an advertising medium in its own right, but it can also host other companies' advertising in the form of 'pop-up' ads and the 'banner' ads. Often, one advertiser's site can be linked to another site that can be reached by the customer (or 'surfer') visiting the website. Measurement of advertising effectiveness is also different on a website. Advertisers look at the 'stickiness' of the website: how long the visitor remains there and the amount of 'clickthrough' that the visitor makes. Measurement can be done in greater detail and can include the number of sales that are made. So, advertising medium and sales medium are integrated in a website. Advertising copy can be changed and upgraded instantly. Consumers can have greater information upon which to base their purchasing choices as a result of websites. Websites have also enabled individual personal advertising on a grand scale. See also INTERACTIVE MARKETING.

13. **Interactive digital television and cable television** changed the way in which the audience interacts with and how they receive associated advertising. Audiences are able to interact with the programmes and information, and also the advertising. There has been a rise in infomercials,

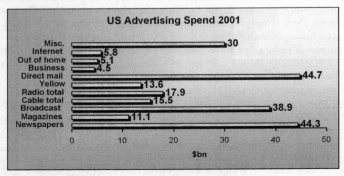

Source: Universal McCann's Robert J. Coen.

that run much longer than traditional adverts and whose punchline always involves a heavy sales pitch and inducement to buy immediately. This also enables customers to buy directly using their television and to view the product before purchase. The cross-leverage of TV advertising and interactive purchase will be a fertile area for future marketers.

The amount spent on media buying for advertising rises each year. The above chart gives an example of the relative amounts spent on advertising by each media channel in the world's largest advertising market, the USA. Direct, or 'below the line' advertising has now exceeded traditional advertising.

THE ADVERTISING CAMPAIGN

The advertising campaign is an interconnected set of creative executions running across multiple media channels for an extended period of time, with a singular theme and aimed at a target audience. This is in contrast to a single advertisement or a series of individual, disconnected adverts.

There are two main types of media strategy that support an advertising campaign:

1. **A burst campaign** is an intensive campaign that concentrates expenditure into promotional 'bursts' of three or six weeks in length. Burst campaigns can be repeated periodically and are often used to launch a new brand or product/service.

2. **A continuous campaign** allows for a constant but less intensive campaign over a longer period of time. This is often used to reinforce an existing brand.

There are several stages of a finite advertising campaign:

Development of an overall positioning strategy to give focus and consistency to the advertising campaign. Often the campaign will be given a theme or a slogan at this stage.

Detailed research on the target audience. Development of an identifiable target audience.

Target audience segmentation based upon the detailed market research and planning.

Overall positioning programmes of a product or service relative to the overall strategy and the knowledge of the target audience.

Setting clear and measurable advertising objectives for the campaign, which will later form the basis upon which the campaign's success is measured.

Developing a set of core messages relative to the overall positioning platform for the campaign.

Sizing and allocation of budget and resources for the advertising campaign (usually within the context of what the client has said that they are prepared to budget for advertising).

Writing the creative brief for the campaign that explains what an advertisement or the campaign has as a strategic context, objective and purpose. It includes the overall objective, desired positioning, the target audience, the core and supporting messages and the overall desired brand essence and personality.

Production of various creative options and copy that bring the creative brief to life.

Testing the various options, usually with a representative cross-section of the target audience and the client.

Selection of the final creative story, artwork and copy for the campaign.

Final agreement with the client on the artwork, copy and media.

Media strategy and selection of the most appropriate media distribution channel. Media purchasing.

Evaluation of any obligations or constraints in the external environment (e.g. advertising standards or prohibitions of types of advertising, local cultural considerations, competitive activity).

▼

Post-campaign testing and evaluation, usually with test groups.

▼

Reporting against campaign metrics, based upon the original objectives set.

EXAMPLES OF
SUCCESSFUL ADVERTISING CAMPAIGNS AND SLOGANS
IN THE 20TH CENTURY

De Beers

(See www.debeersgroup.com)

Diamonds are forever, 1940s

The campaign that effectively invented the diamond solitaire as the engagement ring of choice and established it as a symbol of eternal love. Prior to this campaign, love had been symbolized by all different manner of tokens, few of which were as expensive as a diamond.

An example of the success of this campaign worldwide: prior to the 1960s, less than 10% of the women in Japan wore diamonds. After a custom-made advertising campaign by De Beers evoking the Japanese need to maintain ties to their past and culture, with the premise that diamonds are a perfect symbol of one's love that combines the simplicity of Shinto with the chic of the West, over 60% of Japanese women wear diamonds today, all of which were sold by De Beers. See also brand case study: 'Diamond Mind'.

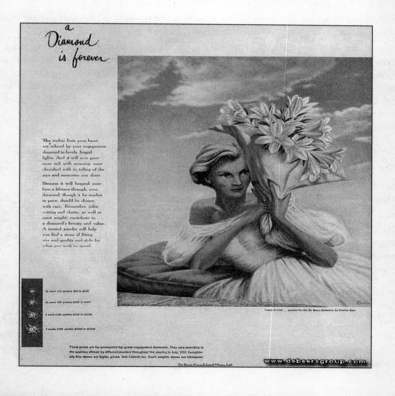

Nike

(See www.nike.com)

Just do it, 1988

One of the more successful advertising campaigns of the later 20th century. It appealed to the mood of the times for action, particularly sporting action, to achieve some purpose in life without hesitation and deliberation. The slogan, combined with the Nike 'swish' logo, became a global icon.

Pepsi

(See www.pepsi.com)

Twice as much for a nickel... 1930s–1940s.

The jingle that accompanied this was played an estimated 6 million times on radio. Later, the direct price comparison was removed when Pepsi could no longer keep their price so low.

You've got a lot to live, Pepsi's got a lot to give, 1960s.

This had clear implications for the generation of Americans living through the trauma of the Vietnam war.

Come alive...the Pepsi Generation, 1964

This slogan had problems in Germany and China where it had connotations of bringing back the dead.

Overall Pepsi, Coca-Cola's great rival, is drunk in as many countries as Coca-Cola, but without the huge advertising budgets. Pepsi also relies heavily on celebrity endorsements and frequently uses comparative advertising under the guise of consumer tests ('The Pepsi Challenge': *Taste the Difference*). The latter led Coke to change the flavour, prompting massive protest, which Coca-Cola turned brilliantly to its advantage.

Broadway Melody

(See Appendix)

All Talking! all singing! all dancing!

This was the first movie with soundtrack and ushered in the era of the 'talkies', bringing to an end the era of silent movies.

The phrase has now become generalized to mean a multi-functional or multi-purpose product or service.

Poster advert for the film, *Broadway Melody, 1929.*

Coca-Cola

(See www.coca-cola.com)

Thirst knows no Season, 1922

The pause that refreshes, 1929

Things go better with Coke, 1963

The Real Thing, 1970

Being the 'real thing' has been a constant message in Coca-Cola advertising since the 1940s, partly because it has so many rivals in the cola market.

I'd like to buy the world a Coke, 1971

Coke Adds Life, 1976

Coke is it! 1982

Invented in 1886 by John Pemberton, Coca-Cola is perhaps the most heavily and most successfully advertised product in history. Its first recorded advertising budget in 1890 was $11,000. It has had many legendary campaigns, including the invention of the modern Santa Claus, with his Falstaffian appearance and red and white (the colours of Coca-Cola) robes for a Macey's store campaign in the 1930s.

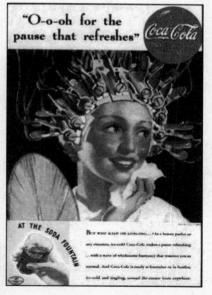

Exxon Corp. – Esso Motor Fuel

(See www.exxon.com)

Put a Tiger in Your Tank

Exxon started to use a tiger in various images from the 1950s. Esso first used the tiger in the early days of branded petrol that followed the end of rationing after World War II. The tiger image has adapted over time, to meet the changing times.

In the 1960s, the tiger assumed the aura of a cartoon , contrasting humorously with the fashion at the time for baffling scientific improvements to the performance of petrol. 'Put a tiger in your tank' became one of the most famous campaigns in advertising history, complete with merchandised 'comical' tiger tail to fix around the petrol cap along with the bumper-sticker proclaiming *'I've got a tiger in my tank'*: 2,500,000 tails were sold.

Esso, the UK brand for Exxon, started to use tiger images in the 1950s, but it was only in the 1960s that it became a craze. A cartoon tiger was used and a whole range of merchandise using the tiger was given away at filling stations. The campaign was also taken to France ('Mettez un tigre dans votre moteur') and to Germany ('Pack den Tiger in den Tank'). In the UK, the campaign then gave way to a real and beautiful tiger, carrying a subtler environmental message.

Republican Party Presidential Campaign for Dwight Eisenhower

I like Ike 1952

This slogan appeared on millions of election campaign buttons and posters and in songs. With its alliteration, it was simple but devastatingly effective. Eisenhower, the supreme commander of Allied Forces in Europe during World War II, was elected twice, at a time of extreme anti–communist hysteria in the US.

New York State Department of Commerce

I love New York, 1977.

The most famous campaign in repositioning a city started when New York was in severe decline in the 1970s, facing bankruptcy and bedevilled by high crime rates. New York, from the 1980s onwards, rebuilt its reputation as one of the world's most dynamic cities.

New York Times

(See www.nytimes.com)

All the news that's fit to print, 1896

This famous slogan, devised by Adolph Ochs, has appeared on the front of every edition of the *New York Times* since 1897.

British Conservative Party campaign poster

(See www.saatchi.com)

Labour Isn't Working, 1978

Saatchi and Saatchi

A campaign that introduced the power of advertising into the world of British politics, seen to have been a decisive contributor to the downfall of the Labour government and the beginning of 18 years in power for the Conservatives under Margaret Thatcher, who became Britain's first woman prime minister. The campaign actually began before the general election of 1979, and was given greater poignancy when Labour called the election during the infamous 'winter of discontent'.

The irony is that the supposed dole queue featured in the ad was, in fact, a group of Young Conservatives from Hendon, who were asked to participate in the shoot. Only about 20 of them turned up, and Saatchi & Saatchi, which became the ad agency of choice for the Conservatives for the next 9 years, had to reproduce images of the same people to create the impression of a snaking queue.

The campaign cost only around £100,000, but gained huge media attention, particularly amplified by the reaction of outraged Labour cabinet ministers.

After the election of 1979, Lord Thorneycroft, Tory party treasurer at the time, claimed that the poster had 'won the election for the Conservatives'.

UK Egg Marketing Board

Go to Work on an Egg, 1957

Allegedly, the British novelist Fay Weldon wrote the copy, which was brought to life by the British comedian Tony Hancock. Despite the salmonella scare of 1988, eggs have remained popular with the British public and for a time had their own little lion logo.

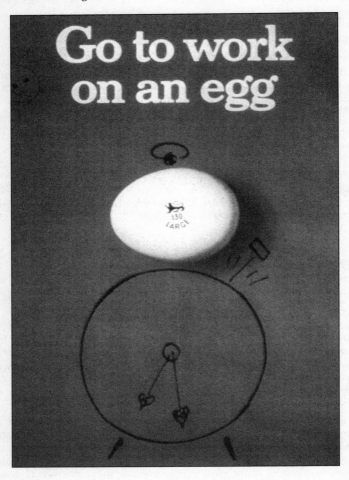

Firestone

Where the rubber meets the road, 1976

A phrase that passed into popular business idiom.

Martini

(See www.martini.com)

The right one, 1970

With a slogan created by Barry Day, the campaign was intended to shift Martini's image from being a woman's drink to being a drink for everyone, particularly younger people. Accompanied by this song and travelogue style adverts in lush and exciting locations, it epitomized the kitsch glamour of the 1970s.

A self-mocking 1990s campaign with a bossy woman giving makeovers to the British public to make them glamorous enough to drink Martini didn't restore sales to its 1970s peak.

In the UK the line 'anytime, anyplace, anywhere' has become generalized as the 'Martini' approach, often with bawdy connotations.

Any time, any place, any where
Try a taste of Martini
The most beautiful drink in the world,
It's the bright one, the right one.
There's much more to the world than you guess,
And you guess it the day you say yes
To the bright taste, the right taste
Of Martini
Any time, any place, anywhere...

Composed by Chris Gunning

Benetton Clothing

(See www.benetton.com)

United colors of Benetton, 1980s

These poster ads by Oliviero Toscano became increasingly shocking as they portrayed AIDS victims, the clothes of dead soldiers, and new babies soaked in blood from the womb, black stallions mounting white mares.

Luciano Benetton summarized his views: 'The purpose of advertising is not to sell more. It's to do with institutional publicity, whose aim is to communicate the company's values ... . We need to convey a single strong image, which can be shared anywhere in the world.'

Oliviero Toscani pursues this : 'I am not here to sell pullovers, but to promote an image...' Benetton's advertising draws public attention to universal themes like racial integration, the protection of the environment, and Aids.

Eastman Kodak cameras

(See www.kodak.com)

You press the button – we do the rest, early 1900s

A phrase that ushered in the age of popular mass photography, led by the Kodak 'Brownie' camera. As with Hoover, people for a while started to call all cameras Kodak.

NEW KODAKS

" *You press the button, we do the rest.*"

Seven new Styles and Sizes

ALL LOADED WITH *Transparent Films.*

For sale by all Photo. Stock Dealers.

THE EASTMAN COMPANY,

Send for Catalogue   ROCHESTER, N. Y.

Kellogg's (Rice Krispies)

(See www.kellogs.com)

Snap! Crackle! Pop! 1940s

Coined in the US in the late 1920s, this simple and enduring slogan was accompanied by a hummable ditty. The advent of commercial television in the late 1940 and 1950s gave this slogan and campaign a vast audience and enduring brand recognition for this Kellogg's cereal over the years. While the look and appearance of the characters has changed over the years, the slogan is etched in the mass memory of consumers.

AT&T, Yellow Pages

Let your fingers do the walking, 1973 –

Designed to inform people about Yellow Pages, and how to use it, as it became a nationally available product.

It then became a global symbol adopted by several telephone companies across the world using the Yellow Pages directory.

Yellow Pages are now available on the Internet, giving a new dimension to the use of the fingers to obtain information.

Listerine Mouthwash

Often a bridesmaid, never a bride, 1925

Stops halitosis! 1921

Milton Feasley, of Lambert and Feasley.

This famous ad campaign appeared in magazines such as *Ladies' Home Journal*. The now famous slogan, 'Often a bridesmaid but never a bride' – quickly became an adage, still in use today. Many people believe that it is an old saying.

Ad caption

Edna's case was really a pathetic one. Like every woman, her primary ambition was to marry. Most of the girls of her set were married — or about to be. Yet not one possessed more grace or charm or loveliness than she.

And as her birthdays crept gradually toward that tragic thirty-mark, marriage seemed farther from her life than ever.

She was often a bridesmaid but never a bride.

That's the insidious thing about halitosis (bad breath). You, yourself, rarely know when you have it. . .

(From the 1925 ad for Listerine that introduced the American public to halitosis.)

Hoover

Beats as it sweeps as it cleans, 1920s

Hoover in the UK became the eponymous word for a vacuum cleaner. It even became an active verb ('hoovering the carpet'). In 1926, Hoover introduced the famous 'beats-as-it-sweeps-as-it-cleans' feature which cleverly incorporated the three established but separate methods of cleaning carpets: beating, sweeping and suction cleaning. This innovation set the standard for the rest of the market to follow and was a feature of Hoover cleaners until the 1980s.

Although Hoover's vacuum cleaners were very expensive, they carried the royal warrant and were used on the prestigious ocean liners of the late 1930s. They were also cleverly marketed under such headlines as 'No millionaire can buy better' (1947) and 'All women are equal in this' (1933), implying that if you had scrimped and saved for the 'Hoover' you were at least equal in this respect to royalty and the well-to-do.

In 1935, Hoover's success was guaranteed by the launching of a British-built, compact, upright cleaner that retained the features and quality of their larger model, but at half the price. The subsequent success of the 'Junior' model (a version of which was still selling in the mid-1980s) was indicated by a biasing of the British cleaner market towards the upright format, in contrast to the rest of Europe.

New designs and materials In the mid-1930s, Hoover USA pioneered the use of professional industrial design in vacuum cleaners by employing Henry Dreyfuss, one of the first industrial designers, to consider the design, manufacture and ease of use of their vacuum cleaner as a whole. The result was a new generation of cleaners, starting with the model 150 (1936), and the 160 (1938), which used fewer components, new light alloys and plastics and had more benefits for the user. This development indicated the fact that by the late 1930s, at least in America, the electric vacuum cleaner was a common-enough product and required a 'design overhaul' to stimulate the next generation of sales. The basic component layout and manufacturing approach of these new models continued until the first 'clean-fan' plastic uprights in the mid-1960s, such as the Hoover Dial-A-Matic (UK-Convertible).

Maxwell House

Good to the last drop, 1959

Maxwell House Coffee is actually named after a hotel, the Maxwell House, in Nashville, Tennessee. Completed after the US Civil War, the Maxwell House became one of the best known hotels in the United States for 100 years. Presidents who stayed there included Rutherford B. Hayes, William Henry Harrison, Grover Cleveland, William McKinley, Theodore Roosevelt, William Howard Taft, and Woodrow Wilson. While staying at the Maxwell House Hotel, President Theodore Roosevelt enjoyed the 'house blend' of coffee so much that he raved about it being 'good to the last drop.' The Check-Neal Company, which supplied the hotel's coffee, wisely saw a good marketing opportunity. They began packaging and selling the hotel's house blend as Maxwell House Coffee, using President Roosevelt's remark in its advertising. Both the coffee and the slogan caught on with the American public.

The hotel was destroyed by fire in 1961, but its name lives on in the Regal Maxwell House Hotel at a different location in Nashville. And, of course, the name lives on in Maxwell House Coffee, which is still advertised as 'Good to the Last Drop.'

Rolls-Royce

(See www.rolls-royce.com)

The best car in the world, 1929

At 60 miles an hour the loudest noise ... comes from the electric clock, 1958

Written by David Ogilvie, this slogan saw sales of Rolls-Royce cars jump by 50% in the following year.

Since 1907, the name of Rolls-Royce has been synonymous with refined and distinctive motor cars that have made it one of the world's most celebrated marques. The famous Rolls-Royce badge has two interlocking letter R's and these simple initials of the founders, Sir Henry Royce and the Hon. Charles Rolls, have acquired significance as an immediately recognized symbol of quality, evoking ideals of precision, integrity and attention to fine detail. The Spirit of Ecstasy mascot, which has adorned the motor cars since 1911, likewise identifies characteristics of Rolls-Royce with a romantic representation of elegance and craftsmanship.

Engineer Royce had focused his unquenchable enthusiasm to improve the mechanical aspects of automobiles. He had firm views on the need for quality and a Victorian fancy for expressing his aims in stirring phrases. 'Small things make perfection, but perfection is no small thing,' declared Mr. Royce. 'Whatever is rightly done, however humble, is noble,' he added. And one of his memorable observations was: 'The quality remains long after the price is forgotten.' Those seeking to emphasize value over price in their marketing often use this phrase.

Clairol (hair colorant)

Does she ... or doesn't she? 1956

Shirley Polykoff

A tantalizing question during the early days of the sexual revolution. Sex became a major part of advertising after this campaign.

The first Miss Clairol ads were originally written 'Does she... or doesn't she? Hair colour so natural only her *mother* knows for sure!' However, Clairol was concerned about alienating the older generation that the word was changed to 'hairdresser'. The final ad read, 'Does she... or doesn't she? Hair colour so natural only her hairdresser knows for sure!' Polykoff insisted the models in the Miss Clairol ads resemble the 'girl next door' rather than the high-glamour women typically portrayed in 1950s ads. The idea was to make hair colouring respectable and mainstream. The print ads typically included a child to undercut the sexual undertones, making it clear that respectable women coloured their hair, not just women of easy virtue as was believed at the time. Also, showing the mother's hair next to the child's hair emphasized the precise colour match by comparison.

Clairol's sales increased by an amazing 413% in just six years. More than 50% of adult U.S. women began using hair colour, up from 7% prior to Polykoff's Miss Clairol campaign. Through her ads, Shirley Polykoff helped transform Clairol from a small business (a tiny division of Bristol-Myers) to a huge international brand by assisting in the creation of a hair-colouring industry.

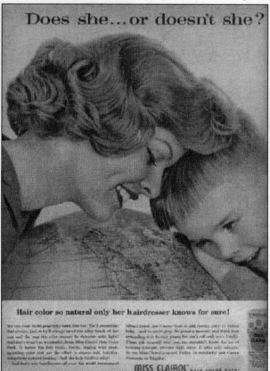

Heineken

(See www.heineken.com)

Refreshes the parts other beers cannot reach, 1980s

A brilliantly conceived and inventive set of adverts that used humour and smartness interchangeably.

For nearly 20 years, Heineken promoted itself as the beer that '...*refreshes the parts other beers can't reach*'. To prove the point, their ads showed situations where the unachievable was achieved with the help of either bottled or canned Heineken. For example, Larry Hagman, who played the legendary screen villain, J.R. Ewing, in the long running soap-opera Dallas, which dominated TV screens in the 1980s. The incorrigible J.R. is progressively made saintly by drinking Heineken. There were multiple variations on this theme, often tailored to local audiences.

Avis

(See www.avis.com)

When you're only No. 2 you try harder. Or Else. 1963

The first campaign to promote the No.2 market position (against Hertz's No. 1 position). This was a new technique at the time and gave Avis a platform to advance their customer service.

BMW

(See www.bmw.com)

The Ultimate Driving Machine, 1975

Puris and Ammirati

The campaign that helped define a decade of conspicuous consumption, particularly in the 1980s.

The campaign focused on BMW's performance and was unashamedly elitist. The ads targeted the affluent and successful professionals who responded to advertising that tapped into their sense of superiority.

The effort that started in the 1970s spanned three decades. BMW remains one of the world's more successful car companies.

Volkswagen

(See www.volkswagen.com)

Think Small 1959 *Doyle Dane Bernbach, NY.*

Part of the campaign that introduced the Volkswagen to America with stunning success. It would appear that the Volkswagen Beetle had little in its favour when entering the US market in the late 1950s. It was still strongly associated with Hitler and the Nazi party who had promoted it as the People's Car (actually designed by Porsche). It was also the complete opposite of the wide bodied, big finned and fendered American automobiles popular at the time. The copywriter, Julian Koenig, together with Helmut Krone and Bernbach himself developed an understated, self-deprecating, counter-intuitive advertising in an age of conspicuous consumption that had characterized the 1950s. Often regarded as the most influential advertising campaign of all time.

Schlitz

The Beer that made Milwaukee Famous, 1895

Milwaukee is actually famous for brewing and is known in America as the 'beer capital of the world'. Cheap, abundant ice from Lake Michigan favoured brewing before the advent of artificial refrigeration. Ice also stimulated long-distance shipping of beer, since rail cars needed to be packed with enormous quantities of ice to prevent spoilage of the beer en route. Compared to other major brewing cities, such as Chicago, Milwaukee's population (and that of its outlying regions) was relatively small. Milwaukee brewers were forced to turn to outside markets to expand sales. This unique problem ultimately transformed Milwaukee's breweries into export-minded organizations. The strategy of long-distance distribution did not cease for Milwaukee's brewers until they had covered the American market.

The large beer-consuming population of Chicago and the easy and inexpensive lake transportation acted as an early stimulant to Milwaukee's brewing industry. The Great Chicago Fire of 1871 boosted sales of Milwaukee breweries enormously. Schlitz's frequent shipments of beer to the devastated city earned it the slogan, 'The Beer that made Milwaukee Famous.' And Schlitz enjoyed a 100% jump in sales.

Grateful Chicago was instantly bonded to Schlitz and before local breweries could rebuild, Schlitz captured the city's beer market. Within a year the company adopted the slogan 'The Beer that made Milwaukee Famous' for all aspects of its marketing.

1918 ad for Schlitz beer.

Guinness

(See www.guinness.com)

Guinness Is Good for You, 1929–1963.

Guinness's advertising agency (S. H. Benson) did some market research during the 1920s to find our what people liked about Guinness. People responded that they felt good when they had their pint and the slogan 'Guinness is Good For You' was born. The slogan is still used in some countries (Africa) that do not regulate advertising claims. Some advertising even features athletes implying that their athleticism can be attributed to Guinness. In the UK, post-operative patients used to be given Guinness, as were blood donors. In Ireland, Guinness is still made available to blood donors and stomach and intestinal post-operative patients. Guinness is known to be high in iron content.

Guinness used the artist John Gilroy to craft a memorable and enduring set of images to develop the idea that Guinness was good for you. Gilroy's first known Guinness poster was produced in 1930. Working with copywriters like Ronald Barton and Robert Bevan, Gilroy produced more than 100 press advertisements and nearly 50 poster designs for Guinness over 35 years. He is perhaps best remembered for his posters featuring the girder carrier and the wood cutter from the *Guinness for Strength* campaigns of the early 1930s and for the Guinness animals. The animals, including a lion, toucan, gnu and kangaroo, appeared, with their long-suffering zookeeper, on posters, press advertisements, show cards and waiter trays from the 1930s to the 1960s. Gilroy continued to produce Guinness advertisements well into the 1960s even though he left Benson's employment as an in-house artist in the 1940s to pursue freelance work.

Guinness today is more focused on the psychological than upon the physical, particularly in relation to men.

H.J. Heinz

(See www.heinz.com)

57 Varieties, 1896

Henry John Heinze, son of Lorenz Heinze of Bavaria who emigrated to the US, was born in 1844. He began the company selling horseradish from the family vegetable patch to his neighbours. Later, they started putting ground horseradish into bottles.

In 1869 he took a partner and founded the firm of Heinz (dropping the 'e') and Noble that sold bricks and horseradish. The company flourished and two years later Heinz opened a food-processing factory where bottled horseradish and bottled pickles were made. After a promising start, the firm was bankrupted in the depression that marked the post-Civil War period and the early 1870s. Heinz borrowed $3,000 from his brother John and his cousin Frederick to relaunch as F & J. Heinz. The new firm introduced tomato ketchup, pepper sauce, vinegar, apple butter, fruit jellies and mincemeat to the US market. In 1886 he visited London and persuaded the famous firm of Fortnum & Mason to sell his goods in the UK, still at that stage the world's richest market.

In 1888 Henry bought out his brother's interests, re-named the firm H.J. Heinz & Company and then bought a new site and started planning to build a new factory.

It was in 1896 that he originated the famous '57 Varieties' slogan which became one of the more famous brand signatures in the world of fast-moving consumer goods. Corporate folklore at Heinz has it that, in 1896, Henry John Heinz noticed an advertisement for '21 styles of shoes.' He decided that his own products were not styles, but varieties. Although there were many more than 57 foods in production at the time, because the numbers 5 and 7 held a special significance for him and his wife, he adopted the slogan '57 Varieties.' So, in fact the number 57 isn't related to the number of products offered by Heinz.

In 1928, it was decided to produce a canned food that became the flagship of the Heinz company, baked beans in tomato sauce. The introduction of baked beans

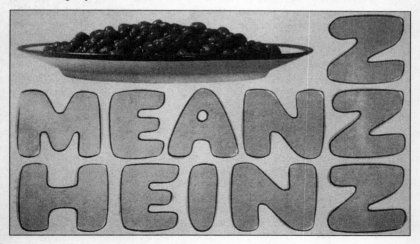

was so successful that it was followed by spaghetti and a variety of soups. During the Second World War the Heinz factory produced food for the armed forces. Heinz became a listed public company in 1946 and continued its global expansion.

H. J. Heinz Company today is an enterprise involving more than 45,800 people in over 200 major locations worldwide, with leading brands on three continents, offering a lot more than 57 varieties – actually more like 5,700 different products in total. It is the world's largest tomato producer.

Apple

(See www.apple.com)

'1984', Chiat Day

A landmark television ad heralding the high point of the first wave of the PC market, and directed by Ridley Scott, this ad cost $1.6 million to make and was inspired by George Orwell's *1984*. The ad, where a young lady silences Big Brother with the aid of a hammer, was only ever shown once, during the US Super Bowl in January 1984, to announce the launch of the Apple Macintosh on 24th January 1984, promising 1984 would not be like *1984*. Despite only being shown once, the ad had one of the highest audience recall figures in America.

This ad is often seen to be the beginning of advertising as a major event rather than just a campaign. The ad launched the Apple Macintosh without even showing the product.

The memorable line, 'Why 1984 won't be like 1984', was written for an Apple II newspaper ad, then rejected, then recycled by copywriter Steve Hayden and art director Brent Thomas in 1983.

The main purpose of the campaign was to stop customers from buying the IBM PC until there were sufficient quantities of the Apple Macintosh on the shelves. The ad was almost not shown. When Apple initially dragged its feet on approving a 60-second version of '1984' at a pre-screening for their board of directors, one board member called for the agency to be fired. Shortly before the Super Bowl, the company decided to sell off its airtime. However, the valuable time could not be unloaded, and the spot ran. Nearly 20 years later, clients spend millions to advertise during the Super Bowl.

Storyboard and text of '1984' Scene reminiscent of 'brainwashing' cinema scene in Orwell's 1984. Voice 1: Today, we celebrate the first glorious anniversary of the Information Purification Directives. We have created, for the first time in all history, a garden of pure ideology where each worker may bloom secure from the pests of contradictory and confusing truths. Our Unification of Thoughts is more powerful a weapon than any fleet or army on earth. We are one people, with one will, one resolve, one cause. Our enemies shall talk themselves to death and we will bury them with their own confusion. We shall prevail!

Female athlete throws a hammer through the screen and smashes the 'Big Brother' face. Voiceover: 'On January 1984 Apple Computer will introduce Macintosh.

And you'll see why 1984 won't be like 1984'.

Pears soap

Cleanliness is next to Godliness, 1880

This was the brainchild of Thomas Barratt, the son-in-law of Andrew Pears, inventor of the famous soap. Barrat was an early advertising genius. He persuaded prominent skin specialists, doctors and chemists to give glowing testimonials to Pears Soap. Such endorsements were boldly displayed in magazines and newspapers, handbills and on posters. Lillie Langtry, a highly popular actress of the day, cheerfully gave Barratt a commendation for Pears Soap. Barrat entered the lucrative American market by persuading the enormously influential religious leader Henry Ward Beecher to equate cleanliness, and Pears Soap in particular, with Godliness. Barratt promptly bought up the whole of the front page of the New York Herald to display the glowing testimonial.

UK Army recruitment poster, 1914

Your country needs you

The resolute face of Kitchener pointing at potential recruits had a massive effect on the British psyche, sending thousands of young volunteers to the slaughter of the trenches. Kitchener drowned, and conscription was introduced in 1916, the volunteer force having been largely wiped out since the beginning of hostilities. The poster campaign remains one of the enduring icons of the 20th century.

US War Department poster, WWII

Loose Lips Might Sink Ships, 1941–45

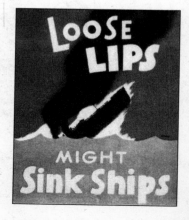

With German and Japanese submarines patrolling American waters after 1942, there was huge concern over security and the need for secrecy to protect shipping. German U-Boats had made a devastating raid on American fleets in the Atlantic and, of course, there was also Pearl Harbour.

This poster was part of a campaign to discourage loose or careless talk about all military matters, both in the public and in the private domain.

UK Recruitment Poster

Daddy, what did You do in the Great War? 1916

By Savile Lumey

A poster commissioned by the British Parliamentary Recruiting Committee in 1915. By 1915 the mood had changed from naïve patriotism to a sense of duty and dark resolution. This ad focused on creating a guilty conscience in those who shirked the call to arms. The little girl has apparently put her father on the spot: was he a 'shirker' during the war, or did he enlist and 'do his bit'? The look on his face suggests he was one of the men who may have elected not to serve his king and country.

A contemporary response quoted by Eric Partridge in his *Catch Phrases* was 'Shut up, you little bastard. Get the Bluebell and go and clean my medals'.

UK Ministry of Agriculture poster, WWII

Dig For Victory, 1940–45

An outstanding example of a public information campaign resulting in positive action. At a time of endangered food supply, the UK started the war with 850,000 allotments and ended with 1.4 million and became almost self-sustaining in food.

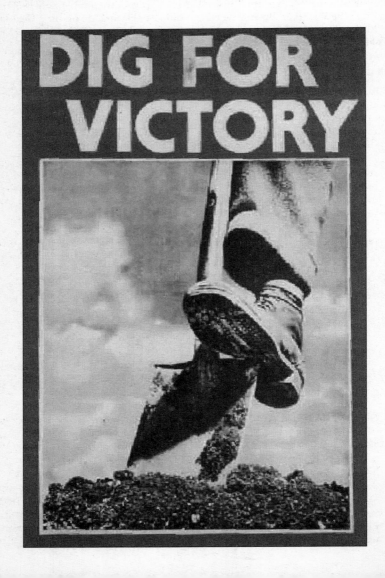

ADVERTISING AGENCY

The primary responsibility of an advertising agency is to gain an understanding of the client's business strategy and imperatives, then to determine what role advertising can play in supporting them, and then to help them execute and measure the campaign. It is usual for companies, organizations and even governments to use external agencies for advertising rather than attempt to do it themselves. External agencies are used because the company's own marketing team do not usually have the resources, time, media purchasing power or expertise to develop the campaign themselves. Agencies are usually selected through competitive tendering that results in a final selection or 'pitch'. Agencies that 'pitch' successfully usually have a distinguished track record and credentials; they can usually demonstrate to the prospective client that they understand their brand and that they have innovative ideas to promote it. Then considerations of price, culture, chemistry between the account team and the marketing group, their international reach and local presence in the prospective clients' target markets are taken into the final selection criteria. Ultimately, business and communications strategies must connect and be mutually re-enforcing.

Advertising, which helped fuel the rise of the global corporations of the 20th century, itself became a global business with the advertising agencies becoming giant corporations. As it stands today, WPP, a highly acquisitive marketing services agency, is among the largest agencies in the world (see table below).

Rank/Company	Headquarters	Worldwide gross income 2001
1 WPP Group	London	$8,165.0
2 Interpublic Group of Cos.	New York	7,981.4
3 Omnicom Group	New York	7,404.2
4 Publicis Groupe (includes Bcom3 Group)	Paris	4,769.9
5 Dentsu	Tokyo	2,795.5
6 Havas Advertising	Levallois-Perret, France	2,733.1
7 Grey Global Group	New York	1,863.6
8 Cordiant Communications Group	London	1,174.5
9 Hakuhodo	Tokyo	874.3
10 Asatsu-DK	Tokyo	394.6

Notes: Figures are in U.S. dollars in millions. Ranked by gross income in 2001 by all marketing-related activities.
Source: Ad Age Agency Report

TYPES OF ADVERTISING AGENCY

Full service agency Often known as an integrated or 'one-stop shop' agency, this can offer clients a full range of promotional services from research, advertising, public relations, direct marketing, digital, media planning/buying and events and promotions as well as account management. These agencies are distinguished by their large range of internal resources that have usually been recruited or else acquired through merger or takeover of other agencies. The trend in recent years is to build full marketing service agencies that continue to have advertising at their core.

Specialist agency These agencies provide a customized service to individual clients. Often this type of agency will focus on the creative aspects of advertising and arrange other parts of the campaign mix through other agencies, affiliated companies and contractors. These agencies are often eventually acquired by the larger agencies.

Functional departments of an advertising agency

Although each advertising agency is organized differently, there are certain core functional departments that most of the larger agencies would deploy.

* *Planning* is generally the department responsible for trying to discover how advertising is received and interpreted and what people find valuable in products and brands. One of the more important elements of the job is to commission, understand and interpret market and audience research. Planners tend to be more analytical and empirical than creative.

* *Creative* is the department where the basic campaign strategy – objectives, positioning, themes, messages – are turned into creative concepts in terms of artwork and copy. A creative team is usually composed of a copywriter and an art director. Creative people tend not to be analytical or empirical. Creatives tend to have a different, less regimented culture than the rest of the agency.

* *Production* is the department responsible for turning the creative concepts into reality and making the advertisement. Often there is an element of subcontracting here, as studios, camera crew and actors may be required.

* *Media planning and buying* is the department that selects the optimum media channels that will have the greatest impact over the longest time period with the intended target, at the lowest possible cost. Having developed that strategy, this department then buys media time and space from the media owner. The media buyers also negotiate slots and prices with the media owners. This area tends to attract tough negotiators.

* *Account management* is dedicated to a particular group of clients or in some cases an individual client. The role of account manager is to be dedicated to individual clients and therefore carry ultimate responsibility for the client's satisfaction. The account manager is also accountable to the agency for revenues and profits generated from their clients. This role has to co-ordinate all specialist functions and activities. They represent the agency to the client, present the agency's findings and outlook and they feed back client comments. They also deal with client dissatisfaction.

The account team must work closely with the client's marketing department. They receive briefing from the client on the overall positioning and strategy. Often the account manager will attend the client's strategic planning meetings.

* *Traffic* deals with delivering the artwork or film to the magazine or TV station on time. When the promotional campaign involves a number of media channels, this process becomes complicated because accurate timing is crucial to successful execution and cost management.

REGULATION OF ADVERTISING

This is usually an activity that is done within a national context and is rooted in the cultural, legal and social interpretations of fairness, integrity, honesty and truth in advertising in the particular country. Each country has different nuances and regulation of advertising standards. For example, some countries allow unsubstantiated claims for certain products (such as 'product X improves your health') whereas others do not. Some countries allow the use of the superlative (as in 'Product X is the best product in the world') while others do not. For example, in the UK the beer company Carlsberg had to moderate its claim to be 'the best lager in the world' with 'probably'.

The advent of Internet-based advertising has also presented regulatory authorities with a range of challenges. There is, as yet, no universally guaranteed way of regulating Internet-based advertising or enforcing penalties against illegal advertising, The regulation of promotion activities is largely based on self-regulatory codes of practice rather than statutory law as there is no one act which covers the entire range of promotional activities. There are no internationally agreed laws on consumer protection, competition and monopoly that can be applied to cyberspace. For example, one of the most exposed areas in the short term is the whole system of quality assurance and control standards of goods and services advertised on the Internet. Goods and service promoted then ordered over the Internet from another country could circumvent the apparatus of quality controls. Quality and safety are national variables. For example, drugs which may be over-the-counter in one country, may be available only by prescription in another. The patient may be able to see them advertised on the Internet, then order them remotely and receive them through the mail, thereby by-passing the local regulations and controls. Digitally distributed content, such as software for example, or the Internet's most advertised product, pornography, could be accepted in one county and offensive or banned in another. There is no standards body to arbitrate over misleading or inaccurate advertising.

Agency self-regulation is self-policing by the advertising industry, which may include ethical issues, certification, standards, and reviews and recommendations by the industry-policing bodies regarding allegedly deceptive or fraudulent advertising.

ADVERTISING MEASUREMENT AND EFFECTIVENESS

There are several methods of measuring the effectiveness of advertising, which is often referred to as the ROAI, or rate of return on advertising investment. The measurement of advertising effectiveness is a perennial source of controversy and has always cast a shadow of doubt on the effectiveness of the advertising industry.

1. **Pre-testing** of advertising is a way of testing how effective it can be prior to full launch, usually involving test groups assessing impact, emotional reaction, communication, image, recall and originality.

2. **Post-test** evaluation of advertisement, which may involve a customer survey, recall tests (in which each respondent or test group is asked about what advertisements he or she has seen recently), and recognition tests (in

which each respondent or test group is shown the actual advertisement and asked if they recognize or recall it and what it meant to them). This is often divided into tests of aided and unaided recall. In aided recall he test group is prompted with cues or lists of the adverts or brand attributes; in the unaided this is not done.

3. **Sales testing** is testing to determine the actual sales or order growth that resulted from the advertising campaign. This is a more difficult type of test because, generally, advertising works more on perception in the customer's mind than on immediate purchase action. It could include sales in total, by customer, or sales by product or service contribution or, in total, by customer and by product and service. It may include a measure of the impact of the campaign on actual expenses versus budgeted expenses on the basis that good advertising ought to lower sales costs.

It may measure the number of new leads, or potential customer interests resulting and, ultimately, the number of new customers obtained. It may be a simpler measure of percentage increase in sales after the advertising campaign compared with the period before the advertising campaign.

4. **Public reaction testing** aims to determine the overall effectiveness of the campaign by, for example, measuring the amount of media space gained, and the number of articles and favourable comments written and made about the campaign.

5. **Offer redemption** refers to the uptake of a special offer promoted in the advertising (such as a discounted product, a special package or deal, a coupon in which the way of reclaiming it is embedded in the advertisement) where the redemption or interest in the offer can be measured directly.

See also DAGMAR, DAR.

ADVERTISING TERMINOLOGY

The following are terms used in advertising, the majority having their origins in the US.

accordion insert an ad inserted in a magazine, with an accordion-style fold.

accumulation an audience-counting method, where each person exposed to a specific vehicle is counted once within a certain time period.

ad blocking the blocking of website advertisements, typically the image in graphical web advertisements. This enables the user to filter out ads while surfing websites. Ad blocking is used by a relatively small percentage of the on-line population. Ad filtering technology is increasingly bundled into other web applications. Those who favour ad blocking say it improves the speed and convenience of the website to visitors, making it less of a nuisance. Those who oppose it say that it deprives website owners of revenue from advertising, as ad-free surfers use valuable resources without indirectly 'paying' in the form of viewing ads. This means that content owners could be forced to charge subscription fees.

adcept a halfway stage of a campaign idea at which it is half advert and half concept: a staging point in the creative process, a time when initial creative ideas are checked with various constituencies, probably including clients, to ensure that the concept is following the overall message and position developed in the creative brief.

ad copy printed text or spoken words in an advertisement.

ad inserts enclosures that are used to relate information as part of an overall advertising campaign.

adjacencies time periods immediately before and after a television programme, normally used as a commercial break between scheduled programmes.

ad network a means of aggregating buyers and sellers for on-line advertising. The network is made up of several websites that sell on-line advertising, allowing advertising buyers to reach broad audiences relatively easily. Advertising networks provide a way for a media buyer to coordinate buys across multiple websites far more efficiently and more cost-effectively than could be done otherwise. Media buys usually focus on running ads over a category or an entire network. Advertising networks can also aggregate visitor information.

adnorm a measure of readership averages for print publications over a two-year period, used as a baseline for comparing specific ads to an average.

ad recall the measured ability of readers or audiences to remember ads they have viewed in various media and programmes.

ad space the space on a web page available for advertisements. In the early days of website design, ad space was not a major factor. Nowadays, it is crucial for sites that are dependent on advertising revenues. One of the challenges of web design is to use ad space in a way that satisfies advertisers without alienating visitors and causing them to leave the site.

ad speak the language, acronyms and idioms used by people in the advertising industry. Many of these phrases have become part of idiomatic language.

adstock a technique developed by The Brand Consultancy to measure the effect and performance of an advertising campaign by focusing on the recall in the minds of target audiences that an advertising campaign has after it has ceased to run.

ad tip-ins inserts placed in a publication, such as extra pages of advertising or subscription return cards.

advertising allowance money provided by a manufacturer to a distributor for the purpose of advertising a specific product or brand.

advertising budget money set aside by the advertiser to pay for advertising. There are a variety of methods for determining the most desirable size of an advertising budget.

advertising elasticity the relationship between a change in advertising budget and the resulting change in product sales. Ideally, more advertising means more sales.

advertising page exposure a measure of the opportunity for readers to see a particular print advertisement, whether or not they actually look at the ad.

advertising plan an explicit outline of the goals that an advertising campaign should achieve, how to accomplish those goals, and how to determine whether or not the campaign was successful in achieving the goals.

advertising specialty the older, but still commonly used, term for PROMOTIONAL PRODUCT (below).

advertorial a paid-for advertisement made to look like a newspaper or magazine editorial. It is normal practice to label these 'Advertising' or 'This is an Advertisement'. An advertorial is the print equivalent of the TV-based **infomercial**. In the printed medium these are fairly easy to distinguish from news or journalism. However, advertorials are now also prevalent on the Internet. The ability to create customized advertising on-line creates another challenge: many Internet surfers are probably not aware that most of the information they get from technology and business news sites is actually sponsored by a corporation. Many surfers fail to distinguish between advertorial and real editorial. On-line magazines work hard to generate an appealing look. These publications try to be consistent and advertisements are often designed to look like the magazine they appear in. Often an advertorial is not labelled as an advertisement (as it is in physical print) but as an Info Site or other misnomer.

advocacy advertising advertising used to promote a position on a political or social issue. For example, Greenpeace may try to create awareness around nuclear testing in the Pacific.

ad volume the amount of dollars or media units (e.g., hours, number of pages) spent on advertising and marketing efforts.

agate line a measure of newspaper advertising space, one column wide and 1/14th inch deep.

agency commission the advertising agency's fee for designing and placing advertisements. Historically, this was calculated as 15% of the amount spent to purchase space or time in the various media used for the advertising. In recent years the commission has, in many cases, become negotiable, and may even be based on some measure of the campaign's success.

airdate the first time an advertisement is broadcast.

airtime the actual transmission time or time allocation for an advertisement.

appeal the advertisement's selling message. This is usually based on deep research into the audience as well as a clear understanding of the overall strategic objective being adopted using the advertising messages.

art proof the artwork for an ad, to be submitted for client approval. This is a visual expression of the overall strategy.

artwork the visual components of an ad, not including the typeset text.

audience the number of people or households exposed to a vehicle, without regard to whether they actually saw or heard the material conveyed by that vehicle.

audience duplication the number of people who saw or heard more than one of the programmes or read more than one of the publications in which an ad was placed.

audilog a diary kept by selected audience members to record which television programmes they watched, as a means of rating television shows. Used by A.C. Nielsen.

audimeter an electronic recording device used by A.C. Nielsen to track when a television set is in use, and to what station it is set.

availability advertising time on radio or television that is available for purchase, at a specific time.

average audience (AA) the number of homes or persons tuned to a television programme during an average minute, or the number of persons who read an average issue of a print publication.

back-to-back refers to more than one commercial advert being run one immediately after another.

bait advertising promoting a product at a very low price, when it is difficult or even impossible to obtain the product for the price advertised. See also BAIT AND SWITCH.

bleed a picture or ad that extends beyond the normal margins of print on a page, to the edge of the page.

body copy the text of a print ad, not including the headline, logo, or subscript material.

bridge a transition from one scene to another in a commercial advertisement or programme.

buried position the position of an ad between other ads in a print publication, so that readers are less likely to see it.

business-to-business advertising advertising directed to other businesses, rather than to consumers. See also BUSINESS-TO-BUSINESS MARKETING under MARKETING SPECIALIZATIONS.

camera-ready art artwork that is in sufficiently finished form to be photographed for printing.

caption an advertisement's headline or the text accompanying an illustration or photograph.

card rate media advertising rates published by a broadcast station or print publication on a 'rate card'. This is typically the highest rate charged by a vehicle.

category development index (CDI) a comparison of the percentage of sales of a product category in a market, to the percentage of population in that market.

circulation the average number of copies of newspapers or magazines that are distributed. Newspapers will often use their circulation figures to market themselves to advertisers, from whom their major revenues come. These numbers are independently audited for accuracy. Circulation does not necessarily imply readership, which is the total number of people who actually read the newspapers and magazines distributed. Increasingly, newspapers are given away free in order to boost circulation, as the major revenue comes from advertising. Also, newspapers do not last much beyond their day of publication, whereas several people can read magazines continuously over a longer period. For outdoors advertising, circulation means the potential number of people who have an opportunity to observe a billboard or poster. This term sometimes is used for broadcasting too, but 'audience' is used more frequently.

classified advertising print advertising that is limited to certain classes of goods and services, such as household goods, local services and personal ads, usually limited in size and content and usually in black and white. They are paid for on a per-word, per-line or per-inch basis. Although very different and less glamorous in style, content and cost from display advertising, the classified advertising market is worth around $50 bn worldwide. See also TYPES OF ADVERTISING.

clearance the process by which an advertising standards body or media channel reviews an advertisement for legal, ethical, and taste standards, before accepting the ad for publication.

closing date the day that final copy and other materials must be at the vehicle in order to appear in a specific issue or time slot.

clutter the density of competing simultaneous ads and messages. When an advertisement is surrounded by other ads, it has to compete for the viewer's or listener's attention, which often reduces its overall effectiveness.

coincidental survey a survey of viewers or listeners of broadcast programming, conducted during the programme.

colour proof an early full-colour print of a finished advertisement, used to evaluate the ad's final appearance.

column inch a common unit of measure by newspapers, whereby ad space is purchased by the width, in columns, and the depth, in inches. For example, an ad that is three standard columns wide and five inches tall (or deep) would be 15 column inches.

combination rate a special media pricing arrangement that involves purchasing space or time on more than one vehicle, in a package deal. This is frequently offered where different vehicles share a common owner.

comparative advertising advertising that consists of explicitly comparing one product brand to a competitive brand. An example would be the Cola wars in which Pepsi 'challenges' consumers to compare the taste of Pepsi to Coca-Cola. Nowadays some advertising directly and indirectly attacks competitors, such as Virgin Atlantic and British Airways. For a long time comparative advertising was prohibited.

competitive parity a method of determining an advertising budget, in which the image, awareness, share of voice and general perceptions of competitors are compared. The rationale is that one company can improve its brand and image awareness by spending more on advertising than another. Although this theory does not always prove accurate in practice, it is used within numerous companies to argue in favour of investing more in advertising.

comprehensive layout a draft layout of an ad designed for presentation only, but so detailed as to appear very much like the finished ad.

consumer advertising advertising directed at a person who will actually use the product for their own benefit (rather than business-to-business or organizational advertising). See also CONSUMER MARKETING under MARKETING SPECIALIZATIONS.

consumer jury test a method of testing advertisements that involves asking consumers to compare, rank, and otherwise evaluate the ads. See also MARKET RESEARCH.

consumer stimulants promotional efforts designed to stimulate short-term purchasing behaviour. Coupons offering price discounts, premiums, two-for-one offers, special sales and samples are examples of consumer stimulants.

continuity the scheduling of advertisements to appear in media channels at regular intervals over a period of time.

continuous advertising the scheduling of advertisements to appear regularly, even during times when consumers are not likely to purchase the product or service, so that consumers are constantly reminded of the brand.

controlled (qualified) circulation publications, generally business-oriented, that are delivered only to readers who have some special qualifications or positions. Generally, publications are free to the qualified recipients. Examples are *CEO Magazine* or the *McKinsey Quarterly.*

cooperative (co-op) advertising a system by which ad costs are divided between two or more parties. Usually, such programmes are offered by manufacturers to their wholesalers or retailers, as a means of encouraging them to advertise the products themselves.

copy all spoken words or written text in an advertisement.

copy testing research to determine an ad's effectiveness, based on consumer responses to the ad, or special panels used to evaluate the ad. Copy testing is an integral part of the creative development process.

corrective advertising an advertisement or messages within advertisements for the purpose of correcting consumers' mistaken impressions created by prior advertising. Public authorities, such as the advertising standards agency in the given country, usually order this type of advertising.

cost efficiency the balance, for a media schedule or purchase, of reaching target audiences at the right frequency relative to the business goals and at the lowest price.

cost per inquiry the cost of prompting one person to inquire about your product or service. This is a standard used in direct response advertising.

cost per rating point (CPP) the cost, per 1% of a target audience, of buying advertising space in a given media vehicle.

cost per thousand (CPM) the cost, per 1000 people reached, of buying advertising space in a given media vehicle.

counter-advertising advertising that takes a contrary position to an advertising message that preceded it. Such advertising may be used to take an opposing position on a polemical subject in a public debate, or to counter an impression that might be made by another party's advertising.

coverage a measure of a media vehicle's audience reach, within a specific geographic area.

creatives the art directors, designers and copywriters in an ad agency, often distinguished from the 'suits' (such as account directors) by their unique culture and attitude.

creative strategy an outline of the positioning message: to whom it should be conveyed, together with tone, substance and objective. This is usually set down in a document called a creative brief, and provides the guiding principles for copywriters and art directors who are assigned to develop the advertisement from a concept to full copy, artwork and campaign. Within the context of that assignment, any ad that is then created should conform to that strategy and creative brief.

crop to eliminate or cut off specific portions of a photograph or illustration.

crop marks marks inserted on a photograph or illustration to indicate which portions are to be used, and which are to be eliminated.

cumes an abbreviation for net cumulative audience. This refers to the number of unduplicated people or homes in a broadcast programme's audience within a specified time period. A.C. Nielsen uses this term. It is also used by many advertising practitioners to refer to the unduplicated audience of a print vehicle, or an entire media schedule.

dailies (also called **rushes**) unedited film, so called because, typically, the film from a single day's shooting is viewed, even if the final commercial or programme will take many days or weeks of shooting and editing with computers.

day-after recall test a research method that tests consumers' memories the day after they have seen an ad, to assess the ad's effectiveness and penetration level.

day part any of the standard time periods into which the day is divided by broadcast media. Cost of purchasing advertising time on a vehicle varies by the day part selected.

decay constant an estimate of the decline in product sales if advertising were discontinued or reduced.

deceptive advertising advertising that misrepresents, omits key facts or information, or any act or practice that is likely to mislead consumers acting reasonably under the circumstances.

directory advertising advertising appearing in a directory, such as a telephone directory or reference brochure.

direct response promotions that enable or request consumers to respond directly to the advertiser, by mail, telephone, e-mail, or some other means of communication. See also DIRECT MARKETING under MARKETING SPECIALIZATIONS.

display advertisement any advertisement in print media other than a classified ad, or an ad that stands alone, such as window sign or a billboard.

dissolve a fade from one scene to another in a film or television production.

door opener a product or advertising specialty, usually given free by a salesperson to consumers to induce them to listen to a sales pitch. The worst examples of this are free gifts given by timeshare salesmen to induce potential customers to listen to a high-pressure sales pitch.

double truck a two-page spread in a print publication, where the ad runs across the middle gutter.

drive time a time band used in radio advertising, which refers to morning and afternoon times when consumers are driving to and from work.

dummy a copy of an ad, or even blank sheets of paper, provided to a printer or artist as an example of the size, colour, or other aspect of the ad to be produced.

duplicated audience the portion of an audience that is reached by more than one media vehicle.

earned rate a discounted media rate, based on volume or frequency of media placement.

electric spectacular refers to outdoor signs or billboards composed largely of lighting or other electrical components.

envelope stuffer a direct mail advertisement included with another mailed message (such as a bill). For example, gas and electricity companies are using their mailing lists to advertise either their own products and services or those of others.

exposure the number of consumers who have seen (or heard or visited) a media vehicle, whether or not they paid attention to it.

eye tracking a research method that determines which part of an advertisement consumers look at, by tracking the pattern of their eye movements.

fixed-sum-per-unit method a method of determining an advertising budget which is based directly on the number of units sold.

flat rate a media buying rate that allows for no discounts.

flighting a time division management system in a media schedule that involves more advertising at certain times and less advertising during other time periods.

focus group interview a research method that brings together a small group of consumers to discuss the product or advertising, under the guidance of a trained interviewer. See also MARKET RESEARCH.

franchised position an ad position in a periodical publication to which an advertiser is given a permanent or long-term right of use.

free-standing insert (FSI) an advertisement or group of ads inserted (but not bound) in a print publication, pages that contain only the ads and are separate from any editorial or entertainment matter.

frequency (1) the number of times that an average person or home is exposed to a media vehicle (or group of vehicles) within a given time period. (2) The position of a television or radio station's broadcast signal within the electromagnetic spectrum.

fringe time a time period directly preceding and directly following prime time on television.

fulfilment house a clearing house for companies that use coupons as an incentive; it receives coupons and manages their accounting, verification and redemption.

full position a position for an ad in which it is surrounded by reading matter in a newspaper, making it more likely that consumers will read the ad. This is a highly desirable location and is usually more expensive.

galley proof typeset copy of an ad or editorial material before it is made into pages for final production.

galvanometer test a research method that measures physiological changes in consumers when asked a question or shown some stimulus material (such as an ad). See also MARKET RESEARCH.

gatefold Double or triple-size pages, generally in magazines, that fold out into a large advertisement.

green advertising advertising that promotes a product or service's ability to improve the environment and conserve the earth's natural resources. For example, in recent years leading petroleum companies, stung by criticism of their harmful effect on the natural environment, have begun to produce ads promoting their environmental credentials. The care and quality of the environment, being one of the great issues of the day, and thereby gaining a great deal of public attention, has attracted the advertising industry.

grid card a broadcast media rate card that lists rates on a grid, according to the time periods that might be selected for the ad.

gross audience the combined audiences of all vehicles or media in a campaign. Some or much of the gross audience may actually represent duplicated audience.

gross impressions the total number of unduplicated people or households represented by a given media schedule.

gross rating points (GRPs) a measure of the advertising weight delivered by a vehicle or vehicles within a given time period, calculated by reach times average frequency.

guaranteed circulation a media rate that comes with a guarantee that the publication will achieve a certain circulation to the target audience.

gutter the inside margins of two pages that face each other in a print publication.

halftone a method of reproducing a black and white photograph or illustration, by representing various shades of grey as a series of black dots.

holding power the ability to hold the attention of an audience throughout a broadcast, rather than having them change channels. It is represented as a percentage of the total audience. With the growing number of media channels this is becoming an increasingly challenging element of the advertising impact.

holdover audience the percentage of a programme's audience that watched or listened to the immediately preceding programme on the same station. Also called **inherited audience**.

hologram a three-dimensional photograph or illustration, created with an optical process that uses lasers and which is increasingly used in advertising and promotional material.

horizontal discount a discount on a media purchase resulting from a promise to advertise over an extended period of time.

horizontal publications business publications designed to appeal to people of similar interests or responsibilities in a variety of companies or industries, for example, purchasing or financial officers.

host/hostess gift a gift from a producer to a consumer who sponsors a sales demonstration party in a domestic or neighbourhood setting with the intention of selling to neighbours, for example household goods, or health and personal care items.

households using television (HUT) the number of households in a given market watching television at a certain time.

house organ a publication owned and operated by an advertiser, and used to promote the advertiser's products or services. Services companies, such as those offering financial services, will often promote their own services under the guise of analysing the market or economy.

ID a station identification during a commercial break in a television or radio programme.

imprinted product a promotional product carrying a company logo or advertising message printed on it.

independent station a broadcast station that is not affiliated with a national network of stations.

infomercial a commercial that is very similar in appearance to a news programme, talk show, or other non-advertising broadcast. The broadcast equivalent of an **advertorial**.

inherited audience same as **holdover audience**.

inquiries consumer response to a company's advertising or other promotional activities, such as coupons. Used for measuring the effectiveness of some promotions.

insert an advertisement, collection of advertisements, or other promotional matter published by an advertiser or group of advertisers, to be inserted in a magazine or newspaper. It may be bound into the publication, or be inserted without binding. See FREE-STANDING INSERT (above).

insertion an ad in a print publication.

insertion order an agency or advertiser's authorization for a publisher to run a specific ad in a specific print publication on a certain date at a specified price.

institutional advertising advertising to promote an institution or organization, rather than a product or service, in order to create public support and goodwill.

international advertising the advertising of a product or service in a country other than where it originates. See also INTERNATIONAL MARKETING under MARKETING SPECIALIZATIONS.

island position a position for a print ad in which it is completely surrounded by editorial material, or for a broadcast ad surrounded by programme content, with no adjoining advertisements to compete for audience attention.

layout a drawing that indicates the relative positions of the elements (e.g., headline, photo, logo, body copy, etc.) of an ad.

linage the size of an ad, based on the number of lines of type taken up.

local advertising (1) advertising to a local merchant or business as opposed to regional or national advertising. (2) advertising placed at rates available to local merchants.

local rate an advertising rate charged to a local advertiser, typically a retailer, by local media and publications, as distinguished from a national rate that is charged to a national advertiser, typically a manufacturer.

mail-order advertising advertising which supplies paperwork for the purpose of soliciting a purchase, made through the mail. See also DIRECT MARKETING under MARKETING SPECIALIZATIONS.

make good (1) to present a commercial announcement after its scheduled time because of an error. (2) to rerun a commercial announcement because of technical difficulties the previous time it was run. (3) to rerun a print advertisement due to similar circumstances.

marginal analysis a technique of setting the advertising budget by assuming the point at which an additional dollar spent on advertising equals additional profit.

merchandising the advertising the promoting of a firm's advertising abilities to distributors.

milline rate a measure of the cost effectiveness of advertising in a newspaper, calculated by multiplying the cost per agate line by one million, then dividing by the circulation. Also referred to as **milline**.

narrowcasting use of a broadcast medium to appeal to audiences with special interests. For example, the Golf Channel would be a narrowcast, because it appeals to an audience with a specific interest.

national advertising advertising which is aimed at a national market, as opposed to local advertising.

net cost the costs of services rendered by an advertising agency excluding the agency commission.

net unduplicated audience the combined cumulative audience exposed to an advertisement.

network a national or regional group of affiliated broadcast stations contractually bound to distribute radio or television programmes for simultaneous transmission.

network option time programming time that a network controls on each of its affiliate stations. Also referred to as **network time**.

Nielsen rating a measurement of the percentage of U.S. television households tuned to a network programme for a minute of its telecast.

noncommercial advertising radio and television advertising that is designed to educate and promote ideas or institutions, e.g., public service announcements.

off card advertising time sold at a rate that does not appear on the rate card.

on-air tests tests measuring recall among viewers of a commercial or programme during a real broadcast of the tested communication.

open end (1) time left at the end of a commercial or programme which is provided for the use of local advertising or station identification. (2) a radio or television programme with no specific time to end.

opticals visual effects used to instil interest as well as portray mood and continuity to a commercial. Dissolves, cross fades, and montages are all opticals.

outdoor advertising any outdoor sign that publicly promotes a product or service, such as billboards, movie kiosks, etc.

out-of-home advertising advertising and mass media to which people are exposed away from their homes. Included are outdoor, point-of-purchase, and radio.

overlay a transparent or opaque print in a design or layout, often one of several that combine to form a finished design or graphic.

package (1) a combination of programmes or commercials offered by a network that is available for purchase by advertisers either singly or as a discounted package deal. (2) a merchandise enclosure or container.

package insert an item of separate advertising material included in merchandise packages that advertises goods or services; also referred to as a **package stuffer**.

painted bulletin a freestanding steel or wooden structure, approximately 50' wide by 15' high, with moulding around the outer edges similar to a poster panel, and including a hand-painted copy message. Bulletins are generally found near highways or roofs of buildings in high traffic areas. See also BILLBOARD.

panel a type of outdoor advertising. A regular panel is only seen during the daytime, while an illuminated panel is seen also from dusk until dawn.

participation (1) announcements made within the context of a programme as opposed to those shown during station breaks. (2) an announcement or amount of broadcasting time that is shared by several advertisers.

pass-along reader a reader who becomes familiar with a publication without buying a copy. These readers are taken into account when calculating the total number of readers of a publication.

payout planning an approach to advertising budgeting in which the money spent to advertise is represented as an investment toward sales and profits.

percent-of-sales method a method of determining the advertising budget based on an analysis of past sales, as well as a forecast for future sales.

per inquiry an agreement between a media representative and an advertiser in which all advertising fees are paid based on a percentage of all money received from an advertiser's sales or inquires.

personalize to add a name or other personal information about the recipient to direct mail advertising.

persons using television (PUT) a percentage of all persons in a certain viewing area that are viewing television during a specific amount of time. Used by A.C. Nielsen.

persons viewing television (PVT) the term used by Arbitron for **persons using television**.

persuasion process the process used by advertising to influence audience or prospect attitudes, especially purchase intent and product perception, by appealing to reason or emotion.

photoanimation a process of creating animation through the use of still photographs.

photoboard any of a set of still photographs made from a television commercial, accompanied with a script, to be kept as records by an agency or client.

picture window an ad layout in which the picture is placed at the top of the page, and the copy is placed below.

piggyback (1) a direct mail offer that is included free with another offer. (2) two commercials shown back-to-back by the same sponsor.

point-of-purchase (POP) display advertising display material located at the retail store, usually placed in an area where payment is made, such as a check-out counter.

post-testing testing the effects of an ad after it has appeared in the media. See also MARKET RESEARCH under MARKETING SPECIALIZATIONS

pre-emptible rate a usually discounted rate for commercial time which is sold to an advertiser and is not guaranteed. As time may be sold to another advertiser who is willing to pay more, the advertiser buying this rate gambles to save money on the spot.

preferred position a position in a printed publication that is thought to attract most reader attention and is sold at a higher rate; for example, the back cover of a magazine.

premium an item, other than the product itself, which is offered free or at a nominal price as an incentive to purchase the advertised product or service.

preprint a reproduction of an advertisement which is viewed before actual publication and is created by an advertiser for special purposes, e.g., to serve as retail displays or to gain support from retailers.

pretesting testing an advertisement or an audience sample prior to placing the ad in the media.

primary demand advertising advertising designed for the generic product category, as opposed to selective demand advertising.

prime time the broadcast periods viewed or listened to by the greatest number of persons and for which a station charges the most for airtime.

professional advertising advertising directed toward professionals such as doctors, dentists, and pharmacists, etc., who are in a position to promote products to their patients or customers.

programme delivery (rate) the percentage of a sample group of people tuned in to a particular programme at a particular time.

promotional product a product imprinted with, or otherwise carrying, a logo or promotional message. Also called an **advertising specialty**.

publicity a type of public relations in the form of a news item or story which conveys information about a product, service, or idea in the media.

public relations advertising advertising by a company that focuses on public interest but maintains a relationship to the company's products or agencies. See also PUBLIC RELATIONS.

public service advertising (PSA) advertising with a central focus on public welfare, generally sponsored by a non-profit institution, civic group, religious organization, trade association, or political group.

pulsing the use of advertising in regular intervals, as opposed to seasonal patterns.

pupilometrics a method of advertising research in which a study is conducted on the relationship between a viewer's pupil dilation and the interest factor of visual stimuli.

rate (1) the amount charged by a communications medium to an advertiser per unit of space or time purchased. The rate may vary from national to local campaigns, or may be a fixed rate. (2) to estimate a particular medium's audience size based on a research sample.

rate card an information card, provided by both print and broadcast media, which contains information concerning advertising costs, mechanical requirements, issue dates, closing dates, cancellation dates, and circulation data, etc.

rating point (1) in television, 1% of all TV households who are viewing a particular station at a given time. (2) in radio, 1% of all listeners who are listening to a particular station at a given time. Both instances vary depending on time of day.

reach the estimated number of individuals in the audience of a broadcast, or of an outdoor ad, that is reached at least once during a specific period of time.

readership (1) the total number of readers of a publication (2) the percentage of people that can recall a particular advertisement, aided or unaided.

recognition the ability of research subjects to recall a particular ad or campaign when they see or hear it.

renewal rate the percentage of individuals that renew their print media subscriptions to extend beyond the previous expiration date.

residuals a sum paid to a performer on a TV or radio commercial each time it is run.

rip-o-matic a very rough rendition of a proposed ad composed of images and sounds borrowed (ripped-off) from other commercials or broadcast materials.

road block a method of scheduling broadcast commercials to obtain maximum reach by simultaneously showing the same advertisement on several different stations.

rotoscoping the process of using live and animated characters within an advertisement.

rough an unfinished layout of an ad which shows only a general conception to be presented for analysis, criticism, and approval.

rough cut a preliminary arrangement of film or tape shots that are roughly edited together without voice-over or music in the early stages of editing.

run-of-press (ROP) a newspaper publisher's option to place an ad anywhere in the publication that they choose, as opposed to preferred position. Also referred to as **run-of paper**.

run-of-schedule (ROS) a TV station's option to place a commercial in any time slot that they choose.

rushes same as **dailies**.

sales-response function the effect of advertising on total sales. Often used as a measure of advertising

seasonal rating adjustments in broadcast media, rating modifications that reflect changes in the season, e.g. weather and holidays.

selective demand advertising advertising which promotes a particular manufacturer's brand as opposed to a generic product. See PRIMARY DEMAND ADVERTISING (above).

sets in use (SIU) the percentage of television sets that are tuned into a particular broadcast during a specific amount of time.

share-of-audience the percentage of audiences that are tuned into a particular medium at a given time, e.g. the number of people watching television between the hours of 8:00 p.m. and 11:00 p.m.

shelf screamer or **shelf talker** a printed advertising message which is hung over the edge of a retail store shelf, e.g. 'On Special,' or 'Sale item.'

signature a musical theme associated with a television programme, radio show, or a particular brand, product or service.

situation analysis the gathering and evaluation of information to identify the target group and strategic direction of an advertising campaign.

slick a high-quality proof of an advertisement printed on glossy paper which is suitable for reproduction.

specialty advertising the use of PROMOTIONAL PRODUCTS (above).

split run the simultaneous running of two or more different forms of an advertisement in different copies of the same publication, used to test the effectiveness of one advertisement over another to appeal to regional or other specific markets.

spot announcements commercial or public service announcements that are placed on television or radio programmes.

spread a pair of facing pages in a periodical, or an advertisement which is printed across two such pages.

staggered schedule a schedule of advertisements in a number of periodicals which have different insertion dates.

Standard Rate and Data Service (SRDS) a commercial US firm that publishes reference volumes containing up-to-date information on rates, requirements, closing dates, and other information necessary for ad placement in the media.

storyboard a blueprint for a TV commercial which is drawn to portray copy, dialogue, and action, with caption notes regarding filming, audio components, and script.

stripping the positioning of film negatives or positives of copy and illustrations for the purpose of creating a printing plate for an ad or page. Also referred to as **image assembly**.

subliminal persuasion an advertising message presented below the threshold of consciousness. A visual or auditory message that is allegedly perceived psychologically, but not consciously. Also called **subception**.

superimposition or **super** a process in TV production where an image, words, or phrases are imposed over another image.

supplementary media non-mass media vehicles that are used to promote products, e.g., point-of-purchase advertising.

syndicated programme a television or radio programme that is distributed in more than one market by an organization other than a network.

tabloid a size of newspaper that is roughly half the size of a standard newspaper. The page size is normally 14 inches high by 12 inches wide. This has also become the generalized name in the UK for popular, sensationalist journalism.

tachistoscope testing a method used in advertising and packaging recall tests to measure a viewer's recognition and perception of various elements within an ad by using the different lighting and exposure techniques of a tachistoscope, a device that projects an image at a fraction of a second. See MARKET RESEARCH.

tag line a slogan or phrase that visually conveys the most important product attribute or benefit that the advertiser wishes to convey. Generally, a theme to a campaign.

target audience a specified audience or demographic group for which an advertising message is designed and positioned.

tear sheet a page cut from a magazine or newspaper that is sent to the advertiser as proof of the ad insertion. Also used to check colour reproduction of advertisements.

teaser campaign an advertising campaign aimed at arousing interest and curiosity for a product. For example, Accenture's campaign when it changed its name in 2001.

thumbnail a rough, simple, often small sketch used to show the basic layout of an ad.

time compression a technique used in broadcast production to delete time from television commercials.

trade advertising advertising designed to increase sales specifically for retailers and wholesalers.

transit advertising advertising that appears on public transport or on waiting areas and bus stops.

unaided recall a research method in which a respondent is given no assistance in answering questions regarding a specific advertisement.

unfair advertising advertising that is likely to harm the consumer. See REGULATION OF ADVERTISING (above).

unique selling proposition (USP) a unique product benefit that the competition cannot claim.

up-front buy a purchase of both broadcast and print early in the buying season.

vehicle a specific channel or publication for carrying the advertising message to a target audience.

vertical discount a reduced rate offered to advertisers who purchase airtime on a broadcast medium for a limited amount of time, e.g., one week.

vertical publications publications whose editorial content deals with the interests of a specific industry, e.g., *National Petroleum Magazine* and *Retail Baking Today*.

voiceover (VO) the technique of using the voice of an unseen speaker during film, slides, or other visual material.

voice-pitch analysis (VOPAN) an advertising research technique of analysing a subject's voice during their responses, to test their feelings and attitudes about an ad.

waste circulation (1) advertising in an area where the product or service is not available or has no sales potential. (2) persons in an advertiser's audience who are not potential consumers.

wave scheduling an advertising strategy that consists of scheduling space in the media at intermittent periods, e.g., two weeks on, two weeks off.

wear-out the point reached when an advertising campaign loses its effectiveness due to repeated overplay of ads.

weight (1) an adjustment made in a survey sample to correct for demographic or geographic imbalances. (2) the number of exposures of an advertisement.

white space parts of a print advertisement where nothing is printed, including between blocks of type, illustrations, headlines, etc.

wipe a transition of scenes in a visual production where one image appears to wipe the previous one from the screen.

word painting a radio technique that uses highly descriptive words to evoke images in reading material in an attempt to place the listener into the scene.

---

affiliate directory a categorized listing of affiliate programmes. Affiliate directories are used to find and compare various merchants' programmes. Directories provide simple text listings, but a few offer more advanced search capabilities. Many include articles, newsletters, and forums.

affiliate marketing a specific type of marketing on the Internet that is characterized by revenue sharing between on-line advertisers or merchants and on-line publishers or salespeople. Affiliates give wider advertising and sales distribution on-line to the merchant's products. Typically, an affiliate model works in the following way: a smaller website owner registers with a larger and better known website (e.g. Amazon.com or some other affiliate programme), the website owner then puts various links, banners, and products on their website. The larger website owner pays the smaller website owner when visitors click through on these links and purchase a product. Benefits of affiliate marketing include the potential for automating much of the advertising process (such as accepting and approving applications, generating unique sales links, tracking and reporting of results) and payment by desired results (sales, registrations, clicks). Affiliate compensation can also be based on attention metrics, such as audience size, registrations, subscribers, click-through and website access. Paying for performance shifts much of the advertising risk from the merchants to the affiliates, although merchants still assume some risk of fraud from partner sites. Amazon.com uses affiliate marketing techniques very effectively. Affiliates are usually small sites run by individual webmasters. However, there is a growing trend for large companies to use affiliates. Some companies even participate as a merchant of their own programme and as an affiliate of other programmes.

affiliate network an intermediary that provides services, including aggregation, for affiliate merchants and affiliates. These services can include providing tracking, sales reporting, payment processing, and access to a large base of affiliates. For affiliates, services can include providing one-click application to new merchants, reporting tools, and payment aggregation.

agent a representative of either the buyer or the seller in a negotiation. See also BROKER and WHOLESALER. There are now many different types of agent:

- **manufacturers' agents** are used to represent one or more manufacturers. Their primary role is to sell the manufacturer's goods, particularly for manufacturers who do not have their own direct sales force or who wish to sell their goods in a territory where their direct sales force does not operate. They usually cover pricing, defined distribution area, order handling, fulfilment, post-sales service, guarantees and commission rates. This type of agent usually handles a number of manufacturers' product lines.

- **purchasing agents** primarily buy for the manufacturer. Often these agents will work for the company buyer. Their main role is to negotiate purchases with suppliers, and to receive, inspect, warehouse and deliver the goods to the company.

- **commission agents** take possession of goods from manufacturers and sell them, taking a commission and expenses following sale.

- **personal agents** are used for high value individuals in the media, entertainment and sports areas. Their main purpose is to negotiate the best possible deals for their clients in terms of fees, long-term contacts, advertising and merchandising and, in sports, transfer fees.

- **intelligent agents** are a new development on the World Wide Web, referring to a non-human software agent taking instructions from a human to search out the best and most appropriate information on the web, customized to the needs of the individual searcher. In future this intelligent agent will become more sophisticated, using intuition to seeking out best information and make purchases for its 'master'.

AGGREGATE DEMAND

Aggregate demand is the total of planned expenditure on goods and services in an economy. This economic measure is used by marketers for a number of tasks: in assessing investments in geographical markets; planning campaigns for specific socio-economic groups; to understand and measure the ability, and willingness, of individuals and institutions to purchase goods and services. Aggregate demand is primarily a measure of the *ability to spend* on goods and services at different price levels and is therefore a measure of purchasing power relative to expenditure and income.

There are four key types of expenditure that constitute aggregate demand:

Consumption expenditure

Of the four components of aggregate demand, consumption expenditure is the largest, contributing to between 60% and 70% of total expenditure in any given economy. This category of expenditure includes private spending on durable goods (for example cars, electronic goods, appliances), non-durable goods (food, clothing, books), and services (housing, healthcare, education, entertainment). Consumption expenditure decisions are strongly influenced by household disposable income, household wealth, savings needs and plans, confidence in the future direction of the economy, and interest rates.

Special attention must be given to the service component of consumption expenditure for several reasons. First, services are the largest component, representing at least 50% of spending. Second, services include housing services (e.g. rents being paid from tenant to landlord). Third, services, unlike durable and some non-durable goods, are difficult to accumulate as inventory.

Investment expenditure

Investment expenditure constitutes a smaller share of the total but tends to be the most volatile component contributing to the cyclical behaviour of aggregate demand. This category of expenditure includes fixed non-residential investment (factories, machines, transport equipment), fixed residential investment (new houses and rented flats), and business inventories. Often, the volatility in investment results from fluctuation in inventory levels as a result of changing expectations about business conditions. Because of the sensitivity of investment decisions to changing interest rates, this category of expenditure is directly affected by monetary policies and activity in the financial sector of an economy.

Fixed residential and non-residential investment refers to the creation of income-producing assets. For example, those assets that will generate net-benefits (such as housing services) in the case of owner-occupied housing or generate profits as part of the production process. These net-benefits and profits depend on the expected revenue generated by the asset as well as the costs of acquiring, maintaining and replacing these assets.

Demand for the production of the asset will directly affect the revenue generated. Strong demand based on preferences, optimism, purchasing power, or demographics will lead to the desire for more investment expenditure.

Acquisition costs include both the purchase price of the asset and the borrowing costs involved, which are both highly sensitive to changes in interest rates and the financial markets. Higher interest rates lead to higher borrowing costs; this, in turn, leads to lower net-benefits or profits. Therefore, the level of aggregate investment expenditure may be reduced. Another factor is the cost of maintenance and replacement costs that are related to the useful life of an asset and also to its rate of depreciation. Assets that wear out very quickly, or become obsolete in a short period of time, have higher costs. This has the same effect on aggregate demand as rising interest rates.

Government expenditure

Government expenditure is a reflection of the fiscal needs and policies of the public sector in a given economy. This type of expenditure might be in reaction to the demand for public infrastructure investment and services by citizens and businesses either through electoral voting or other types of political activity. In addition, government expenditure could be used as a directed public policy to increase incomes in the hope of stimulating aggregate demand. This has, been used from time to time (famously in the US in the 1930s) to help national economies recover from depressions.

Net export expenditure

Net export expenditure is based directly on service and merchandise flows across international borders as well as capital flows into and out of a particular country. Merchandise flows are sensitive to domestic income levels and preferences for foreign-made goods. In addition, these flows are influenced by exchange rates that determine the domestic price of goods and services produced abroad. Capital flows depend on interest rate differentials among nations as well as exchange rates that affect the domestic price of a foreign asset both at the time of purchase of that asset and at the time of sale.

AIDA (Attention Interest Desire Action) one of many models that analyse and measure the customer's journey from ignorance to purchase. The AIDA model is simple, which partly explains its longevity and widespread use.

The model was developed in 1898 by St. Elmo Lewis in an attempt to explain how personal selling works. The model laid out a sequence that describes the process a salesperson must lead a potential customer through in order to achieve a sale. The stages, Attention, Interest, Desire, and Action, form a linear hierarchy. In order to be motivated to actually make a purchase, customers must progress from being aware of a product's existence to being interested enough to pay attention to the product's benefits and advantages, to having a desire to benefit from the product. Lewis believed that the fourth stage, Action, would come as a natural result of movement through the first three stages.

Although Lewis's work was primarily focused on helping the personal selling process, it was avidly taken up by marketing and advertising theorists over the next half-century. The action stage became the ultimate goal of all marketing and all advertising. This is also fundamental to the understanding of the HIERARCHY OF EFFECTS theory. Later theories distinguished the role of marketing as moving the consumer to action from that of advertising, whose main purpose was to move consumer through the sequence toward action.

If the seller can successfully gain the consumer's attention, then the next stage is to stimulate interest in the product. For example, what special features or benefits does the product have? What special needs does it address? How might it satisfy any one of the needs and wants that the consumer might have? During this stage the consumer develops a reaction to the product, usually either favourable or unfavourable. If the response is favourable and the advertisement is successful in awakening interest, it then attempts to create in the consumer's mind a desire to purchase. It does this by successfully connecting the benefits of the product with the consumer's needs and wants. This is often the most difficult aspect of advertising design. Portraying a product in an attractive manner that stimulates interest in consumers is the easier part; it is more difficult to persuade consumers to buy it. Advertising rarely makes the sale on its own. So, this phase of advertising has to both show consumers that there is a product available which will satisfy their needs, and show them that they can satisfy that need by purchasing the product in question. This leads to the final stage, action, where consumers actually get up, go out, actively seek the product and buy it.

See also ADOPTION, DAGMAR, HIERARCHY OF EFFECTS, THREE ORDERS MODEL.

Ansoff matrix (also known as the **directional matrix**) a model for analysing the approach to product-market growth strategies developed in 1965 by H. Igor Ansoff in his book *Corporate Strategy*. The main axes of the matrix are new or existing products and new or existing markets. The matrix has four quadrants: *market penetration*, existing products and markets; *new product development*, which involves new products introduced into existing markets; *market development* which involves finding new markets for existing products; *diversification*, which involves new products in new markets. The modern day marketing practitioner may find the matrix useful mainly for well-defined markets and tangible products. The matrix framework can be used to develop product strategies for various market growth strategies:

1. *market penetration strategy*, or penetrating the existent market with existing product, is regarded as the lowest risk strategy. This could involve more aggressive marketing and sales campaigns around the existing product. Results could include increased purchase and usage from existing customers encouraged by attractive pricing or discount offers or discounts on multiple purchases. It could be as a result of more intensive customer research and focused action such as targeted mailing of customers with relevant offers.

Alternatively, it could be achieved through aggressive market share building, ie winning customers from competitors in the existing market.

2. *market development*, developing new markets with existing products, is higher risk. This strategic approach seeks out new market sectors that are underdeveloped, or which are less price-conscious than the existing market. This may involve the development of new distribution channels or new retail outlets. It may also involve new geographic markets for the existing products, for example through licensing, agent or distributor arrangements.

3. *new product development*, developing new products for existing markets, can often be the heaviest investment programme because of the cost in involved in producing and marketing a new product. This may involve the development of products based upon new and untried technologies.

4. *Diversification*, developing new markets with new products, is regarded as the highest risk. It will take the company into markets and product development cycles in which it is inexperienced. It may also lead the company into making acquisitions or merging with other companies in order to gain either market or product assets.

Product \ Market	Present	New
Present	Market Penetration	Product Development
New	Market Development	Diversification

anticorporatism a protest movement targeted against major international and global corporations, particularly those believed to be using cheap labour to create their primary branded product, those whose operations cause harm to the natural environment or its creatures, and those involved in harmful trades, such as arms, tobacco or certain types of drugs and chemicals. As the focuses of the protests are those companies who have global brands, this is an important social and political movement and trend for marketers to understand, especially when designing campaigns. It shows that consideration of brand reputation must now go beyond the simply commercial dimension of a company.

The global brand image can be a surprisingly complex business to handle, and can be affected adversely in many ways. Nike, for example, became the focus of worldwide protests when it became apparent that Nike trainers are produced by workers in conditions that are characterized in the media as 'sweatshop labour'. Nike responded to this attack by saying they were providing jobs where no one else was, but also seemed to be saying that in any case most trainer manufactures produced their shoes in the same way, so why did Nike get the bad publicity. The fact remains that many consumers are now aware of the low pay earned by the workers who manufacture their shoes, and there seems little doubt that Nike has been damaged by the many campaigns on low manufacturing pay in the industry. There is also no question that the growing 'anti-globalization' movement has hurt many firms with an international image that once seemed impregnable, a notable example being the McDonald's chain, which has been particularly attacked for its strong propogation of a fast food culture. Being American, with American values. also comes under attack. This is a factor that has also damaged Coca-Cola in the Middle East, where rival local brands explicitly position themselves as opposed to the all-American appeal of Coke. As in martial arts, size and power can sometimes be turned by even tiny pressure groups against the large corporations, the perceived 'David and Goliath' syndrome, except in this case David has little to lose, while Goliath can suffer a severe setback to its brand image. A classic example here is the so-called 'McDonalds libel trial'. The case was brought by McDonalds against Greenpeace activists Helen Steel and David Morris after London Greenpeace issued a pamphlet 'What's Wrong with McDonalds? Everything they don't want you to know'. The pamphlet accused McDonalds of a wide range of abuses, from animal welfare failings to the exploitation of children. After a trial lasting 313 days (making it the longest-ever English libel trial) the judge found that McDonalds had indeed been libelled, but also found the company responsible in variable degrees for a wide range of abuses, including animal cruelty, misleading customers about nutrition, paying low wages and child exploitation. Unsurprisingly, the trial is now widely perceived as a huge PR disaster for McDonalds. The image implications for companies with cases such as the McDonalds libel trial are of course enormous and it can be incredibly difficult to undo the harm done. Similarly, even the most powerful oil company will find that its image suffers disastrously every time there is an oil spill. For all the power and spin capacity of large commercial enterprises, a photograph of one oil-drenched seabird has the power to negate massive image-building campaigns.

APIC a set of core marketing management activities defined by Philip Kotler as Analysis, Planning, Implementation, and Control.

applications service provider (ASP) a type of business characterized by the hosting and distribution of third-party applications or services. These applications or services are distributed over the Internet to many customers in exchange for a stream of smaller payments as opposed to one fixed, upfront price. The business model is based upon customers paying a monthly service fee to use proprietary software developed by major brands, such as Oracle and Microsoft, instead of licensing software and having to support it themselves. Application service provider is a very general term; there are many different types of ASPs that share very few common characteristics. Many sub-acronyms are currently being introduced in an attempt to better make distinctions, but few of the terms have gained general or major brand recognition.

approvers see DECISION-MAKING UNIT under BUYING PROCESS FOR ORGANIZATIONS OR INDUSTRIAL BUYERS

article a piece of non-fiction text written for inclusion in a journal, newspaper or other publication.

atmosphere a part of retail image that is created by a blend of sensory effects intended to create a specific shopping mood.

atmospherics a term coined by Philip Kotler in *Journal of Retailing* in 1973 that described how retail environments could affect shopping behaviour and eventual purchase. There has been much psychological and market research into the practice and effect of the total shopping experience and how it can be best created. Atmospherics may involve music, lighting, scent, the provision of food and beverages, entertainment, and display. There are now many agencies that specialize in the design of retail interiors around a central concept, and the use of atmospherics is core to the design.

attention an important development of management theory that has direct applicability to marketing. The capturing and retention of customer attention is an increasingly difficult task that is breeding different types of new marketing technique and practice. In an age of impatience and shortening attention spans, increases in the number of communications channels, and the vast availability of information, the impact of traditional mass marketing has, to some extent, been undermined. Attention grabbing is much more difficult than it used to be; attention holding is even more difficult. We are now in the age of customer attention deficit and new techniques that can gain and hold attention need to be developed. Modern-day citizens are faced with the paradox of the Information Age: they are overloaded with information, but are unable to absorb and classify it, and continue to generate even more. This places a higher premium than ever on the marketers' ability to gain attention. Attention has become a key source of value in the economy of the Information Age. The Web involves exchanges of attention between individuals. The proponents of the Attention Economy argue that attention is a scarce resource, and therefore has and will increase in economic value. It is causing increasingly creative and outlandish marketing campaigns.

An increasing proportion of our society lives and works through the processing of information: fewer workers are directly involved in the production, transportation, and distribution of material goods, but instead earn their living managing or dealing with information in some form. The Information Age has created an abundance of unstructured information with no overall ideological, schematic or intellectual framework through which the information can be processed. In the past most sources of information, such as printed books, radio and television broadcasts, were one-way dissemination media. Nowadays an increasing proportion of the media channels are interactive. Therefore, interactivity is becoming an increasingly important part of gaining and holding attention. (See also AIDA, PERSONAL SELLING under SALES, DIRECT MARKETING and INTERACTIVE MARKETING under MARKETING SPECIALIZATIONS).

attitude a position that an individual has adopted in response to a theory, belief, object, product, service, event, or another person. It is a relatively consistent predisposition to behave in a certain way. There are three components to an attitude: a *cognitive component* which is what the individual knows or believes about an object or act; an *affective component* which is what the individual feels emotionally about an object or act; a *cognitive component* which is how the individual is disposed to behave towards an object or act. See also CONSUMER BEHAVIOUR.

audience the person or persons who are receiving a transmitted marketing or informational message. All good marketing communications should begin with a thorough understanding of the target audience and assumptions made about them. In all aspects of marketing communications, the definition of the target audience, the determination of attitude and value systems, and the positioning and development of relevant and appropriate messages for them is critical.

awareness see marketing communications, DAGMAR.

awareness-trial-reinforcement (Ehrenberg's process) a process suggesting that a trial purchase may proceed from awareness of a brand, or confrontation with a product in a retail outlet, after which the consumer gets to know the product and develops an attitude towards it.

B

baby boom the increase in births that started in 1945, when World War II ended, and extended into the early 1960s.

baby boomers the large generation born after World War II, particularly those born between 1946 and 1964. In market targeting, the baby boomers are among the wealthier and more influential groups in the advanced economies. For example, baby boomers comprise 15% of the on-line population and control a disproportionate amount of the wealth in North America. They constitute 36% of the cinema audience in North America.

baby bust the decrease in births between 1965 and 1976. People born in this period are often referred to as **generation X.**

Backer, Bill (1926–) during his 25-year career with the advertising agency McCann-Erickson Worldwide, New York, Backer created some of the more successful advertising campaigns in history. For example: Campbell's Soup's 'Bring on the Campbell's, Soup is Good Food;' Coca-Cola's 1971 'Hilltop' anthem, 'I'd Like to Buy the World a Coke' and Coke's 'It's the Real Thing' jingle (see ADVERTISING above); and Miller Lite's 'Tastes great/less filling' celebrity 'feud' series that ran for years and put Lite atop a new beer category. In 1979, Backer left McCann as vice chairman-creative director and, with Carl Spielvogel, Interpublic vice chairman, opened Backer & Spielvogel. Saatchi & Saatchi acquired the agency in 1985 for $100 million.

backward invention the process of redesigning and producing a product for foreign markets after it has become obsolete in advanced economies.

bait and switch the practice of enticing or 'baiting' the potential customer with a misleading advertisement (e.g. offering goods deceptively cheap) then persuading them to buy something more expensive ('switching') or more than they originally intended.

Bait advertising, specifically, is an alluring but insincere offer to sell a product or service that the advertiser does not really want to sell. The real purpose is to switch consumers from buying the advertised merchandise in order to sell something else, usually at a higher price, which is more advantageous to the advertiser. The primary aim of a bait advertisement is to obtain leads that can be 'switched' to buying something else. A range of techniques are used to cause the potential customer to 'switch'.

This practice is now illegal in certain markets, notably the USA. In the US, advertisements cannot contain an offer to sell a product when the offer is not a bona fide effort to sell the advertised product. No statement or illustration can be used in any advertisement that creates a false impression of the grade, quality, make, value, currency of model, size, colour, usability, or origin of the product offered. Nothing that could lead to a misrepresentation of the actual product is allowed. Interviews or contracts that switch the customer to another product are prohibited. No act or practice to discourage the purchase of the advertised merchandise as part of a bait scheme to sell other merchandise is allowed. Advertising authorities look at the following warning signs of a bait and switch manoeuvre:

(a) the refusal to show, demonstrate, or sell the product offered in accordance with the terms of the offer;

(b) the disparagement by acts or words of the advertised product or the disparagement of the guarantee, credit terms, availability of service, repairs or parts, or in any other respect, in connection with it;

(c) the failure to have available at all outlets listed in the advertisement a sufficient quantity of the advertised product to meet reasonably anticipated demand, unless the advertisement clearly and adequately discloses that supply is limited and/or the merchandise is available only at designated outlets;

(d) the refusal to take orders for the advertised merchandise to be delivered within a reasonable period of time;

(e) the showing or demonstrating of a product which is defective, unusable or impractical for the purpose represented or implied in the advertisement;

(f) use of a sales plan or method of compensating or penalizing salesmen designed to prevent or discourage them from selling the advertised product;

(g) 'unselling' a product and substituting a different or higher priced product or service in its place;

Among acts or practices that are considered in determining if the initial sale was in good faith are, for example:

(a) accepting a deposit for the advertised product, then switching the purchaser to a higher-priced product;

(b) failure to make delivery of the advertised product within a reasonable time or to make a refund;

(c) delivery of the advertised product that is defective, unusable or impractical for the purpose represented or implied in the advertisement.

Example: bait and switch on the internet

A notorious e-mail scam offered free video-game consoles but instead routed people to a pornography website at expensive cost-per-minute rates. Consumers received unsolicited spam e-mail messages claiming that the recipients had won a free Sony PlayStation 2 or other prize through a promotion supposedly sponsored by Yahoo. In fact, the e-mail messages directed consumers to an adult Internet site through a 900-number modem connection that charged them up to $3.99 per minute of use. When consumers responded to the e-mail informing them that they had won the game system, they then were routed to a Web page that imitated an authentic Yahoo page. That page then instructed consumers to download a program that would purportedly permit them to connect to a 'toll-free' website where they could enter their name and address to request a PlayStation. When consumers adhered to these instructions, they were connected to a pornographic site by way of a 900-number, where they then incurred per-minute charges. A legal case was brought against the operators by the US regulatory bodies. The practices of the defendants were asserted to be deceptive *and designed to mislead consumers with respect to supposedly winning a prize, Yahoo purportedly sending the e-mail, and the connection supposedly being toll-free. The operators did not disclose the cost of connecting to the website and did not provide an audio introductory disclosure message when consumers connected via the 900-number.*

banner ad a graphical advertising unit especially created for use on the World Wide Web. These have become the dominant form of advertising on-line. The accepted standard size is 468x60. Banner ads were initially measured for performance on the basis of the click-through rate (CTR) achieved. Banner ads have been controversial with many detractors claiming that they do not achieve the required result. Some of this is related to the demise of the CTR as an effective measure of on-line advertising. Consequently, banner ads have declined in price. On-line marketers now seek to combine low-cost banner ad rates with above-average response rates as their prime return on investment metric in this medium. See also ADVERTISING, POP UP WINDOW, INTERACTIVE MARKETING under MARKETING SPECIALIZATIONS.

banner blindness the tendency of web visitors to ignore banner ads, even when the banner ads contain information visitors are actively looking for. This is a major issue for on-line advertisers to overcome.

banner exchange a network where participating sites display banner ads in exchange for credits that are converted (using a predetermined exchange rate) into ads to be displayed on other sites.

bargain (in marketing terms, rather than stock exchange terms) is either a discounted price for a product or service or a high-value product or service at a good price relative to competitor prices. Bargains can often be an important part of consumer marketing. Non-financial factors, such as the concept of fairness, play an important role in bargain hunting and consumer satisfaction. Consumers often derive pleasure or satisfaction from the idea that they are paying a fair price rather than a highly reduced price. They can derive pleasure or satisfaction from getting a good deal or 'fair' price even when there was no major cost saving at stake. Price discounts are important in creating a sense of fairness: the percentage discount offered is an important factor in consumer satisfaction and sense of value. Even if the amount of money involved in a discount is relatively small, a higher percentage discount, 40% for example, leads people to infer that they are getting a fair price.

bargain basement originally the name given to the lower floor of a department store where excess or end of line merchandise was offered to the public at prices well below that which they had when they were on the other floors of the store. It has since become a generic term for low or sell-off prices.

barriers to entry economic or technical factors or costs that make it difficult for new firms to enter a market against other competitors. The term was popularized by Michael Porter in his classic works *Competitive Strategy* (1980) and *Competitive Advantage* (1985). Companies with high barriers to entry and high market share are in a stronger position than companies with high market share in which barriers to entry are much lower. This is an important element in overall marketing strategy. Barriers to entry reduce the level of competition in a market, often enabling higher-than-competitive prices.

Some factors that prevent competitors from entering a particular market are:

- cost advantages on the part of the company with market leadership, or costs that are so high that it prevents major new entrants. For example, it is relatively easy to enter the retail industry, either through purchase of a retail outlet or, increasingly, setting up as an on-line retailer. On the opposite extreme, entering the oil business or car production business requires a level of capital investment that deters most new entrants. Only large companies, often backed by governments, can meet the entry costs into such industries. For example, there have been relatively few new entrants to the oil, aerospace or car manufacturing industries over and above those already established since the war.

- sunk costs (those that aren't recoverable) can often be a barrier to entry. If a railway owns a rail track or a water company owns a reservoir, it is very difficult for a competitor to enter the market place. This makes certain types of business a 'natural monopoly' – such as the provision of drinking water to a certain region. To some extent, sunk costs represent the difference between the purchase price and the resale price of capital equipment and the costs of advertising. High sunk costs will act as a barrier to entry as the cost of failure is so great. Conversely, low sunk costs will encourage firms to enter an industry, as they will have little to lose.

- marketing costs, as huge spending by firms leads to consumer loyalty. New entrants have to at least match this level of marketing if they wish to persuade consumers to buy their product. High marketing spending makes it prohibitively expensive for new companies to enter the market and establish themselves. For example, the movie industry increasingly now spends equally high amounts on the marketing and merchandising of movies as it does in producing them. This makes it very difficult for small or independent movie studios to recapture their investments in movie making because they normally don't have the marketing power to secure major audiences. The vast amount spent by the perfume industry to merchandise and market its products, relative to the costs of production of a bottle of perfume, makes new entrance prohibitively expensive.

- technological advantage, often protected by patents, prevents competitors catching up. Increasingly, however, simple technological advantage is unlikely to be a sustainable barrier to entry unless a continuous stream of innovation supplements it.

- monopolistic or oligopolistic practices governing strong distribution channels that give access to end-users. An example of this has been the failure of the cable companies and telecom start ups in Europe to compete effectively against the former state monopoly telecom. providers. One of the reasons that is often cited for this is the fact that the former monopolies controlled the local loop, which was the 'last mile' of local exchange and distribution channel to domestic customers. Another example is the diamond industry, which even managed to shut out GE when it discovered a synthetic, low cost way to make diamonds.

- the vast economies of scale that some incumbents in industries are able to establish, meaning that the minimum efficient scale (MES) barrier to new entrants is very large. It would take many years to reach the necessary level of output. Existing firms who have the lower costs would be able to win any price war against a new entrant.

- legislative barriers, often created by government licences, can prevent other firms from providing service, for example, commercial television and radio, the national lottery, delivery of letters by Royal Mail and the production of nuclear energy. Additionally, tariffs and quotas imposed by governments on imported goods and services can act as a barrier to entry as they prevent firms from competing in a particular national market.

- restrictive practices – for example, a manufacturer's refusing to supply a retailer who stocks a competitor's product, or a firm refusing to sell one product unless the buyer purchases a whole range of goods.

- firms lowering the price so much that competitors are driven out of the market. Also known as **predatory pricing**.

See also PORTER, COMPETITION, MARKET STRATEGY.

Barton, Bruce (1886–1967), of Batten, Barton, Durstine & Osborn (BBDO) Agency, New York is one of the pioneers of the advertising industry in North America. He discovered the iconic American artist Norman Rockwell and, during World War I, worked on United War Work campaigns with copywriters Roy Durstine and Alex Osborn. They opened their ad agency in 1918, merging it in 1928 with George Batten Co. to create BBDO. BBDO became known for writing hard-hitting copy. Barton's 1925 bestseller, *The Man Nobody Knows* portrayed Jesus Christ as an advertising salesman. He also wrote many newspaper columns as well as other books and had a political career. After surviving a sensational blackmail scandal, Barton returned to BBDO in 1940.

belief the underpinning value of brand image. The set of beliefs that the consumer holds about the brand determine its overall brand image. The beliefs that the consumer holds about a brand are not necessarily aligned to what he thinks are the most important attributes of the brand. Loss of belief in a brand is perhaps more dangerous than temporary falling sales of a brand. See also BRAND, CONSUMER MARKETING.

below-the-line refers to promotions that use directly targeted promotional techniques (such as direct selling initiatives, database marketing, direct mail marketing, telemarketing and, increasingly, interactive or 'permission' based techniques using the Internet) as opposed to advertising in mass media channels (above-the-line). Certain aspects of public relations can also qualify as below-the-line promotions. In the late 20th century, total spending on below-the-line promotions came to exceed above-the-line promotions in the mass media. See also ADVERTISING, ABOVE-THE-LINE, DIRECT MARKETING under MARKETING SPECIALIZATIONS, PERSONAL SELLING under SALES.

benchmarking a technique by which a company tries to emulate or exceed standards achieved, or processes adopted, by another company in order to improve its own performance. Sometimes referred to as best practices, exemplary practices, or business excellence, benchmarking is used in marketing to decide on comparative advantages of competitors and to advise on gaps in the marketplace between competitors. It can also be a collaborative process among a group of companies to focus on specific operating practices, compare measures and results and identify improved processes within their organizations. In more recent times it has become an analytical tool to help companies improve their business processes. Most business processes can be benchmarked. One of the main benefits of benchmarking is that it encourages companies to look externally and comparatively in order to find best practice and high performance and then to measure actual business operations against those goals. One of the mistakes people make when beginning their benchmarking project is that they only look to benchmark some company within their own industry. Worse yet, some people think they must benchmark their main competitor. The danger here is that the competitor is often a lower performer than the company doing the benchmarking. Therefore, only companies that show excellent performance and are well known for being a good model ought to be benchmarked. Companies initiating a benchmarking study have to decide on the most compatible company to benchmark, who they need to conduct a full benchmark study and the best format for conducting the survey (in person, by telephone, by e-mail or by survey instrument). Most business processes are common throughout industry. For example; NASA has the same fundamental Human Resources requirements for hiring and developing employees, as does American Express. British Telecom has the same Customer Satisfaction Survey process as Brooklyn Union Gas. These processes, from different industries, are similar and can be benchmarked very effectively.

Key components of benchmarking
- data gathering in the form of detailed surveys of measures and processes;
- identification of best performers; and
- site visits to the best companies.

Benchmarking and best practices
- internally among divisions;
- within the industry; and
- outside the industry.

See also MARKET RESEARCH under MARKETING SPECIALIZATIONS.

benefit in marketing terms, the principal or major benefits sought by customers in making a purchase decision. These benefits are different depending on the customer segment, each of whom perceives different benefits from the same product or service and ascribes a different values to them. Ultimately, benefits must be seen to satisfy an unmet portion of customer need.

benefit segmentation the idea that consumers can be grouped according to the principal benefits that they seek from products or services. Different people buy the same or similar products for different reasons. For example, women may purchase a Volvo car for safety and comfort; men may purchase it for it durability and practicality. Use of different types of segmentation variables could lead to the conclusion that the main criterion for segmentation is the *principal benefit sought*. Hence, although this approach acknowledges the fact that no single variable is likely to be of sufficient discriminatory power to segment a market on its own, it regards the *benefit sought* as the main variable. See also MARKET SEGMENTATION under (TECHNIQUES OF) MARKET RESEARCH.

Bernays, Edward L. (1891–1995) regarded as the founding father of public relations. Lacking his uncle's renown outside the world of business history, this nephew of Sigmund Freud was among the most influential people in the 20th century. Well versed in the then-new science of psychiatry and mass psychology, Bernays, from the 1920s onwards, helped to consolidate a fateful marriage between theories of mass psychology (that had previously been used by government propaganda agencies) and schemes of corporate and political persuasion and the creation of popular consent for causes, products and ideas. While there had been major press agencies before Bernays, he was the first to adapt the theories of psychology to the formation of mass public opinion. He defined public relations as 'a vocation applied by a social scientist who advises a client or employer on the social attitudes and actions to take to win the support of the public upon whom the viability of the client or employer depends'. He viewed the public relations professional as one of the intellectual elite shaping the opinions and consent of a democratic society. He founded his own public relations firm in New York in 1919 and he gave the first-ever lectures in public relations in New York University in the 1920s and published the seminal *Crystallizing Public Opinion* in 1923 as well as *Propaganda* (1928) and *The Engineering of Consent* (1947). Bernays, in his career, advised US Presidents Coolidge, Wilson, Hoover and Eisenhower, legendary individuals such as Edison, Henry Ford, Eleanor Roosevelt, Freud, Caruso, Diaghilev and Nijinsky, as well as large corporations such as General Motors, Procter & Gamble, R. H. Macy & Company, Cartier, MGM and heads of government outside the US. His legendary public relations campaigns included creating favourable public opinion to America's entry into World War I, a campaign to get children to like soap, the election of Herbert Hoover, the building of Route 66 across America, the joys of having bacon for breakfast, convincing women to like Lucky Strike cigarettes in the 1930s, then in a famous volte-face, creating anti-smoking campaigns when the link between smoking and cancer was made in the 1960s.

Bernays, who died aged 103 in 1995, became extremely concerned at the 'monster' that he had helped to create. ' Public relations today is horrible. Any dope, any nitwit, any idiot can call him or herself a public relations practitioner. Some people just use public relations as a euphemism for press agentry,' he declared. 'A firm sends articles or press releases to newspapers to win favour for a client and it usually ends up in the trash. It's not only not good P.R.; it intensifies the antagonism toward the product. I'm pleased to be known as the father of public relations when the field is taken seriously, like law or architecture.'

See also PUBLIC RELATIONS.

Bernbach, William (1911–1982), joint founder of the Doyle Dane Bernbach agency in New York in 1949. Often regarded as the most influential figure in the 20th-century advertising industry, Bernbach is remembered for his creative campaigns characterized by their freshness, relevance, lack of pretension and tonal harmony between product and copy. 'Advertising doesn't create a product advantage. It can only convey it', was a typical Bernbach view of the advertising industry. He was an advocate of advertising as an art form and the (then) radical notion that the general public was intelligent. Underlying respect for the public, in his view, would encourage favourable reactions to intelligent and imaginative advertising. Bernbach always insisted on first learning how his client's products related to their users, and what human qualities and emotions came into play. The next stage was to decide on how best to communicate those elements to the consumers through various media channels, gaining the consumers' understanding and support. His most legendary campaign was for Volkswagen's introduction to the USA, involving a range of print and TV commercials. In print, VW's 'Think Small' ad challenged the acquisitive tendencies that had been characteristic of American advertising in the 1950s. The Beetle became the first successful import car and the ad campaign altered the overall approach to advertising for all time. He had very successful TV advertising campaigns: Volkswagen's 'Funeral' and 'Snow plow' stories as part of the overall Volkswagen campaign; 'Mamma mia' and 'Poached oyster' for Alka-Seltzer; 'Visit to Grandpa' plus Laurence Olivier for Polaroid; 'Italian wedding' for Rheingold beer; 'Mikey' for Life cereal; 'Gorilla' for American Tourister luggage; 'Card game' and 'Sharing,' with Jack Gilford, for Cracker Jack; 'Burning egg' for GTE; and stop-motion 'Contrasts' for Jamaica Tourist Board.

See also ADVERTISING, BRAND.

beyond-the-banner describes on-line advertising not involving standard GIF and JPEG banner ads. See also BANNER AD, POP UP WINDOWS.

bidding the process in which potential suppliers submit their offers (or tenders) in response to a published requirement. This process is normally competitive. Competitive bidding is one dimension of selling, particularly in a business-to-business market. There are always judgments to be made around the balance of value, price, actual cost and the desire to win the contract. For many, the physical and oral presentation of the tender to the potential client is the 'sharp end' of marketing, when the potential client judges all attributes of the potential supplier, including the specific proposal. Competitive bidding principally benefits the buyer, given that it creates an impartial environment that is likely to drive value for money efficiency. It also helps to 'educate' the buyer by giving him a lot of information on various competitors and their offerings. This process is increasing for large-scale purchases, and is almost mandatory for large government contracts. See also SALES.

billboard the board on which posters, or bills, are pasted. It can also be known as a hoarding or poster site. The billboard is one of the oldest advertising media and is still among the most popular.

billing a marketing term that tends to be used as a measure of a marketing agency's (particularly an advertising agency's) total revenues. In an advertising agency it is the term used for the total value of business undertaken by the agency. A **billing rate** is the individual price of each expert in an agency charged externally, usually on an hourly or a daily basis.

black box model a model of consumer behaviour in which the mind of the consumer is likened to a 'black box' that cannot be penetrated to find out what is inside. Such models focus on the **input** or stimulus (for example, advertising) and the response or **output** (purchase behaviour). See also CONSUMER BEHAVIOUR.

blog/blogging blog is an abbreviated term for a Weblog. A blog, or the act of 'Blogging' is defined by its existence and transmission rather than by a predetermined format. In essence, it is a highly personalized point of view, usually written chronologically, on a defined subject area, and posted on a website that hosts fellow 'bloggers'. A blog can take the form of a personal log, journal or diary, and often interspersed personal emotions with the subject matter. Most 'blogging' discussions are moderated. The benefit to the 'blogger' is the sharp and near instant feedback received from fellow bloggers. Good examples of websites that host blogging discussions on focused subject matter are: Ecademy.com and Slashdot.org. Blogging can be variously interpreted as 'Internet journalism', or how the Internet has enabled individuals to go beyond the traditional journalism of the offline world, or, less favourably, as vanity publishing enabled by the Internet and the web.

blurb a short description of a book that appears on the cover. It can also mean the effusive endorsements of a book or a play or a film that are usually printed on the cover or poster.

booklet a small and concise version of a larger text, often presented in bound or leaflet form. Alternatively, it could be a short piece of presentational material summarizing essential features and benefits.

bookmark a link stored in a web browser for future reference. It is the main way in which people personalize their favourite sources of information on the vast World Wide Web.

Boston Consulting Group (BCG) matrix a model developed by the consultancy of the same name in the 1970s. It is focused on the cash flows generated by products and businesses portfolios as a result of relative market share and growth. Market share is measured relative to the product's largest competitor. This technique became a staple of market strategies in the 1980s. In the Boston matrix products are classified according to their ability to either generate or to consume cash. These are the main categories with their famous labels for each dimension of the matrix.

Cash cow a product or business with high market share and low market growth;

Dog one with a low market share and low growth;

Problem child (or question mark) one with low market share and high growth potential.

Star one having high growth and growing market share, but not as high a share and therefore not as cash generative as a cash cow.

The matrix is not static and the interrelationship between the various classifications makes the model very useful, particularly for developing market strategies. For example:

Stars are businesses or products with outstanding opportunities that do not generate excess cash because they are still growing market share in face of competition. They may well be self-financing. Stars of today may become cash cows of the future. Excess cash is provided by the *cash cows* that are entering a period of low growth in mature markets but which need relatively little cash investment. Cash cows are assumed to enjoy lower cost, economies of scale and high profit margins. *Dogs,* by contrast, have low market shares in low-growth markets and tend to generate either a loss or a relatively low profit. They typically take up more management time than warranted and, unless they can be strategically justified, such as contributing to overheads, are potential candidates for divestment. *Problem children* (or *question marks*) need considerable cash investment because they have a low relative share but high growth prospects. They are therefore cash users and could one day become stars of the future. Management must choose between further speculative investment and even withdrawal, depending on their prospects in their target markets.

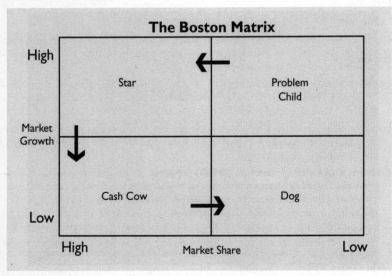

Figure supplied by courtesy of marketingteacher.com

The BCG remains a useful framework for portfolio analysis. It has, since the 1980s, been subject to various criticisms of its shortcomings and has become less reliable as a framework for practical marketing action. The main criticism levelled at the matrix is the assumption that all of a company's products and business units work in an interconnected life cycle. In this life cycle, the mature and profitable funds and fuels the new and growing while the old falters and eventually is terminated. Another one of the problems that practitioners have with the BCG matrix is that it is difficult to delineate and define what a 'market' is, and, consequently, to measure market share precisely. It does not take into account technological discontinuities that can alter the entire shape and dynamics of a marketplace within a very short space of time. Beyond that, some critics have also pointed out the underlying assumption that cash generation is always organic with a company and does not take into account many other 'inorganic' or external cash generating instruments that are available which could affect a portfolio and market position. Also, one would have to be careful in its uses – particularly using it as a guide to divestments and product withdrawals – as it offers an overly simplistic formula to determine 'dog' status. General Electric Corporation developed a more sophisticated analytical matrix model (known as the GE matrix) that used *industry attractiveness* and *business strengths* as the main axes of analysis.

boutique a specialist agency or consultancy that employs deep experts and creative specialists who offer a range of discrete marketing and professional services, such as market strategy, branding or creative writing.

boycott the refusal of a government or public groups and consumers to buy certain goods from a country or company.

BRAND

A combination of attributes that gives a company, organization product, service concept, or even an individual, a distinctive identity and value relative to its competitors, its advocates, its stakeholders and its customers. The attributes that make a brand are both tangible and intangible: a name, a visual logo or trademark, products, services, people, a personality, reputation, brand loyalty, mental associations, culture and inherent values which, together, create a memorable, reassuring and relevant brand image in the eye and mind of the beholder. The overall value of brand to the business results in what is often known as **brand equity**, which is the total value that the brand brings to a company over and above its net book value.

The relationship between consumer and brand is often emotional rather than rational. The brand is often something that lives as a perception in the mind of the beholder. As the famous advertising guru Leo Burnett said in 1955, 'Before you can have share of market, you must have share of mind'. Branding facilitates memory recall, thus contributing to preferred selection and improving customer loyalty. Also, brands can be more enduring. *Products have life cycles; brands can last forever.* That was the argument made in 1931 by Neil McElroy to executives of Procter & Gamble Co. He advanced the vision that each brand within the package-goods company needed to be managed by a team whose sole focus was driving that brand into a No. 1 position in its category. At the time this was a revolutionary idea, because until then marketing had been about pushing products through retail channels to customers – and branding was viewed as making this an easier process. This would make the brand an area of marketing promotions against which investments were made in order to create the supreme market position. Moreover, and this certainly proved to be the case with Procter and Gamble, it assured certain brands enduring distinctiveness. This formed the basis of what is now known as **brand management**, one of the more powerful functions of marketing.

In the 1990s brands took on a new dimension of meaning. Branding became the most powerful aspect of the marketing mix. Advertising spending, which increased exponentially after the early 1990s recession, fuelled the cult of branding. Brand expanded its frontiers. Companies used advertising and sponsorship to develop *brand meaning* rather than simply using brand to push products and services. Companies invested heavily in brand to the extent that their products and services (once the centrepiece of their marketing efforts) became merely tools in promoting the overall brand values, experience and personality. For example, companies such as Nike, the Gap, the Body Shop and Starbucks developed the notion in the 1990s that buying their otherwise ordinary and basic products was a lifestyle statement and choice, endowed with higher meaning than simple satisfaction of customer need for simple consumable goods. Branding started to extend beyond the product and services themselves and into the entire retail outlet and often the public space itself. Suddenly, there appeared entire stores dedicated to Nike, the GAP, Starbucks and Disney, selling only one branded range. More and more ingenious ways are found to completely encircle the consumer with the brand experience and personality. The management guru, Tom Peters, even produced a book advising on how to make oneself a brand.

Distinctive and successful brands usually have the following qualities:

1. They are differentiated from competing brands. In an age of increased customer choice, over-supply and growing clutter and clamour in the marketplace, a differentiated brand (and the investment that is required to build and grow it) is necessary to survival and prosperity. The more that brands deliver against the expectations of what customers have of them, the deeper the trust; the longer the survival, the greater the value.

2. They are both relevant and desirable to their target market. They have a deep emotional resonance with their customers (rather than just vast recognition and awareness of name and logo). Great brands are usually perceived to have some involvement in the fabric of consumers' lives by the consumers themselves. GE always promoted the idea that its products and services touched multiple aspects of American daily lives and made them easier.

3. They enjoy public esteem and have a 'legendary' status, perhaps having passed from generation to generation. There is constant investment in keeping them fresh without departing from the core values of the brand. Occasionally, their decline and revival contribute to the mythology of the brand. Examples include Perrier's perilous situation when benzene was discovered in the drink and it was recalled; Coca-Cola's near-disastrous attempt to change its flavour and its dramatic recovery of its position

after mass protest; Apple's role in the creation of the PC market, then its decline, followed by its revival in the late 1990s with the innovative iMac designs.

4. The very great brand can dominate and change the nature of an entire segment of the market. Examples are IBM's domination of the information technology market for most of the second half of the 20th century; Kodak's domination of camera film processing; Disney's constant pushing back the frontiers of family entertainment since the 1930s.

5. At the more advanced levels the greatest brands ultimately become global brands, even if their origins are very national. For example, Kodak, Coca-Cola, McDonalds, Sony, Disney, Microsoft, Rolls-Royce, BMW, Volkswagen, Gucci, Ferrari, the BBC, Mercedes, Nike, and Intel all began as domestic, national brand names and have now become global.

Brands that have such emotional resonance, personality and customer connection can have huge power and economic value. A typical measure of such brand strength is their ability to command a price premium, to inspire customer loyalty or to dominate a market through higher market share.

There are many reasons to have a strong brand and branding strategy. A strong brand gives a product or service a sustainable advantage in a competitive market, market share increase and, often, economies of scale and improved profitability. Brands differentiate and subsume products and services. Brand helps to create an acceptance of and intimacy with the product and service in the target consumer. Brand reduces price pressures, particularly against competing products of similar quality. They ensure longevity and repeatability and diminish risk. For marketing management purposes, a strong brand enables greater negotiating power with channels of distribution; display space is more easily obtained and point-of-sale promotions for branded product can be made more prominent in retail outlets. Companies can use strong brand names to increase their shareholder value. The brand is the bellwether of a company's reputation. Some of the most recognized brands such as Disney, Microsoft, Dell, Sony, Nike and Mercedes Benz have vastly increased their market value. Nike, for example, during the promotion of the *Just Do It* advertising campaign, saw its market value increase from $750m in 1987 to $4bn in 1994.

In addition to regular advertising activities, companies also use corporate sponsorship to increase brand awareness. Companies sponsor charity events, the arts, sporting events and venues as well as various tournaments. Corporate sponsorship provides a double dose of advertising and brand awareness. People attending the event become more aware of the corporate brand. In addition, as a corporate sponsor, a company will typically have access to special lounges or areas or may have a table at a dinner. This provides a good opportunity to bring existing or potential clients to these events and build a rapport that can also lead to more business.

Harley-Davidson, an outstanding case of brand revitalization in its own right, used a novel approach to building their brand name. They developed a programme aimed at new riders. Participants in the programme spent time in the classroom as well as on the road learning about technical details. Bike safety was presented and there was even an opportunity to try on motorcycle gear, which was, of course, covered in Harley-Davidson logos. New riders who graduated from the class remembered the Harley-Davidson brand name, and the majority of those buying bikes bought Harleys. Starbucks, once a Seattle-based coffee company, has become a global brand, but without major spending on advertising. Under Scott Bedbury's marketing leadership since 1995, the company has taken an innovative and a collaborative approach to building its brand. It negotiated an agreement with United Airlines to serve Starbucks on all United flights; it collaborated with Redhook Ale Brewery Inc. to introduce Double Black Stout, a malt beer flavoured with coffee; it created a joint venture with Pepsi Cola Co. to market Starbucks's Frappuccino drink in supermarkets; it joined with Dreyer's Grand Ice Cream to introduce six flavours of Starbucks Ice Cream. Starbucks coffee shops create a comfortable overall brand experience, and these have been opened across the world, from Seattle to Tokyo, expanding the Starbucks company to 1100 outlets with 22,000 employees and serving coffee to 4 million people each week on branded cups.

Other advantages of branding include obtaining legal protection for products and services. Branding also makes it easier to link advertising to other marketing communication programmes and it can reduce the overall cost of personal selling and persuasion. Finally, a strong brand gives a foundation from which a company can launch new products and services as extensions of the brand.

BRAND TERMS

brand environment the physical manifestations of the brand, such as the graphics, logo and their application to physical space. It is important for a brand to have consistency of design, look and feel, whatever the environment in which it is projected. A brand has to be displayed in the right environment and in the right media. There has to be harmony between them.

brand cannibalization the extent to which one brand gains recognition and esteem at the expense of other similar brands from the same company.

brand collaboration or co-branding the bringing together of two well-known brands to endorse a new product or service in which they have a mutual interest.

brand descriptor a specific attribute, offering or benefit of the brand.

brand equity the value added to a range of products and services that is over and above the net book value of the company, or the cash flow from products and services with the brand name compared with the cash flow without the brand name. The effects of strong equity can manifest themselves in the overall value of a company or in the higher prices that a company can charge for its products and services. Brand strength has a direct impact on revenues and profits and can only be sustained with appropriate levels of investments in sustaining and growing it. So far, despite multiple models that can quantify brand valuation in monetary values, there is as yet no single, universally agreed methodology to measure the value of a brand.

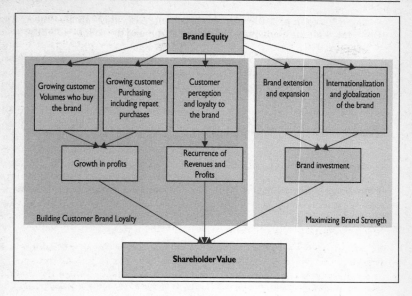

Brand Equity Components

brand essence the expression of the total attributes, tangible and intangible, of a brand as a core concept.

brand experience the total experience the customers have of the branded product and service. For example, Virgin Atlantic view the total customer experience for business class customers as an end-to-end experience. Customers are picked up from their appointed destination by a limousine, they are checked in without leaving the car, they go the well-branded Virgin lounges where they enjoy complimentary food, drinks, shoeshines, massages, haircuts, manicures, pedicures; where they can listen to music, work on their computer, use a small office, make calls, surf the Internet, read in the library. In the flight itself, there is also a complimentary massage and manicure service. Some planes have an open stand-up bar, as well as a wide range of food that can be taken at any time, innovative entertainment and then a complimentary limousine pick-up after checking through customs to go to the final destination.

brand extension the use of an existing brand for a new product or service offering a distinctive benefit to a new set of target customers. The belief is that the core attributes and essence of the original brand can be transferred to a new product or service. French couturiers such as Dior and Chanel have been particularly adept at extending their brand name to perfume and retail goods and apparel. Disney has extended its brand, developed in film, into theme parks, holidays, cruise ships, merchandise, and resorts.

brand identity how the various elements of a brand are made to appear externally, by means of a corporate logo or symbol, a product, service, packaging, slogan or a physical environment. Also, this can also mean the sum total of all the elements of branding that make the unique identity.

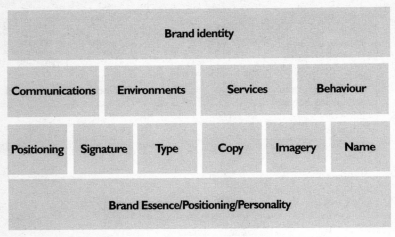

Source: Accenture: Fundamental Elements of Brand Management System.

brand image one of the major roles of brand management is to create positive perceptions in the minds of target customer groups. Taken together, these perceptions constitute the brand image. A key measure of the success of the brand image is the preference that customers show this brand over other competing brands. This is closely connected to **brand loyalty** and repeat purchases of the branded products and services by the customer.

brand interactive or **interactive branding** the use of websites and interactive techniques to enhance the overall power of the brand.

brand loyalty a measure of the consumers' unwillingness to switch to a competing product or service. Successful brands are characterized by high levels of customer satisfaction and repeat purchases of the branded goods or service by existing customers over a long period of time. The cost of winning new customers is much higher than retaining and cross selling to existing customers, so brand loyalty is an important economic factor in profitable brand development. There are several methods of measuring customers' brand loyalty and preference, but few of the methods have managed to capture all the factors involved in the decision. For example, straightforward repeat purchase measurement does not always capture customers' purchase of other brands. Also, customers may be loyal to a brand because choice is limited, special pricing deals are used, or the brand dominates a given channel of distribution.

brand management brings together a range of marketing disciplines. Good and systematic brand management is indispensable to the longevity of a brand. Brands do not 'naturally' survive and prosper; they have to be actively managed and invested in. The brand is perishable unless investment continues and it is actively managed through a range of appropriate managed programmes. The brand can act as the focal point for the entire range of marketing activities. Successful brands have a strong, well-integrated brand management system that covers all aspects and dimensions of the brand as an asset, as a guide to action and behaviour and with a full range of protection over the use of the brand both by the brand owner and by associated third parties.

brand mark, icon or **symbol** the part of an overall brand that can be recognized but which is not written as the brand name. These symbols or characters give instant recognition of the brand. Examples are the Metro-Goldwyn-Mayer roaring lion, the Nike swoosh, Mickey Mouse, the Marlboro Man, Tony the Tiger, the Coca-Cola dynamic curve, and the Michelin man (from 1898).

brand name letters, words or groups of words, which can be written or spoken. Names can include a manufacturer's name in which the brand name is owned by the company making the individual branded product (e.g. Dulux, Persil, Maxwell House); a family brand name in which the brand is projected onto all products sold by the company (e.g. Microsoft, Kodak, Heinz, Campbell's); a category brand name for a range of products within the same category, such as household appliances (e.g. Hotpoint, Hoover, Whirlpool) or a specific product name combined with the company name (e.g. Mars Bar, Hershey Bar, Kellogg's Corn Flakes). A private label brand is one in which the company making the product does not have title to the brand name.

Most brand names are legally protected trademarks. One of the more famous brands, Coca-Cola, is fiercely protected, but it cannot have exclusive use of the second part of the name, cola, because this is viewed as a generic category name that is now used by many competitors. Generic names are difficult to protect because legal and regulatory authorities view them as being in the public domain. The same applies to names of cities, rivers, countries and mountains.

Selection of new brand names has become increasingly complex. A new brand name with trademark now must also be registered for use as a website or domain name on the Internet. There are over 20 million commercial domain names already registered on the Internet. This narrows the chances of creating a new name that is clear and descriptive of the product or service. As a result, new or rebranded companies often sport a range of fanciful or compound names with no direct relevance to the product or service delivered (e.g. Consignia, previously the Royal Mail, Innogy, previously National Power). See also LOGO and TRADEMARK.

brand revitalization the injection by a company of new energy into its brand, either by changing its overall positioning, or by investment in regenerating the various types of brand execution. Inevitably, all brands become tired and revitalization becomes necessary. For example, Volkswagen AG's new brand strategy for Audi is to market it as a sportier brand. In the past, Audi had been viewed as too conservative. Audi is now developing high-performance cars that challenge BMW as part of a brand revitalization strategy to make Audi a premium luxury brand in Europe, thereby differentiating itself from the other VW brands. Lucozade, formerly perceived as a medicinal drink usually administered to people recovering from colds and flu, was completely revitalized and repositioned and is now known as a high-energy drink for athletes. Harley-Davidson, once the motorbike of choice of Hell's Angels, then languishing in the shadow of Japanese and European motorcycle brands, kicked itself into life as a lifestyle choice for prosperous, active, middle-aged Americans, with a entire range of Harley-Davidson clothes, accessories, restauraunts and retail outlets.

brand strategy a necessary element in the development of a successful brand. The brand must be closely aligned to the company's overall business strategy and market positioning. It must be integrated into all other marketing and communications programmes. Objectives for the brand are set and an investment plan for the brand is created. Positioning, or repositioning, is at the heart of a successful brand strategy. A full brand communication strategy and programme is developed to build awareness of the brand attributes. If it is a consumer brand, this will involve a sales incentive programme, trade promotions, merchandising and retail display to create brand recognition and customer demand for the brand. A wide distribution network must be built up and the brand must be made known and understandable to the retailers. Finally, full ranges of evaluations are put in place in including sales volumes, cost efficiencies, volume building, and improved profits.

brand switching movement from one brand preference to another. Potential reasons for brand switching are: dissatisfaction with the current brand and its experiences; curiosity about another brand, possibly a newer one; an inducement to move from one brand to another; availability of a new or substitute brand, often making claims of superior performance or benefit; a move to multiple brand choices for reasons of variety, risk management, price consciousness or simple indifference; coping with multiple preferences in the buyer group or as a way of capitalizing on various brand promotions at the same time.

brand valuation the premium attributed over and above a company's net book value, often taken as a part of the goodwill value of a company. This collection of intangible value added is often known as the brand value, or equity. In the modern economy, brand is one of the major intangible assets to which marketers can directly contribute. There is much debate on the right way to value a brand, and this is compounded by the fact that there are different methods and standards of accounting in each country. Although there are many theories and techniques for valuing a brand, there is no single agreed method of valuation that is supported by accountants to include it on the balance sheet. See also BRAND EQUITY.

BRAND CASE STUDIES

DE BEERS

Diamond Mind: Anatomy of a 20th century marketing campaign

The market for diamonds has never been characterized by free, dynamic and open competition. Everything about the diamond industry is manipulated: supply, pricing, processing and retailing. The leader of the diamond industry is De Beers, a company that produces half of the world's high-quality diamonds. This case explores the impact of marketing on the diamond market and how it helped to shape the public perception of diamonds as a desirable gift over the course of the 20th century.

As we have already seen (see ADVERTISING), De Beer's 'Diamonds are Forever' advertising campaign, which started in the 1940s, was to become one of the most effective of the 20th century. It enabled De Beers to manipulate demand as well as supply. With the help of their agency, they created a mindset, which later swept the world, in which diamonds came to be perceived, not simply as precious gems (of which there are many) that could be traded according to volatile market prices, but as an inseparable part of life. Most specifically, diamonds became a significant love token, marking the engagement that could lead to married life. It is now difficult for courting couples to contemplate engagement without, at some stage discussing, the purchase of a diamond solitaire ring. Anything less would appear to devalue the courtship, and be a less than permanent token. The size of the diamond, or its number of carats, was somehow perceived to signify the grandeur of the affection. It was a potent place to occupy in the mass consciousness.

Before the 1940s, however, diamonds were not held in such high esteem and did not hold such a cherished place in the minds of women. The idea of a long historical tradition of giving a diamond ring for an engagement was a post war invention. The giving of diamonds to mark an engagement had been around since the 19th century, but it was a low key, optional activity. In Germany, Austria, Italy and Spain, the notion of giving diamond rings to commemorate an engagement was not even entertained. On the eve of the Second World War, Germany saw diamonds as important for industrial and military purposes; given it is the world's hardest substance. In the UK and France, before the war, diamonds were perceived as a jewel for the upper classes. In America, the gift was usually confined to a lower quality, inexpensive diamonds. Diamond sales had actually been declining in America since the early 1920s, both in quantity and value.

The man who decided to change the pattern of demand for diamonds was Harry Oppenheimer of De Beers. Oppenheimer was at the time concerned by the post depression collapse of diamond prices, despite the best efforts of the DeBeers cartel to manipulate prices by control of supply. He selected the N.W. Ayer advertising agency in New York to achieve this extraordinary piece of marketing manipulation.

N. W. Ayer, following extensive research, very typical of the early days of 'scientific' advertising, came up with a plan to change the attitudes of American public towards diamonds. The dominant characteristic of half a century of diamond marketing is the direct and manipulative association of diamonds and romance. It was a long-term strategy – to change a mind set and behaviour pattern – rather than an attempt to drive short-term sales of diamonds. Therefore, marketing of diamonds was essentially an appeal to emotions, rather than a focus on the product itself. Through multiple messages and images the world would begin to perceive diamonds as the jewel of romance, esteem and enduring love.

As a result of such marketing, the diamond market developed in a curious pattern: for such an icon of female decoration, the market is mainly composed of men as buyers – 90% of all diamonds are bought by men for women. Yet the wearers are almost always women; women rarely buy diamonds either for themselves or for others. Moreover, women are rarely involved in the selection or purchase of the diamond. The reaction of the woman, rather than the object itself, is the primary driver in the male purchasing decision. The element of surprise following the presentation of the diamond ring to the woman, and the gushing delight as it is received is an abiding mental image, portrayed in many films and television shows.

The result of the first 40 years of marketing, was that Ayer helped De Beers expand its sales of diamonds in the United States from $23 million in 1939 to over $2 billion by 1980. In the same period, expenditure on diamond advertising for De Beers in North America increased from $200,000 a year and to $10 million.

How did they do it? Ayer sought out the glamorous role models who were able to influence the purchasing habits of Middle America. In the 1940s, movie stars had a huge bearing on American society. The agency began negotiations with Hollywood to use diamonds in the titles of their movies. Movie scripts started to include the leading man using diamonds to make marriage proposals. News stories and society photographs were planted that emphasised the link between diamonds and romance. In 1946, the agency began a weekly service called Hollywood Personalities, which published stories in 125 leading newspapers with descriptions of the diamonds worn by major movie stars. In 1947, the agency produced portraits of socialites showing off their diamond rings for recent engagement. Nationwide lecture tours were organized to introduce high school girls to different ranges of diamonds and to start to plant the idea in the minds of the young. Fashion designers were encouraged to use diamonds in their new creations. The British royal family were even used to enhance the status of diamonds: for example, Oppenheimer presented Queen Elizabeth II with prize diamonds during her trip to South Africa.

The De Beers advertising campaign continued unabated during the Second World War, although diamond mines being closed all over Africa and cutting centres in Europe being abandoned. Ayer even promoted the message that diamonds were contributing to the war effort and, consequently, buying diamonds was equated with patriotism. By 1941, the campaign was starting to show results: the sale of diamonds had increased by 55 percent in the United States. After the war, the Ayer agency focused upon the millions of American servicemen returning from the war.

The American market for diamonds was around 70 million people in the immediate post war period. The agency, on behalf of De Beers, sought to influence men to buy more, and bigger, diamonds in the name of an invented 'tradition' that was linked emotionally to romance. In 1948 an Ayer copywriter came up with the legendary and enduring slogan: "A Diamond Is Forever". Within a year, it became the official signature of De Beers, and it remains so today.

In the 1950s, the era of conspicuous consumption in America, N.W. Ayer used the new medium of television to influence American public opinion. Famous actresses and other celebrities displayed diamonds to the television audience. A diamond not only became a way of legitimising a romance, of finding a man, it also became a status symbol in a status hungry culture. The more the carats, the deeper the love, the more enduring the relationship, the greater the prestige. A famous song of the time stated, 'diamonds are a girl's best friend'.

During all this time the agency also promoted the idea that De Beers diamonds were authentic and that they were made from the rarest stones. This enabled them to fend of the challenge of synthetic diamonds (such as the process developed by GE in the 1950s).

In the 1960s the agency proposed the global expansion of the idea that they had so successfully nurtured over a 20-year period in the United States. They proposed the invention of the same 'tradition' in other countries where it did not previously exist. Japan, Germany and Brazil were targeted. Within ten years, De Beers succeeded even beyond its most optimistic expectations in creating a billion-dollar-a-year diamond tradition in Japan.

Once the international market had provided expanded sales, the agency promoted the idea of buying a second diamond ring as a symbol of 'renewal' of marriage and of long-term love. These became known as 'later in life' diamonds. This came at a time as diamond production expanded and there was a risk of flooding the market.

With the production of diamonds of smaller caratage in the Soviet Union (which De Beers distributed), the company now had to make small diamonds respectable. The average size of a diamond, which was one carat in 1939, fell to one-quarter carat by the late 1970s. The consequence of this was to diminish the market for large diamonds, which came to be seen by the American consumers, who had become gradually accustomed to the idea of buying smaller diamonds, as gaudy and brash. Conversely, the demand for smaller diamonds started to outstrip supply.

Today, the diamond market is a low growth market, and in recent times the diamond mining industry has come under greater scrutiny. De Beers has taken the decision to re-invent itself as a luxury goods company.

VOLKSWAGEN

The story of Volkswagen (see *www.volkswagen.com*), the car as famous for its appearance as it is for its advertising, is strongly intertwined with the history of the last century. It is also one of the greatest brand successes ever.

The Volkswagen Company was originally operated by the German Labour Front (Deutsche Arbeitsfront), a Nazi organization specifically charged with the organization of the German workforce without trade unions. The legendary German car designer, Ferdinand Porsche, designed the original 'People's Car' during Hitler's tenure of power. Nazi propaganda heavily promoted the Volkswagen as a symbol of German progress and community. World War II interrupted production of the Volkswagen. By 1945, both the Volkswagen factory and its home city of Wolfsburg were in ruins. Volkswagen was seen through its association with the Nazi regime as having a tainted brand and, for some, an unsaleable brand. The British, who administered the region in the postwar period, refused to transfer the plant to the UK. The French tried to get the British to sell the equipment to France, but that did not happen. The machinery was also taken as payment in kind for war reparations. The British occupiers looked for a car company to manage the Wolfsburg plant. The Ford Motor Company was contacted and Henry Ford II assessed the plant. Their opinion was that the Volkswagen was not worth their investment. Eventually, and despairingly, the plant was turned over to German management under Heinz Nordoff. The Volkswagen Corporation that we know today was born. Exports to most parts of the world grew in strength. However, the vast market of the US remained elusive until the 1950s. The Volkswagen car's unusual rounded appearance, its engine in the rear, together with its historical connections with Nazi Germany originally proved a disincentive in the US. This changed in 1959, when the New York advertising agency, Doyle Dane Bernbach, began a landmark advertising campaign, dubbing the car 'the Beetle' because of its shape and pointing to its size as an advantage to the consumer. This campaign was very successful, and for some years following, the Beetle was the leading automobile import sold in the United States. It was the 'hero' of the popular Disney 'Love Bug' movie series.

Although the German government had founded the company, in 1960 the state essentially denationalized it by selling 60% of its stock to the public. Volkswagen acquired the Audi auto company in 1965. Volkswagen and its affiliates operate plants throughout most of the world. In addition to cars, the company produces vans and minibuses, automotive parts, and industrial engines. It owns several other auto companies, including Audi in Germany and SEAT (Sociedad Espanola de Automoviles de Turismo) in Spain, and it also makes and markets cars with Fiat of Italy and Skoda of the Czech Republic.

The Volkswagen hardly changed from its original design, however, and by 1974, with increasing competition from other compact foreign cars, Volkswagen came near bankruptcy. This spurred the company to develop newer, sportier car models; among them were the Rabbit and its successor, the Golf. In 2000 the Beetle design was revived with a new engine, with great international success. Billboards in New York for the new Beetle read ' The World's Cup is half full Again'. See also ADVERTISING: Volkswagen's 'Think Small' campaign.

NOKIA

Founded in 1860, Nokia Corporation (see *www.nokia.com*), headquartered in Helsinki, is the world's leading mobile phone supplier. It is also a leading supplier of mobile and fixed telecommunications networks, including related customer services, and supplies solutions and products for fixed and wireless data-com and multimedia terminals, and computers. Nokia accounts for almost a quarter of Finland's exports, and nearly 4% of its GDP.

Nokia is an outstanding example of re-invention and brand positioning.

In 1865 the Finnish mining engineer Fredrik Idestam established a wood-pulp mill in Southern Finland and began manufacturing paper. Named after the river Nokia, where its lumber mills were sited, Nokia started off in forestry, and later moved into making paper, rubber, and electrical cables. The Finnish Rubber Works, initially opened in 1898, established a factory on the river Nokia after its executives passed through the area and recognized the value of the hydroelectricity available there. In the 1920s, the Finnish Rubber Works started to use Nokia as their brand name. In addition to footwear and tires, the company later went on to manufacture rubber bands, galoshes, industrial parts, raincoats, and other rubber products. The company that later became known as the Finnish Cable Works opened in 1912 in Helsinki. The increasing need for power transmission and telegraph and telephone networks meant that the company grew quickly. After World War II, the Finnish Rubber Works bought the majority of the Finnish Cable Works' shares, and gradually the ownership of these companies consolidated. Finally, in 1967 the companies were merged to form the Nokia Group. The company evolved dramatically, growing first into a conglomerate encompassing diverse industries. However, by the 1980s it was an unfocused conglomerate that made everything from galoshes to TVs. Nokia's operations had rapidly expanded into too many business sectors, countries and products. The strategy was to expand relentlessly on all fronts. In 1988, Nokia was Europe's third-largest television manufacturer and the largest information technology company in the Nordic countries. During the deep recession in Finland at the beginning of the 1990s, the telecommunications and mobile phone divisions were the supporting pillars of the company. Despite the depth of the recession, Jorma Ollila was appointed to head the entire Nokia Group. Nokia made the major strategic decision to divest its non-core operations and focus on mobile telecommunications.

The groundwork for the shift to mobile communications had been laid in the 1960s, when Nokia's electronics department was researching radio transmission. Nokia started to make mobile phones for the military, which took off after the establishment of a multinational cellular network by a consortium of Scandinavian state operators. This network gave the Scandinavians an advantage when it came to setting up Europe-wide networks, based on the digital GSM standard in the early 1990s.

Nokia took a major gamble and it paid off. Under Ollila's leadership, Nokia became focused on being a mobile phone company with a global brand. Nokia has led the mobile phone industry by emphasising its brand and its design — mobile phones are fashion statements — with easy-to-use software. The company has also positioned itself to take advantage of the coming convergence between mobile phones and the Internet.

VIRGIN ATLANTIC

Virgin Atlantic (see *www.virgin-atlantic.com*) was born in the 1980s. Richard Branson, the British entrepreneur, had already created a successful brand with the Virgin Group, particularly in the music business. He had founded the group when he was 20 as a mail-order record company and shortly after opened a music shop in London's main shopping thoroughfare, Oxford Street. The original brand slogan of these stores was 'Cheap and nasty'. A music studio was built in Oxfordshire in 1972, where one Mike Oldfield recorded his massively successful album *Tubular Bells* for the Virgin Records label. This album sold 5 million copies and was the catalyst for Virgin Records, which signed a range of successful artists, including The Rolling Stones, Culture Club, Janet Jackson, Peter Gabriel, Simple Minds and The Human League.

Virgin was to become one of the six biggest record companies in the world. By the early '80s Virgin Group was well established. Branson developed the idea of operating a Jumbo jet passenger service between London and New York in 1984. Freddie Laker had already tried to create a low-cost transatlantic airline to rival the incumbents, but this ultimately failed.

An aircraft was found, staff were recruited, licences obtained and, thanks in a great part to Richard's infectious enthusiasm, the airline took off on deadline. On the 22 June 1984 a plane packed with friends, celebrities and the media set off for Newark, New York. Since then, Virgin Atlantic has become the second largest British long-haul international airline, operating services out of London's Heathrow and Gatwick to 18 different destinations all over the world, from Shanghai to the Caribbean. Virgin Atlantic has won numerous awards for its customer service.

In 1992, Branson consolidated, selling Virgin Music for $1bn to Thorn EMI and invested the profits back into Virgin Atlantic. In December 1999 Branson signed an agreement to sell a 49% stake of Virgin Atlantic to Singapore Airlines to form a unique global partnership. The deal valued Virgin Atlantic at a minimum of £1.225 billion. In 1999, the combined sales of the different Virgin holding companies were around £3 billion.

ADIDAS

Beginning as a cobbler in Herzogenaurach, Germany, Adidas (see *www.adidas.com*) founder Adolph Dassler, built one of the world's most popular and well-known brands of sports shoes and apparel. Growing up in poverty-stricken post-World War I Germany, Adolph (nicknamed Adi) joined his family in making and selling homemade house slippers. Dassler began producing training shoes in 1920 when he was only 20 years old. He later began to manufacture soccer, tennis and running shoes. To ensure that each shoe would be both safe and performance-enhancing, Dassler used his own athletic experience and the input of doctors, trainers, coaches and other athletes to guide the design of his shoes. Dassler's athletic shoes were first worn in Olympic competition in 1928. Henceforth, Adidas shoes and equipment were used by Olympic athletes and national soccer teams. Jesse Owens wore Adidas track shoes during his spectacular Olympic performance in Berlin in 1936, where he earned four gold medals. Armin Hary was the first athlete to run the 100m sprint in 10 seconds, also wearing Adidas shoes. In 1949, Dassler created the first soccer shoe with moulded rubber studs and, for the first time, adopted the trademark three stripes. The German National team won in the1954 World Cup final wearing Adidas soccer boots with screw-in studs, which enabled the game to be played under vastly different conditions without slipping.

One of Dassler's goals in producing athletic shoes was to design them according to each sport's specific demands, a goal that resulted in more than 700 patents among which were nylon soles and running spikes. Today Dassler is known as the founder of the modern sporting goods industry.

The Adidas brand logo

The 'Trefoil' was adopted as the corporate logo in 1972. In 1996, it was decided that the Trefoil would only be used on heritage products such as the classic running shoe. The Adidas Equipment line was launched in 1991. In

January 1996, the Three-Stripes brand mark became the worldwide Adidas corporate logo. This logo is used in all advertising, printed collateral and corporate signage.

XEROX

THE DOCUMENT COMPANY

XEROX.

Chester Carlson, a patent attorney and part-time inventor, made the first xerographic image in his laboratory in Astoria, Queens, in New York City, on Oct. 22, 1938 (see *www.xerox.com*). He spent years trying to sell his invention without success. Business executives could not be persuaded that there was a market for a copier; typed carbon copies, although labour intensive, were viewed to work well. The prototype for a facsimile copier was unwieldy and messy. There was no interest from the leading companies of the time, including IBM and General Electric.

In 1944, the Battelle Memorial Institute in Columbus, Ohio, contracted with Carlson to refine his new process, which Carlson called 'electrophotography.' Three years later, The Haloid Company, a maker of photographic paper in Rochester, N.Y., approached Battelle and obtained a licence to develop and market a copying machine based on Carlson's technology. Haloid later obtained all rights to Carlson's invention. Carlson and Haloid agreed the word 'electrophotography' was too cumbersome. A professor of classical languages at Ohio State University suggested 'xerography,' derived from the Greek words for 'dry' and 'writing.'

Haloid coined the word 'Xerox' for the new copiers. In 1948, the word *Xerox* was trademarked. In 1958 it became Haloid Xerox Inc. The company became Xerox Corporation in 1961 after wide acceptance of the Xerox 914, the first automatic office copier to use ordinary paper.

September 1999 marked the 40th anniversary of the Xerox 914, aptly named for the size of paper it used: 9x14 inches. More than 200,000 units were made around the world between 1959 and 1976, the year the company stopped production of the 914. Xerox adopted 'The Document Company — Xerox' as their corporate signature logo in 1994 to better reflect what has always been the company's core business: document management. At the same time, Xerox launched the 'digital X' as its marketing symbol/logo. The symbol's upper right quadrant depicts the pixels of digital imaging and the movement of documents between the paper and electronic worlds.

IKEA

Founded in Sweden by Ingvar Kamprad, IKEA (see *www.ikea.com*), a home furnishing retailer, has grown from the most unlikely local circumstances to become both a global brand and a retailing phenomenon. IKEA is headquartered in Amhult (known locally as IKEA town) in a forest in southern Sweden. Kamprad started his first furniture catalogue in 1951 and was an early user of flat packing, which was devised in the 1950s. Since it opened its first store outside Sweden in 1963, IKEA has grown to have 170 stores in 22 countries, employs 70,000 people and uses 2000 different suppliers around the world. Their famous catalogue, which has 7000 photographs in each edition, runs to 110 million copies annually, making it one of the world's most widely circulated publications. It consumes around 50% of IKEA's total marketing budget. It does not target any particular market segment and is distributed randomly. Such a lack of classic segmentation has not impeded IKEA: their worldwide customer base is estimated at 260 million.

IKEA has capitalized on the postwar market trends of demand for home living design, wide range of choice and customer self-service and self-help. Its global brand is built around a combination of their design skill, their products, their stores and the marketing of all of these via their catalogue. The IKEA success formula is based on simplicity in the design of its furniture and then packing the furniture into flat packs (first done in 1956) for its retail outlets that enable the consumers to transport it and assemble it themselves. (Also since the 1950s onwards the majority of consumers have cars that can carry IKEA flat packs back to their homes.) Flat packing also enables IKEA to make major cost savings, both in terms of storage and delivery, which are passed onto customers in terms of lower prices. IKEA's giant stores are usually based near large urban centres where there is a high demand for home furnishings. This gives IKEA huge cost advantages and appeals to the consumers' home design needs. Also, IKEA's retail stores are very innovative: they give consumers ideas for home design and decoration; they display entire room concepts rather than just the individual furniture components. IKEA also provide wide choice with an average of 10,000 lines available in each store, of which 20% are changed each year. However, IKEA only employ around 15 permanent designers supplemented by 80 freelance designers around the world. The designers are constantly employed in thinking through innovative ideas – from furniture design to new ways of flat packing that are based on what customers need for convenience and quality.

ACCENTURE

Innovation delivered.

Accenture (see *www.accenture.com*), a brand that was born on the first day of 2001, has already established global recognition in a relatively short time period. Accenture is the pioneer in professional services brand and image building.

The antecedents of Accenture's brand building were unique: it was formerly the consulting practice of the accounting firm Arthur Andersen and was separated to form an independent business unit. In a bold and unprecedented step the firm began, in 1989, to market itself as an organization that helped companies apply technology to create business advantage. It became a top quality consultancy brand by the end of the 1990s. In a decade it had achieved the extremely difficult task of positioning itself in the information technology professional services market space. It had, simultaneously, created a separate identity from its accounting roots with Arthur Andersen.

In order to build this new identity, the firm had taken the pioneering step of using sophisticated marketing techniques to develop and build a professional services brand. It was the professional services industry's first large-scale advertising campaign used to promote name, market positioning and brand image. Before this, the professional services category had formal rules that prevented advertising, and was known for its outmoded and archaic approaches. Most professional services firms chose not to advertise, feeling it was inappropriate, or even unprofessional.

Between 1990 and 2000, as the market for technology, systems integration and management consultancy boomed, so the firm grew from an accounting firm's offshoot into the world's largest management and technology consulting organization.

On August 7, 2000, Accenture was notified of the successful outcome of arbitration against Andersen Worldwide and Arthur Andersen. As part of the final award that released Accenture from all further obligations to Arthur Andersen and Andersen Worldwide, Accenture was required to cease using the Andersen Consulting name by December 31, 2000.

This confronted the 11-year-old firm with a branding challenge on a gargantuan scale. After spending an estimated $7 billion building their brand over a decade, the company now had to find, implement, and introduce to the world a new name in a matter of months. Never before had a rebranding of such scope been implemented over so short a timeframe.

The rebranding as Accenture – the largest rebranding initiative ever undertaken by a professional services firm – was successfully implemented across 47 countries in just 147 days. Accenture launched worldwide on January 1, 2001. The name Accenture was invented by an employee following an internal competition, and is a fusion of 'accent' and 'future'. Accenture planned a two-phased marketing strategy for introducing itself to its global audience. The aim of both phases was to surround the company's target audience – including its 40,000 clients and prospects, 70,000 employees, 1.5 million potential recruits, as well as world-wide press and media – with messages informing them about the new name and new positioning. As well as rebranding, the objectives included a desire to reposition the company in its target markets: focusing on its ability to deliver innovative solutions to its clients across its breadth of services in Consulting, Technology and Outsourcing. It adopted the 'Innovation Delivered' signature in all its advertising. Another objective was to transfer brand equity to Accenture (which was important because the company became a public corporation later in 2001) and to eliminate residual confusion with Arthur Andersen. Ironically, in the same period, its former parent, Andersen, which had opposed the separation, collapsed in a welter of financial scandals triggered by that of Enron. The Accenture rebranding was not only highly successful; in retrospect, it was an act of extraordinary business prescience.

breakeven analysis in essence, the study of the interrelationships between costs, sales volume and prices at various levels of activity. The breakeven point is the time at which the fixed and variable costs involved in the production and distribution of a product are matched by its overall sales: the point at which total costs are exactly equal to revenues. Beyond this point, when revenues exceed total costs, there lies profitability. To understand the breakeven analysis it is necessary to appreciate fixed and variable costs:

Examples of costs that are typically 'fixed':

- salaries of personnel
- sales administration
- advertising investments ('above-the-line')
- capital costs, such as building and plant

Examples of costs that are typically 'variable':

- commissions to agents and brokers and salesmen
- delivery costs
- after-sales maintenance and service
- credit
- order processing

- invoicing
- non-advertising marketing costs ('below the line')

In physical volume terms, the usual formula for the breakeven point is:

$$breakeven\ point = \frac{Fixed\ cost}{(Sales\ revenue - Variable\ cost)/Units\ sold}$$

The main purposes of a breakeven analysis for a marketer are to provide information about cost behaviour for new product marketing activities and to determine specific decision-making. A marketer of a new product needs to know what volume of sales is needed at any given budgeted sales price in order to break even. The product marketer needs to identify the 'risk' in the budget by measuring the margin and to calculate the effects on profit of changes in variable cost, cost of sales ratios, sales price and volume and product mix.

Care should be taken in applying the breakeven analysis to real-life marketing, particularly in a dynamic market environment. The breakeven point contains some risky assumptions: for example, sales prices are assumed to be constant and fixed costs are assumed to remain stable. A breakeven calculation only holds for circumstances where efficiency remains constant, notwithstanding increased productivity. Since there is a direct relationship between purchases and sales, then all that is manufactured can actually be sold and the sales and marketing mix will be maintained at the same levels throughout the initial launch.

Although the breakeven analysis lends itself to product marketing, it can also be applied to services. For example, if a company is arranging a large entertainment event, it is important to know how the fixed and variable costs of producing and marketing the event are linked to the sale of tickets to the event. Dividing the fixed and variable costs of an event will give an indication of how many tickets need to be sold and at what price in order to make the event break even.

brief a concise and short statement of strategy, positioning, objectives, factual information that is agreed between a client organization and its marketing agency as a prerequisite to a campaign being formulated. See also ADVERTISING.

broadband various transmission technologies that enable users to view content across the Internet such as large files and multimedia such as video, audio and 3D. Broadband can also refer to an increased ability to do so. (The term narrowband can refer to the inability to do so.) A user's broadband capability is typically governed by the connection to the home, the connection between the service provider and the user. As broadband becomes more widely available to consumers and businesses, it will enable new types of media and marketing techniques, as well as becoming a much more widely used commercial channel for the delivery of digitized products and services. The advent of mass availability of broadband connections that are 'always on', will have a profound effect on direct marketing. Early tests show that consumers with broadband access to the Internet tend to spend 40% more time online than those with 'narrowband' or dial-up connections. Recent projections by industry analysts are not, however, optimistic that broadband will penetrate much more than 10% of domestic households in Western Europe before 2006. High access prices, technical difficulties in setting up broadband access software, as well as a perceived lack of a 'must have' mass application are cited as reasons for the slow pick-up. In contrast, the US, where prices are lower and there is a more developed PC-based culture, is experiencing far faster domestic penetration.

Types of internet access in selected countries
Year-end 2001

	France	Germany	Britain	United States
Total households	24.8m	37.7m	25.7m	105.0m
Internet households	4.5m	10.3m	8.8m	63.0m
Broadband households	0.5m	1.0m	0.2m	13.8m
Internet access				
Percentage of households	18%	27%	34%	60%
Broadband access				
Percentage of all households	2%	3%	1%	13%
Percentage of Internet households	8%	9%	2%	22%

Source: GartnerG2 2002

It is unlikely that the greater uptake of broadband will, at least in the short term, provide on-line companies with the same level of advertising revenues to be able to sustain themselves as with print and broadcast media. While broadband may not create enough advertising revenue to sustain an e-commerce business model, the entertainment sector will probably be able to develop a new business model. Broadband's fast downloads will act as a new sales and delivery channel for non-interactive, non-Web-based digital entertainment. Streamed and downloaded music has already proved its popularity on-line, and streaming video and downloadable games are likely to follow. Both music and video could also be stimulated by broadband uptake. On-line gaming will also benefit from broadband uptake, with tests indicating a 35% increase in on-line gaming for those who have broadband access. Games in which thousands of people play against one another can be offered only on-line. They are already successful as a niche; as broadband usage increases, subscriptions should also increase. Broadband-based games are also likely to make it easier for casual gamers to participate on a pay-per-play basis. An even bigger opportunity will come from casual gamers (more than half of all time spent on broadband entertainment is devoted to casual gaming) if companies can find a way to persuade them to pay for the opportunity to play games such as backgammon. The third business model, marketing off-line entertainment (such as movies) on-line, is already working. The cult movie, *The Blair Witch Project*, was mainly marketed over the Internet, rather than by classical advertising. Producers of off-line entertainment now use the Internet as a key part of integrated marketing campaigns for movies, music and TV programmes. The Web is one of several marketing channels.

As broadband penetration increases, these types of business and potentially others will enjoy an increasing likelihood of success. Connectivity will evolve as companies find new ways to integrate broadband technology into televisions, digital video recorders, personal digital assistants and audio equipment. Eventually, home networks will offer a more compelling entertainment experience. As new standards are created, even more opportunities for the digital delivery of entertainment to consumers' homes, offices and even cars will emerge.

broker a market intermediary whose function is to bring buyers and sellers together and to assist in negotiation. A broker assumes no risk, does not finance deals and does not take title to goods. The party on whose initiative they are acting usually pays them. See also AGENTS and CHANNELS OF DISTRIBUTION.

brown goods (now largely outdated) those domestic appliances that used to be encased in brown veneer, such as old radios, televisions and Hi-Fi systems. With the advent of multi-coloured plastics this term has only historical interest. This contrasts with WHITE GOODS, which continues to be a relevant term for domestic appliances.

B2B abbreviation for Business to Business, referring to an enterprise that sells products or provides services to other businesses rather than to consumers. Examples would be an aerospace engine company such as Rolls-Royce or GE selling aircraft engines to the world's leading airline carriers, or a management consultancy selling strategic advice to major banks or industrial manufacturers. Intel is also a business-to-business company that sells semiconductor components for information machines and systems, yet manages to have a visible brand.

B2C abbreviation for Business to Consumer, referring to a business that sells products or provides services to the end-user consumers or audiences. Examples would be food retailers, cinemas, domestic appliance retailers or individual life insurance providers.

bundling or **bundle pricing** the technique of combining different products and services at a unified price in order to achieve market prominence, to outsmart or destabilize a competitor, or to reward valuable customers or buyers. Bundling involves combinations of products, or products and services (for example 'free' software bundled with a PC), often at discounted or tiered prices. In services businesses the need to add greater value to the customer often leads to 'extras' being bundled into the price of the core service offering. For example, a cable company may offer free telephone services and Internet connection time to those subscribers who buy a digital television package. However, at another extreme, some service industries, seeing the larger profit potential, go in for 'unbundling' of services in which individual services are separated out and priced, allowing consumers to mix and match their service purchases. See also PRICING.

Burnett, Leo (1892-1971), founder of the Leo Burnett Advertising Agency, headquartered in Chicago, in 1935. Founder of the 'Chicago School' of advertising, Burnett, brought drama to advertising through shared emotions and experiences drawn from mid-western American values. He created such famous brand icons as the Jolly Green Giant, Pillsbury Doughboy, Charlie the Tuna and Tony the Tiger. His Marlboro campaign, a legendary, if controversial, example of advertising's power to build a global brand, ultimately became a target for legislative restrictions on tobacco industry marketing. See also ADVERTISING.

business cycle or **trade cycle** the periodic fluctuation of levels of economic activity that affects overall output, profitability, productivity and employment. At a macro-economic level the business cycle is the cyclical, periodic or regular fluctuations of economic activity and income through boom, downturn, recession and upturn. Finally, the business cycle can be a definition of the progression of events from business formation that starts with the establishment of a new business, products or services and continues through their growth, maturity, and decline. It has many parallels with the PRODUCT LIFE CYCLE.

An understanding of the business cycle is particularly important to market planning and investment. Below are general elements and characteristics of the business cycle and the different types of marketing management technique that may be used in its various phases:

downturn a period when consumer demand starts to fall away and markets stop growing. Consumer confidence starts to decline and there is rising job insecurity. Prices stabilize or start to fall. As demand drops, there is heavy discounting in the marketplace and consequently business profit falls. Marketing managers must in this period be very attentive to the balancing of supply and demand. The major danger in this period for a product business is the accumulation of excess unsold inventory; for a service business, excess capacity and people without enough fee-earning work. This is a time to review product and service portfolios and channels of distribution. Recruitment of new marketing staff should be halted and no further long-term commitment taken on.

recession technically a stage that is reached in the business cycle where Gross Domestic Product has fallen for two consecutive quarters. Domestic consumption falls off. Company investment becomes very tightly controlled as companies struggle to maintain sales volumes and profit margins. Speculative investments are usually cancelled and productive capacity is brought in line with decline in market demand. Lay-offs are frequent and overall unemployment rises. Inevitably, some businesses fail completely and are either taken over or seek protection from bankruptcy. During this time marketing usually focuses on fundamentals, such as directing marketing investment to core markets and clients and to be on constant alert for signs of economic and market recovery. It is important during this period to retain core skills and assets. Strong management and cost control over suppliers, agencies and contractors is also advisable in this period.

recovery is characterized by returning consumer confidence, then spending, then rising market demand. New investment begins. Employment rises, although slowly at first, as employment usually lags behind a recovery by one year. Profits rise for companies that are able to take early advantage of the recovery. Overall business confidence grows and is often witnessed by mergers and takeovers. Prices start to rise. Marketers must be ready to take immediate advantage of the upswing. Those in product marketing would start to build up their stock in anticipation and to sell off their redundant stock to discounters, perhaps by organizing special sales initiatives. They can take advantage of lower prices for stock and for resource contracts. Marketing programmes should be aggressive and confident. This may also be a time to attack competitors who have been very weakened in the recession.

boom is characterized by consumer spending rising so fast that it is fuelling concerns about inflation and rising debt. Productive capacity rises and there are key skills shortages. Productivity gains are sought to offset labour shortages and market demands. Investment spending is high and frequently speculative. Use of external contractors and agencies is much less controlled than hitherto. Increases in market demand now stimulate price rises and, consequently, profits rise. Marketers should encourage the sale of surplus in order to realize top prices. Retention of top quality marketing skills is at a premium. New market entry and new product or service line introduction may be explored. However, the marketer should be judicious in the expansion knowing that a downturn will inevitably follow.

business ethics an enquiry into the moral dimensions of business activities and conduct, an increasingly important aspect of corporate governance and public reputation. Business ethics are notoriously difficult to define in a standardized way and do vary from culture to culture. With the recent wave of accountancy scandals, however, business ethics and financial probity has become an international issue of major importance, both in terms of markets and economic systems and beliefs. For example, an unethical business would be prepared to go to any length and to condone any actions that contribute to the achievement of its corporate aims and objectives. Other organizations respect the laws but not necessarily the spirit of the law, if that conflicts with economic performance. Other companies, believing that there is much to be gained from ethical behaviour, actually communicate their ethical behaviour and in some cases actively market it. Other organizations take an active (rather than reactive) interest in ethical issues. (An example would be *The Body Shop*.) At the most advanced level, some organizations are entirely driven by an ethical platform, informing everything that the company does and involving a commitment of the part of everyone to carefully selected core values.

business to business see B2B.

business to consumer see B2C.

button ad an on-line graphical advertising unit that is smaller than a banner ad. Button ads measure typically 120x90, 120x60, 125x125 and 88x31. Whereas banners are often placed at the top or bottom of a page, buttons are often placed towards the middle of a page on the left or right sides. See also ADVERTISING.

button exchange a network where participating sites display button ads in exchange for credits, which are converted (using a predetermined exchange rate) into ads to be displayed on other sites. See also ADVERTISING.

BUYER AND BUYING BEHAVIOUR (INDUSTRIAL AND CONSUMER)

Buyer and buying behaviour is one of the more fervently studied subjects in marketing. To understand buyer behaviour is the ultimate goal of all marketers. Buyers are crucial in managing the relationship between an organization of the company, the enterprise and its suppliers. Effective marketing plans and programmes must be based upon a sound and thorough understanding of the buyer, the buyer's behaviour and the buyer's values. While complete knowledge of buyer behaviour is unattainable, this has not prevented many marketers, academics, and psychologists attempting to model repeatable buyer behaviour.

Buyers in consumer markets

Philip Kotler (in his book *Marketing Management*) identified several types who can play a role in an overall buying decision in a consumer market:

- the *Initiator* who can first suggest the idea of buying a product or service;
- the *Influencer* whose personal authority or knowledge can influence the outcome of the buying decision;
- the *Decider* who eventually decides on whether to buy, what to buy, where to buy from, and how to buy;
- the *Buyer* is the person who actually makes the buying transaction;
- The *User* is the person who actually uses the product or consumes the service.

A marketer, equipped with knowledge of the various roles that people play in the buying process, can shape his marketing programmes around these buyer types. We see, for example, huge effort expended on marketing toys to children during children's television commercial breaks, in the complete knowledge that the child is unlikely to be either the decider or buyer, but is most certainly going to be the initiator, possibly the influencer, through pestering the parent, and certainly the final user.

Kotler also outlined a 5-stage model for the buying process:

problem recognition the first stage of the buyer's decision process in which the consumer recognizes a problem or need. The recognition of the need become a drive to satisfy that need. The task for the marketer at this stage is to identify the circumstances and stimuli that trigger that particular need and use this knowledge to develop marketing strategies and plans to develop consumer interest.

information search the stage of the buyer decision process in which the consumer is aroused to search for more information. The intensity of the information search is partly determined by the level of the consumers' drive to satisfy their need. For example, the consumer may simply have heightened attention or may conduct an intensive information search. The task of the marketer is to decide which major information sources the customer will use at this stage: for example a) personal sources (such as friends, family, neighbours, work mates), who may be the most trusted sources but may not be the most expert; b) commercial sources (such as salespeople, websites, dealers, advertising or marketing information), which may be the most expert sources but not necessarily the most trusted; c) public sources (such as published studies that evaluate various products on behalf of consumers); d) experiential (such as personal use of the product during a demonstration or a trial period); this could be the final stage when the buyer decides to 'see for himself'.

alternative evaluation the stage of the buyer decision process in which the consumer searches out and uses information to evaluate alternative brands. It is vital for the marketer to know what attributes are important to the buyer during this stage. In fact it is possible, if the knowledge is deep enough, to segment buyers according to the importance they place on each product or service attribute. Also, some marketers attempt to predict, using statistical probabilities and game theories, what the buyer will actually choose given a set of options and variables. The actions that professional marketers might follow at this stage in the buying process are to obtain as much information directly from potential buyers about what attributes that they value in specific branded products and services. Having analysed the responses, the marketer can:

- modify the existing brand by altering beliefs about the brand (*repositioning*);
- alter beliefs about the competitor's brands (*competitive depositioning*);
- alter the buyers' weighting of attributes by trying to persuade the buyer to attach more importance to the key attributes of their company's brand;
- call attention to attributes that have been neglected, perhaps because of imperfect information or knowledge, or, most difficult of all,
- attempt to shift the buyer's ideas, beliefs and perceptions of the brand (*psychological repositioning*).

purchase decision the final stage in the buying process. The purchase decision follows from the evaluation of alternatives stage during which a purchasing intent is made. Between the formation of a purchasing intent and the completion of a purchasing decision the buyer can again change course and make different choices. Another party can influence the buyer, either positively or negatively, and this can result in a changed choice of brand. The second is unanticipated factors that did not exist when the purchasing intent was made, such as a change in financial circumstances.

Kotler points out that a buyer making a final purchasing decision actually makes five decisions, or sub-decisions: they choose a brand; they choose a retailer or dealer; they make a decision on quantity; then the timing of the purchase; finally the payment method.

post-purchase behaviour the stage of the process in which the buyer takes further action after purchase based on their satisfaction or dissatisfaction with their purchase. If they are dissatisfied, they may return the product, complain, or else avoid repurchase; if they are satisfied, or if their initial expectations are exceeded, then they may repeat the purchase, or, in a best case for a marketer, become a living advert for the product and spread the word to their friends and associates. Buyer satisfaction depends upon the alignment of initial expectations and the perceived product or service performance. In some cases the buyer expectation could have been set too high (for example by the salesman 'overselling' the product or service). The marketer's role must extend into this period, as it is a crucial determinant of the buyers' repurchase decisions. They ought to be aware of the ways in which buyers express dissatisfaction and be prepared to handle the various ways in which a buyer will demonstrate dissatisfaction. Post-purchase communication with the buyer is vital.

Factors influencing consumer buyer behaviour

Consumers' buying behaviour and the resulting purchase decision is strongly influenced by cultural, social, personal and psychological characteristics. An understanding of the influence of these factors is essential for marketers in order to develop suitable marketing mixes to appeal to the target customer:

• Factors include a consumer's culture, subculture and social class. These factors are often inherent in our values and decision processes.

• Factors include groups (reference groups, aspirational groups and member groups), family, roles and status. This explains the outside influences of others on our purchase decisions either directly or indirectly.

• Factors include such variables as age and lifecycle stage, occupation, economic circumstances, lifestyle (activities, interests, opinions and demographics), personality and self-concept. These may explain why our preferences often change as our `situation' changes.

• Factors affecting our purchase decision include motivation (Maslow's hierarchy of needs), perception, learning, beliefs and attitudes.

Types of consumer buying:

Buying tends to be more complex with the size of the purchase. The size of the purchase usually determines the number of people involved in the buying process.

Consumers buy in different ways:

• **complex buying** when the consumer is highly involved in the purchase and has much information about different brands and is aware of differences between them. This buyer spends much time in evaluation and choice selection;

• **habitual buying** when the consumer has low involvement and is not aware of significant differences between the brands. Brands are usually bought on the basis of their familiarity rather than their perceived attributes;

• **variety buying** when the consumer has low involvement in the purchase but is aware of high brand differences. These consumers tend to switch brands frequently.

Buyer types have also been divided into various categories among which are:

- **the loyal,** who repeat purchase the same brand for long periods;
- **the opportunistic,** who change brands and suppliers on the basis of their own long-term interests;
- **the dealer,** who concentrates on the best deal available at the time;
- **the creative,** who ask the seller to customize the product, service and price precisely to their needs;
- **the trader,** who asks for extras and mutual favours in exchange for their purchase;
- **the negotiator,** who constantly demands extra discounts on pricing;
- The **no-frills** buyer, who buys products on the basis of the quality of their construction.

Buying decisions

As illustrated below, the consumer is subject to several influences in the pathway to a final decision or group of decisions.

There are two overall types of buyer influence:

1. The marketing input that introduces the product or service to the buyer and draws the buyer's attention. If this is done well it should appeal to the buyer's needs, wants and desires. How the product or service is packaged, priced and distributed are also key influences in the final buying decision.

2. Secondly, and more intangibly, are the psychological factors that include cultural (such as the culture of the country of the buyer, perhaps the subculture, religion and social class); social (such as peer group, the family, social reference groups that confer status, education and socio-economic groups); psychological (such as needs, motivation, perception, learning, beliefs and attitude); personal factors (such as the buyer's age and where they are in their life cycle, their occupation, their economic status, their personality and how they view themselves in terms of lifestyle).

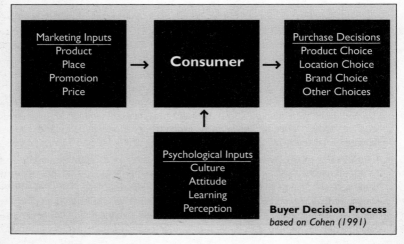

Buyer Decision Process
based on Cohen (1991)

Buyers in Organizations

In an organization a buyer is the person or group responsible for the purchasing policies and management of the purchasing functions of an organization. A buyer can be an individual, a department within a company, or a group from various parts of the company that is brought together to make a buying decision. This is often referred to as the **buying group** or the **buying centre**. The buyer, or buyers, can be a direct purchaser themselves for their individual use (for example an Information Technology manager buying a range of PCs for his own staff); they can be influencers (for example an Information Technology manager who provides an evaluation of various PC suppliers to management to supply the entire organization); deciders (for example an Information Technology manager who decides on the entire supply of PCs on behalf of his organization based upon the evaluations and recommendations of third parties, or perhaps a competitive tendering process); or they can be gatekeeper (past whom a PC supplier must go in order to gains access to management who can decide on the overall purchase).

Different types and size of purchase will require different types of buyer and buying process. Normally, the larger the purchase, the more buyers become involved and the more complex the buying process.

Industrial (organizational) buying

industrial market the acquisition of goods and services that enter into the production of other products and services that are sold, rented, or supplied to others. Goods and services are usually purchased for organizations. There are few buyers but many decision-makers. Buying volume can be very large and there are close supplier-customer relationships.

industry structure the organizational and competitive characteristics of an industry including the number and size distribution of buyers and sellers, the nature of the product and the size of any barriers to entry. There are both fragmented industries that are populated by a large number of small and medium-sized companies and concentrated industries that differ from fragmented industries in that they are dominated by a small number of large firms. These concentrated firms are able to exercise a significant buying influence over the market as a whole.

Types of industrial/organization buyer

Organizational buyers can be:

- manufacturers,
- wholesalers,
- operational users or
- retailers.

Retailers are the last destination before the final user. Physical retailers buy, display, merchandize, service and sell the products to the final user and give it local context and a highly targeted approach to local buyers.

On-line retailers, whilst losing the local point of presence and sale, can develop direct relationships with their buyers based on a number of indirect channels (phone, internet/e-mail, websites). On-line retailers normally sell at a discount to physical retailers.

Wholesalers are in the stage before the retailers in the value chain. The characteristic of the wholesale purchase of products is high volume. The purpose of the wholesaler is to be able to access the retail markets in a cost-effective way. Wholesalers sell to the retailer, either physical or on-line.

Buying process for organizations or industrial buyers.

Kotler identified the following stages in industrial buying process:

- **problem recognition** the first stage of the industrial buying process in which someone in the company recognizes a problem or need that can be met by acquiring a good or a service.

- **general need description** the stage at which the company describes the general characteristics and quantity of a needed item.

- **product or service specification** the stage at which the buying organization decides on and specifies the best technical product characteristics for a needed product or service. The major activity is the design and development of product specifications designed to solve the problem previously identified. Often this will involve assistance from third parties prior to this being put out to contract.

- **products and suppliers search** the stage at which the buyer looks to match suppliers with the detailed specification. This is the point at which the reputation, track record and awareness of potential suppliers becomes important.

- **proposal solicitation** the stage in which the buyer invites qualified suppliers to submit proposals. This is the stage at which the selling abilities of the supplier organization are vitally important. This may also involve the issuing of an invitation to tender, depending on the size and scale of the purchase.

- **selection and ordering** the stage at which a selected group of suppliers are assessed, terms negotiated, selection made and contracts offered. This process tends to involve several experts – purchasing, legal, selling, commercial contracts, and finance. See DECISION-MAKING UNIT (below).

- **performance review** (evaluating the product and supplier) the stage at which the buyer rates their satisfaction with suppliers, deciding whether to continue, modify, or drop them.

The **decision-making unit** (DMU) in an industrial purchasing process consists of all those individuals and groups who participate in the buying decision, all of whom share some common goals and are knowledgeable about the risks arising from decisions.

Although each decision-making unit is different, these are the usual roles:

1. **Initiators** are a group within the DMU who begin the process of considering a purchase. This group help the decision-makers by gathering information.

2. **Influencers** are a group within the DMU who help define the specification and also provide an input into the process of evaluating the available alternatives.

3. **Deciders** are a group within the DMU who have the responsibility for deciding on product requirements and suppliers.

4. **Approvers** are a group within the DMU who authorize the proposals of deciders and buyers.

5. **Gatekeepers** are a group within the DMU who, by controlling the flow of information, may be able to stop sellers from reaching individuals within the buying centre.

6. **Buyers** are a group within the DMU who have the formal authority for the selection of suppliers and negotiating purchase terms.

7. **Users** are a group within the DMU who may initiate the buying process and help define purchase specifications.

Functionally, these decision-makers might be Operation Managers who use the product in the organization's processes and who are seeking greater efficiency and effectiveness; Technical Managers who might test and approve the product and who will be seeking quality and reliability; the Senior Executive who may approve major expenditure or choice of supplier; the Purchasing or Commercial Manager who negotiates terms, approves conditions of purchase and monitors supplier performance; the Legal Manager who draws up or approves legal contracts with the supplier; the Finance Manager who approvers expenditure and controls.

Types of organizational buying:

New task **purchase**. The organization is facing a need or a problem for the first time and the full organizational buying process will probably occur.

Modified re-buy **purchase**. This is when something about the buying situation has changed, but a lot still remains the same.

Straight re-buy **purchase** occurs when the buyer routinely purchases the same product under the same terms of sale.

Contrast between industrial/organizational and consumer market buying

There are fundamental differences between the individual consumer buying process and the organizational buying process.

An obvious difference is that the individual buyer is normally spending his own money; in organizational, or industrial buying, the purchase is made with organizational money.

The number of customers is much smaller in industrial markets.

The buying decision in organizations and industries is more complex and the influences are different. Those in consumer markets tend to be individual or family-based with fewer decision points.

Organizational purchases tend to be larger than individual consumer purchases.

Purchases in industrial markets tend to be contract-based rather than straightforward money or credit purchases. Price decisions in industrial markets are negotiated beforehand and terms are important whereas in consumer markets prices are normally pre-set and fixed and bargain discounts are important.

Suppliers to industrial markets tend to have deeper, longer-term relationships with organizations than they do with individuals.

The nature of demand in industrial markets is dependent on demand in consumer markets. This is usually known as derived or joint demand (in consumer markets this is known as primary demand).

Buying motivations in industrial markets are usually in support of a company's operations and its longer range needs, while those in consumer markets are for immediate individual or family needs.

Product specifications in industrial markets are usually technically sophisticated whereas in the consumer market the technical content is lower.

In terms of marketing and sales the emphasis in industrial markets is on personal selling, whereas in consumer markets the emphasis is on mass media advertising.

Distribution decisions: in industrial markets there are a limited number of large buyers and simple channels; in consumer markets there are a large number of small buyers and complex channels.

Customer service: this is critical to success in industrial markets and less important in consumer markets.

buying association an informal group of retailers, usually in a specific geographic locality, who group together to enjoy the economies of scale accruing from bulk purchases from wholesalers and manufacturers.

buzzword a short-lived word or phrase that is used more to impress than explain. A buzzword may be a newly coined word or an old word used in a new way. Buzzwords are part of the fashion of a living language, more about style than substance. Some buzzwords are actually useful for a period of time, but the object they describe eventually becomes less useful. Other buzzwords are simply confusing or inaccurate. A buzzword spends only a fraction of its lifespan being used; the rest of the time it is being abused. The result is a phenomenon known as buzzword backlash, whereby the tide turns against a buzzword and it starts to fade from usage.

cable an important medium for direct advertising, interactive marketing and Internet access. Increasingly cable is the focus of 'triple play' – telephony, digital television and high-speed Internet access. See also BROADBAND.

caching the storage of Web files for later re-use at a point more quickly accessed by the end user. Caching can happen at many places, for example the user's local computer. The objective is to make efficient use of resources and speed the delivery of content to the end user. While caching can have a positive impact on the user's experience, it can have a negative impact for site publishers, resulting in undercounts of page views and ad impressions. In response to this problem, sites have implemented various cache-busting techniques to better ensure that all performance statistics are accurately measured.

call planning the detailed preparations made by a salesman in preparation for a client meeting. Call planning can almost be viewed as a type of single campaign for a single client on a single occasion. See also PERSONAL SELLING under SALES.

campaigns see ADVERTISING.

cannibalization describes how and when a new product or service line takes away sales or market share from other products in the existing product or service line of the same company. It is incumbent upon marketers to guide their range of products and services away from cannibalization, which is very damaging to their portfolio.

capital equipment for example, industrial machinery, tools, office equipment or transport vehicles that are purchased infrequently and are used to produce goods, to provide a service, or to support the day-to-day operation of an organization.

capital items industrial goods that enter or become part of the finished product, including installations and accessory equipment.

cartel an association of suppliers whose purpose in cooperating is the fixing of variables, such as price and output levels. This places a limitation on free market competition and pricing. Cartels are subject to legislative action in the major economies. Although becoming a cartel would make a marketer's life much easier, cartels are inimical to the marketing profession and process.

Case, Steve (1958–) American entrepreneur and founder in 1991 of AOL (America Online). AOL became one of the first Internet companies to make the Fortune 500 list, the company's success in large part being due to a marketing strategy based on supplying free AOL disks in stores, through the mail, and with magazines. AOL subsequently merged with Time Warner to become one of the world's most influential media empires. In 2003, following the failure of the merger, Steve Case stepped down as head of AOL Time Warner.

cash cow see BOSTON CONSULTING GROUP MATRIX.

cash discount price reduction to buyers who pay their bills promptly or to buyers who pay their bills in cash rather than on credit. This is used as an instrument of competitive marketing as well as financial management.

cash refund offer or **rebate** a guarantee to refund part of the purchase price of a product after the purchase to consumers who produce a 'proof of purchase' such as an original receipt. This can often be a market differentiator for retailers whose policies create good word of mouth marketing, such as Marks and Spencer in the UK or Nordstrom in the US.

catalogue an important channel of direct marketing and also one of the earliest ways in marketing techniques for increasing distribution channel and reach, particularly to those buyers who were unable to visit the retail store or factory outlet. Catalogues display a variety of merchandise available from a manufacturer or retailer. Originally intended to service remote and rural areas that were far from department stores, catalogues have now entered a new era of commercial development. Electronic catalogues are also available on the World Wide Web and this has extended their reach even further, enabling even more direct marketing than ever. See also BRAND (IKEA).

catalogue marketing direct marketing using catalogues mailed to a select list of customers or made available in retail outlets. Retail catalogues often employ agents at a local level who organize purchase and delivery of goods as well as collecting and remitting moneys in exchange for commission from the catalogue company. See also DIRECT MARKETING under MARKETING SPECIALIZATIONS.

catalogue showroom a retail operation that sells a wide selection of consumer goods (usually at discount prices) that can be identified in the retail catalogue. This is, in the age of electronic shopping, a surprisingly popular way of shopping.

causal research research that helps marketers identify a specific factor that causes an effect in the marketplace. See also DIRECT MARKETING under MARKETING SPECIALIZATIONS, MARKET RESEARCH.

cause-related marketing see MARKETING.

caveat emptor Latin for 'let the buyer beware', from the principle that the buyer alone is responsible if dissatisfied.

caveat vindictor 'let the seller beware'.

CD-ROM a compact disc with read-only memory, forming a cost-effective and secure information storage device with multimedia capabilities. With the increase of new media, computers and games consoles, CD-ROMs are used frequently for marketing promotions such as moving image and testimonial and for the delivery of market data, such as research. Direct marketing often involves a CD-ROM being sent rather than a physical brochure. See also DIRECT MARKETING.

celebrity testimonial an advertisement or promotion featuring endorsement of products by a well-known personality from the field of entertainment, sport and politics. See also ADVERTISING.

chain store any of multiple outlets that are commonly owned and controlled, have central buying and merchandising, and sell similar lines of merchandise. The most common type of chain store is the corporate chain store that is made up of retail outlets that are owned by a single company. Marketing of these chain stores is usually done centrally. Wal-Mart, Tesco and Sainsbury are examples of such chain stores. The next most common type of chain store is the franchise outlet such as The Body Shop or Burger King or McDonalds.

CHANNELS OF DISTRIBUTION

Channels of distribution are the means by which a seller of goods or services connects with their target customers. The management and development of these channels is a key part of the marketing mix. There are wholesale and retail channels, direct and indirect channels, narrow channels and broad channels.

A distribution channel can be any channel used by the product or service creator to get produce to the end customer. Distribution is a key element of the marketing mix. There are direct and indirect channels of distribution. Marketers can use multiple channels to get their products and services to market, but must avoid channel confusion or conflict in order that the channels work efficiently.

Direct channels are characterized by the producers of goods and services interacting directly with the end consumer. Examples include:

• personal selling

• retail selling

• direct mailing

• mail order

• telesales

• taking orders over the Internet.

The direct sales force is among the oldest channels. Although declining as a volume channel relative to other channels to market, the personal sales channel is one of the more effective and most expensive to run. Increasingly, direct personal selling is being used for major complex sales rather than the sales of consumer goods and services.

The retail channel markets, sells and services consumers directly. They will often offer credit to the customers. The retail channel determines the final price of the good or service to the customer. Retail channels can take the form of stores, catalogues, franchises, websites, telesales, mail order, and home shopping channels. Retailers act as a channel for multiple brands, but can themselves also be a brand – sometimes much more powerful than the brands that they distribute and sell. See also BRAND and CONSUMER MARKETING under MARKETING SPECIALIZATIONS.

The retail channel is highly managed and often controls other parts of the supply chain. For example, an in-store EFTPOS (Electronic Funds Transfer at Point of Sale) system can immediately collect and transfer information about purchases to warehouse and distribution centres that can dispatch new supplies when they are needed in the retail store. This system eliminates the need for stockrooms within the retail outlet and allows the entire space to become retail outlets serving customers. Retail channels can exercise enormous power over pricing and product design and quality.

The Internet represents a powerful intermediary channel. It has possibly the widest geographical reach of the channels to market. It can enable niche products to reach a vast audience. It is a relatively low-cost channel with low entry barriers. It uses on-line payments to enable purchase.

Indirect distribution channels are characterized by using a third party as an intermediary between the producer of the goods and services and the end consumer. Examples are:

- wholesalers
- agents
- brokers
- resellers
- dealers.
- aggregators.

Indirect distribution channels are used most efficiently when they can access either more customers than retailers or can sell more efficiently (such as to a diverse base of smaller retailers in a large geographical area) or can add more value (such as customization of product) for the retail outlet that serves end customers.

A wholesale distribution channel is formed between the producer and the retailer. Wholesalers generally do not sell to the end consumer, but to the retail channel. Wholesalers take ownership, or title, to the goods that they buy. They provide storage facilities. Wholesalers usually buy goods from a range of manufacturers at a substantial discount and then sell on to retailers who in turn sell them to end consumers. Wholesalers can service multiple small retailers who do not have sufficient purchasing power on their own to deal directly with the manufacturer. Occasionally, wholesalers produce marketing materials, such as brochures, catalogues, websites and price lists, but they are not so active as the retailer.

Another type of indirect distribution is agents and brokers, who largely sell on behalf of the producer without taking possession of and title to the products: they bring together the producer and the buyer and they are mainly compensated on a commission basis. Agents secure orders and take commission but do not take ownership or title to the goods themselves.

Another channel of distribution is the reseller. These tend to be used for international marketing. See also INTERNATIONAL MARKETING under MARKETING SPECIALIZATIONS.

The chief purpose of the dealer is to buy goods, add value to them, then resell them with post-sales service.

Channel conflict is disagreement among marketing channel members on goals and roles in a channel of distribution: on who should cover which territory, who should sell what, to whom, and for what rewards. It can also occur between manufacturers and retailers over who controls volumes and pricing in a specific channel. It can involve field sales forces who have to sell different products by different means in the same territory. Examples of industries facing significant channel conflict include insurance, music, airlines, computer manufacturers, appliances, furniture and securities trading.

New types of distribution channel:

Example: Amazon.com and E-Trade.com

Both of these new companies have demonstrated that they can grow an on-line business in a market that had been hitherto dominated by physical, non-electronic distribution channels. Amazon does not support a chain of bricks-and-mortar bookstores. E-Trade has no network of commissioned brokers to acquire their customers' business.

Amazon and E-Trade were able to avoid channel conflict because they developed new channels. The degree and type of channel conflict in the electronic marketplace varies across industries and individual companies. The key for these companies was to develop strategies that minimize the impact of channel conflict. However, both of these successes caused the traditional competitors (e.g. Barnes and Noble in bookselling) to develop online distribution and marketing channels to implement their physical businesses.

Channel conflict is not a new business phenomenon. For example, during the 1980s manufacturers faced channel conflicts when outlet and discount superstores expanded and started to harm the trade of traditional department stores. Recognizing the demand for outlet stores, manufacturers began to use them to reach new customers and sell different products, creating mutual benefit for themselves and their distribution channels.

Companies that do not own, or closely control, their non-electronic distribution channels risk damaging long-standing relationships and revenue streams. For example, when Compaq started allowing on-line sales of its computers at discount prices, traditional retailers threatened to stop selling its products. As a result, Compaq ceased selling through on-line discounters and was forced to re-evaluate its relationships with all distribution channels. Hewlett-Packard has recently acquired Compaq.

On the other hand, companies that control their own channels risk cannibalizing off-line revenues with on-line revenues. This takes customers away from existing channels, decreasing the older channels' profitability. For example, as more consumers use on-line banking, commercial banks have been unable to justify maintaining as many physical branches. In the UK there have been waves of bank branch closures in the UK retail-banking sector.

However, in the Internet economy, channel conflicts are intensified by the unique characteristics of the electronic marketplace. Companies now have to contend with a business environment characterized by new consumer expectations, new competitors, and a faster time to market.

Ideally companies facing channel conflict will devise strategies to minimize it, while simultaneously creating value on the Internet. To do this, companies need to determine the level of channel conflict they may incur.

Some products and services are appropriate for electronic channels, and some are not. For example, books and music sell easily on the Internet. However, service businesses, such as hair salons and car repairs, cannot transfer entirely to the Internet, but might use it for customer service, marketing or appointment setting.

Secondly, the level of channel control that a company exercises is also important. Channel control can be defined in two different ways. For manufacturers, channel control is the extent to which they control the relationship with their retail channels. For retailers, channel control is better defined as the power they have in the market in which they compete. Companies with easily transferable businesses, and little control over their channels, may face significant channel conflicts. Companies with easily transferable businesses, but high channel control, face moderate levels of channel conflict, most often related to cannibalization of existing channels. Industries in this area include many retail chains (e.g., office supplies, books, toys), mobile telephone providers and many franchise organizations. Companies in this category often *link* their existing channels with the on-line channels to enhance the benefit of having all channels together.

Companies with businesses that do not transfer to the Internet, and that have little control over channels, face minimal channel conflict. These companies' channels will likely view electronic commerce as a threat to their control of the customer relationship.

It is unlikely that companies that have control over their channels, but do not easily transfer to the Internet, will experience channel conflict. Examples of industries in this area include: pharmaceutical companies, law firms, accounting firms and other professional service firms.

character symbol a historical figure, animated character, animal, or object used to advertise a brand and that comes to be associated with the brand, e.g. Joe Camel for Camel cigarettes, the lion in MGM movies, Tony the Tiger for Exxon, Charlie Chaplin (played by an actor) in 1980s IBM ads.

Chiat, Jay (1931–2002) Chiat/Day Agency, New York
Jay Chiat created an innovative style of advertising fused with popular culture that revolutionized the industry in the 70s and 80s. His agency, Chiat/Day, grew from its single Los Angeles office in 1968, to an international agency with 1,200 employees and billings of $1.3 billion in the early 90s. His agency, known for creativity and innovation, introduced the British discipline of account planning to the US; he set up unconventional work environments like the 'virtual agency' in the company's New York offices.

Born Morton Jay Chiat in the Bronx on October 25, 1931, he worked on recruitment advertising for Aerojet General, an Air Force contractor, and then joined a small advertising agency in Orange County, California. He opened Jay Chiat & Associates in 1962 before merging with another small agency,

Faust/Day, in 1968, which became Chiat/Day. He sold his advertising agency to the Omnicom Group in 1995. Chiat/Day earned the coveted title of agency of the decade from *Advertising Age* magazine, as well as agency of the year in 1980 and 1988. In 1998, Chiat became acting chief executive of Screaming Media, an Internet content distributor, and took on the role of chairman in 1999. *Advertising Age* named him one of the top 10 on a list of 100 top players who had shaped the course of advertising history.

Chiat introduced Apple Computers' Macintosh PC to millions of viewers with his celebrated '1984' commercial during Super Bowl XVIII (see also ADVERTISING). While the mini-film was shown on national television only once, it set the tone for future Super Bowl commercials. With Chiat's influence, Nike became the 'unofficial' footwear of the 1984 Summer Olympics after he ran a campaign that featured Randy Newman singing 'I Love L.A.' Five years later, he made the popular Energizer bunny commercial.

choice one of the greatest dynamics behind consumerism in the post-war period. In recent time consumer choice has been greatly widened through the advent of global markets and the Internet. Greater access to information on products and services has not only given the consumer greater choice, it has also given them greater power. This power shift has resulted in an increased focus on the consumers rather than the producer. Consequently, marketing is starting to transform the entire range of its techniques, which were originally developed to serve the producer interest. See also CONSUMERISM, INTRODUCTION.

cinema a major medium and outlet for marketing programmes. Advertising is an obvious beneficiary of cinema. The advantages of using advertising through cinema are that the audience, although relatively small compared to a television audience, is captive and has a higher attention span. The size of the screen and the audio quality can give a memorable impact on the audience. Often, the type of movie being shown enables the advertiser to target the messages and the ad to the audience. Advertising can be customized to either regional or local culture in the local cinema area in which the movie is being shown. The cinema can also be an advertising location for the company that owns the cinema, such as Warner Brothers.

Increasingly, as product merchandising (such as T-shirts, dolls, computer games and derivatives) is becoming an important element in the total marketing of a movie, the cinema can often act as a retail outlet for merchandised goods. Increasing percentages of the total budget of a movie are being spent on advertising. In the last few years, websites have become part of the marketing mix for the promotion of new films by movie companies. Major films these days reach the local cinema with a website promoting the film concurrently. It is a much less expensive promotional technique than traditional media. The cost of creating these websites is a fraction of the cost of a full TV or radio advertising campaign. There is a high correlation between Internet users and moviegoers, making websites a targeted and cost-effective medium for creating awareness for their films. Unlike a traditional promotion, a website can continue to generate awareness over a sustained period. Movie websites are not only building awareness for a movie before and during the cinema distribution, they continue to promote once the mass media advertisements have stopped running and the movies have moved on to ancillary markets. In addition to generating buzz and hype, film websites can also engage the viewer and enhance the experience. The most recent 'Star Wars' website created an on-line community before the movie was even shown. These communities are where visitors can find more information, take part in interactive activities, subscribe to newsletters, and chat with other like-minded individuals, with the eventual aim of creating greater audience loyalty.

Example

Vodafone released a cinema ad in the UK to show that ring tones are part of peoples' personalities. The 60-second animated advert was created to support the phone company's youth website. The ad follows two girls, Stacey and Mandy, who are enjoying a night on the town. They meet the man of their dreams in a nightclub but are disappointed when they see him again, having reapplied their makeup in the lavatories. The handsome stranger picks up a call from a friend called Steve, and in doing so reveals that his ring tone is 'YMCA' by the Village People. The commercial ends with the strap line: '2LET YR RNG XPRESS U'.

circulation the number of copies of a publication that are sold both directly and through subscription. The circulation number remains one of the main measures of the success of newspapers. The reason for this is that circulation number is directly linked to advertising rates: the greater the circulation to an identifiable audience, the greater the advertising rate that can be charged. There are frequent outbreaks of 'circulation wars', or extreme competition between newspapers. Weapons in these wars can involve 'scoop' stories, shock stories, eye-catching features, increased number of extra sections, lowered prices, competitions and games, or even poaching well-known journalists and writers from each other.

Increasingly, more heavyweight newspapers are emphasising their 'quality' of readership and using that to market directly to advertisers.

LARGEST US DAILY NEWSPAPERS BY AVERAGE DAILY CIRCULATION[1]	
The Wall Street Journal	1,752,693 (m)
USA Today	1,671,539 (m)
The New York Times	1,086,293 (m)
Los Angeles Times	1,078,186 (m)
The Washington Post	763,305 (m)
Daily News, New York	701,831 (m)
Chicago Tribune	657,690 (m)
Newsday	574,941 (m)
Houston Chronicle	542,414 (m)
The Dallas Morning News	490,249 (m)
Chicago Sun-Times	468,170 (m)
The Boston Globe	462,850 (m)

San Francisco Chronicle	456,742 (m)
New York Post	438,158 (m)
The Arizona Republic	433,296 (m)
The Star-Ledger, Newark	407,129 (m)
The Philadelphia Inquirer	399,339 (m)
Denver Rocky Mountain News	396,114 (m)
The Plain Dealer, Cleveland	386,312 (m)
The San Diego Union-Tribune	376,604 (m)

[1] *Average for six months ended. Source: Audit Bureau of Circulation, 2000*

NEWSPAPER ADVERTISING COMPARED TO OTHER TYPES OF ADVERTISING IN THE US

	National advertising (millions)	Retail advertising (millions)	Classified advertising (millions)	Total Newspaper advertising (millions)	GDP (billions)
1965	783	2,429	1,214	4,426	719
1970	891	3,292	1,521	5,704	1,036
1975	1,109	4,966	2,159	8,234	1,631
1980	1,963	8,609	4,222	14,794	2,754
1985	3,352	13,443	8,375	25,170	4,181
1986	3,376	14,311	9,303	26,990	4,422
1987	3,494	15,227	10,691	29,412	4,692
1988[1]	3,821	15,790	11,586	31,197	5,050
1989	3,948	16,504	11,916	32,368	5,439
1990	4,122	16,652	11,506	32,280	5,743
1991	3,924	15,839	10,587	30,349	5,917
1992	3,834	16,041	10,764	30,639	6,244
1993	3,853	16,859	11,157	31,869	6,553
1994	4,149	17,496	12,464	34,109	6,936
1995	4,251	18,099	13,742	36,092	7,254
1996	4,667	18,344	15,065	38,075	7,636
1997[2]	5,315	19,242	16,773	41,330	8,111
1998	5,721	20,331	17,873	43,925	8,511
1999[3]	6,732	20,907	18,650	46,289	9,256

Sources: NAA, U.S. Department of Commerce

[1] The 1988 category figures are not directly comparable to previous years due to a change in methodology.
[2] Revised data.
[3] Preliminary data.

click-through the process of clicking through an on-line advertisement to the advertiser's destination, such as a website or on-line service. The click-through is the most common way in which on-line visitors connect with an advertiser's website. Alternatively, visitors can also choose to visit the website directly by typing the URL directly into the browser bar, or typing the company's name into a search engine box.

click-through rate (CTR) the most immediate response to an advertisement as well as the prime measure of an on-line ad's success. Accurate counting methods of click-throughs are very importance when CTR is used as the measurement on which on-line advertisers' payments are based. See also ADVERTISING.

client account see ACCOUNT.

cluster analysis a multivariate statistical classification technique for discovering whether the individuals of a population fall into different groups by making quantitative comparisons of multiple characteristics. The differences within any group should be less than the differences between groups. This analytical technique is often used for consumer segmentation and brand positioning. See MARKET RESEARCH.

clutter all non-programming time on radio and TV; this includes time given to advertising commercials, station or channel promotions, station or channel identifications and programme credits. Excessively high clutter levels may result in audience dissatisfaction or alienation. See also ATTENTION, ADVERTISING.

code of practice a voluntary guideline to encourage desirable modes of behaviour. See also ADVERTISING (REGULATION).

cognitive dissonance a theory developed by Leon Festinger, a social scientist from Stanford University, in 1957. It is concerned with the relationships among cognitions. Cognition is any type of knowledge. The knowledge may be about an attitude, an emotion, behaviour, a value. People hold a multitude of cognitions simultaneously, and these cognitions form irrelevant, consonant, or dissonant relationships with one another. Festinger considered the human need to avoid dissonance as basic as the need for safety or the need to satisfy hunger. (See also Maslow's Hierarchy under HIERARCHY OF NEEDS.) It is an aversive drive that pushes us to be consistent. He claimed that people avoid information that is likely to increase dissonance. Not only do we tend to select reading material and television programmes that are consistent with our existing beliefs, we usually choose to be with people who are like us. The tension of dissonance motivates us to change either our behaviour or our beliefs in an effort to avoid a distressing feeling. The more important the issue, and the greater the discrepancy between behaviour and belief, the higher the magnitude of dissonance that we will feel. In a marketing context, cognitive dissonance arises after a major purchase when alternatives are recommended, or if dislikes emerge after the purchase choice has been made. To eliminate the discomfort of dissonance, the consumer will seek to rationalize the original choice, in other words, find positive advantages and ignore negatives.

cold calling the practice of making a sales call on a client without an appointment. This can be done either in person or by telephone. Cold calling is often seen as a necessity to make new sales or to develop new prospects, but it is often a source of major criticism, particularly when made through telesales, obtrusively and at unwelcome times. Examples are double-glazing and replacement windows salespeople in the UK or telephony services supplies in the US. See also DIRECT MARKETING under MARKETING SPECIALIZATIONS.

Cold calling give the sales world a very unpalatable reputation. The consumer generally detests cold calling. Equally, few practising sales people actually like cold calling, at best seeing it as a means to an end. It is the type of selling that has the highest rejection rate and often incurs hostility. So why does cold calling exist? Here are some potential reasons:

- Sales managers think that cold calling develops character and technique among salespeople. Those making cold calls have to deal with rejection and often hostility. In the sales mindset this is good for personal growth and development.
- Cold calling is supposed to keep the salespeople sharp and involved.
- Cold calling is a way to educate and teach salespeople in the fundamentals.
- Cold calls are a supplement to other marketing and sales approaches. Frequently, the purpose of cold calling is to get an appointment for a salesperson; in fact it enables direct personal selling.
- Cold calling is often a way to establish the needs and problems of a group of clients. Once these are established, a more effective way of marketing, based on detailed knowledge can be adapted.
- If the information gleaned from cold calling is analysed on a database, one can track changing needs. This tracking can open new market potential. Today's modern sales process requires multiple contacts.
- Cold calling can actually be used as a form of market research. Depending on the industry, gathering information by cold calling gives first hand customer and competitive intelligence.
- It is a way in which some sales managers track the performance of their salespeople in advance of selling.

colour an extremely important dimension of marketing, particularly in branding. Much of marketing is visual as well as psychological. Colour is a powerful means of communicating emotion, which is a driving force behind decision-making. Colour is used in logos, signage, marketing packages and material, graphics and illustrations. Company brand systems usually ascribe different moods and meanings to colour. For example, the Kodak logo is inextricably linked to the yellow background, IBM to a blue logo, Coca-Cola to red, Marks and Spencer to green in either background or foreground. Colour also has different connotations in different cultures.

Marketers and advertisers have to be very sensitive to how colours are received by the audience. Red is a controversial colour (for example it is often said that red cars have more accidents). As far as humans are concerned the visible spectrum consists of the rainbow. However, because our retinas have only three types of light/photo receptors (the cones), we actually detect only three of these colours: red, blue and green. They are called the additive primaries because mixing them to create other colours has the effect of adding energy together. Combinations of these primary colours produce all the colours we see. Because we have two eyes, which look in the same direction, we can also distinguish depth up to a distance of about six metres. This is called stereoscopic vision. The photosensitive part of the eye is a mosaic of receptor cells: the rods and cones of the retina. Rods are sensitive to small amounts of light but do not have any colour perception. It is the cones that are responsible for our colour vision. In one eye we have about 7 million cones. Our eyes adapt differently to colour and brightness differences because both eyes operate independently. If we look at large areas of colour for even a short period of time our eyes become tired and we become temporarily blind to that colour. Our brains piece together the information gathered by our eyes, and then make guesses about the world around us.

COMMUNICATIONS

Communications is one of the more important elements of the marketing mix. Marketing communications usually constitutes the largest component of an overall communications budget, but an important element is also corporate communications, which had its roots in the public relations industry, and whose primary purpose is to educate investors, consumers and the general public about what this company is, what it does and what it stands for. Towards the end of the 20th century, with the fragmentation of markets and the introduction of new communications media and technologies, communications were able to be more customized, more targeted and more interactive than the classic forms of mass communication. There have been in some companies attempts to integrate all communications in support of the overall brand rather than seeing them as separate functional domains. In recent times, in terms of expenditure, direct marketing communications have surpassed all other forms of marketing. The advent of globalization has also posed some challenges for communications, in terms of language, medium, culture and tone. More and more communications systems have become global while the messages and content are adapted to local language and culture. The phenomenon of globalization has placed greater emphasis on the communication of the global brand, which can often transcend cultural and geographical barriers.

There are multiple types of communication, both external to an enterprise and internal to it, those based upon mass communications systems and those based upon more direct, interpersonal communications. In the broadest sense, it covers the transmission or exchange of information to a target audience. In the context of marketing, the substance of communications is all-encompassing, covering all advertising, press releases, press and analyst communication and interaction, internal communications, websites, marketing materials, sales presentations, management communications, formal documents such as the company annual report, all branded materials and messages that present the company and its products and services internally and externally, price lists, product catalogues, service descriptions and guarantees, market research questionnaires, letters, interviews on all forms of media, internal and external formal announcements, presentations to investors, recruitment literature and the conduct of recruitment campaigns, speeches by company staff as well as all external publications by and on behalf of the company. In short, the totality of how the company, its people, services and products are made known internally and externally. For the marketer, communications is the way in which the company or enterprise communicates the benefits and differences to target markets and customers.

Increasingly, modern communications techniques attempt to share meaning within a defined context. Each market demands a different type of communication message, context of meaning and medium. For example, industrial markets demand a higher level of personal communication (such as personal selling) than consumer markets that demand a higher degree of non-personal communications (such as advertising). There are an increasing number of communications media that have dramatically broadened the ways in which audiences receive and understand meaning and messages. These have complicated greatly the techniques of the marketer and public relations expert in the transmission of messages to target audiences.

The communications media available to the marketer have grown significantly in the past years, and this has changed the nature of marketing communications. The array of media available often outpaces the ability of the marketer and public relations expert to adapt messages in the right format. Messages can be transmitted through face-to-face communication, formal meetings, conferences, events, interviews, oral communication, the telephone and the multi-party conference call, long, short and FM wave and internet-based radio, television, video-conferencing, written communication (in physical and in electronic format), letters, external mail system, internal mail system, e-mail, chat lines, formal reports and memoranda, forms, lists, catalogues, notice boards, journals, newspapers, internal bulletins, newsletters, broadcasts, webcasts, narrowcasts, manuals, visual communication aids (static, pictorial and animated), presentation charts, films, corporate videos, electronic data interchange. At the beginning of the 21st century, the average consumer in the advanced economies can be exposed to an average of 3000 commercial messages a day.

Despite the multiplicity of media and the vast amplification of 'noise' created by modern communications, the purposes of communications remain relatively constant: to inform, to initiate actions, to communicate decisions, to motivate people, to find out, then make known needs and requirements, to exchange information, ideas, attitudes and beliefs, to establish understanding and sometimes meaning, and also to initiate, develop and maintain relations.

Schramm's Communication model outlines a simple model and process for communications flow:

The process begins with a desire to communicate: the **sender** sends the message to the other party. The **sender** is alternatively known as the communicator or the source. It is normal at this stage to have a purpose, or target destination, for the message. The **encoding** stage of the process imbues meaning with symbolic form (such as words, signs, sounds etc.). At this stage, it is important to understand both the context – which gives meaning to the message – and also the audience whom the final message is intended to reach and to influence. Next stage is the selection of the **media,** that is the communication channel or channels through which the message moves from sender to receiver. It is most important at this stage to select the most important medium to enhance the message. A good message can often be

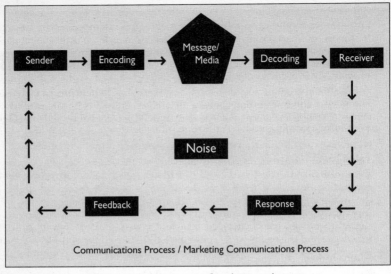

Communications Process / Marketing Communications Process

Figure supplied by courtesy of marketingteacher.com

undermined by a poor communications medium. **Decoding** is a process carried out by the **receiver** who converts the symbolic forms transmitted by the sender into a form that has meaning and that makes sense to him. This is one of the more difficult stages in the communications process, as much can change between message transmission and message reception. Often the most well-crafted messages through the most impactful communications medium will have an altogether different effect from that intended by the sender. The **receiver** is the party who receives the message, also known as the audience or the destination. They will often interpret the message and its meaning in their own context and their own circumstances. This often results in a single message having multiple meanings to the same audience. The impact and effect of the message is gauged by the **response** process that measures the reaction of the receiver to the message communicated. This is when the receiver can be transposed into the sender.

Often there is immediate polling of a sample audience immediately after a keynote political speech to determine if the messages transmitted had any resonance in the minds of the receiver. This leads to the **feedback** stage, that is the part of the receiver's response that the receiver communicates back to the sender. **Noise** is a modern description of all those factors that prevent the decoding of a message by the receiver in the way intended by the sender. This is also known as message distortion.

In communications, much can go wrong between the transmission of the message and its reception. One of the core problems faced by the modern marketer is that the attention span of the receiver is either short or very selective, given that the receiver is bombarded by a constant stream of messages on a daily basis (see also ATTENTION). The second problem is that the receivers, being human, have a complex array of cultures, preconceived notions, beliefs and opinions that are unique to them and which cause them to distort the information or messages received in order to fit into their belief or value system. The next problem is the receivers' memory – both the short-term memory and the permanent memory. Studies have shown that receivers retain in their permanent memory only a small fraction of the messages that reach them. Beyond that is the more complex phenomenon of message rehearsal, a phenomenon in communication whereby the receiver elaborates on the meaning of the message in a way that brings related thoughts from the long-term memory into his short-term memory.

FUNDAMENTAL TYPES OF COMMUNICATION

One-to-many

This type of communication is normal for mass communication. Content is generated from a single broadcast point and is then made available over airwaves or in mass print runs. One-to-many is an appropriate model for news distribution and other situations in which discussion and dialogue are not necessarily desirable. It is not interactive or tailored to individuals.

Many-to-one

Many-to-one is often linked to one-to-many communications. Examples include a freefone number, an invitation to return a pre-paid envelope, or a reply button on an e-mail: all techniques of engendering bi-directional communication from mass communications.

One-to-one

The most intensive communication 'transactions' occur at a one-to-one level. For example, a sales presentation, a negotiation over price, or direct delivery is almost always done on a one-to-one basis. For value-based products and services one-to-one communication is preferred. Most one-to-one communications take place face to face. On the Internet the most common type of one-to-one communication takes place in transaction-centred e-mail, where a buyer and seller communicate directly. Another example is instant message 'chat' channels, which are becoming hugely popular in business.

Many-to-many

On the Internet the main outlet for many-to-many communications has been in community building such as on-line forums, real-time chat rooms, 'blogging' web sites, discussion boards on issues of common interest. The principal value of many-to-many comes from the participants' ability to exchange ideas and experiences.

Immediacy and longevity

Each type of communication is time-based. All of the communications models listed above lend themselves naturally to different types of 'time'. Some communications fade quickly from memory; others linger longer and have lasting impact. For example, one-to-one communication channels tend to be focused on the here-and-now. At the other extreme, many-to-many channels tend to focus less on urgency and more on reference. Meanwhile, many-to-one and one-to-many have varying levels of immediacy, but almost never have any sort of permanence. These two dimensions, immediacy and longevity, are responsible for defining the underlying *value* of any communications medium.

The tools available in the many-to-many category have the broadest range of time-based attributes. Real-time chat offers immediate communications with almost no inherent longevity at all, while discussion boards and moderated newsgroups offer slow interaction. Newsgroups and on-line forums also offer a certain amount of archival capabilities, providing other users with an additional source of knowledge and expertise. A website is by definition a one-to-many forum, while real-time chat is an immediate, impermanent, many-to-many tool.

company culture an intangible system of values, collective personality and beliefs shared by people in an organization: the company's collective identity and meaning, often described to outsiders as 'the way we do things around here'. This can be the product of the company's history or of a strong leader or founder. A company's culture shapes the way that it treats its customers and goes to market. This is important for the business-to-business marketer to understand in the same way that the consumer marketer seeks to understand the mind of the individual consumer. See also CORPORATE CULTURE.

company forecast the expected level of sales for the company based on a chosen marketing plan and an assumed marketing environment. Frequently these forecasts are given within a relative context, such as market share, or measured against previous years' growth.

comparative advantage the principle that companies and countries are best employed in activities that they undertake and execute relatively better than their competitors. For example, in the economics of international trade, a country has a comparative advantage in producing good X over good Y if it can produce good X at a low opportunity cost relative to good Y. It follows that a country will benefit from specializing in producing goods in which it has a comparative advantage over other countries. See also FIVE FORCES MODEL, COMPETITION AND COMPETITIVENESS, COMPETITIVE ADVANTAGE.

comparative influence a type of influence exerted on consumers by their reference and peer groups. Comparative influence occurs when the reference group provides the means by which consumers compare their beliefs, attitudes and behaviour. When there is similarity between a consumer's opinions and those of the peer or reference group, the greater the comparative influence of that group. See also CONSUMER BEHAVIOUR.

COMPETITION AND COMPETITIVENESS

Competition is the rival activities between enterprises trying to increase sales, profits, or market share while addressing the same set of customers within a similar target market. Competition is critical in a free-market economy and is the dynamic that drives marketing processes.

A market displaying characteristics of *perfect competition* (which rarely ever exists) would include the following assumptions:

- There are many companies each selling an identical or indistinguishable product (lack of differentiation is much more difficult in the area of services, which are delivered mainly through people, all of whom are different).
- There are many buyers for these products.
- There are no restrictions on entry to the industry or marketplace.
- Firms in the industry have no advantage over potential new entrants.
- Firms and buyers have complete information about the market.

Since in *perfect competition* there are many firms selling a homogenous product, no single firm can influence the market to a greater extent than any other. Therefore, all firms must accept the 'natural' market price for their product.

The short run and the long run

The short run, under perfect competition, is the period during which there is too little time for new firms to enter the industry. In the short run, the total number of firms is fixed. Firms could be making large or small profits, breaking even or making a loss.

The long run under perfect competition is the period of time that is long enough for new firms to enter the industry.

- In the long run the level of profit will affect the entry or exit of firms.
- Normal profit is the level of profit just sufficient to persuade firms to stay in the industry, but not high enough to attract new firms. This level of normal profit will vary from one industry to another.
- Supernormal profit is any profit above normal profit. If economic profits are being made, new firms will be attracted into the industry in the long run. This will have the effect of increasing supply and reducing price and profit for those firms already in the industry.

Short run equilibrium of the firm

The diagram overleaf shows the short run equilibrium for a firm in perfect competition.

Price is determined by industry supply and demand curves. The firm in a market of perfect competition faces a horizontal demand curve (or average revenue) at this price.

In the diagram, the y axis represents the natural market Price and the x axis (Quantity) represents supply.

Output Profits will be maximized where marginal cost (MC) equals marginal revenue (MR). Whilst MR is greater than MC total revenue is increasing at a faster rate than total cost, thus profits will be increasing. Where marginal cost is greater than marginal revenue, total cost is increasing more quickly than total revenue and therefore profits are declining.

Profit – at the profit maximizing output average cost (AC) (which includes normal profit) is below average revenue and therefore the firm is making supernormal profits. The firm's short run supply curve will be its (short run) marginal cost curve. A supply curve relates quantity to marginal cost.

Long run equilibrium of the firm

In the long run, if typical firms are making economic profits, new firms will be attracted into the industry or existing firms will increase the scale of their operations. The industry supply curve will shift to the right, leading to a fall in price. Supply will go on increasing and price falling until firms are only making normal profits. This will be where the demand curve for the firm touches the lowest point of its average cost curve. This can be seen in the second diagram.

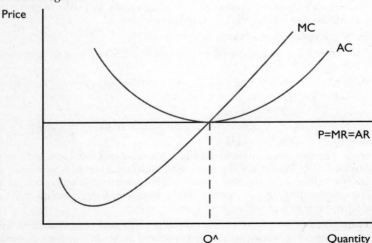

In the long run if the price falls below the average cost of producing the goods, then firms will make a loss and will leave the industry. If firms leave the industry, supply will decrease and the price will rise until firms are just making normal profit, that is where the demand curve touches the lowest point of the average cost curve. Therefore, under perfect competition output will always tend towards this long run equilibrium. Long run equilibrium is therefore where AR = MR = MC = AC

Exit point

We can find the short run breakeven price, and the short run exit price, by comparing the price with average variable total costs. Profit maximization occurs where MC=MR. Since the average total cost (ATC) includes all the relevant opportunity costs, this equilibrium is the short run breakeven point where normal profits (zero economic profits) are being made. As the price falls, the firm will carry on producing, but will only be achieving below normal profit. However, if the price falls below the average variable costs, then it will not be worth the firm producing any more products, as they will be making a loss larger than their fixed costs. The exit point from an industry therefore comes when average revenue (AR) is equal to average variable cost (AR=AVC).

See also BREAKEVEN ANALYSIS, PRICING.

Perfect competition and the public interest

The nature of competition is very important to the overall economy and therefore to the public interest of a country or grouping of nations. Perfect competition carries both advantages and disadvantages:

Advantages

- Price equals marginal cost. Given that price equals marginal utility (that is, how much satisfaction a consumer places on a good), marginal utility will equal marginal costs.
- If a firm is less efficient than other firms it will make less than normal profit and be driven out of business. If it is more efficient it will earn supernormal profits. Thus competition will act as an incentive to efficiency within an industry.
- The desire to earn supernormal profits and to avoid making a loss will encourage the development of new management techniques, processes and technology.
- The lack of advertising (all goods are homogenous) will lower firm's costs.
- The long run equilibrium is at the bottom of the firm's long run average cost curve and, therefore, will produce at the lowest cost output.
- The consumer gains from lower prices, since not only are costs low, but there are no long run supernormal profits.
- If consumer attitude towards a product changes, the price change will lead to the firm responding.

These last two points are said to lead to the dominance of the consumer. Consumers through the market decide what, and how much, is produced.

Disadvantages

- Even though firms may have developed new technology, they may not be able to afford the necessary research and development.
- Perfectly competitive industries produce undifferentiated products. This lack of variety may be seen as a disadvantage to the consumer.

Obstacles to efficiency

The two main obstacles to efficiency are:

1. External costs and benefits and

2. Existence of monopoly.

The model of perfect competition allows us to understand important features of real world markets even though most markets do not have perfect competition.

---

competitive activity the actions taken by businesses to improve their profitability at the expense of rivals. Marketing activity should always be considered in a relative position to that of competition. Often the marketing activities of one company (such as price discounting, new product introduction or market expansion) may trigger a reaction in competitors.

competitive advantage the factor which enables a firm to compete successfully with competitors on a sustained basis particularly to satisfy consumer needs and wants. This leading theory and models of competitive advantage (both of industries, and then of nations) were advanced by Michael Porter in the 1980s. They have had an enormous influence on market strategy and planning.

- There are many sources of competitive advantage, among which are:
- superior skills, or resources, such as salespeople;
- expenditure on advertising and sales promotion;
- range and reach of distribution channel;
- expenditure on, and successful exploitation of, research and development;
- the scale and efficiency of productive capacity;
- financial resources, such as deep reserves of investment capital or strong cash flows;
- powerful brand equity;
- market relevant capabilities and expertise;
- a superior supply chain with world-class in-bound and out-bound physical distribution;
- cost-effective and low-cost operations;
- effective marketing;
- excellent customer service;
- efficient procurement and low cost sourcing;
- valuable use of technology to improve business process;

- recruiting the best people;
- a solid enabling infrastructure.

competitive (and anti-competitive) behaviour the conduct of businesses in market situations involving actions and reactions to achieve advantage over rivals. Strong competition is usually beneficial to the consumer. Most governments in the advanced economies are dedicated to inculcating competitive behaviour and in discouraging anti-competitive behaviour (such as monopoly, cartels, collusion to limit supply, predatory pricing to drive competitors out of business and price fixing). Strong and unbiased enforcement of competition policy is one of the key elements in the creation of a modern market economy. Effective marketing depends upon a strong climate of competition and effective regulation of anti-competitive practices that are inimical to consumer interests. The EU and the US have learned from experience that lively domestic competition leads to greater international competitiveness. Weak enforcement of competition policy all too often hinders innovation or else leads to inefficient allocation of resources in the economy and high input costs for business, and hits the defenceless consumer hardest. EU regulatory bodies on competition can fine a company up to 10% of its total world turnover for anti-competitive behaviour and actions. See also CARTEL.

Example: The Microsoft Case

The Microsoft court case, which is not finally resolved, illustrates the phenomenon of a company that has been so successful in the marketplace that it exerts a virtual monopoly and controls the development of new but related markets as well as the overall nature of the industry. It is, also, an example of how the state (in this case in the form of the US Justice Department) intervenes in the late 20th and early 21st century to ensure competitive behaviour and practice. By the end of the 20th century, Microsoft had risen to be one of the world's largest companies by market value. Its founder, Bill Gates, had become the world's richest man. Microsoft, one of the pioneers of the computing revolution that had started in the early 1980s, had come to dominate the market for PC operating systems, where it had 80% share of the worldwide market. Microsoft also became one of the world's largest suppliers of software applications: spreadsheets, word processing and increasingly Internet browsers. Any software, such as games or business applications, therefore had to be compatible with the operating system for them to work, or indeed, to be marketed effectively. Because Microsoft's Windows operating system is so dominant, companies or individuals writing software have to write software that will run on the Windows operating system, rather than for rivals such as Apple, who have a different operating system. The result is that software applications are written for the Microsoft operating system, which has the effect of enforcing Microsoft's market domination. This dominance also affects the PC manufacturers, who decide to install the Microsoft operating system in their products because they know that it is likely to be the bestseller.

The US Justice Department as well as 19 US states brought the original case against Microsoft. In the initial ruling against Microsoft, US judicial authorities deemed that Microsoft had abused its dominant market position in operating systems to disadvantage its rivals and to inhibit competition. For example, Microsoft licensed its operating system more cheaply to computer makers such as Dell and Compaq, if they exclusively installed its software. The key element for the prosecution case was the way in which Microsoft forced its Internet Explorer (IE) browser to leadership in a market that had been dominated by Netscape's Navigator. The prosecutors demonstrated that Microsoft not only gave away Internet Explorer, but also 'bundled' it into its Windows operating system, forcing manufacturers to pre-load it on to their computers. If users wanted to use Netscape's Navigator browser instead of Internet Explorer, the user found that the performance of the alternative browser was not as quick. Internet Explorer, which was given away freely, would be triggered as the default browser for a variety of functions. Microsoft also encouraged Apple to pre-install Internet Explorer on its PCs, even though it used a different operating system. As a result, Microsoft swiftly succeeded in winning 50% of the emerging web browser market. Microsoft was also alleged to have modified Sun Microsystems's Java products so that they ran only on Microsoft's operating system despite the fact that Java had been designed to be a language that could run on all operating systems.

In 1995 the US judicial authorities, upon hearing evidence from Microsoft's rivals, ordered Microsoft to scrap terms requiring PC makers to install Internet Explorer, which was seen Microsoft trying to monopolize Internet access. In 1997, the US Justice Department claimed that Microsoft violated an earlier court order and ordered Microsoft to supply Windows 95 without the Internet Explorer browser. In1998, the US attorney general and 20 US states launched further anti-trust lawsuits against Microsoft. In April 2000 Microsoft was found guilty of anti-competitive behaviour and of breaking US anti-trust laws. In June 2000, following this ruling, Judge Thomas Penfield Jackson ordered the dismantlement of Microsoft Corporation. He ordered that Microsoft be split in two separate businesses for abusing its dominant market position. One part was to be the businesses for the Windows operating systems; the other, the software applications such as Microsoft Office, Excel and the Internet explorer web browser.

Judge Jackson also said the action was needed to ensure that the company did not operate as a monopoly. He also ordered Microsoft to modify its competitive behaviour to give its competitors a better chance of selling their own software. This modification of competitive behaviour involved giving computer makers such as IBM more flexibility in configuring their systems and in selling and promoting non-Microsoft software; it enforced early release of Microsoft's technical information to other software vendors at the same time as it released it to its own personnel; It forced Microsoft to charge a uniform price for the Windows operating system to the top 20 computer makers and to charge the same price for past supported versions of Windows, as was the Microsoft practice for the most current version of the operating system

Following a Microsoft appeal against the Jackson ruling, however, the appeals court overturned Jackson's enforcement of a break-up of Microsoft in 2001. The appeals court did, however, uphold the view that Microsoft had improperly monopolized the computer operating market. By 2002, the US government reached a settlement deal with Microsoft over the claim that the company had acted as a monopoly, making it difficult for other manufacturers of software to put their products on personal computers running on Windows. Microsoft was found guilty of violating US anti-

trust law. A new judge was appointed to rule in the Microsoft case and he now has to approve the out-of-court deal reached by the new Bush administration team at the Justice Department and Microsoft. The case now goes to a new district judge, who will take a fresh decision about how to 'remedy' Microsoft's anti-competitive behaviour.

Microsoft may still be absolved of the original charge, especially as the dynamics of the software and Internet markets have changed so dramatically since the days of the browser wars, which were at the heart of the court case. For example, the growth of the Internet, and mergers between rivals such as AOL and Netscape (and now Time Warner) means Microsoft's position is not a monopolistic as it was five years ago.

competitive bidding a process in which buyers request potential suppliers, who are direct competitors, for a proposed purchase or contract. There is usually a short list of suppliers who are requested to submit bids simultaneously by means of a request for proposal. The request for proposal usually includes a detailed specification of the requirement, the standards sought, the terms of delivery, the contract and the due date of the bid. This is the usual way of winning business in a business-to-business environment and less used in a consumer environment. Competitive bidding is the preferred way of government and public authorities' buying processes. It is usually accompanied by intensive negotiations and presentations.

competitive depositioning a set of actions attempting to change the beliefs of buyers about the attributes of a competitor's product. The attempt may be especially useful in cases where buyers generally have an inflated perception of the quality of a competitor's product. This can also involve comparative advertising. See MARKET POSITIONING.

competitive environment that part of the company's external environment where other firms are vying for the same market. The competitive environment is also a description of how the companies compete within a defined market place – the distribution channels, collaborations between suppliers, competitors and distributors, the pricing methods, the level of promotion etc. It is determined by how the competing companies are positioned relative to the **Five Forces.**

competitive equilibrium a market situation of relatively stable competitive position and activity.

competitive forces or **Porter's five forces** see STRUCTURAL ANALYSIS, COMPETITIVE STRATEGY and (MICHAEL) PORTER.

competitive myopia short-sightedness in regard to the activities of competitors by incumbent market players. For example, this may involve an over-concentration on a single competitor to the exclusion of, say, new competitors or rising competitors or it could also mean completely ignoring competition in the marketplace. Often, existing competitors become so fixated by each other that they fail to see new competitors entering their markets in unexpected ways.

competitive niche a defined segment in a market in which a company can compete effectively and possibly win a major share of the market. Here an organization focuses effort and resources on a narrow, delimited segment of a market in which competitors have less strength. Competitive advantage is generated specifically for that market niche. Smaller firms often use a niche strategy. A company could use either a cost focus or a differentiation focus. With a cost focus a firm aims at being the lowest cost producer in that niche or segment. With a differentiation focus a firm creates competitive advantage through differentiation within the niche or segment. There can also be potential problems with the niche approach; for example, if the niche is so small or so specialized that it does not give an adequate return to the companies that serve the niche. See also COMPETITIVE STRATEGY, FIVE FORCES MODEL.

competitive parity budgeting a method of allocating a promotion budget based on matching the activity of a major competitor. See also MARKETING COMMUNICATIONS.

competitive position (competitiveness) a range of measures that assesses the overall competitiveness of one company relative to another company operating in a defined market. Traditionally, competitive position can be measured by means of a combination of the following variables:

1. Relative market share of the competitors. Here it is important to emphasize relativeness: the reason for this is that an apparently high market share of say 20% can be relatively weak if the nearest competitors have 40% and 35 % of the same market; alternatively an apparently low share, of say 8%, can be the dominant share in a highly fragmented market where no-one commands more than 10% of the total market.

2. Costs (either of production, running the enterprise or marketing and selling, or a combination of all three), which are particularly important in price-sensitive and mature markets where consumers are looking for higher quality at lower cost.

3. Price of goods and/or services. Although this depends on the price elasticity of the market, prices have always tended towards affordability as the market expands. Only the most exclusive luxury brands and services can afford to ignore prices.

4. Quality of goods and services. As has often been said, the memory of price fades faster than the memory of poor quality; equally, exceptional quality will quickly erode the memory of high prices.

5. Accumulated experience of a service delivery or product, which factors into a lower and more effective way to serve the market. Experience and expertise in products and service delivery is a distinct competitive advantage, which can often enable higher prices to be charged for a rival product and particularly a service. 'They're not cheap, but they are good' is a familiar refrain for this type of company.

6. R & D performance: good research and development is critical to the development of good products. The linkage between marketing and R&D is often neglected, given that marketing, being in regular touch with the market, can often inform where and how research investment ought to be spent. This prevents what is often known as an 'engineering' or 'technology' centric culture, that emphasizes the technical features and benefits of the product

rather than tuning it to the needs of the marketplace. This mindset turns marketing and sales into blind functionaries who have to market and sell whatever is developed. There is always a fine line to tread between slavishly following the market and allowing research that leads to innovative products. The sales and marketing community is often fond of pointing out the examples of technically good products that, because they were developed in a market vacuum (e.g. K5, Ford Edsel, Concorde, nuclear power stations, Betamax, Visicalc, the Apple Newton), were market failures, whereas the engineers can point to the Sony Walkman, the laser, penicillin, the telephone, etc. that were developed without the assistance of market research and analyses.

7. Production effectiveness and capacity. Again, the efficiency of production determines the price and therefore the market competitiveness. A good product cannot survive if the costs of production exceed the amount of return that can be gained from the product. See also BREAKEVEN ANALYSIS.

8. Distribution channel and network; effective distribution is crucial to effective marketing, particularly for products in either consumer or business-to-business markets. Good products need to reach their target audience at the right time, place and cost. Increasingly, there are many new channels of distribution, or new ways of reaching audiences, such as the World Wide Web, that can reduce the costs of engaging audiences with products on a worldwide scale that were previously beyond the reach of a single country or local producer. See also CHANNELS OF DISTRIBUTION.

9. Brand and image reputation relative to competition; in a world where it is increasingly difficult to sustain product and service differentiation, and where consumers are increasingly discerning, better informed, the image and brand of a company are vital to retaining customer loyalty. A powerful brand and reputation in professional services is now an indispensable necessity to be able to compete. The recent fate of Andersen shows how a once venerable business can be completely wiped out in a very short space of time when trust in the brand is lost in the minds of clients and markets.

10. Competitive scope, meaning, for example, the breadth or narrowness, of an organization's focus as measured horizontally by the range of industries, market segments, or geographical regions that the company targets, with its range of products and services. Alternatively, competitive scope can also refer to the degree of *vertical integration* that a company has relative to other competitors in the same marketplace. For example, one company in the paper industry may be vertically integrated if it owns the forests, pulp mills, paper-making factories, distribution systems and outlets for its paper products relative to another competitor that only manufactures paper but does not own the raw materials or the means of distribution and sale.

11. Competitive dynamics, which means the overall standing of a company or organization in its markets, relative to the standing of its competitors, when all competitors are described in terms of their size, resources, capabilities, product range and quality, marketing strategies, opportunities, goals, intentions, behaviour and similar variables. Usually the dynamics of a market are those special or unique ingredients that cause the market to operate as it does and which tend to favour one competitor over another.

Also, competitive market dynamics are constantly changing, therefore competitiveness can often be defined by the company that adapts more efficiently to changing market dynamics.

See also COMPETITIVE ADVANTAGE.

competitive strategy the way in which a company chooses to compete in the marketplace and the method and approach that a company adopts relative to its competitors' strategies. For example, a Competitive Attack Strategy uses various methods for attacking a competitor, many of which are derived from military strategy, including a frontal attack (head-on), a flanking attack (attack at a point of weakness), an encirclement attack (attack on several fronts at once), a by-pass attack (attack by diversifying into new territories, products or technologies) and a guerrilla attack (attack by waging small, intermittent skirmishes with unconventional marketing methods).

Michael Porter has defined several strategic approaches to competitive strategy:

- *Differentiation* is an approach which offers leadership or focus products which can be regarded as unique in areas which are highly valued by the consumer, creating consumer loyalty which protects the firm from competition. This enables the producer to sell at premium price to consumers who perceive deep value in the product or service.

- *Niche focus* is an approach to serve particularly attractive or suitable segments or niches (to differentiate within one or a small number of target market segments).

- *Cost leadership* attempts to control the market through being the low-cost producer in a given market.

Summary of Porter's competitive strategy classifications:

Type of Competitive Strategy	Skills & Resources	Organizational dimension	Associated Risks
Overall Cost Leadership	Sustained capital investment and access to capital	Tight cost control	Technological change that nullifies past investments or learning
	Outstanding process engineering skills	Frequent, detailed reports on costs and productivity.	Low-cost learning by industry newcomers or followers through imitation, or through their ability to invest in state-of-the-art facilities
	Intensive supervision of labour by management.	Structured organization and detailed responsibilities	
	Products designed for ease of manufacture	Incentives based on meeting strict quantitative targets, usually financial.	Inability to see required product, service or marketing change because
	Low-cost distribution system to access the market.		

Type of Competitive Strategy	Skills & Resources	Organizational dimension	Associated Risks
			of the attention placed on cost. Organization becomes too tactical, run by short-term financial considerations.
			Inflation in costs that narrow the firm's ability to maintain enough of a price differential to offset competitors' brand images or other approaches to differentiation.
Differentiation	Strong marketing capability. Product design and engineering. Creative flair and innovation. Strong capability in basic research. Corporate reputation for quality or technological leadership Long tradition in the industry or unique combination of skills drawn from other businesses. Strong cooperation from channels.	Strong coordination among functions in R&D, product development, and marketing. Subjective measurement and incentives instead of quantitative measures. Amenities to attract highly skilled labour, scientists, or creative people. Focus on unique competencies of the organization.	The cost differential between low-cost competitors and the differentiated firm becomes too great for differentiation to hold brand loyalty. Buyers thus sacrifice some of the features, services, or image possessed by the differentiated firm for large cost savings. Buyers' need for the differentiating factor falls. This can occur as buyers become more sophisticated. Imitation narrows perceived differentiation, a common occurrence as industries mature.
Focus	Combination of the above policies directed at the particular strategic market target.	Combination of the above policies directed at the particular strategic market target.	The cost differential between broad-range competitors and the focused firm widens to eliminate the cost advantages of serving a narrow target,

Type of Competitive Strategy	Skills & Resources	Organizational dimension	Associated Risks
			or, to offset the differentiation achieved by the focus.
			The differences in desired products or services between the strategic target and the market as a whole narrows.
			Competitors find niche markets and sub-segments within the strategic target and out-focus the focusser.

Other individual elements that can be included in a competitive strategy or that may affect the nature of competition:

1. Creation of cartels (International cartels: *OPEC* (oil), and *De Beers* (diamonds));

2. Product differentiation through design, quality, packaging, brand name, delivery, after-sales service); for example, Dell and Apple computers.

3. Price. Using customer credit and payment terms, credit allowances and trade-in values;

4. Promotion that supports differentiation (e.g. sales force, advertising);

5. Distribution in which one company can dominate a market through superior distribution channels, reaching a greater number of customers than their competitors can.

6. Acquisitions, merger and economies of scale;

7. Creation of barriers to entry to other competitors. For example the world's top oil companies.

8. Innovation. For example 3M, Sony, Xerox

competitor analysis an analysis of competitors' strengths and weaknesses, strategies, assumptions, resources, market positioning from all available sources of information, in order to identify suitable market strategies. Competitor analysis is an integral part of market planning. See also COMPETITOR INTELLIGENCE and MARKET RESEARCH.

The process of competitor analysis:

1. Identify competitors within a target market (products, product substitutes, services, generics, new entrants);

2. Audit competitor capabilities (financial, technical, managerial, marketing assets, strengths and weaknesses);

3. Relate the competitor capabilities to those of the enterprise to determine

competitive advantages and disadvantages. Infer competitor objectives and strategic thrust of competitor;

4. Deduce competitor strategies (target segments, differential advantages, competitive scope, cost leadership);

5. Estimate competitor response pattern to the company's marketing strategy (retaliatory, complacent, hemmed-in, selective, unpredictable).

See also SWOT ANALYSIS, MARKET RESEARCH and COMPETITIVE ADVANTAGE.

competitor intelligence the systematic collection and analysis of data about a firm's competitors, with the goals of understanding the competitors' positions in the market and of formulating strategies in response. Competitor intelligence is also the process of monitoring the competitive environment. It enables senior managers in companies of all sizes to make informed decisions about everything from marketing, R&D, and investments and long-term business strategies. Effective competitor intelligence is a continuous process involving the legal and ethical collection of information, analysis and controlled dissemination of actionable intelligence to decision makers. It is also important to study the competitor's likely responses to a given course of actions as well as the facts and data about its actual performance.

Sources of competitor intelligence

Annual reports and accounts are generally available for public companies. Company and financial analyst reports on sales, market share, costs, profit levels, return on capital invested, cash flow, profitability by segment. Where these are available, they can be a good source of background financial information on the competition and also give their own interpretation of their marketplace as well as the assets and companies that they own.

Published market research and industry analyst reports. These can be used to assess one's own market share and often industry forecasts are given. Equity analysts' reports are useful, given that the authors' assessment of the company is usually a guide to potential equity investors and shareholders. Analysts – industry and financial – prepare detailed and in-depth reports on competitors, many of which are available on the World Wide Web. The Internet has become a major information source on competitors. For example, it is possible in a very short space of time to find out all public statements that have been issued by and about a particular competitor.

Salespeople can be a very good source of competitor information, as their livelihood depends on outselling the competitors. Whether field sales, or sales office based, they will have the opportunity to pick up intelligence from customers. Although a certain amount of information might be offered, salespeople might need encouraging in asking the right sort of questions and probing when chance comments of comparisons with the competition are made. They also might need some incentive to pass these on to the managers in the company or to place them on a competitive database.

Competitors' agents, dealers and representatives who are trained to talk constantly about the company's products and services. They are particularly informative at trade shows and exhibitions where competitors have exhibits.

Trade magazines and quality newspapers. These sources often contain features that will be written about different companies within the industry. New developments may be detailed or how the sales force is organized.

Trade associations. These voluntary associations will provide details of members and set them in the context of their industry. These associations tend to be national or locally organized. They also give industry context to a competitor evaluation.

Websites and directories. Depending on which directory source or website is chosen, these can be used to assess the size, turnover, number of employees etc. of a competitor. Websites have become increasingly informative, particularly the investor relations sections as well as the sections on products and services and often recruitment.

Competitive literature or catalogues and price lists. These allow a sales/marketing manager to assess the competition's strengths and weaknesses in terms of the product range. They also give a fair indication of how the competitor wishes itself or its products and services to be perceived by the marketplace.

The competition's products. A visual examination or trial could provide a certain amount of information. Certain companies undertake 'reverse engineering' which involves a complete and detailed stripping down of the product by experts to examine the components and how they are put together.

Customers are often an excellent source of competitor information, giving insight into how they are perceived and how they perform relative to the marketplace. This will also give some indication of the level of brand loyalty shown to a competitor and its products.

Suppliers can also give much indirect information on the strength of competitors: it may be that your sources of certain raw materials or equipment also supply the competition. Knowing how much of a certain raw material, or semi-finished goods, are used annually could help assess product portfolio and market potential.

Former employees of the competitor. Although it is unethical to advertise a non-existent job to attract applicants from the competition just to quiz them on their companies, there is no reason why ex-employees of a competitor who now works for the company or enterprise should not be engaged and they can provide a valuable insight into competition.

Areas to investigate for competitor strengths and weaknesses

Fundamental elements of competitor intelligence are:

Assessing the strengths and weaknesses of competitors: these assessments would generally include the competitors' ability to understand and serve their customers, the loyalty of their customer base, their distribution channel and coverage; their marketing mix and the resources that they commit to a given marketplace.

Financial and asset strength and weaknesses: this assesses the competitors' financial stability, their profitability, their innovative response to customer needs, their time to market for new products, their intellectual property, their technical manufacturing skills, their infrastructure, their workforce and their quality standards.

Further areas to assess competitor strength and weakness are:

- the corporate culture and the overall capabilities of the competitor and its ability to compete overall;
- the competitor's overall strategy and its success in implementing it: is the competitor trying to win by lower prices, product and service differentiation?; are they growing by acquiring market share or by making acquisitions?; are thy competing on the basis of superior quality, customer service, product offerings etc.?
- management capability and attitudes to risk, for example investment risk;
- production processes and quality of technologies employed;
- capacity levels and utilization of productive capacity;
- operations and logistics and delivery capability;
- product quality, prices and catalogues, for an understanding of the range of products and new developments;
- dealer networks and distribution channels;
- the competitor's alliances and partnerships as well as its potential acquisitions;
- marketing and selling capabilities and effectiveness;
- human resource capability as well as resource and recruiting patterns;
- advertising and promotions, which give an indication of how the competitors wish to present themselves and their capabilities to their target markets. See also MARKET RESEARCH, under MARKETING SPECIALIZATIONS.

complaint an expression of customer dissatisfaction which can directly affect the company or organization's permanent reputation. The management and handling of complaints is increasingly the focus of marketing interest because the way in which complaints are handled and resolved is critical to the image and reputation of a company or organization in the eyes of its customers. One badly handled situation with a customer complaint can forever injure the reputation of the company with that customer. See also CUSTOMER LOYALTY under CUSTOMER.

complements goods are complements of each other if changes in the demand for one will have a complementary effect on the demand for the other: for example, compact disc players and compact discs, cars and petrol, printers and ink.

concentrated marketing marketing focused on a small part of the market with a single or limited line of similar products. It can be used by firms with limited resources or in markets with specialized customer segments. It enables deep concentration of resources in a highly defined market space, with the objective of gaining leadership. It is better known now as **niche marketing**. See also MARKETING.

concentration ratios the proportion of firms holding most of the market (e.g. the top two firms hold 20%). In the United States, the US Census Bureau covers this.

concept testing and development the testing of a new product concept with a group of target consumers to learn whether the concepts have wrong consumer appeal and should be developed further. See also MARKET RESEARCH under MARKETING SPECIALIZATIONS.

Fundamentally, concept testing and development are techniques that attempt to predict the success of a new product idea before it is actually marketed in order to mitigate the risk of a misplaced launch. The research usually involves getting people's reactions to a statement describing the basic idea of the product. The concept is ultimately 'bought' in the minds of people who will not be the ultimate consumers. It is also important to gauge the reaction of those who will ultimately influence the product concept.

Care should be taken with concept testing that the original idea is not lost: a more fruitful approach is to use testing as part of the gradual development and refinement of new ideas into a form that is most likely to be accepted in the marketplace. Testing can also provide guidance for the communication of relevant benefits, uses, packaging, advertising, sales approaches, product information, distribution, and pricing. People find it more difficult to hypothesize and, generally, test groups react better to actual products than to conceptual ideas about new products. Also, they tend to be sceptical about new ideas, and often hostile to them. Radically new products shake up people's established way of doing things, putting them at or over the edge of their own incompetence. So, new ideas are unsettling at best, and a threat at worst. People often do not have the imagination to see how the new product would benefit them.

For these reasons, good ideas which were ultimate successes, like automated teller machines, extended battery-life pacemakers, VCRs, and the Walkman had major problems when they were first described to people in the concept testing stage of development. New product ideas presented in the form of a half-page concept statement run a terrible risk of being killed prematurely. Concept testing is sometimes practised rather naïvely. All too often, a couple of focus groups are assembled, read a simple description of the concept and people are then asked for their reactions. This approach can often be dangerous. Many underdeveloped, defenceless concepts are killed when in the early stages by being concept tested by few groups of people

However, concept development and testing can be a very powerful tool. It has saved hundreds of millions in investments. It helps marketers avoid false starts, wrong positioning, poor strategy and selling in a misdirected way to the wrong parts of the market. It is not only vital insurance, but also more importantly, it acts as a guide throughout the entire concept development process, from original thinking to successful launch. The idea is not the product. It is disastrous to believe that a new product will sell itself. It is absolutely necessary to see the product from the point of view of the customers. A new product is unsettling to most people. It usually requires a new way of doing things.

Consumers only change to new products when they perceive that there is a significant benefit or gain. They have to believe it is more valuable than the money, time and comfort that they will have to give up in order to purchase it. Marketers have to convince people that it will ultimately be an improvement over what they have now, it is worth changing from what they already have, there is a relatively simple way to verify its superiority, that it will live up to the promises implicit in the claims made for it. Marginal improvements rarely succeed in displacing a market leader. Different people will perceive even the most straightforward product differently. It can be seen from various perspectives, used for a variety of purposes, in different contexts, with different expectations. Most products require a prototype and initial testing in the real world.

Focus groups are an effective way to test new products and services. People are motivated to communicate in focus groups: an experienced moderator can infer what is going on through the implicit and explicit language of the focus group. What the participants say is important, but how they say it, what is behind what they say and what is not said are also just as important. Surveys of people voting on whether or not they would use the product are usually very misleading. In these surveys, a test is something that passes or fails, or that gets a score. Concepts, however, must be developed and nurtured. Concept development is a more accurate name for the process than concept testing. Also, concept development is a process of successively refining, amplifying and enhancing the basic idea of the product.

While concept development and testing is often conducted haphazardly, it can and should be a highly organized process:

1. Assess the present situation

You must thoroughly understand what people are doing now. You want to know their present satisfaction levels, whether they perceive a problem for which your product may be a solution, and what are their present beliefs, misconceptions, attitudes and emotions. Look particularly for the issues that they have the most energy around, rather than what they tell you is important. You want to know the words they use, and the way they categorize and conceptualize the area. More often than not, people will not make the same distinctions and discriminations the manufacturers make. Users' concepts will be much more use- and function-oriented. The manufacturers' concepts will be more product- and feature-oriented. Sometimes people say that they don't need the product when it is the kind of product that solves a problem that they don't see, or are embarrassed about, or don't want to acknowledge. Such a response does not mean that your concept is dead. One of the roles of the experienced marketer is to get them to acknowledge that there is a problem. Product rejection is a normal initial reaction, when the respondents take professional pride in their ability to overcome the difficulties that your products will eliminate

2. Concept statement

This step is the most difficult in the concept development and testing process. The way the concept is presented is crucial.

The statement ought to be more than just a straightforward 'objective' description of the features of the product, and it should not make claims that cannot be backed up in reality. Instead, a balance must be struck between a specification and a sales document. It should begin with a brief description of the present situation, in words the target audience uses. It is usually best to describe the concept as a solution to a problem; then the product or the service itself, and, importantly, how the product's claims will be substantiated.

3. Refine and elaborate the statement with subsequent testing with different groups

The concept statement is written and rewritten, for successive groups, continually taking into account what has been learned before. Each time it is presented, the marketer will elicit qualms, objections and concerns as well as praise, new uses and new ways of describing it. You take the positives and incorporate them into the concept statement. With the negatives, the marketer will look for ways to turn them into benefits. The marketer will find out directly from participants how the product can be made more appealing.

The psychological atmosphere of the focus or test group is as important as the concept statement itself. Participants must clearly understand what the task is, how you want them to approach it, and you must make it desirable and safe to do so. It is important to create an atmosphere of trust and constructive helpfulness. It ought to be made clear to the participants that they are there to help develop the basic idea into something genuinely useful for them. Suggestions, recommendations and constructive criticisms should be sought out. The marketer conducting the focus group is primarily looking to obtain their immediate first reactions. People should be encouraged to think creatively and hypothetically. This will avoid an over-detailed focus on the physical characteristics of the eventual product. It is also important for the group to be able to express dissenting opinions or contrary experiences, even if a single individual expresses them.

Almost every good concept starts off with strong scepticism, which can be devastating to the client unless the process is understood. Sometimes concept testing is unfortunately stopped at this initial flood of objections. However, objections are actually desirable, because in the first sessions you want to understand people's concerns. As successive focus groups begin to become more positive, it is important to re-iterate the negatives encountered in former groups and ask them how they would answer such objections. Shifts of opinion, however subtle or implicit, should be closely monitored. These shifts of opinion, either from positive to negative or vice versa, are often intimations of how the product will be received in the real marketplace.

For concept work, a skilled marketer or facilitator is needed – especially someone with experience of product introductions, successful as well as unsuccessful. The facilitator should also have extensive experience in creative idea generation sessions.

What to avoid in a concept testing and development focus group:

- letting the participants take a product, rather than market, focus;

- using a moderator inexperienced in concept development;
- adopting a 'Testing' mindset rather than one focused on concept development;
- testing products that are not comprehensible to the focus group, such as products that can't be produced in prototype, or ideas that are so vague that they cannot yet be communicated meaningfully;
- waiting until it is too late to do concept development. This is sometimes the case in the pharmaceutical industry where many products are tested only after the clinical trials are arranged;
- killing the concept at the first sign of either negative or sceptical reaction;
- taking votes for the purpose of projecting whether the concept will be successful. Much can be extrapolated from groups, but this ought to be based on opinions and reactions;
- taking what people say at face value, rather than looking for deeper reactions and contexts for what they are saying. See also MARKET RESEARCH.

conditioning learning to associate a stimulus with a response.

conglomerate diversification making or acquiring new products for new markets, particularly in a large and diverse company with multiple products in multiple markets. A conglomerate diversification merger or takeover is where businesses in completely different industries merge together, for example if a leisure company merged with a computer firm.

conjoint analysis see MARKET RESEARCH.

CONSUMERS and CONSUMER SOCIETY

consumer the end user of a product or service. The consumer may or may not be the actual buying customer. A consumer is different from either retail or wholesale buyers in that the consumer tends to buy for personal use rather than for resale.

Consumer activity, in terms of saving and spending, is a bellwether of confidence that is much observed and studied in the modern economy. See also BUYING.

consumer behaviour a process through which an identifiable group of consumers actually make buying decisions. Any study of consumer buying behaviour must also include the forces that influence them in making their decisions in their final choice of a brand at a given time, place and price. Deep study of consumer behaviour is a separate discipline within marketing and has grown in sophistication since its origins in the 1960s.

In the quest of understanding why consumers behave as they do, what their mental processes are and what influences them, mny academic models and theories of consumer behaviour have been elaborated. These various models show how the consumer develops and grows towards a decision, using information, knowledge and experience, and then how these decisions are either reinforced or rejected over time. Many of these models go into the roots of human psychology, sociology, economics and learning. Some models involve differential calculus, mathematical modelling, computer simulation techniques, econometrics, Freudian analysis, sociology, statistical analysis and even game theory.

The theories of consumer behaviour explore the various drivers, fundamental and secondary, that impel consumers toward their choices. Some of these choices can be highly rational, in that they seek to satisfy their needs within their disposable income range to the best of their knowledge; others are more emotional, in that they are actually attempting to satisfy some subconscious desire deep within their psyche.

Consumer behaviour is analysed using one or several of the following general models:

CONSUMER BEHAVIOUR AND MOTIVATIONS MODELS

The Stimulus-Response Model Behaviour is determined by learned experience through exposure to a set of stimuli and their associations. A focus on human drives – both primary and secondary. Secondary drives are learned drives (pride, covetousness, status, fear) that are acquired in order to satisfy primary drives (safety, need to belong etc.). Various stimuli are focused on satisfying these drives and can result in brand loyalty. These stimuli (including those created by marketing) activate the drives and the response made by the consumer to these various stimuli. Various types of reinforcement also condition the consumer to respond in similar ways again over time, for example to buy the same brand again.

Psychological Models These theories attribute complex motives to buying, including an intermingling of functional and symbolic drivers. For example, someone who buys a Rolex watch may say that the motive is for the precision of its timekeeping whilst the real reason is to display social status. The fundamental role of the psyche is, therefore, not always made known to marketers with various research survey instruments, because consumers are not always prepared, or not always conditioned, to say what their deeper psyche is really wanting. This may account for some of the many new product launches that fail, despite market research giving every indication of potential success.

See also Maslow's Hierarchy under HIERARCHY OF NEEDS.

Sociological Model This model espouses the view that consumers' behaviour is primarily determined by the social forces that act upon them. These are, for example, the culture and value system of the society that the consumer lives within; the sub-culture which is a group within the dominant culture whose values are somewhat at variance with the mainstream. Social class is a grouping where individuals in a given society share similar values, education, income levels and lifestyles; reference groups which shape the individual's behaviour and from whom the individual seeks validation

Economic Model Is founded on the concept of utility maximization, in which the individual seeks to maximize his self-interest within his economic means. This model views the consumer as mainly rational, and one who tends to spend within reason and according to their means.

Many of these consumer behaviour theories are predicated upon the availability of information to the consumer and various other stimuli that are derived from the industrial world. They make assumptions in that context about how the consumers are equipped to analyse and evaluate available information and then make choices and final purchase decisions. However, many of these models and theories were developed before the commercialization of the Internet via the World Wide Web. In the present times, the Internet has made the consumer much more powerful in terms of information, accessibility and range of buying choices available, but it is too early to tell if it has made buying decisions more rational. Consumers often delegate the processing of available information and the evaluation of competing products and services because their knowledge is imperfect, and often the glut of information has made the buyer less sure of their overall knowledge and, as a result, has modified their decision making processes.

consumer goods goods made for the household consumer, which can be used without any further commercial processing. Convenience goods are generally purchased in small units of low value (e.g. milk, sweets). Shopping goods have higher unit values and are bought less frequently (e.g. clothes, furniture). Specialty goods are those of high value, which a customer will know by name and go out of his or her way to purchase. See also MARKETING, CONSUMER MARKETING under MARKETING SPECIALIZATIONS.

consumerism (1) advocacy of the rights of consumers, as against the efforts of advertisers and producers (see CONSUMER RIGHTS). (2) the emphasis of advertising, public relations and marketing efforts toward creating consumers (see CONSUMER SOCIETY). These two definitions are almost opposite in meaning, but the former is commonly used today, while the latter was common prior to the 1970s.

consumerists groups and organizations who exert legal, moral and economic pressure on business to account the interests of consumers over profit.

consumer market a market characterized by the purchase of goods for personal consumption, of mass buyers, of one or few decision makers in the purchasing decision, of small purchasing volume, of separation of the producer, as the consumer mainly interacts with the retailer.

consumer panel a form of sample surveying where data is collected from the sample of consumers on more than one occasion. These panels are used to test new products or to modify or improve existing ones. These can often happen in person as well as remotely. Information technology has made the job of the panel members a lot easier. See MARKET RESEARCH and CONCEPT DEVELOPMENT AND TESTING.

consumer rights rights designed for the benefit and protection of consumers and to force the producers and providers to take the consumer's perspective. The various laws and protective bodies augment the rights and powers of consumers in relation to sellers up to the point where the consumer is able to defend his interests.

John F. Kennedy's Consumer Bill of Rights in 1962 is the landmark legislation in this area and defined the four fundamental principles and rights of the consumer:

1. The right of consumers to be protected from defective goods and services and unscrupulous or illegal traders.

2. The right of consumers to be to be informed about what they are buying, the price, quality, contents and guarantees for the product or service.

3. The consumer's right to choose and to have a range of competing choices and prices.

4. The consumer's right to be heard by producers and retailers and to have means of redress against them if required.

Consumers' rights are, in the advanced economies, becoming as important as political, social and human rights, and have gained a further stimulus as a result of new trading patterns resulting from globalization and the Internet.

consumer society the organized pursuit of getting and spending on a mass scale: a social and economic phenomenon that expanded continuously throughout the 20th century. The United Nations reports that world consumption expanded at an unprecedented pace over the 20th century, with private and public consumption expenditures reaching $24 trillion in 1998, twice the level of 1975 and six times that of 1950. In 1900 real consumption expenditure was $1.5 trillion.

Prior to the 20th century, consumerism as a lifestyle activity was confined to social elites. For the mass of the people, buying was based on necessities. Cultures and religions were not favourable to consumer society. Many of the Christian denominations frowned upon 'luxury' and encouraged frugality. Gradually, some religions and belief systems promoted some limited, careful consumption for all and protested disparities in consumption between rich and poor. Excessive or conspicuous consumption, particularly by the rich, was often recognized and criticized in pre-industrial societies.

The rise in mass consumerism that started in the late 19th and continued throughout the 20th century was caused by over-production of goods by new technologies without enough people to buy them. Resources were scarce prior to systematic and mass production of goods. However, technological advances and innovations in production changed situation from dearth to one of abundance. Raw materials and resources become more accessible than ever before. These advances were supplemented by the expansion of new trade routes with modern transport, military conquest, the growth of urban centres, and the wealthier nation states experiencing second waves of industrialization.

Convincing people to buy more goods beyond those needed to sustain them, by generating a new ideology of pleasure and leisure, was part of the birth of modern marketing. Active consumption was encouraged. The barriers to a consumer society were gradually removed; there were changes in attitude and lifestyle, higher standards of living, a new approach to international commerce, as well as changes in the law, and, notably, higher wages and the extension of mass credit. The effect of this credit was to increase consumer debt, while creating mass markets for consumer goods that stimulated economic growth.

The role of marketing was to promote the idea that those goods that were previously regarded as luxuries of the rich, were now necessities for everyone. (See, for example the case on Diamonds Marketing under ADVERTISING.) This was a trend that has continued, fuelled by marketing, up to the present day. Conspicuous consumption became the hallmark of wealthy countries and their citizens.

One of the early engines of mass consumer society was the department store. Department stores were created to constantly display goods on a scale never previously imagined and to encourage people to buy them. There were also developments in the concept and practice of 'customer service' – where people who bought in department stores were flattered with levels of service hitherto reserved for the social elite. The shopping malls that succeeded the department store, and the hypermarkets that succeeded the supermarket, are carefully designed to create appropriate moods to indirect encourage buying. Also, as home ownership rose, the home and the family became a focus of mass consumption. Shopping was done increasingly from the home – through catalogues, by mail, by telephone, by television and latterly over the Internet.

Also, the profession and the techniques of advertising grew rapidly in and helped to shape a new commercial culture aimed at the masses. In the United States in 1880, only $30 m was spent on advertising; by 1910, $600 m (then 4% of national income) was spent; today the US spends $120 bn and worldwide $250 bn is spent on advertising. Advertisers helped to create the concepts of fashion and fashionability and obsolescence – creating a constant restlessness about needing to have new and up to date possessions; buying for style rather than for need, in order to remain 'fashionable'. See also ADVERTISING.

Education services also began to embrace business and to create learning in marketing, sales, accounting, and communications. Governments set up departments and chambers of commerce to promote consumption of commodities. In the US, government-sponsored consumer research began in the 1920s; in the UK, it did not begin until the 1950s. These surveys detailed what citizens consumed and where and how they purchased.

Consumerism and the cult of individualism became intertwined. The discipline of psychology, pioneered in the 20th century, contributed to understanding and promoting individualism. From its social and political activism beginnings, individualism became used and understood by corporations to create more diverse products for consumers. There is overwhelming pressure to consume and to be seen to be consuming. Some people resort to what psychologists term as 'compensatory consumption', that is, consuming even more to feel better, or as it has become popularly known, shopping therapy.

Individualism became good for business and marketing shaped its messages around this new individualism. Corporations supported individualism, but detached it from strong political and social activism. The 1960s generation, once concerned with social issues, started to focus on exploring and fulfilling their individual desires through the purchase of material goods.

Consumption became a definition of identity: 'I shop, therefore I am'. Democratic participation increasingly became about expressing needs and wants rather than supporting great causes.

The consumer society has evolved in such a way that consumption and consumerism (for good and bad) is identified as being at the core of a modern culture and society. Right-wing governments in Europe and America continued to champion and support individualism throughout the 1980s. The collapse of the Soviet Union and the Soviet bloc was seen in the west as much as a triumph of consumerism, and people's desire to go shopping, as much as of ideology. China opened its markets and encouraged a far greater degree of consumer demand than hitherto. Corporations began to globalize. Consumerism became a global phenomenon rather than just the preserve of the wealthy nations. Global brands, global production and distribution were everywhere. Governments now constantly monitor consumer debt and behaviour as this has the power to destabilize – or in some cases, prop up – an overall modern economy.

The rise of consumer society has had many critics, both in the capitalist and non-capitalist worlds. In the 20th century a worldwide battle for access to and control of consumable resources has driven many conflicts and conquests. Conquest and control of oil supplies, for example, was a major factor in the military and political strategies of combatants in both world wars. Unequal trade between unequal regions has led to a massive imbalance that is reflected in differentials in consumption. There has been much protest that the poorer countries end up servicing the consumption of the wealthier countries. Globally, 20% of the world's people in the highest-income countries account for 86% of total private consumption expenditures; the poorest 20% a minuscule 1.3%. The richest 20% of the world consume 45% of all meat and fish, the poorest 20%, only 5%. The richest fifth consume 58% of total energy, the poorest fifth less than 4%. The richest fifth have 74% of all telephone lines, the poorest fifth only 1.5%. The richest consume 84% of all paper, the poorest fifth 1.1%. And the richest own 87% of the world's cars while the poorest fifth less than 1%.

In the 1960s, there was a growing student-based and civil right movements in the advanced consumer economies among whose targets were corporations who were exploitative in their drive for profits, and who encouraged mass consumerism that was creating conformity. With increasing activism, this had a possibility of threatening political stability for power holders, and economic stability for corporations in nation states, as students and the young are the consumers of the future.

In the early 21st century there is in the advanced economies another backlash – similar in some ways to the 1960s backlash against the materialist, mass consumer society – but now more focused on globalization, particularly its effect on the environment, global resources, the exacerbation of inequality and in the destruction of local ways of life. How we consume, and for what purposes, drives how we extract resources, create products and produce pollution and waste. Issues relating to consumption hence also affect environmental degradation, poverty, hunger, and even the rise in obesity that is nearing levels similar to the 'official' global poverty levels. Global brands – particularly those that use low-paid foreign labour in the manufacture of their products – are particularly vilified. Marketing, seen as the handmaiden of the consumer society, has also suffered in the backlash against global brands and the cult of 'spin'. See also ANTI-CORPORATION, PUBLIC RELATIONS.

Consumers' Association a UK interest group representing consumers; conducts product tests and comparisons, lobbies government. It also publishes a range of consumer publications.

contest a promotion, such as a sweepstake, prize draw, lottery, or quiz, that offers a prize and may or may not require a purchase for prize eligibility. These are often linked to direct below-the-line marketing.

contingency within a marketing plan, this is action to be implemented only upon the occurrence of future events other than those in the accepted plan.

continuous research a research activity planned to provide regular information from systematic ongoing data collection from key sources. This could, for example, include: sales quantity and value by individual customer; sales quantity and value by product; profitability by customer; profitability by product. This research is then used to inform and shape marketing programmes. See also MARKET RESEARCH.

contractual marketing system defined by Philip Kotler as a vertical marketing system in which independent firms at different levels of production and distribution join together through contracts to obtain more economies or sales impact than they could achieve alone.

contribution a financial measure of sales value less variable cost of sales. More generally it can be anything that adds value or benefit, either tangible or intangible.

contributions centre a profit centre where expenditure is reported on a marginal or direct cost basis.

convenience goods consumer goods that the customer usually buys frequently, immediately, and with the minimum of comparison and buying effort. Alternatively they are relatively inexpensive products that buyers or users choose frequently with a minimum of thought and effort. See also BUYING, CONSUMER MARKETING.

convenience store a small-scale retail outlet, usually located near a residential area, serving a local market, open long hours, seven days a week, and carrying a limited line of high-turnover goods that are more convenient for customers to buy locally than in a major supermarket or mall. See also CONSUMER MARKETING under MARKETING SPECIALIZATIONS and BUYING.

conventional distribution channel a channel consisting of one or more independent producers, wholesalers, and retailers, each a separate business seeking to maximize its own profits even at the expense of profits for the system as a whole. See also CHANNELS OF DISTRIBUTION.

conversion rate a measure of the number of on-line visitors to a website who take a specified action (expressed as a percentage of the total number of visitors). These actions could typically be sales of products, membership registrations, newsletter subscriptions, software downloads or polling.

A high conversion rate depends on several factors, such as the attractiveness of the site, the offer, the interest level of the visitor, the ease of using the buttons, the quality of the navigation guides and speed of loading. See also INTERACTIVE MARKETING.

cookie information stored on a user's computer by a website in order that website preferences are remembered on future requests. Cookies are passed from a Web server through a Web browser to the user's hard drive. This information is essential for many of the features taken for granted on the Web, such as shopping cart credit information and personalized portals. Privacy advocates and guardians have raised concerns over the role of cookies in on-line advertisements. They fear that large companies could piece together information that could be used against individuals, especially if off-line information is merged with on-line information. Cookies are not universally used. Estimates vary, but some percentage of the Web population browses with cookies turned off. Cookies can be blocked completely via the browser, or selectively via a cookie manager.

co-operative campaign collaboration of two or more advertisers and advertising in which the manufacturer of a product provides materials to and reimburses a retailer for part or all of the retailer's advertising expenditures. See also ADVERTISING.

copy the words that make up the substance of all advertisements – usually text and headlines. It does not include the actual artwork and graphics although in more recent times copy is often used to mean the finished work. See also ADVERTISING.

copy date the date at which the finished advert must be delivered to the publisher or broadcaster.

copyright the exclusive legal right to reproduce, publish, and sell the matter and form of a literary, musical, or artistic work. Copyright laws were developed over the last century for the physical, controllable world; however, the world of the Internet with instant publication and vast distribution channel has challenged the existing copyright laws and the copyright owners' ability to police and enforce them. An example of the new threat to old copyright processes was the huge popularity of the free music file-sharing Napster website and its major challenge to the assumptions of the music industry. Napster, which itself was bought by a large media conglomerate, raised many questions about the nature of artistic property rights in a digital medium where copying and file sharing are made possible on a massive scale.

copy testing the testing of the effect of an advertisement on a selected test panel before or after it is printed or broadcast.

copywriter the person in an advertising agency who writes the words that are in an advert.

core customers a company's more important customers, distinguished from the rest by their long-term value to the company. The standard wisdom is that the core customers never usually constitute more that 20% of the total customer base of a company. See also CUSTOMER LOYALTY.

corporate appraisal a critical assessment of the strengths and weaknesses, opportunities and threats in relation to the internal and environmental factors affecting an entity in order to establish its condition prior to the preparation of the long-term plan. See also SWOT ANALYSIS.

corporate culture the culture of an organization, perhaps influenced by its founder, dominant group, history, structure and systems, leadership and management style. It is often described as 'the way we do things here'.

corporate sponsorship corporate financial backing for a project or event, in return for public exposure and goodwill. Often referred to as 'as brought to you by company X' in the advertisements for cultural events. This is now seen to be a field of mutual interest. The UK national lottery, for example, the largest business to consumer business in the UK, donates the majority of its profits to good causes that might otherwise be funded by private charity or the taxpayer. See also MARKETING.

corporate strategy a total strategy for the business as a whole, including all strategic objectives and all aspects of investment and execution programmes, including marketing. Successful marketing is usually deeply integrated into the corporate strategy.

cost benefit analysis primarily a method of measuring resources used in an activity and comparing them with the value of benefits. Marketing is frequently one of the costs measured and its benefit is not always easily expressed in straightforward financial terms.

cost leadership the attempt to control the market through being the low cost producer (lowest cost position). See also COMPETITIVE STRATEGY and COMPETITIVE ADVANTAGE.

A business obtains low cost leadership by focusing attention on it at every functional level of the organization. Low cost leaders typically (1) optimize the operating efficiency of facilities; (2) pursue cost reductions through tight procedural controls, and avoidance or elimination of marginal customer accounts; and (3) minimize costs in areas like research and development.

Many businesses have grown from small to very big over the years using low cost leadership as a strategic tool. Some of the more famous examples include Briggs and Stratton, Texas Instruments, Black and Decker, Du Pont and Wal-Mart. Low cost leadership is certainly a proven approach to successful competition in the marketplace.

cost of ownership the total cost of acquiring and owning a product; it includes the search costs, the purchase price, and any other expenses related to installation, maintenance, service, and replacement. It is traditionally used by businesses to help control costs and make strategic decisions. Product salesmen often use it, particularly those selling computer systems, to indicate total costs to potential customers.

cost of sales the sum or variable cost of the total value of the goods and services that were sold to customers. Typically, this refers to businesses that buy inventory for resale or a manufacturer who builds items for resale. Total revenue less cost of goods sold equals gross profit.

cost per action (CPA) an on-line advertising payment model in which payment is based solely based on qualifying actions such as sales or registrations.

cost per click (CPC) the cost or cost-equivalent paid per click-through on a website.

cost per thousand a measure of media and advertising cost-effectiveness, in terms of the price paid to reach a target audience of one thousand readers. See also ADVERTISING.

cost plus pricing a method of determining the price of a good by adding a percentage mark-up to the average variable cost. See also PRICING.

cost pool a group of all costs that are associated with the same activity or cost driver.

cost-push inflation inflation resulting from an increase in the costs of production of goods and services, either from prices of imported raw materials or from salary increases.

cost unit a unit of product or service in relation to which costs are ascertained.

countertrade a reciprocal and compensatory trade agreement in the purchase of goods or services between the seller and the buyer of a product, or when the seller assists the buyer in reducing the amount of net cost of the purchase through some form of compensatory financing. Countertrading is now a sophisticated international activity with multiple types of trading activity determined by the trading party and the economies in which they trade. It has been compared to a modern type of the barter system which was one of the older forms of international trading. For example, in trading with countries who do not have 'hard' currencies, exchange of goods or services of equivalent value can take place without the use of currency. A computer system may be sold in exchange for uranium, nickel, wood or rubber.

One of the main uses of countertrade is in defence and aerospace deals. For example, advanced industrial economies will often use reciprocal trade agreements using industrial goods and services in compensation for military-related export sales and services. This is known as an *offset deal* and can be divided into two categories, *Indirect offset* and *direct offset*. The former is when goods and services unrelated to the aerospace or defence material are sold in exchange; the latter is when compensation is in related goods and usually involves a licence or joint venture.

Another type of agreement is one in which the exporter either buys, or undertakes to find a buyer for, a specified amount or value of unrelated goods from the initial importer during a specified time period. This is known a counterpurchasing.

Also, often as part of an offset agreement, other than coproduction or licensed production, some level of technology transfer is agreed. It may be in the form of research and development, technical assistance and training, or patent exchange. This is important to many Third World enterprises, both public and private. See also EXPORTING, INTERNATIONAL MARKETING.

coupon a legal certificate offered by manufacturers or retailers that entitles the bearer to a discount on an item at the time of purchase; includes rebates.

Alternatively, they can be certificates that give buyers a saving when they purchase a product. A coupon is a very frequent technique in consumer goods marketing. It usually takes the form of a voucher with money off the purchase price, with the purpose of encouraging greater amounts of purchase or else as a way of rewarding consumer loyalty. There is always a vast disparity between the number of coupons issued and the number redeemed, usually in the range of 10-15%, suggesting that this is not a very efficient way of marketing.

coverage a measure of the percentage of the specified target that see an advertisement at least once during a defined time period of an advertising campaign. Also known as **reach**. See also ADVERTISING.

credit (and the availability of credit) a component of market demand. The rise of easily available credit to individuals and to business has gone hand in hand with the rise of the consumer society. Governments and their economic agencies now closely monitor the levels of consumer credit and debt – partly with a view to controlling inflation. Raising interest is one way of controlling spiralling credit; reducing interest rates or easing credit might be to encourage a higher promotion of bad debts or to increase sales volume. As advanced economies have moved from a cash to a credit economy this has created different types of commercial relations between buyers and sellers and consequently, different approaches to marketing. See also CONSUMERISM.

creditor a person or company who extends credit and to whom money is owed.

crisis communications immediate actions taken by a company or organization to maintain its credibility and good reputation after a situation has occurred that may adversely affect the company and its reputation, increasingly a core activity of the corporate communications or public relations team. Often the failure of a company to communicate effectively in a crisis can cause immeasurable damage. The process, characterized by rapidity of response, involves: the fast identification of the problem; articulating the problem in a way that both addresses the problem and mitigates risk to the company or organization's reputation without altering or covering up the facts; identification of right level of spokesperson; speech and message development for key spokespersons; the development of a full media briefing plan and interview; media explanations and articulation of a plan for future prevention or mitigation. See also PUBLIC RELATIONS, COMMUNICATION.

Example: Exxon Corporation and the Alaskan oil disaster

This is the case in which the tanker Exxon Valdez owned by the Exxon Corporation spilled massive quantities of oil into a bay in Alaska causing massive ecological damage. The net effect of this in the media was that of an uncaring global company that had damaged the natural environment and its wildlife and the local economy. It was also a disaster for Exxon's reputation. The Exxon Valdez disaster demonstrates the need for companies to have media crisis-management plans in place well before any such disaster strikes. This requires advanced planning and strict discipline in the execution. It is a good example of how NOT to do Crisis Communication.

In this case, Lawrence Rawl, chairman of the Exxon Corporation, is viewed as having handled this crisis very poorly. What did he do wrong and what could he have done better?

- *Immediate response: Rawl's public response time was regarded as inadequate relative to the severity of the crisis and the spiralling world media coverage of the incident and its consequences. Rawl, for example, did not visit the site of the disaster immediately and was very slow to address the media on Exxon's response. The Chairman did not seem to have a grasp of key messages, both in the acknowledgement of the disaster and in the formulation of a reassuring response to it.*

- *Round the clock crisis centre: Rawl failed to establish a 24-hour crisis-management command centre in New York as a centralized repository for fact gathering and responding to rumour.*

- *Communication with public authorities: ultimately governments, national and local, are responsible for the nation's territory and its people. Exxon did not set up a liaison office to brief government agencies about the company's efforts and to request governmental assistance.*

- *Consistency and clarity of communications: Exxon should have established a news centre to act as a clearinghouse for statements, briefings and status reports from the company to ensure consistency of response to the media and the public. Consistency and clarity of response are vital in a crisis. It is also necessary to avoid conflicting statements, particularly as the media are trained to look for inconsistency.*

- *Frequency of communications: the media are also hungry for briefings when a story is hot. Exxon should have had, at a minimum, at least two briefings a day with journalists. Rawl, as chairman, would have to be present and deliver the briefing personally at least once a day. Another co-ordinated briefing ought to have come from the location of the disaster by a senior Exxon official.*

- *Advanced planning and testing: Exxon had a crisis-management plan that claimed that an oil spill could be contained within five hours. However, this plan had never been tested in practice. In reality it took nearly 2 days to begin to staunch the outpouring of oil into the sea. The gap between the stated theory and the reality led to a media as well as an environmental disaster. Exxon's image was as damaged as the oil-sodden Alaskan bays.*

critical path analysis (CPA) a project management technique, often used on large scale marketing projects, that maps the sequential relationships between different tasks in a project in order to assist planning, and to find the shortest possible time for doing them and to manage costs effectively. The main benefit of the CPA approach is to create the shortest possible time horizon for a project by identifying activities to schedule simultaneously. This, in turn, enables the most effective allocation of resources to the various strands of the project.

cross elasticity of demand a measure of the responsiveness of demand for one good to changes in the price of another: the percentage change in the quantity demanded of one good divided by the percentage change in the price of the other good.

Elasticity is a measure of responsiveness. It tells how much one thing changes when you change something else that affects it. For example, the elasticity of demand tells us how much the quantity demanded changes when the price changes. The elasticity of demand measures the responsiveness of quantity demanded to changes in the price charged. See also PRICE and ELASTICITY OF DEMAND, under PRICING COMPETITION.

cross impact analysis a qualitative forecasting technique that involves the assessment of the impact of key trends. This is a relatively inexpensive technique that allows regular updates as situations develop. See also MARKET RESEARCH.

cross selling selling by a salesperson of some part of the company's total product range for which another division or salesperson has prime responsibility. This is a frequently used technique to increase total sales volume to the same customer. See also SALES and DIRECT MARKETING under MARKETING SPECIALIZATIONS.

cue a signal communicated by a person, a product or a service, usually non-verbally.

cultural environment a combination of the various institutions and other forces that control and affect society's basic values, perceptions, preferences, and behaviours.

culture a high determining factor in marketing, particularly in the interplay between international and local marketing. Marketers must be sensitive to the reigning aspects and dimensions of culture: shared values, beliefs, religion, language, laws, rituals, attitudes of mind, traditions, customs and behaviours learned by members of society from family and other important institutions. In some societies, religion is the dominant cultural force; in others, it is institutions; in others, the family. There are multiple examples in consumer and industrial goods of products failing in one country that have been successfully marketed in another because of culture. There are many well-documented cases of McDonalds having to modify highly standardized fast-food packages because of very different eating habits around the world. Even in services, this can also be prevalent. For example, the marketing of professional advisory services that are intangible, such as management consultancy, is very difficult in Asia because local cultures do not normally pay for discrete advisory services; they are normally given 'free' as part of a more tangible purchase.

CUSTOMER

customer traditionally regarded as the actual or intended purchaser of a product or service. The customer is always the buyer, although not always necessarily the consumer. See also CONSUMER. There have been several extensions of the customer concept, even within an organization, in which employees are also seen as customers of the various internal services of the company, or where citizens are viewed as customers of government services.

customer acquisition cost calculated by dividing total costs of acquiring a new customer by the total number of customers. Generally, it is much less expensive to develop and grow an existing customer than to acquire a new one. This, of course, varies from market to market and by channel for accessing customers. However, there are different opinions as to what constitutes an acquisition expense. For example, rebates, loyalty schemes and special discounts do not represent an actual cash outlay, yet they have an impact on cash and customer mindset.

customer care a fundamental approach to the standards of service quality. It covers every aspect of a company's operations, from the design of a product or service, to how it is packaged, delivered and serviced, for the pre- and post-sales periods.

Governments and their agencies have ensured a steady stream of laws and regulations (for example, in air travel, financial services, communications, energy supply) to improve customer choice, to deregulate previous monopolies and to encourage competition. This has brought increased benefit, choice and strength to the customer. It is now recognized that customer care directly affects continuing profits and brand strength. Therefore, the company is highly dependent upon the customer service agents who deal regularly with the customers as well as the systems that support them in dealing with customers. These systems can be call centres, customer databases or electronic information systems. It is now an all-too-frequent occurrence for customer service agents to deal with their computer rather than directly with the customer.

Consequently, customer care has become one of the toughest battlegrounds in modern business, particularly in those businesses whose products and services are otherwise undifferentiated from those of their competitors. Suppliers of customer care systems have themselves become major businesses in their own right. Customers, increasingly powerful, are very aware of their multiple choices and have rising expectations of excellent customer care. To some extent, that which delights customers today becomes a standard expectation tomorrow. Therefore, customer care is something that requires continuous attention and work. It is particularly important to care for long-term customers and to work assiduously at building long-term relationships with them. The cost of growing revenues from existing customers is far smaller than the cost of acquiring new customers. Good customer care means repeat customers and customers who will buy more products and services. See also RELATIONSHIP MARKETING under MARKETING SPECIALIZATIONS and CUSTOMER LOYALTY.

The essential elements of superior customer care are a mindset of putting the customer first and at the centre of all operations of the company, gaining a deep knowledge, understanding and insight into the customer, a high degree of sensitivity to customer needs supported by good ability and willingness to listen to customers and to respond to what is heard, a general persuasion to please the customer at all times and be accessible whenever and however the customer needs service and be generally easy to interact with. The higher dimension of customer service is when the customer is actually delighted rather than merely satisfied.

Key elements of an effective customer care programme are a major investment area and include the following:

1. Identify key dimensions of service quality. This is done usually through some form of customer research, particularly focusing on the key encounters and interactions that a customer has with the organization, what they buy, how they buy it, how it is delivered to them and how they are looked after beyond the delivery. It is important to get first-hand accounts from the customer and to listen to their feedback directly. Often the company's customer service agents and sales people contribute to this research, being on the front line of customer interaction.

2. Set standard for customer service delivery. It is vital to identify and examine all areas of customer interaction and delivery of service, such as understanding the services and products offered to the customer; the delivery systems and channels; the delivery environment; the employees and customer service agents doing the delivery, as well as the interdependencies between them. This will also involve translating the customer needs into precise product and service experiences and packages.

3. Analyse employee-training needs to meet the customer service delivery system. Getting service right first time is important. The human factor in customer service is paramount, despite the growing use of automated machines and computers in customer care.

4. Develop a system for handling customer complaints, for identifying gaps and failure points in customer service. This will involve both customer databases and also a clear process map of all customer interactions and encounters.

5. Develop customer care training programmes to include deep business and product knowledge, customer awareness and interpersonal skills.

6. Internal education and communication programmes to employees, celebrating customer care and success. The old adage that people buy from people has never been truer than in customer care. Marketers must be increasingly aware that the brand of a company is actually brought to life through the actions of its frontline staff, particularly those working with customers. Therefore, the motivation of staff through celebration of, and reward for, excellent customer service, is becoming an increasingly important part of the marketing mix.

7. Measure and monitor customer service, employee performance and satisfaction, customer expectation and perceptions of actual service quality. This should not be reduced to a mechanical scoring system, but should be used as an opportunity to have a continuous dialogue and conversation with customers.

8. Performance-related pay and recognition system for employees who deliver customer service.

9. A customer-centric culture that puts the customer at the heart of everything done by the company.

Many organizations appoint a very senior director who has responsibility for customer service and who regularly monitors performance as well as a dedicated staff who are fully trained and who have expertise and who are always available to handle customer issues, complaints and requests for information. All contemporary evidence suggestion that customers prefer to speak directly to another person rather than to use automated information systems.

It is important to resolve customers' problems as fast as possible, with resolution being made closest to where the complaints originate by staff with the power to resolve them. Additionally, there ought to be a published customer service policy that is well understood and acted upon, backed up by a customer charter and code of practice that is adhered to. Finally, it is important to have a continuous dialogue and feedback from customers and to act upon – and to be seen to be acting upon – their suggestions.

customer lifetime value a technique for analysing all the potential purchase values from a single customer over the lifetime of a relationship with a supplier or service provider. This moves the focus away from looking at customers in terms of single purchasing transactions and, equally, gives an assessment of the cost of losing a potentially lifetime customer. Lifetime value calculations depend upon a thorough understanding for the target customers' lifecycles because customer behaviour changes over time. Even though a transaction, or 'snapshot' approach to customer value behaviour can be modelled at a given point in time, it is far more powerful to look at the total value over a time period.

The old ways of mass marketing were predicated on treating all customers the same – and consequently offering the same price and promotions to everyone. When a sale or promotion is launched, everyone gets the sale price – loyal customers and occasional transaction buyers. New techniques of marketing, notably the use of customer research and databases, have caused a more sophisticated approach to customer targeting. For example, some retail outlets are now issuing their customers with proprietary shopping cards and rewarding them for using them. The cards then become the basis of the store's customer database. With the database set up, the retailers can ensure that different customers receive different offers. Occasional, unknown customers pay full price. Loyal, regular customers pay a lower price on certain merchandise, or on all merchandise. Furthermore, the loyal customers are made aware that they are the favoured. They are treated like gold card customers on major airlines. Retailers have discovered is that they can modify customer behaviour by appropriate application of rewards. Customer lifetime value stresses that existing customers should be encourage to spend more with the same supplier over a longer lifetime. This is different to the more traditional approach of taking customers away from competitors. Marketers using lifetime value approaches to customers tend to reduce their advertising outlay because they know the low profitability and low loyalty of the promiscuous shoppers who are attracted to their stores by heavy advertising. This leads to an approach in which low margin offers are not made to unprofitable customers. The best customers get offered the most aggressive pricing and special promotions and are treated more specially.

customer loyalty the ability to retain customers and to keep them buying what is on offer over a longer period of time than competitors. Recent trends point to growing customer dissatisfaction and turnover. Loyal customers are increasingly hard to develop and keep.

Aspects of building customer loyalty include delivering a quality product or service which meets the customer expectation, and ensuring that customers are valued and looked after effectively.

As far as benefits of customer loyalty are concerned, research has shown that it can be up to six times more expensive to acquire a new customer than it is to retain an existing one. Customer loyalty is extremely important and highly profitable to a company. A continuous dialogue with customers gives increased contact and knowledge of customer needs and this understanding of customer needs means fewer returns and complaints and costs. Happy customers generate positive word of mouth recommendation that improves a company's competitive position and lowers marketing costs. Finally, well-serviced and satisfied customers are always less sensitive to price, enabling greater profitability.

customer orientation a management philosophy, and often a culture, based on the idea that the customer is central to everything the company does and that the processes of a company begin with, and are designed around, the customer. A customer orientation is not necessarily the same as a market orientation: often a market orientation begins with the producer and examines the best way, using various channels, to get products and services to the customers. A customer orientation adapts to the way that the customer wishes to deal with and interact with the producer or supplier. Some companies have detailed customer measurement systems indicating their share of total customer expenditure that they are able to address and detailed revenue and profit from each customer relationship.

customer satisfaction the main way of measuring the quality and effectiveness of the customer care delivery system. There can be measures of both meeting expectations and also, more desirable, exceeding customer expectations. This gives management an immediate view of the organization's performance relative to customer expectations, and enables them to track customer response and perception over time, which helps with market planning. It also enables cross-comparison of customer service centres, and in some cases, can help with remuneration schemes, where remuneration is connected to excellent customer service. Those with the better customer satisfaction scores are given bonuses.

Services can usually only be measured for customer satisfaction after consumption. Also, as customers become aware of, or actually experience, alternatives, their expectations will change and rise over time. Jan Carlzon, when CEO of the SAS airline, called the encounter between a service provider and the customer a 'moment of truth'. These are the crucial interactions or touch points at which the customer forms an impression of the service provider; for example, at an airline check-in desk, being greeted at a restaurant or dealing with a bank teller.

customer value analysis analysis conducted to determine which benefits or features that target customers value and how they rate the relative value of various competitors' offers. See also MARKET RESEARCH (particularly **conjoint analysis**).

customs long-established business practices and modes of customer behaviour (e.g. half-day closing, religious holidays, social taboos). They represent culturally approved ways of responding to given situations: usual and acceptable ways of behaving. They comprise folk history, idioms, literature, song, conventions, mores and laws. These can often determine the success or failure of a marketing programme conducted from outside the territory. Global marketing often becomes a series of adaptations to local customs and cultures.

cycle analysis a time series correction technique that adjusts forecasts for movements in the overall economy. See also BUSINESS CYCLE and DEMAND.

D

DAGMAR (Defining Advertising Goals for Measured Advertising Results). Developed by Russell Colley in 1961, its purpose is the measurement of advertising effectiveness. Its central idea is that the audience moves through phases of awareness of an **advertising campaign** to comprehension, to conviction that the product can meet their needs, to eventual action, or purchase. See also ADVERTISING.

daily activities report a record of a salesperson's activities on a day-by-day basis, showing clients visited, products presented and results; it may also include reasons for the failure to sell. This is often used a measure of sales productivity before measurement moves to actual tangibles such as orders and revenues. See also SALES.

daily sales plan a record of a salesperson's intended sales calls on a day-by-day basis, listing the clients to be visited, the objectives of each call, and the anticipated outcomes. This is often referred to as a marketing plan for a single customer.

database an ordered collection of data, stored on a computer medium, with a dedicated software program, that can be used for multiple purposes. The advent of the database has transformed various marketing techniques and channels to market. For example, the increasing sophistication of databases has enabled marketers to gather and process data with greater precision on different types of customers. In particular, market analysts can clearly see the differences between high spending and low spending customers. Such depth of knowledge enables marketers not only to see patterns more clearly, it also allows more targeted marketing programmes to be executed. See, for example, DIRECT MARKETING, E-MAIL MARKETING, INTERACTIVE MARKETING under MARKETING SPECIALIZATIONS.

database management the task of storing, modifying, and retrieving database information to produce reports, answer queries, and record transactions.

data warehouse a collection of data designed to support management decision-making. Data warehouses contain a wide variety of data that present a coherent picture of business conditions at a single point in time. Development of a data warehouse includes development of systems to extract data from operating systems plus installation of a warehouse database system that provides managers with flexible access to the data. The term data warehousing generally refers to combining many different databases across an entire enterprise. See also MARKET RESEARCH.

DAR (Day After Recall) a method for analysing and assessing the impact of television advertising one day after it was first broadcast. See also ADVERTISING.

deceptive advertising advertising intended to deceive consumers with false or misleading claims. This is prohibited in most of the advanced economies. See ADVERTISING.

deceptive packaging packaging intended to deceive the purchaser; for example excessive ullage creates the impression that the volume of the contents is greater than it actually is.

deceptive pricing the pricing of goods and services in such a way as to cause a customer to be misled. An example of deceptive pricing is BAIT-AND-SWITCH PRICING.

decision tree an analytical tool for classifying the choices, risks, objectives, gains and information needs involved in different courses of action.

decision makers see BUYERS.

Delphi technique a forecasting method in which a coordinator seeks predictions from experts who revise their opinions in light of the opinions of the others until some degree of consensus is reached. The technique is based on the Hegelian principle of achieving a consensus through a three-step process of thesis, antithesis, and synthesis. In thesis and antithesis, all present their opinion or vision on a given subject, establishing views and opposing views. In synthesis, opposites are brought together to form the new thesis. All participants must then accept ownership of the new thesis and support it, changing their own views to align with the new thesis. Through a continual process of evolution, a consensus or oneness of vision occurs. This technique uses expert judgment and anticipation of the future without empirical hard data, for example long-term strategic planning using scenarios of future events. Stage 1 is to poll experts, anonymously and separately. In stage 2, the results are consolidated and fed back to the experts as a group. Stage 3 polls them individually again, in the light of peer group opinion. A forecast of the future is prepared which has the acceptance of all or most of the panel of experts,. When there is some uncertainty among the experts, probability weightings might be given to different possible future scenarios or events.

demand the creation of market demand is an objective of all marketing professionals. At the core of the marketer's task is the acquisition of new customers, keeping existing customers and growing the overall demand of each customer for the company or organization's products and services. This may also include increasing demand by taking an innovative approach to the way in which traditional products and services are delivered to customers, which has the effect of expanding demand. For example, Amazon.com delivers traditional products in an innovative way, thereby increasing its total market demand to a far greater level than a local or national book seller. It can also involve extending the company's brand into new products and services that are based upon its core competence. For example, Disney has a core competence in entertainment that started in animated films, then extended into general movie production, theme parks, music and book publishing, television broadcasting, retailing and merchandising, tourist and holiday packages (such as cruises) and property development, such as resort timeshares. The Disney brand is used to develop new market areas and generate overall demand for the Disney Company's overall products and services.

The assessment of demand is also crucial, particularly in terms of strategy and pricing. There are five types of demand:

Historic demand is based on the extrapolation of historical market demand data from customers who have bought a product or service in the past, and is often used as a guide to future demand, which can cause problems, as it does not take into account discontinuity in market demand.

Existing demand uses data from customers who are currently buying the products and services.

Latent demand is a reference to inactivated demand that could be developed if certain marketing strategies and programmes were developed but which otherwise remains dormant.

Potential demand makes a forecast based upon customers who might buy products and services in the foreseeable future if the circumstances (such as their disposable income, or special offers, or prices) are right and the market environment is favourable.

Price-related demand is the main instrument available to marketers to convert latent or potential demand into existing demand. This makes use of the instrument of pricing to increase market demand for given products and services. The law of demand states that quantity demanded varies inversely with price. Economists expect that demand will diminish if prices increase. The maximum price a buyer is willing to pay for a good or a service, rather than do without, is called the *reservation price*. As a group, buyers' reservation prices for a given quantity of a good can vary because of differences in their preference for the good or service, their knowledge of the price of substitute or complementary goods and services, their disposable income, and their expectations about what will happen to their income or the price of the good in the near future. The quantity of a good demanded by buyers in a market varies with market price, if all these other influences are held constant. As market price rises, fewer buyers will have a reservation price high enough to make the purchase worthwhile. That's because as price rises, *substitutes for the good* start to look more attractive. As price falls, more buyers will have a reservation price low enough to make the purchase worthwhile. That's because as price falls, *substitute uses for this good* start to look more attractive.

Demand can vary over time and according to the changing nature of markets, technologies and lifestyles. Historic demand is always an imperfect source of demand information and trends for the marketer. Equally, an innovative new product or service will have no historical demand data or trends, and the marketer must therefore use other techniques – including guesswork, hope and instinct. See also AGGREGATE DEMAND, PRICING, COMPETITION, DISPOSABLE INCOME, COMPETITIVE ADVANTAGE.

demarketing an attempt to temporarily or permanently reduce demand and limit future growth. It is mainly an inverse marketing technique to dissuade the public from doing something, for example, government warnings against smoking, drugs, drinking and driving, AIDS or overuse of water during a drought. Special interest groups can also launch campaigns to dissuade the public from buying certain types of good or service, for example from a totalitarian regime. It may also be used if a product is found to be faulty and the producers of the good do not wish to risk their reputation by continuing to sell it – for example in the recall of benzene-infected Perrier Water or Tylenol in the US.

demography the study of human populations in terms of size, density, location, age, sex, race, occupation, and other statistics. It is also the description of the vital statistics or objective and quantifiable characteristics of an audience or population. Demographic designators include age, marital status, income, family size, occupation, and personal or household characteristics such as age, sex, income, or educational level. Demographics are used extensively in marketing. See also GEODEMOGRAPHICS.

department store a retail organization that carries a wide variety of product lines, typically clothing, home furnishings, personal care products, accessories and household goods; each line is operated as a separate department managed by specialist buyers or merchandisers. The department store was an invention of the 19th century that has survived into the 21st century despite many competing retail outlets, both physical and on-line.

The world's first department store, *Au Bon Marché*, was opened in Paris in 1852 and by 1877 had become the world's largest department store. The first department store Santa Claus appeared in the 1870s Macy's. See also CONSUMER SOCIETY and CONSUMER MARKETING under MARKETING SPECIALIZATIONS.

An 1896 advertisement for Mitsukoshi, the Japanese department store which, like many Japanese department stores, began life as a kimono seller.

A 1920s postcard of the Mitsukoshi main store in Tokyo.

depreciation a measure of the loss of value due to wear and tear, consumption, or other reduction in the useful economic life of a fixed asset, whether arising from use, affliction of time or obsolescence through technological or market changes. In accounting, it is an allowance made for a loss in value of property, such as a machine or vehicle. To encourage companies to maintain their capital stock, governments usually allow for depreciation when calculating corporation tax. In economics, it is the reduction in the purchasing value of money.

See also CONSUMER SOCIETY.

derived demand the mechanism through which demand for industrial goods is derived from consumer market demand. If demand for end-product consumer goods falls, then this has an effect along the production supply line to all the inputs. Derived demand emphasizes the relationship between the price of the industrial good, and the quantity of the good demanded by firms employing it in production of the final product. It is directly dependent on consumer demand for the final product(s) the industrial good is used to produce.

For example: if, for some reason, the demand for personal computers increases so that more PCs than before can be sold at any given price, then the derived demand for semiconductor chips used in making PCs will also increase. As a result, semiconductor manufacturers will be able to sell more chips at any given price. The key is the change in the price of the final product brought about by the shift in demand for it. If the demand curve for personal computers shifts to upwards and the supply curve remains unchanged, then the equilibrium price and quantity in the PC market will now involve both a higher price for PCs and a larger quantity of PCs being produced and sold to the public. Because of the price rise, the marginal revenues earned by the manufacturers per additional PC sold will be higher. So, consequently, their desire to maximize profits will lead them to produce additional PCs until the marginal cost for the last PC rises to equal the new higher price. Producing more PCs than before will require more production capacity than before, which they will want to purchase from their suppliers, shifting the demand curves for each of the semiconductors upwards. This increase in demand for the semiconductors in turn will tend to raise their prices and to increase the quantity of chips sold, which then affects the semiconductor manufacturers' demand for their own necessary inputs (such as silicone and gallium arsenide) and brings about further price-and-quantity adjustments throughout the economy in an ever-widening, derived demand ripple effect. See also DEMAND, BUYING.

description tag – HTML a tag used to by Web page authors to provide a description for search engine listings.

design a generic skill that can be applied in many different professions and contexts and has at its core the visualization of ideas, concepts, drawings, plans and models and turning them into real and desirable things. Design quality and profitability are directly linked. In marketing, these design skills can be applied to the creation of an overall advertising or publicity campaign, a corporate identity, a brand logo, an exhibition space, a brochure, a poster, a product, a website. Design is extremely important to product differentiation. For marketers, design is often what brings the intangible to life.

The management of design gives a company a visual way of expressing the nature of the organization. Design is very closely linked to brand management. Packaging, advertising, company logo, merchandise, products, buildings, office space layout, staff uniforms and collateral, should all be designed with an overall theme and with a view to projecting the personality and essence of the company.

designer label a company logo usually attached to a piece of apparel or merchandise to indicate a higher value product that comes from a top quality designer. The French couturiers have been especially adept at extending the designer label concept across a range of fashion items. At some point between the 1970s and 1990s marketers convinced the public to wear these labels (previously worn on the inside) to the outside, making each consumer a walking advertisement.

desk research secondary research, literally done at a desk from secondary sources. See MARKET RESEARCH.

diffusion the process and stages by which a product innovation spreads throughout a market. It is the overall cycle from creation to use. Successful diffusion leads to acceptance and to eventual adoption. See ADOPTION.

direct mail an element of direct marketing involving the sending of promotional material directly to the home address or electronic mailbox of the target consumer. Direct mail is seen to be a lower cost way of promoting goods and services and allows a high degree of targeting, as well as eliminating the middleman. Direct mail can increasingly be personalized to the target. However, consumers continue to reject the bulk of what they describe as 'junk mail' and few direct mail campaigns ever reach higher than a 5% response rate. See also BELOW-THE-LINE, DIRECT MARKETING under MARKETING SPECIALIZATIONS, and JUNK MAIL.

discount any reduction from normal list price offered to customers. Negotiated discounting is more a feature of industrial markets; price discounts on goods are more of a feature of consumer markets. The main purposes of discounting are: to encourage greater volume sales; to get rid of end of line or discontinued stock; to try to win market share from competitors, or to respond to competitor price cutting; to increase purchase in low season periods (such as winter holidays or January sales); or to provide an incentive for another 'bundled' product (for example, if a consumer buys this product he gets a discount on that product or service). See also PRICING, BARGAIN.

discriminant analysis a multivariate technique for analysing the predictive value of a set of independent variables. See MARKET RESEARCH.

disintermediation in general, the removal or supplanting of the middleman in any commercial supply and demand chain. The elimination of middlemen was seen as one of the dividends of the new network economy; the Internet would enable a direct path from producer to consumer with consequent cost advantages for the producer (who no longer had to pay intermediaries' commission) and price advantages for the consumer (who was not paying higher prices that producers passed on to customers to cover the costs of the middlemen). This new form of commerce particularly altered the model for selling basic financial services such as banking and insurance. However, the new economy did not eliminate the intermediary; it simply caused intermediaries to adapt and form new types of intermediary in the new economy, such as the information aggregator and the portal site.

Following the demise of the dot.com companies, it is now evident that disintermediation has not doomed distributors, retailers, wholesalers, and all other intermediaries between producers and the ultimate customer. The Internet has transformed but has not eliminated intermediary distribution channels. The reality is that customers need a significant amount of value to be added to most products before they can buy and use them.

For example, the car industry is an example of the change in emphasis rather than the total disintermediation that was predicted at one time. During the dot.com boom many on-line companies started with the intention of offering customers direct sale of cars at much lower prices than traditional car dealers, who were viewed as inflating the prices of cars. However, customers still wanted to test-drive cars, despite being concerned about dealer's markups and often their sales methods. So what tended to happen was that the car buying customer researched cars using the Internet, then did a test drive one at a dealer, then ordered it over the Internet from the manufacturer who would build it to order, then collected it from the dealership, which provided local servicing of the car over its lifetime. (Actually dealerships make more profit from servicing cars than they do from selling them.) Thus the actual value that is created by the dealer buying the vehicle from the manufacturer and then reselling it to the customer is lower that the ongoing servicing relationship. Instead of making profit on a car sale transaction, the dealership will be paid a commission by the manufacturer as a reward for the services it provides. Therefore, the dealership is not eliminated; it simply adds value in a different way, in this case by test driving, collection and servicing. It is a demonstration centre rather than a sales point, a delivery site, and a service centre.

disposable income the income available to persons for spending or saving after taxes have been deducted. A subset of disposable income is discretionary income, which is the portion most often targeted by marketers. Encouraging target consumers to spend a greater percentage of their discretionary income is the target of most consumer marketers. It can vary from market to market and is closely related to demographic changes in markets. For example, the over-40s market (see also BABY BOOMERS) has the highest percentage of disposable and discretionary income and has not until recently been targeted by advertisers.

domain name the identity and location of an entity on the Internet. There are different levels of domain, and examples are as follows:

Top-level (TLD): .com, .net, .org, .edu, .gov

2nd-level: business, shopping, search (2nd-level may contain letters, numbers, and hyphens)

3rd-level: www1, www2, keyword (optional)

The selection of domain names is a major consideration when doing business on line, and it is often one of the first issues to be addressed. While a good domain name won't guarantee success, it can have a positive (or negative) impact on almost every aspect of on-line business. A good domain is one that is easy to remember and minimizes confusion. If you are acquiring a name that has the potential to cause confusion, it is generally recommended that you obtain the most logical variations. This often includes non-hyphenated and hyphenated variations, along with words that are phonetically similar and common misspellings. With the commercialization of the World Wide Web it is estimated that there are around 25 million commercial domain names registered, making domain names an increasingly valuable commodity. There have been instances of domain name 'squatters' who have registered the names of famous companies as domains of their own – causing them to come up on Internet searches – which they then sell back to the companies at exorbitant rates.

doorway domain an Internet domain used specifically to rank the addressee well in search engines for particular keywords, serving as an entry point through which visitors pass to the main domain.

doorway page a web page made specifically to rank well in search engines for particular keywords, serving as an entry point through which visitors pass to the main content.

double jeopardy a term for a marketing problem in which smaller brands are bought both less frequently and by fewer people. This usually marks the beginning of a spiral of brand decline. Brands with a large market share have a huge benefit over smaller brands in stable markets. This results from the double jeopardy effect that demonstrates how big brands that have more customers (who buy more often) have the double benefit effect and smaller brands have the double jeopardy effect. Buyers buy from portfolios of brands in most market categories. This tends to be in a fixed ratio in which their favourite brand is bought the most often and their third or fourth favourite only 10% or so of the time. In a stable market, the biggest buyers are buying a number of brands and the marketer's goal is to get them to buy their brand repeatedly. Therefore, brands that are lower than fourth preference for the bulk of buyers inevitably fail to gain any real share. The benefits for big brands ensure that new small brands simply have no real chance, unless they truly disrupt the market.

downmarket the opposite of upmarket, describing something or some place that is seen to be for mass consumers, low priced and low quality. Both upmarket and downmarket are based on the simplistic notion that markets have upper and lower ends and that quality and exclusivity are at the top and cheapness and mass accessibility are at the bottom.

drip campaign infrequent use of advertising over a long period of time. See ADVERTISING.

dumping an export practice in international trade of selling goods in an overseas market at a much lower price than in the domestic market. The World Trade Organization has prohibited this practice. See also INTERNATIONAL MARKETING under MARKETING SPECIALIZATIONS.

E

early adopters See ADOPTION.

e-commerce the short term for electronic commerce. This refers to commerce, such as the buying, selling and trading of information, goods and services, over the Internet by means of the World Wide Web. Electronic commerce has risen dramatically since the commercialization of the Internet in the mid-1990s. Within five years 2 million companies had websites. This can include retailing over the Internet (known as e-tailing), business-to-business commerce (B2B), business-to-consumer (B2C), Intranets and extranets, on-line advertising, and on-line presences of any form that are used for some type of commercial relations (for example, customer loyalty programmes and customer services).

economic environment the external elements that must be taken into consideration in the environmental section of market strategy and planning. The economic environment ought to include macro- and microeconomic factors, as well as global, regional, national and local economic environments. It is important to set the wider context of macroeconomics even when developing the most focused marketing plans in very specific market segments. Macroeconomic factors can affect many dimensions of marketing, most specifically demand.

EFTPOS (Electronic Funds Transfer at Point Of Sale) a networked system through which funds are transferred electronically from the customer's account to the retailer's account, usually involving some sort of credit or debit card. Developed in the mid-1980s, this has become indispensable both for retailers and customers in the sales and purchase of goods and services. For example, these systems are linked to EPOS (Electronic Point Of Sale) systems that record the goods sold by reading the bar codes on the goods. This enables management information to be transmitted to help with in-store merchandising, rapid replenishment of goods that are selling fast, as well as overall inventory and cash flow control. Retailing has become much more efficient as a result of these systems. It has also helped marketers analyse how and what each customer spends, on what and with what frequency and where.

Eisner, Michael (1942–) Walt Disney Corp. Eisner took over the legendary company in 1984 as chairman-CEO of Walt Disney Productions. A former ABC programming chief and Paramount Pictures executive, he revitalized and expanded to mega-status Disney's motion picture production, theme parks and merchandising activities. He renewed and expanded Disney product merchandising; spread Disney's family amusement park reach to Europe, Japan and South America; moved Disney onto Broadway and into cable, vacation-business travel-destination packaging, arcades and Internet marketing. He also engineered the ABC-Disney merger. Committed to promotion, marketing and advertising, Eisner led Disney to new heights as a major cultural force and multimedia powerhouse.

Elasticity See PRICING.

electronic shopping direct marketing through a two-way system that links consumers with the seller's computerized catalogue by cable or telephone lines.

e-mail the short name for electronic mail, probably the most successful, and certainly the most widely used, application on the Internet since its inception. E-mail, is, quite simply, electronically transmitted mail on your computer. E-mail is a very versatile medium. Its speed and broadcasting abilities give it numerous advantages over traditional mail. Unlike traditional physical mail, e-mail enables instantaneous transmission of messages anywhere in the world, at any time, to anyone for less money than it would cost to mail a letter or call someone on the telephone. Linked by high-speed data connections that create a global network, e-mail permits message composition and transmission in seconds to one or more recipients. Businesses and consumers have enthusiastically and universally adopted e-mail across the world. It has become a new means of communication and is a major marketing tool. See also INTERACTIVE MARKETING.

e-mail spam unwanted, unsolicited e-mail, especially unsolicited commercial messages sent in bulk by organizations and people usually unknown to the receiver. (Spamming refers the process of sending this.) There is no agreed upon definition of e-mail spam because it is in the eye of the individual beholder. Some argue that e-mail spam is the electronic equivalent of traditional junk mail. Spam mail is, however, much cheaper than junk mail. The cost of sending e-mail spam is very small, and people other than the sender pay most of the costs. The lack of significant barriers to entry (i.e. cost of sending) is often cited as a key problem with e-mail spam. It has bred a range of hucksters and fraudsters on the Internet. With traditional junk mail, a direct marketer must ensure that the offer and the response from customer targets are enough to offset the costs of mailing. With e-mail spam there is no such accountability. Spamming has been used unscrupulously to defraud on-line consumers. It is one of the negative byproducts of the Internet age.

embargo a prohibition on the export of a particular good or classes of goods to certain countries, usually for political reasons. This can have significant impact on international trade and the economic wellbeing of a country. It is closely linked to foreign policy. For example, the continuing US embargo of Cuba, which originated in the politics of the Cold War, is a major controversy at present. There are many embargos placed upon regimes regarded as dangerous to international security, such as the various embargos on weapons technology to Iraq in the aftermath of the Gulf War of the early 1990s.

emotional model a model developed in 1984 by Peggy Kreshel to examine the influence of emotions on buying behaviour. This extended the range of prior models, such as the hierarchy of effects model, that had emphasized cognition as the spring source of purchasing behaviour. In the 1980s there was a growing recognition that many of the academic models had, for the most part, ignored emotion as a significant factor in consumer response. Throughout the 1980s numerous new models of consumer response were created which held emotion to be the underlying element that shaped all subsequent responses. Peggy Kreshel suggested that cognition could alter affect (as in previous models) only because of the affective connotations carried by the cognitive process. In other words, information is relevant primarily because of its affective impact. Or, put another way, it is impossible to separate our emotional connections to a stimulus from the stimulus itself.

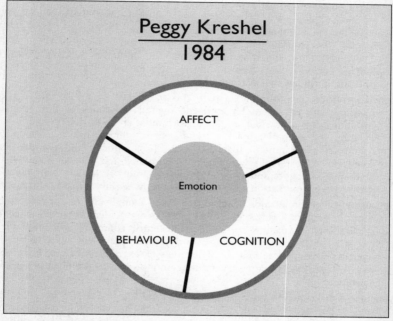

See also AIDA, DAGMAR, BUYING, MARKETING COMMUNICATIONS, ADVERTISING, HIERARCHY OF EFFECTS.

empty nesters families whose children have left home and set up their own homes. This is a group with high disposable and discretionary income, caused by no longer having to support children and also possibly from the sale of the original or inherited family property. Increasingly, marketers target this once ignored group because of their rising economic power as well as their more active lifestyle and aspirations following the departure of their children.

end user the person who actually uses a product and service. The end user is not necessarily always the customer. For example, end users include children who are bought toys and clothes by their parents, or business users who have their equipment and services bought for them by their company purchasing departments. End users always certainly influence the purchasing decision, even if they do not always make it themselves. This is an important element for marketers to understand as they segment their markets and target their campaigns.

Engel's Laws differences noted more than a century ago by Ernst Engel in how people shift their spending across food, housing, transportation, health care, and other goods and services categories as family income rises.

environmentalism an ethos that puts fundamental importance on the relationship between human beings and their actions with the physical environment (ecology). Consumers are showing an increasing desire for environmentally friendly products and are prepared to pay a premium price for them. The reputations of companies can be injured if they damage the environment and their reputations can be enhanced if they are perceived as helping the environment. Environmentalism must therefore be a major consideration for all marketing and corporate reputation building. Products that are perceived to be harmful to the environment will prove increasingly difficult, if not impossible, to market.

environmental scanning an activity taken as part of the overall market planning process to understand the overall dynamics of the external environment within which market opportunities are to be determined. It will include, for example, market trends, sizes, demographics, economics, resources, environment, technology, politics, culture, and competition. Analysing the external environment gives context and substance to various marketing strategies and plans. It is indispensable in today's complex and ever-changing markets in a globalizing economy. See also MARKETING STRATEGY.

ethnocentrism an attitude of mind that holds a single culture (or race) to be superior to such a degree that other cultures are denied any importance. In international marketing terms, an ethnocentric company will often view overseas operations as secondary to domestic operations, often using the overseas operations as a means of dumping excess domestic stock. For global marketing ethnocentrism is a very dangerous attitude and limits the scope of operation.

exclusive distribution the right given by a producer to a retailer or other type of distributor to be the sole distribution channel in a determined territory. In return, exclusive distributors or retailers are usually required to provide exceptional and far-reaching service to customers.

exclusivity a binding contract term in which one party grants another party sole rights with regards to a particular business function. Some advertising networks demand exclusivity with a client. Some do not demand exclusivity, but offer a higher rate for an exclusive deal than the standard rate given to non-exclusive deals. Most reputable firms require exclusivity as a result of the in-depth relationships they have with publishers. Some demand exclusivity when sponsoring events or charities. A couple of affiliate networks demand exclusivity of their merchants, but other affiliate networks have tried to exploit this by promoting their non-exclusive terms. Some affiliate programmes demand exclusivity within their product category, but they are exceptions, as few affiliate programmes are in a position to make extra demands.

exhibition a large-scale venue for the demonstration of goods and services from numerous producers, usually brought together around a single theme or industry. These are an effective part of the overall marketing promotional mix. Exhibitions are dominated by business-to-business marketing, although there are many exhibitions for consumers also. In the US the trade show is an indispensable part of marketing. There are several factors that determine whether or not it is a good use of resources to get involved in exhibitions:

1. The right location: there are some places that excel at exhibitions, such as Las Vegas and Orlando

2. The exhibition hall or show area has to be impressive and well laid-out.

3. The stands, including the documentation, advice, personnel, gifts and interactive displays, have to be attractive and compelling.

4. The exhibitors have to be worth seeing – either for their products and services or even for the quality of their stand.

5. The quality and quantity of the visitors is important: how many of them could be prospective clients? How many existing clients? How many buyers? How many potential visitors will see my competitors' goods if we do not exhibit?

6. The technological and industrial environment: does it make attendance at a trade show compelling?: Are important new products going to be on display or launched?

Marketers have a range of different motives for displaying at an exhibition:

- To maintain market share, particularly in mature markets. For example, car companies MUST display at various car shows in order to keep their shares of markets against competitors.

- Market penetration: often exhibitions can be an integral part of attacking a new market or launching a more intensive attack on an existing market.

- Business developments: certain exhibitions, particularly in consumer markets, are places where deals are done, alliances signed and contracts are won.

- Market research: exhibitions are often places where marketers can find out a great deal about competitors in a relatively short time.

- Sales promotion: exhibitions are pre-eminently places where salespeople ply their trade and promote their goods, services and their company. For example, sales literature will be produced especially for the exhibition. This can take the form of: special format literature, catalogues, event brochures, pamphlets, data sheets, special covers and folders and wallets, self-binders and ring-binders, special packing and bags for transport. These may be dispensed from the stand, with literature and for added publicity. Gifts and promotional goods are also distributed from the stand.

- Media and public relations: often attendance at an exhibition is done deliberately to stir press interest and to create a public awareness. Journalists hold various press conferences at exhibitions. See also MARKETING MIX.

expectations these are important to marketers, especially customer and market expectations. Customers' expectations of goods, services and information are rising all the time and it is the task of the marketer both to anticipate customer expectation and to manage their expectations. There are few more damaging consequences for a company than disappointed or unfulfilled expectations. Therefore expectation management – particularly the art of not over-promising what cannot be delivered – is a subtlety that is often lost even on the most seasoned marketers.

experience curve a model developed that showed that real unit costs decline systematically with increases in cumulative volume production. The antecedent of the experience curve is the production learning curve, first observed in the 1930s as a systematic decline in the number of man-hours required to produce an aeroplane in American factories. It was only in the mid-1960s that the notion of the learning curve was generalized by the Boston Consulting Group to encompass the behaviour of all value-added costs and prices as cumulative volume or experience increases. Complete acceptance of this model is now waning. The application problems were always formidable, but now there is a growing suspicion that some of the key strategic implications may be invalid. The rise of innovative technologies that can substitute for human experience accumulation have undermined the universal application of the model.

EXPORTING

exporting a discipline within international marketing that concentrates mainly on the sale of products created in the domestic market to overseas markets. Exporting is usually the first stage in full-scale international marketing and foreign market entry. Exporting is also a central component of international trade negotiations as well as multilateral and bilateral trade agreements. Exporting is also a barometer of the strength or weakness of the domestic economy and partly determines the balance of trade.

There are several ways to export. The way in which a company chooses to export its products can have a significant effect on its international market strategies. The basic categories of exporting all relate to the exporter's level of involvement in the export process. There are at least four approaches, which may be used alone or in combination:

Passive exporting in this approach, orders are received from foreign buyers and fulfilled domestically and shipped to the buyer. Alternatively, sales are made to domestic buyers who then export the product to overseas buyers. These sales are indistinguishable from other domestic sales as far as the original manufacturer is concerned. Someone else has decided that the product in question meets foreign demand. That party takes all the risk and handles all of the exporting details, in some cases without even the awareness of the original seller.

Active exporting this approach is when the company seeks out domestic export merchants or agents or companies who represent foreign customers. These buyers are a large customer market for a wide variety of goods and services. In this case, a company knows that its product is being exported, but it is still the intermediary who assumes the risk and handles the details of exporting. This is known as *indirect exporting*. The chief characteristic of indirect exporting is that the export of products is carried out through intermediaries. It is also a lower risk and lower cost option for international exporting. It involves no direct investment in the foreign markets. With this approach, a company engages the services of an intermediary firm, agents or merchants capable of finding foreign markets and buyers for its products. Export management companies, export trading companies, international trade consultants, and other intermediaries can give the exporter access to well-established expertise and trade contacts.

Direct exporting this approach is the most ambitious and most difficult, since the exporter personally handles every aspect of the exporting process from market research and planning to foreign distribution, fulfilment and collections. Consequently, a significant commitment of management time and attention is required to achieve good results. It also requires greater investment and research to be successful. However, this approach may also be the best way to achieve maximum profits and long-term growth and grow into a fully international company. The direct exporting company will most likely set up an export department within its own company. Additionally, the company will set up sales offices in foreign markets to handle storage, distribution, sales, servicing and marketing. Alternatively, the company may recruit foreign sales agents who exclusively represent the product in that territory.

There are also potential combinations of export strategy. For example, a company may choose to export to adjacent or neighbouring markets, or an economic free trade area, or economic community zone, directly, then use export agents and intermediaries where it is less familiar with the culture and language and customs, or where the market potential is smaller but still significant.

Other approaches to exporting may involve **licensing** products, processes, trademarks, patents, and intellectual property in exchange for a royalty or fee. This is lower risk than setting up a full infrastructure in the foreign territory. It can also be lower risk for the licensee as the expertise or product is already tried and tested.

Deciding when to export

There are several ways to gauge the overseas market potential of products and services.

Domestic success of a product or service is no guarantee for success overseas. Market differences may inhibit repeatability of success that was known in domestic markets. Those differences may be cultural, environmental or social factors. There may be problems with local availability of raw materials or product alternatives. There may be lower wage costs or lower purchasing power. There could be a lack of convertible currency or the availability of foreign exchange (rather than hard currencies like the dollar, the British pound, and the Japanese yen). There could be government import controls or restrictive labour laws.

Some countries impose tariffs on foreign exports in order to protect their domestic markets or to raise revenues. Some countries have strict import quotas in order to protect their domestic markets or to preserve their foreign currency reserves. At worse, the exporter can face an embargo, or total ban, on foreign imports. There are also non-tariff barriers, such as demanding extraordinary safety features that it is impossible for certain exporters to provide, that have the effect of discriminating against certain export products from foreign countries.

If a product is unique or has important features that are hard to duplicate abroad, the chances of finding an export market overseas may be good. For a unique product, competition may be nonexistent or very slight, while demand may be quite high.

If sales of a product are declining in the domestic market, sizeable export markets may exist, especially if the product once did well in the domestic market but is now losing market share to more technically advanced products. Countries that are less developed than the domestic market may not need more advanced products and may be unable to afford the more advanced and expensive products. Such markets may instead have surprisingly healthy demand for products that are older or that are considered obsolete by domestic market standards.

export-led growth an economic approach adopted by some countries who are seeking to promote economic growth by exporting to wealthier countries.

extended guarantee the guarantee that the manufacturer offers at additional cost to the customer that extends beyond the timescale of the original guarantee. This can be quite lucrative for the manufacturer and plays on the customer's fear of breakdown. This is often called selling the customer 'peace of mind'. Guarantees are an integral part of consumer goods marketing and can also be applied to leased equipment as well as purchased equipment.

external audit see MARKETING AUDIT, MARKETING STRATEGY AUDIT, ENVIRON-MENTAL SCANNING.

extranet a group of websites belonging to independent entities that are combined together in order to share information. This is in contrast to an intranet, which is a private site that is only accessible for employees of an entity. Extranets are used in the supply chain to allow for more effective communications. They are replacing proprietary standard networks that are considerably more expensive to establish, and therefore are only used by large organizations.

e-zine an electronic magazine, whether delivered via a website or in the form of an e-mail newsletter. E-zines range greatly in size and scope, from irregular newsletters reaching a handful of subscribers to daily journals reaching hundreds of thousands of subscribers. Some e-zines are strictly non-profit. Some are extremely profitable. Others are for-profit but don't make any profit because they are unable to attract the necessary audience and advertisers. Additionally, companies are starting to use internal e-zines to communicate information to employees in a relative low-cost way.

e-zine directory a directory of electronic magazines, typically those that are delivered by e-mail.

F

fact book a file of information and intelligence on products, countries, markets or a range of areas of expertise. An example could be the *Economist* Intelligence Unit reports on various countries and their economies.

fad a short-term obsession with a style, product, idea or concept. Fads are characterized by high adoption (expressed in either increased sales or publicity or word of mouth) and equally fast disappearance and obsolescence. Whether marketing actually creates fads or merely exploits and amplifies them is a moot point.

family the basic unit of social organization in most countries in the world and also the main focus of consumption; as such it is very important to consumer marketers. In recent years the home has become increasingly the focus of direct marketing. The combination of the home as a purchasing unit as well as rising family income make the family a powerful economic force, and also one with a tremendous influence on buying behaviour. There is market influence from both parents and children. Demographic changes as well as changing social habits (such as the rise of extended, 'second' families, divorce, single-sex marriage and cohabitation) mean that marketers can no longer assume the classic nuclear family as the basic unit of social organization when preparing their marketing messages and products.

family life cycle a way of segmenting the family market at different stages of the life cycle to determine what products and services that members buy at each stage and also their levels of disposable income. This segmentation charts the stages through which families pass as they age.

The main variables are age, marital status, career and disposable income as well as presence and absence of children in the family home. Stages of the family life cycle are as follows.

1. Single young people not living at home. Typically they would have few financial burdens and marketers would focus upon their interests in fashion, leisure, basic household items, cars, equipment, and holidays. Financial services marketers increasingly target this group at the student level and as they gain their first jobs, hoping to build a lifelong relationship with them as their financial needs grow.

2. Newly married couples that have no children. Typically these couples are wealthier than the singles group. The main focus of the marketer is their initial purchase of starter homes, household and consumer durable goods, holidays and financial services.

3. Full nesters stage I. Couples with children under six. This group is very focused on home purchase but tend to have low levels of disposable income and savings, usually because of mortgage commitments, or the wife having taken time off to have children. This group is a target for marketers selling

financial services, typically credit products, such as cards, loans and overdrafts. The main focus of disposable income is the children and this group is therefore the main target for baby products and clothes, as well as children's toys and books.

4. Full nesters stage II. Couples with youngest child, six or over. Usually, if the job market is good, this couple's financial position is better, perhaps through pay rises, perhaps because of wives' return to work. Children continue to dominate the decisions of the household. Marketers focus on this group for consumer goods, clothes, bicycles, sports gear, musical instruments and lessons, and activity holidays.

5. Full nesters stage III. Older married couples with dependent children, perhaps in full-time higher education or first jobs. The financial position of this group continues to improve, but could also be offset by rising financial demands of children's education. Wives are working. The main focus is on schooling, educational attainment and educational costs. The marketer focuses on this group buying new, more tasteful furniture, luxury goods, boats, timeshares and exotic holidays.

6. Empty nesters stage I. These are older married couples, no children living with them but with the parent(s) still working. Their mortgage payments are less onerous and they may be thinking of trading down their house. They have a high degree of savings and disposable income. They are interested in unique travel experiences, possibly a second home in a foreign country, sophisticated leisure and self-education. They observe their children gain qualifications and move to the first stage of the family cycle. The marketer targets this group as perhaps the wealthiest of all, buying luxury goods, expensive home improvements, specialist holidays and possible top end of the range cars. See also EMPTY NESTERS.

7. Empty nesters stage II. These are older married couples, with no children living at home, but with the main breadwinner retired. This group experiences a significant cut in income and is heavily dependent upon the pension provision that they have made. They tend to spend less on leisure and buy more medical appliances or medical care products. They cease to help their children financially and are constantly concerned with levels of savings and pension. This group is no longer a main focus of the marketer except in financial services (such as annuities, income-generating plans) and providers of hobbies and pastime products.

8. Solitary survivor stage I. Still working, but may have divorce and maintenance costs to bear. Income is still adequate but is likely to sell family home and purchase smaller accommodation. Is worried about security and dependence. Some expenditure is made on hobbies and pastimes and specialist holidays catering for singles. This group is not a top target for the marketer.

9. Solitary survivor II (retired). Has a significant cut in income and requires increasing amounts of care, particularly medical, and special attention and security. Possibly dependence on other family members for personal financial assistance, in the same way as children were dependent on them for

assistance. This group is no longer a target of marketers, but their relatives may be, particularly for financial services, such as insurance and also for medical care services.

fashion a currently accepted or popular style in a given field. Fashion, that is, apparel, accessories and jewellery, is a huge industry in its own right. Marketing the fashion apparel of a haute couturier – such as Dior, Lagerfeld or Yves Saint Laurent – is more to promote the brand than to promote the clothes. Usually, the couturier part of the fashion business is unprofitable; the extensions of the brand, for example to perfume or accessories, are where the profits are made.

fast-moving consumer goods (FMCG) consumer goods that usually sell in retail outlets and which, literally, move off the shop shelves quickly because they are highly consumable.

favourite see BOOKMARK.

feel-bad factor a term used for describing depressed consumer and business confidence that results in a psychological withdrawal of consumers into a pessimistic state, resulting in flat or falling spending on products and investment goods. Because consumer confidence is so vital to a modern economy, the contrary condition causes much concern to politicians and businessmen. See also CONSUMER MARKETING.

feel-good factor a term for describing buoyant consumer and business confidence, which results in high spending and confidence about taking on extra credit facilities. For example, it is a well known factor in the UK that if homeowners feel that property prices are rising, and therefore their net wealth, they will spend much more freely on consumer goods, household furnishings and leisure services.

field research see MARKET RESEARCH.

first-mover advantage the advantages gained by the first significant company to enter a new market in a substantial way, often with a new service or product that has no previous track record. First-mover advantage was initially thought to be a crucial and necessary marketing strategy in the Internet economy, but experience has now shown that this has not always been the case. First-mover advantage can be instrumental in building market share, but the early years of the Internet economy have not shown conclusively that this leads to business success. EBay and Amazon.com are examples of on-line companies that have gained successful early-mover advantage. There is no single reward for early movers. Some industries reward first-movers with near-monopoly status and higher margins. Other industries do not necessarily reward the first mover, allowing late-movers the chance to compete more effectively and efficiently against early entrants.

FIVE FORCES MODEL

Developed by MICHAEL PORTER, this model provided a framework for an overall set of competitive rivalries within an industry structure. Marketers seeking to develop a competitive advantage over competitors can use this model to better understand the industry context in which the firm operates.

The model is illustrated, then expanded upon, overleaf:

Five Forces analysis

Threat of
new entrants

Bargaining
power of
suppliers

COMPETITIVE
RIVALRY

Bargaining
power of
Buyers

Threat of
substitute
products

Adapted from M.E. Porter, Competitive Strategy, Free Press, 1980.

If rivalry among firms in an industry is low, the industry is consider to be disciplined. This discipline may result from the industry's history of competition, the role of a leading firm, or informal compliance with a generally understood code of conduct. When an important rival takes an action that precipitates counter-moves by other firms, rivalry intensifies. The intensity of rivalry is classified into various ranges, based on the firms' aggressiveness in attempting to gain an advantage.

In pursuing an advantage over its rivals, a firm can choose from several competitive strategies:

• Pricing: raising or lowering prices to gain a temporary advantage.

• Improving product differentiation.

• Creatively using channels of distribution: using vertical integration or using a distribution channel that is novel to the industry.

• Exploiting its relationships with its suppliers.

Various industry characteristics that affect the intensity of rivalry:

A *larger number of firms* increases rivalry because more firms must compete for the same customers and resources. The rivalry intensifies if the firms have similar market share, leading to a struggle for market leadership.

Slow market growth causes firms to fight for market share. In a growing market, firms are able to improve revenues simply because of the expanding market.

High fixed costs result in an economy of scale effect that increases rivalry. When total costs are mostly fixed costs, the firm must produce near capacity to attain the lowest unit costs. Since the firm must sell this large quantity of product, high levels of production lead to a fight for market share, resulting in increased rivalry.

High storage costs or highly perishable products cause a producer to sell goods as soon as possible. If other producers are attempting to unload products on the market at the same time, competition for customers intensifies.

Low switching costs increases rivalry. When a customer can freely switch from one product to another there is a greater struggle to capture customers.

Low levels of product differentiation are associated with higher levels of rivalry. Brand identification and loyalty, on the other hand, tends to constrain rivalry.

Strategic stakes are high when a firm is losing market position or has potential for great gains. This intensifies rivalry.

High exit barriers place a high cost on abandoning the product. The firm must compete. High exit barriers cause a firm to remain in an industry, even when the venture is not profitable.

A diversity of rivals with different cultures, histories, and philosophies make an industry unstable. There is greater possibility for mavericks and for misjudging a rival's moves. Rivalry is volatile and can be intense.

Industry shakeout. A growing market and the potential for high profits induces new firms to enter a market and incumbent firms to increase production. A point is reached where the industry becomes crowded with competitors, and demand cannot support the new entrants and the resulting increased supply. The industry may become crowded if its growth rate slows and the market becomes saturated, creating a situation of excess capacity with too many goods chasing too few buyers. A shakeout ensues, with intense competition, price wars, and company failures. It is clear that market stability and changes in supply and demand affect rivalry. Cyclical demand tends to create intensive competition.

Threat of substitutes

In Porter's model, substitute products refers to products in other industries. Substitute products affect a product's price elasticity: as more substitutes become available, the demand becomes more elastic since customers have more alternatives. A close substitute product constrains the ability of firms in an industry to raise prices.

The competition engendered by a threat of substitute comes from products outside the industry. While this typically impacts an industry through price competition, there can be other concerns in assessing the threat of substitutes. For example, the transmission of television signals was once done in a single way: from local transmission stations by airwaves via an aerial to a TV receiver. Now there are substitute alternatives: transmission via cable, satellite, and even high-capacity telephone lines. The new technologies available and the changing structure of the entertainment media are contributing to competition among these substitute means of connecting the home to entertainment.

Buyer power

The power of buyers is the impact that customers have on a producing industry. In general, when the power of buyers is strong, the relationship to the producing industry is characterized by a market in which there are many suppliers and one buyer. Under such market conditions, the buyer sets the price.

Buyers are strong if:

Buyers are concentrated in a given market: there are a few buyers with significant market share;

Buyers purchase a significant proportion of output, particularly standardized product which enables them to switch suppliers;

Buyers possess a credible backward integration threat: they can threaten to buy producing firm or rival.

Buyers are weak if:

Producers threaten forward integration, i.e. producers can take over own distribution/retailing;

There are significant buyer switching costs: for example, products not standardized and the buyer cannot easily switch to another product.

Buyers are fragmented (many, different); in this case no buyer has any particular influence on product or prices.

The producers supply critical portions of the buyers' input, for example in the distribution of purchases.

Supplier power

A producing industry requires raw materials, such as labour, components, and other material supplies. This requirement leads to buyer-supplier relationships between the industry and the firms that provide it with the raw materials used to create products. Suppliers, if powerful, can exert an influence on the producing industry, such as selling its raw materials at a high price, expropriating some of the industry's profits. An example of this is the car industry that clearly dominates its distribution channels and dealers.

The following outlines some factors that determine supplier power.

Suppliers are powerful if:

There is a credible forward integration threat by suppliers, for example car companies taking over direct selling and servicing of their vehicles;

Suppliers are concentrated in a market;

There is significant cost to switch suppliers – to some extent the suppliers have locked in their buyers;

Customers are powerful.

Suppliers are weak if:

There are any competitive suppliers – the product is standardized;

The buyers purchase commodity products which can be found easily elsewhere;

There is a credible backward integration threat by purchasers;

There are concentrated purchasers;

Customers are weak.

Barriers to entry/threat of entry

It is not only existing competitors that pose a threat to firms in an industry; the possibility that new companies may enter the industry also affects competition. In theory, any firm should be able to enter and exit a market, and if free entry and exit exists, then profits always should be nominal. In reality, however, industries possess characteristics that protect the high profit levels of firms in the market and inhibit additional rivals from entering the market. These are *barriers to entry*.

Barriers to entry are more than the normal equilibrium adjustments that markets typically make to control the entrance of new suppliers. For example, when industry profits increase, one would expect additional firms to enter the market to take advantage of the high profit levels. Over time, the entry of new competitors and suppliers would drive profits down for all firms in the industry. When profits decrease, we would expect some firms to exit the market and this would restore market equilibrium. Falling prices, or the expectation that future prices will fall, deter rivals from entering a market. Firms also may be reluctant to enter markets that are extremely uncertain, especially if entering involves high start-up costs. These are normal accommodations to market conditions. However, if firms individually (collective action would constitute illegal collusion) keep prices artificially low as a strategy to prevent potential entrants from entering the market, *such entry-deterring pricing* establishes a major barrier to market entry.

Barriers to entry are unique industry characteristics that define the industry. Barriers reduce the rate of entry of new firms, thus maintaining a level of profits for those already in the industry. From a strategic perspective, barriers can be created or exploited to enhance a firm's competitive advantage. Barriers to entry arise from several sources:

1. *Government creates barriers.* Although the principle role of the government in a market is to preserve competition through anti-trust actions, government also restricts competition through the granting of monopolies and through regulation. Illustrative of this kind of barrier to entry is the local cable company in the UK. The franchise to a cable provider may be granted by competitive bidding, but once a community awards the franchise a monopoly is created. Similarly, the government grants various types of licence that enable entry into a market, such as broadcasting and wireless telephony.

2. *Patents and proprietary knowledge serve to restrict entry into an industry.* Ideas, processes, techniques, expertise and knowledge that provide competitive advantages are treated as private property when patented. This prevents others from using the knowledge and creating a barrier to entry.

3. *Asset specificity inhibits entry into an industry.* Asset specificity is the extent to which the firm's assets can be utilized to produce a different product. When an industry requires highly specialized technology or plant and equipment, potential entrants are reluctant to commit to acquiring specialized assets that cannot be sold or converted into other uses if the venture fails. Asset specificity provides a barrier to entry because when firms already hold specialized assets they fiercely resist efforts by others from taking their market share. New entrants can anticipate aggressive rivalry. An example is control of the 'local loop' telephone exchanges by incumbent communications companies that make the final connection to domestic customers. All competing communications companies have to use these local loops in order to serve local customers.

4. *Organizational (Internal) Economies of Scale.* The most cost efficient level of production is termed *Minimum Efficient Scale* (MES). This is the point at which unit costs for production are at minimum, i.e., the most cost-efficient level of production. If the MES for firms in an industry is known, then it is possible to determine the amount of market share necessary for low-cost entry or cost parity with rivals. The existence of an economy of scale creates a barrier to entry. The greater the difference between industry MES and entry unit costs, the greater the barrier to entry.

We can generalize about an industry's barriers to entry/exit, as follows:

Easy to Enter if there is:	**Difficult to Enter if there is:**
Common or standardized technology	Difficulty in brand switching, or extreme brand loyalty
Little brand franchise	Patented or proprietary know-how
Access to distribution channels	High scale threshold to enter the market.
Low scale threshold to enter the market.	Restricted distribution channels
Difficult to Exit if there are:	**Easy to Exit if there are:**
Specialized assets	Saleable assets
High exit costs	Independent business
Interrelated businesses	

See also COMPETITION and COMPETITIVENESS.

---

flagship the pre-eminent or best-selling product, service or retail outlet of a company. For example, retailers with high-visibility retail outlets on 5th Avenue in New York, Oxford Street in London or the Champs Elysées in Paris could refer to these stores as flagships, because their main purpose is to display the brand.

flanker brand a new brand introduced into the market by a company that already has an established brand in the same product category. The new brand is designed to compete in the category without damaging the existing item's market share by targeting a different group of consumers. Flanker branding is important because it allows a company to attract new customers from various market segments. This technique is also known as multibranding and is used to achieve a larger total market share than one product could achieve on its own. An example is diet Coke that extended the Coca-Cola brand for the growing weight-watcher part of the market. Companies with multiple brands in a single product category generally have a premium brand that offers high quality at a higher price in their overall portfolio. They usually own one or more 'value' brands offering a slightly lower quality or a different set of benefits for a lower price.

The main brand of a company's portfolio should target the market segment containing the most consumers. Another brand can then be positioned to convert users from other market segments by using a different set of benefits or product characteristics. A flanker brand should attract customers from competing brands and not from the main branded product.

There are a number of advantages to developing a flanker brand:

- In consumer goods a flanker brand can gain more shelf space for the company, which increases retailer dependence on the company's brands.

- Flanker brands can capture those consumers who like to switch brands by offering several brands.

- Creation of internal competition within the product portfolio between the different brands without harming the overall brand. Giving a product its own unique name means it will not be readily associated with the existing brand. This reduces risk to the existing brand if the product fails.

- Companies with a high-quality existing product can introduce lower-quality brands without diluting their flagship brand names.

- Introducing a new brand is costly. Creating another independent brand requires name research and substantial advertising expenditures to create name recognition and preference for the new brand. One thing that has to be considered is the extent to which the new brand will have unique qualities that will appeal to a separate group of consumers and provide additional value over and above the existing brand. An assessment of the impact of the new brand's impact on existing brands has to be made and considered as well as the new brand's impact on competitors' brands. And finally, will the cost of new brand development, launch and ongoing promotion be recouped by the sales of the new brand?

See also BRANDING.

flash a multimedia technology that allows interactive images to be created within a relatively small file. It can be used to create entire websites or to add interactive elements to standard HTML websites. Non-flash sites accompany some flash-only sites in an effort to cater to a wider audience. Flash technology can also be used in interactive banner advertisements.

flash pack a package upon which a sales promotion message features prominently.

flighting the overall approach and execution of media strategy in terms of timing, seasonality and level of repetition, particularly for commercials running on print and broadcast media. In broadcast media, inventory is purchased by 'day part,' that is, a certain time block during a 24-hour period. Overnight day parts (which are not even measured by ratings) are much less expensive than, say, prime-time (8 p.m. to 11 p.m.) day parts.

See also ADVERTISING, MEDIA.

focus group a structured form of interviewing which consists of inviting six to ten people to gather for a few hours with a trained interviewer to talk about a product, service, or organization. The interviewer 'focuses' the group discussion on important issues. Focus groups are useful in providing the researcher with qualitative data. It is important that these sessions are used for ideas and product development rather than to kill off new ideas.

See also MARKET RESEARCH.

fold the section of a web page that is visible without scrolling. The fold varies depending on the resolution settings on a visitor's monitor. At lower settings (i.e. 640x480) the fold is relatively high on the page. At higher settings (i.e. 1280x1024) the fold extends much further down the page. Decisions concerning what goes above or below the fold are often made based on a minimum targeted resolution. Advertisers often look favourably at *banner ad* placements that are high on the page, assuming that their ads will be viewed and clicked more often.

FORECASTING

forecast a statistical synthesis of probabilities and expert opinion that attempts to define an outcome either in terms of numbers or actual courses of action. Forecasts range from the short-term (usually up to three months), the medium-term (normally covering one or two years) and the long-term (three years plus). Market forecasting is one of the most difficult arts of the marketer; no matter how well-informed the underlying data. Investments in product and services launches are usually made on the basis of market forecasts.

forecasting the identification of factors and quantification of their effect on an entity, as a basis for business planning and investment. Forecasting approaches include quantitative (objective) and qualitative (subjective) estimates of the future. Forecasting is important because, by predicting future sales, the company can estimate revenue and therefore plan production, capital and human resources accordingly.

Sales forecasting is critically important to overall marketing investment. It is a time series model that takes historical data and projects trends into the future (for example, previous sales figures, moving averages, seasonal aspects, cyclical fluctuations). It can also include causal models, for example those models that relate sales to relative prices, complementary goods sales and promotional advertising. There are other forecasting models that are qualitative – for example those that rely on expert opinions to predict the future. Sales budgets are usually based on company forecasts of future sales, but may be adjusted to take a prudent or conservative view of the expected volume and value of sales.

The following factors are used to determine a sales forecast:

1. Past sales patterns, often risky as in today's economy previous sales patterns are an unreliable guide to the future.

2. The economic environment, particularly factors that affect investment and growth, or which affect demand, directly or indirectly, of the goods being sold.

3. Results of market research, particularly research into buyer intentions over defined time periods.

4. Anticipated advertising during the budget period, which could act as a fillip for sales.

5. Competition, and its intensity in the defined market where the sales force will operate.

6. Changing consumer tastes: these can totally wreck a sales forecast that is based upon historical patterns of consumer taste.

7. New technology, which can often change the pattern of market demand or create new demand.

8. Distribution and quality of sales outlets and personnel: for example, an increase in either volume or quality of direct and indirect sales can have a positive effect on total sales volume.

9. Pricing policies and discounts offered: often creative pricing and discounting can increase sales volumes, if not always profits.

10. Legislation either local or national.

11. Environmental factors, for example the rise in organic food can increase sales to retail outlets.

Sales forecast accuracy

Sales forecasts are rarely 100% accurate. There are some factors that can help improve their accuracy:

- Good, up-to-date internal data and market intelligence are needed to make an accurate forecast, which reduces the use of 'gut feel' or approximation based upon personal hunches.

- Sales statistics should be available in a suitable format and easy to understand.

- All the factors affecting sales, including external market conditions, should be understood by the people involved in the forecasting process.

- Appropriate methods of forecasting should be used, whether quantitative or qualitative or a combination of both.

- Assumptions made in the sales forecast (such as the rate of inflation, exchange rates, rate of adoption of a product, increase in a competitor's promotional activity etc.) ought to be clearly stated so that changes can easily be made to the forecast if the assumptions change.

- Sales forecasts should be reviewed regularly and should take into account any new information in order to keep them up to date and accurate

- An organization's own marketing strategy must be taken into account. Increased advertising, sales promotions or a new price list must be considered when making sales forecasts.

- Accuracy can be improved by combining a number of different methods such as quantitative methods (essentially extrapolations of past sales levels) with qualitative methods (based more on judgment and personal interpretation).

The consequences of inaccurate sales forecasting are punitive. For example, sales forecasts that are too ambitious can lead to over-stretching and unrealistic sales targets for the sales force. Inaccurate sales forecasts can also set wrong expectations not only for management but also for investors in the company. For example, if the company is quoted on the stock exchange, the effect on the investor community of overstating the forecast and having to issue a profits warning may lead to a loss of confidence that could adversely affect the share price.

Sales forecasts feed into manufacturing production plans. Over-optimistic forecasts can lead to excess inventory in the company warehouse. The excess inventory situation ties up working capital and can also increase the likelihood of damage and waste. Extra staff may have been taken on in sales or production to cope with the expected level of sales and, if this does not materialize, there may need to be redundancies that can be very demoralizing to the rest of the workforce. Additionally, relationships with suppliers of materials could be disrupted and damaged if expected forecast levels are not met.

forum an on-line community where visitors can read and post topics of common interest. Forums can be useful for anyone doing business on-line, both in terms of reading the content and actively participating in the discussions. Reading a forum's archives can be a good way to obtain a basic knowledge about a topic, as well as providing an historical perspective on trends and opinions. Participation, whether as a member, moderator, or owner, can help one achieve recognition within an on-line market or business community, and may even generate highly qualified business leads. Forums differ, however, in their treatment of self-promotion; some disallow any hint of self-promotion, some are geared specifically towards self-promotion, and many fall somewhere in between, limiting URLs to an off-the-page member profile. It is very important to read the terms and conditions of each particular forum for a basic guideline as to what is acceptable. Failure to do so can have negative consequences, including tarnishing your site's reputation and being permanently banned from the community.

frames a structure that allows the division of a web page into two or more independent parts.

franchising a marketing and sales arrangement in which the franchiser contracts to the franchisee to market and sell his products and service, with strict controls on supply of product, use of the franchiser's logo and quality control over product and services. The franchiser provides the franchisee with marketing services; in return the franchisee purchases equipment and supplies and pays the franchiser a percentage of revenues and a franchise fee. The franchisee has exclusive marketing and retail sales rights in a designated area or location.

Franchising is a fast-growing and lower-risk form of business expansion. The main characteristics are: the franchiser sells the right to market a product under its name to a franchisee; the franchiser and the franchisee are separate entities but interdependent businesses. It can lead to rapid growth, especially in consumer goods retailing. It is a ready-made opportunity for an entrepreneur with capital wishing to minimize risk of a new venture and to use a tried-and-tested brand rather than create a new one. McDonalds and the Body Shop are franchised businesses.

See also CHANNELS OF DISTRIBUTION.

free website promotion a range of techniques where websites work co-operatively to promote each other's sites. This acts effectively as free promotion for the various websites. Often this co-operation is based upon mutual deals that do not involve exchange of money.

Some techniques of co-operative website promotion are:

Banner exchange: a network where participating sites display banner ads in exchange for credits which are converted (using a predetermined exchange rate) into ads to be displayed on other websites.

Button exchange: a network where participating sites display button ads in exchange for credits that are converted (using a predetermined exchange rate) into ads to be displayed on other websites.

Text link exchange: a network where participating sites display text ads in exchange for credits which are converted (using a predetermined exchange rate) into ads to be displayed on other websites.

Web ring is a means for navigating a group of related sites primarily by going forward and backward.

frequency the number of times the average person in the target market is exposed to an advertising message during a given period. See also ADVERTISING.

fulfilment the processing and delivering of orders received from a direct campaign. This is usually contracted out to a third-party *fulfilment house.* It is rare for the producer to act as its own fulfilment house. See also DATABASE MARKETING and DIRECT MARKETING under MARKETING SPECIALIZATIONS.

Gallup, George (1901-1984), Gallup & Robinson. A pioneer in the methods and techniques of public opinion polling and analysis, creator of the Gallup Poll, Gallup was a firm believer in the concept that consumer attitude research had to precede creative work. On leaving Young & Rubicam in 1947 with Claude Robinson, Gallup established his Gallup Poll and 'impact' evaluations as national influences. Gallup started in 1922 as an interviewer for D'Arcy Advertising, St. Louis, and later proposed research approaches in his University of Iowa PhD. thesis. At Northwestern University in 1932, his male-female copy appeal ratings (economy, efficiency, sex, vanity, quality) caught Ray Rubicam's attention and Gallup then joined Y&R. The copy research department he created and ran for 16 years also trained research leaders.

gap analysis a process for identifying gaps in the market and the methods by which those gaps might be closed. It is an integral part of marketing strategy. Gaps in the market tend to be caused by customers not having their needs or expectations met by current market providers and suppliers. Gap analysis proposes that customer perceptions of the quality of a product or service are determined by degree to which they believe it meets their expectations. Gap analysis measures levels of satisfaction, identifies the source of dissatisfaction when it occurs, and then makes recommendations about how to eliminate the gap. Gap analysis often leads to the development of new products or services, or new combinations, designed to meet these unfulfilled needs. See also MARKETING STRATEGY.

gatekeepers individuals who control access to an organization and its decision makers and, consequently, control the flow of information in and out of an organization. Many personal salespeople, for example, initially concentrate upon their target buyers' gatekeepers, who can range from senior management to personal secretaries, as they control direct access to the target buyer and the communications and visitors that he receives. See also BUYING and SELLING.

Gates, Bill (1955–) American computer software executive and founder (in 1975) of Microsoft Corporation, the world's most powerful computer software company. Gates's central early insight was that personal computing would expand enormously and that his future would lie in creating the software to drive these PCs. This insight led to near-total dominance of the PC and operating system software market. His books include *Business @ the Speed of Thought* (1999). Microsoft have also become a major gateway to the Internet. Gates regularly gives away large amounts of his enormous personal fortune to charity, through his $24 billion dollar Bill and Melinda Gates Foundation. (See also Microsoft case study.)

Generation X a term coined by Douglas Coupland to describe the generation born in the 1960s and up to 1980, the post-**baby boom** generation. This group is characterized by its political disengagement (in contrast to their parents' generation of the same age) and their lack of focus on career (in contrast to their parents in mid-life); they exhibit less social trust or confidence in government, have a weaker allegiance to their country or to political parties and are more materialistic than their parents' generation. They are seen as the generation behind the dot.com boom (and bust). They are also the most indebted generation of all, running up huge amounts of personal debt in an age of freer credit and higher consumption. In terms of disposable income they have less available than the baby boom generation. See also BABY BOOMERS.

generics consumer goods that are sold without major investment in their packaging or promotion. They are often referred to as 'no-frills' goods. See also CONSUMER MARKETING under MARKETING SPECIALIZATIONS.

geodemographics the technique of classifying consumer groups by a combination of geographic and demographic variables. This is a popular segmentation technique, particularly for consumer marketers, in the US. It is predicated on the concept that people living in the same district or neighbourhood will have similar lifestyles and buying characteristics. See also CONSUMER MARKETING under MARKETING SPECIALIZATIONS.

Geodemographics databases have been created in recent times but, in that time, they have matured and become more sophisticated in their applications. Some database applications are used for market research and product sampling, new retail outlet location, direct mail campaigns and overall marketing planning, particularly for consumer marketing.

Geodemographics have their limitations: it is not always the case that people living in the same location have the same lifestyles or buying tendencies. Often the information on the databases is outdated after the two or three or three years and is not constantly refreshed; the information is not in-depth enough to form more sophisticated profiles.

Geodemographic databases can link together data from the national census with other information, for example for credit ratings or investor registers, to enable identification of different types of households. Using cluster analysis, the geography can be broken down into neighbourhoods of around 150 households. The basic assumption is that two people living in the same neighbourhoods are more likely to be similar than two people chosen at random. In the UK there are programs such as **ACORN** (A Classification of Residential Neighbourhoods) that divides up the entire UK population in terms of the type of housing in which they live. For each of these areas, a wide range of demographic information is generated. The system allows assessment of product usage patterns, dependent upon the research conducted within national surveys. There are 54 separate groupings including for example:

(i) wealthy suburbs, large detached houses;

(ii) private flats, elderly people;

(iii) gentrified multi-ethnic areas;

(iv) rural areas, mixed occupations;

(v) council areas, residents with health problems etc.

These geodemographic categories are also classified and segmented as: Thriving, Expanding, Rising, Settling, Aspiring and Striving. See also MARKET RESEARCH.

Another database is CCN's **MOSAIC**. This has started to build classifications within Europe. This system also analyses information from various sources including the census, which is used to give housing, socio-economic, household and age data; the electoral roll, to give household composition and population movement data; postcode address files to give information on post-1991 housing and special address types such as farms and flats, as well as credit search information and bad debt risk.

Another is **PINPOINT**. Pinpoint Identified Neighbourhoods utilizes information from disparate sources and overlays this with Ordnance Survey data to target individual.

FiNPiN. Financial PIN, uses data not only from census, but data from the Financial Research Survey which comprises 30,000 respondents. It was intended to segment the financial services buyers' market. Information concentrates upon details of financial holdings and usage patterns, so that FiNPiN neighbourhoods are able to describe financial activity as well as demographics. Data sources include: the number of company directors, the level and value of share ownership, the demand for various types of financial service, such as household insurance, home ownership, mortgage holding, and county court judgements.

globalization a trend that has been revolutionizing the practice of marketing since the mid-1980s. Technological and economic forces that reduce the costs and mobility of products, services, people, knowledge and money across geographical borders drive globalization. However, world markets have not been entirely globalized and some economists argue that the world trading system was more openly globalized in the late 19th century than at any other time. There are some barriers to globalization (both tariff and non-tariff) which are increasingly exercised by regional trading blocs such as NAFTA, the EU and ASEAN rather than individual nation states which are no longer powerful enough to resist globalization.

Since the 1990s marketing agencies and marketing teams within large companies have stressed the global nature of their marketing programmes and capabilities. In one dimension, global marketing is the next evolutionary stage and extension of international marketing: thinking of, and treating, the world as a single market rather than as confederations of separate national markets. This has proved less difficult for products and brands than it has for services. There has been a consequent rise in placing production facilities in low-cost countries but making distribution global; the trend has also been accelerated by the globalization of capital markets and investment, the increased numbers of cross-border mergers, acquisitions, joint ventures, licensing agreements, the global superhighways, deregulation of industries, reduction of trade barriers, digitization and a marketing and executive management cadre that thinks and acts increasingly globally.

Concurrently, there has been the rise of global brands. This has been led by consumer goods such as Coca-Cola, McDonalds and Kodak film. Increasingly, branding has become the most visible global marketing programme, whilst other aspects of marketing remain stubbornly local. There has been a globalization of certain media broadcasting channels, such as CNN and the BBC, but print media remains at best regional. Most of the top titles (e.g. *The Financial Times*, *The Wall Street Journal*, *The Economist*, and *The New York Times*) have developed excellent websites which give them greater global reach access than their print titles. Within companies, there has developed a huge tension between globalization and localization. Most companies still struggle at being global within their internal organization. There is a constant reversion to multi-domestic approaches. An international company is primarily focused on exporting to foreign countries something that has been successful in their domestic market; a multinational company attempts to attack the market in each country with the same intensity, usually creating an infrastructure in each country to do so; a global company treats the world as a single market, irrespective of geographical boundaries and focuses on the trends and markets that are global. See also MARKETING and INTERNATIONAL MARKETING under MARKETING SPECIALIZATIONS.

group think a tendency for groups to reach consensus at any cost, thereby filtering out any views that might conflict with the prevailing consensus. This is seen an inimical to innovative or radical thinking. Group thinking is deadly in a marketing environment.

guarantee (or **warranty** in the US) an assurance, written or implied, that a product is as represented and will perform satisfactorily. This is mandatory for product sales. Guarantees are necessary for the marketing of consumer durables. Some manufacturers have created a profitable secondary revenue stream by offering EXTENDED GUARANTEES.

habit buying the repetitious purchase of the same brand without question, showing a high degree of brand loyalty. See BUYING, BRAND, CONSUMER MARKETING under MARKETING SPECIALIZATIONS.

hard sell anything that is interpreted by the customer as aggressive or undue sales pressure to force them to buy. This type of selling was characteristic of the production era but is gradually eroding in face of consumer distaste for it. The dividing line between hard selling and misleading selling can often be very narrow. Whilst hard-selling salesmen were often lauded and promoted by product and commodity companies, they are now discouraged, with most market-driven companies now preferring an more sophisticated approach based upon satisfying customer needs rather than trying to shift product. See also SALES.

harvesting the last stage of the product life cycle, when marketing and promotional support is effectively withdrawn from the product and it is 'harvested' for profits prior to full withdrawal from the market. See also PRODUCT LIFE CYCLE and BOSTON CONSULTING GROUP MATRIX.

heavy user the segment of the market where the main concentrations of product sales are made.

Herbert, Ira C. 'Ike' (1927-1995) Coca-Cola. Initially a brilliant account supervisor with McCann-Erickson on the Coca-Cola account, Herbert was recruited to Coca-Cola in 1965. During his 27-year career there, he served as brand manager, marketing director, president of Coca-Cola Foods, president of North America soft-drinks operations and president of Coca-Cola USA. Herbert played key roles in the launching of 'Things go better with Coke,' the brand's first global campaign; the follow-up classic, 'It's the real thing'; and the widely honoured offshoot spot, 'I'd like to teach the world to sing.' Herbert, who retired in 1991 as Coca-Cola's deputy to the president, started his career in 1951 at Chicago's MacFarland Aveyard and was at Edward H. Weiss & Co. from 1956-63.

hierarchy of effects a communications model developed by Lavidge and Steiner and published in 1961 as 'A Model for Predictive Measurements of Advertising Effectiveness' in the *Journal of Marketing*. This model builds on earlier work such as the AIDA and DAGMAR models and describes the stages that a customer passes through, from awareness to purchase. Lavidge and Steiner suggested that advertising effectiveness should be measured in terms of progression through the hierarchy rather than just on its ability to cause purchasing action in the consumer. Additionally, the new model of the hierarchy took into account theories and models from the field of psychology that attempted to describe learning itself as a process. These stages are broadly described as: *cognitive*, in which the customer becomes aware of the product and gathers knowledge about it, *affective*, where the customer starts to react emotionally with the product or service, *conviction*, where the customer develops a preference for the product, and *conative*, where the customer finally purchases the product. Lavidge and Steiner divided each category into two corresponding mini-stages and presented a model of the hierarchy with the following ordered phases:

Awareness, Knowledge, Liking, Preference, Conviction, and Purchase

The developed model required the consumer to pass through all six of the stages, in the given order, before reaching the final stage (action). They did, however, address some possible criticism of sequential models by stating that stages are not necessarily equidistant, that it is possible to move up several steps simultaneously, and the greater the psychological and economic commitment, the longer it takes to move upward on the hierarchy.

Hierarchy of Effects Model

Lavidge & Steiner's
Hierarchy of Effects Model

- Awareness (think)
- Knowledge (think)
- Liking (feel)
- Preference (feel)
- Conviction (do)
- Purchase (do)

Reproduced courtesy of marketingteacher.com

See also ADOPTION, ADVERTISING, AIDA. DAGMAR, THREE ORDERS MODEL, MARKETING COMMUNICATIONS and CONSUMER MARKETING.

hierarchy of needs a hierarchical view of human need developed by Abraham Maslow, often used as the start point or background to understanding basic consumer motivation. In this model, only a few people get to satisfy their higher level needs. The most basic need is to fulfil survival necessities such as food, air, water, and heat. Once a level of safety and survival has been attained, we need to fulfil our social needs: to belong to a community, to marry, or join groups of friends and like-minded associates. The final two levels are esteem and self-actualization. Fewer people satisfy the higher level needs. Esteem means that you achieve something that makes you recognized within and even beyond your community and gives personal satisfaction. Few achieve self-actualization, regarded as the highest need of all. Although a venerable model for generations of psychology and marketing students alike, Maslow's hierarchy is now seen to be overly simplistic for marketing analysis.

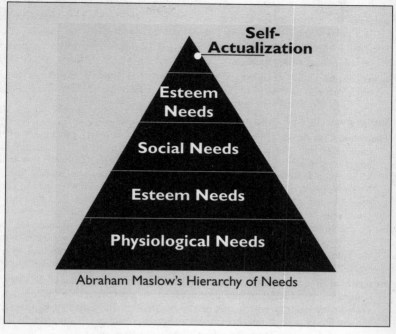

high involvement products those which consumers deliberate for a long time about. They tend to be expensive products that directly affect their image or lifestyles, such as houses, cars, holidays, major household improvements. See also CONSUMER MARKETING under MARKETING SPECIALIZATIONS, PRODUCTS and BUYERS.

high street a UK term that means the concentration of shopping outlets in the centre of a town, suburb or city. High-street retailing has come under greater pressure as more and more major shopping centres move outside of the city where they can have a larger scale display of goods, wider choice and better parking facilities. It also remains to be seen if on-line and teleshopping can displace the physical shopping habits of the majority of consumers. See also RETAILING, DEPARTMENT STORE.

hire purchase a type of customer credit in which the customer effectively 'hires' the product for a given period of time, making stage payments that are divisions of the overall retail price. With the final payment the 'hired' product becomes a 'purchased' product and is owned by the customer. The extension of hire purchase terms to a mass of consumers from the 1950s onward was a massive boost to consumerism and to market development. See also CONSUMERISM, CONSUMER MARKETING under MARKETING SPECIALIZATIONS, CREDIT.

hit a request of a file from a web server. In on-line marketing, the term is often mistakenly used to mean unique visitors, visits, page views, or all of these. It is often used as a measure of attractiveness of a website or its content.

hit rate the rate at which sales calls are converted into actual sales, expressed as a percentage ratio. See also TELE-MARKETING and SALES.

hoarding another word for BILLBOARD. This is one of the oldest and most popular marketing channels.

home audit a type of MARKET RESEARCH conducted in the respondents' home, office or premises, so as to determine the extent of purchase and ownership of certain products and brands.

home page the first or main page of a website.

Hopkins, Claude C. (1866-1932) Lord & Thomas. An early proponent of the viewpoint that the main purpose of advertising is to sell something, his hugely successful copy (notably his Schlitz beer slogan, 'The beer that made Milwaukee famous') led Lord & Thomas' Albert Lasker to recruit him. In 1907, Hopkins insisted copywriters acquire detailed knowledge of client products and produce brief, dry, rational copy. He also promoted couponing, premiums, free samples, mail order and copy testing, which were innovations at the time. For Pepsodent toothpaste, he 'discovered' plaque; he then invested in the company and made another fortune. His classic work, *Scientific Advertising*, was published in 1923, after he retired from L&T, where he had served as president and chairman. See also ADVERTISING and BRANDING.

horizontal integration the acquisition of competitors in the same industry, or companies producing similar products in the same industries (in contrast to vertical integration which means the acquisition of suppliers in the same industry). At some point, horizontal integration brings the attention of those public bodies that regulate competition in a market.

horizontal marketing system a negotiated arrangement in which two or more companies in the same channel join together to follow a new marketing opportunity. See also MARKETING.

house ad a self-promotional ad that a company runs on its media outlets with the objective of putting unsold inventory to use. Many ad spaces are relatively fixed, and house ads are often the logical solution to fill the space. House ads are often used to promote new features, other in-house revenue generators, and other media properties. See also ADVERTISING.

household all of the people who live in the same house, the fundamental unit of consumer market research. In marketing the term is often used to measure the greater parts of goods that are bought more for consumption by a household than for an individual within that household. See also CONSUMER MARKETING under MARKETING SPECIALIZATIONS.

HTML (Hypertext Markup Language) a coding language for web-based text. The World Wide Web Consortium governs HTML language and standards. HTML was crucial to the commercialization of the Internet in the period after 1994. This language made the Internet user-friendly for a mass audience.

HTML banner a banner ad using HTML elements, often including interactive forms instead of (or in addition to) standard graphical elements. They are often used for pull-down menus and search boxes, allowing interaction before the visitor even reaches the destination site. This interactivity often results in higher response rates than purely graphical banners.

HTML e-mail e-mail that is formatted using Hypertext Markup Language, as opposed to plain text e-mail.

hybrid model a combination of two or more on-line marketing payment models. A hybrid campaign might be a mix of impression-based (CPM) and performance-based (CPC or CPA), or a mix of two performance-based models. Hybrid deals are sometimes seen as a way to split the risk between publishers and advertisers. Advertising campaigns sometimes bundle CPM and CPC in a hybrid buy, and sometimes even CPA. Affiliate programmes have been known to offer a few cents per-click in addition to paying for a sale, lead, download, or other conversion activity. See also ADVERTISING.

image the way in which the customer or public perceives a company, product, service, individual or brand. It is the place that they occupy in the mind of the target audience. Image can be communicated through a number of marketing tools, including public relations, sponsorships, advertising, web marketing, the performance of products, the performance of customer service, the behaviour and culture of staff, and the 'history' of a company. While much work has been done on the development and management of image overall, it is, however, essentially in the mind of the beholder. Image, therefore, should not be confused with identity or brand that are within the power of the individual or company to change and reposition. Image which leads to a powerful and sustainable reputation is indispensable in services marketing. See also ADVERTISING, BRAND.

impact an estimate of the number of exposures to advertising. See also ADVERTISING.

import substitution an approach adopted by developing countries whereby local production facilities are set up to avoid imports that can lead to inflation. As a means of ensuring development and growth it has been a less successful technique than export-led growth. Import substitution characterizes many third world economies. Local producers may not be large enough to produce efficiently, and are not subject to competitive discipline. See also EXPORTING.

impulse buying the decision to buy goods without much deliberation or research. These tend to be low-cost consumer goods that are used regularly. Many supermarkets surround their point of sale with impulse purchase goods that catch the customer's attention whilst queuing. This contrasts with HIGH INVOLVEMENT PURCHASES. See also PRODUCT, BUYING, CONSUMER MARKETING under MARKETING SPECIALIZATIONS.

impression is a single instance of an on-line advertisement being displayed.

inbound communications are responses from potential buyers following a direct solicitation through advertising in various media, telephone, e-mail or direct mail. The number of these inbound communications is often used as a measure of the success of the overall communications campaign. See CONSUMER MARKETING under MARKETING SPECIALIZATIONS, DIRECT MARKETING under MARKETING SPECIALIZATIONS, DATABASE MARKETING, and ADVERTISING. See also COMMUNICATIONS.

inbound link a link into a website from another.

incentives techniques that encourage consumers to buy more, including price discounts, special offers, coupons, free samples etc. They can also refer to compensation plans for salespeople, management and distributors to achieve higher sales goals. See also SALES.

incentivized traffic visitors who have received some form of compensation for visiting a website. The danger of incentivized traffic is when third-party promoters compensate people for visiting a website without disclosing that information to the visitor. Incentivized traffic is widely regarded as of a much lower quality than unincentivized traffic. Incentivized visitors typically do only what is necessary to gain the incentive and nothing more. Incentives may come in the form of cash, points, or other benefits such as software. While incentivized clicks/traffic is the most notable incentive-based action, other forms exist such as incentivized registrations. See also INTERACTIVE MARKETING.

indirect communications types of communications that are not personal, face-to-face and direct, such as mass media advertising, radio, newspapers, sales promotion or packaging. See also MARKETING COMMUNICATIONS.

inertia selling a form of selling in which unsolicited goods are sent to potential customers on a sale-or-return basis, without their prior consent or knowledge. This method is especially prevalent with book, record, and video clubs or, often, insurance products. Usually, following a 'special offer' the customer agrees to buy at least four products (typically books or CDs) a year from a wide range of choice that will be offered each month. Each month the customer receives a recommended choice from a selection. In the event that he or she does nothing (i.e. does not inform the company that the recommended choice is not wanted) then the product is sent and assumed to be sold, unless returned within a defined time period at the customer's expense. Certain types of inertia selling have been prohibited in the European Union. Also known as **negative option selling**.

influencers those who influence, but do not make, the final purchase in an organization or a family. Influencers can also be those people in a buying system in a large company who have major influence over the buying group. See also BUYING, CONSUMER MARKETING and INDUSTRIAL MARKETING under MARKETING SPECIALIZATIONS.

infomercial a television commercial, typically presented in a casual talk show format, that is designed to look like an ordinary programme but is actually a strong promotion of a product or service. Infomercials must carry a labelling identifying them as paid advertising. See also ADVERTORIAL, ADVERTISING, MEDIA.

innovation the process through which new products, concepts, services, methods, or techniques are developed. Innovation, particularly technological innovation, can cause 'discontinuities' in a market that may lead the market to be radically different from one responding to a classic product life cycle. The major variables with innovations are the speed and scale of their adoption in the marketplace. (See also ADOPTION.) The graph below shows the various levels of penetration of the marketplace by discontinuous innovations throughout the 20th century and how long it took them to be adopted. The rate of early adoption of, say, the Internet was much faster than with electricity or the telephone, but had much more market to penetrate to catch up with these innovations.

Comparison of Various Technology Adoption

The diffusion of innovations in communications and media has been much more accelerated than of those that drove the industrial economy of the 20th century. For example, it took almost 50 years for electricity to be widely used in households and factories; it took 40 years for radio to gain 50 million listeners; television took 15 years to reach 50 million viewers. In contrast, the Internet reached 50 million users in four years once it had been opened to the general public (1994). The population connected to the Internet has grown from 40 million in 1996 to a current estimated 300 million worldwide and now rivals the population of all but the largest nations. Usage of the Internet has been doubling every 100 days. If current growth of 'Internet Population' continues, there will be 1 billion people connected to the Internet by 2005. The other interactive network – the global telephone network – is also growing. Usage has grown from 4 billion minutes in 1975 to 100 billion minutes in 2001. Communications costs are collapsing; a transatlantic telephone call now costs 1.5% of what it would have cost 60 years ago. This trend, combined with increasing computing power available for lower prices, is a powerful dynamic. Personalization of communications is another important trend: there are more than 200 digital mobile communications networks, operating in 100 countries, with over 55 million users. As well as the Internet and the global fixed and mobile communications networks, there are now a plethora of satellite-based systems impacting the global communications market. Broadband multi-media services delivered by satellite are expected to reach 16% (50 million) of total users by 2010.

Companies must be able to change rapidly in order to benefit from these innovations. It also necessary for marketers both to respond and to be alert to such changes and, if possible, to anticipate them. Responding to innovations should be a key part of all good market strategy. Technological innovation has caused greater speed in new product introduction and substantially shortened their life cycles. See also ADOPTION.

insert a detailed promotional copy or material inserted into a newspaper, magazine or journal. See also ADVERTISING.

instalments a credit arrangement in which the seller allows the buyer to pay for goods in instalments over an agreed period of time, either with or without interest payments. Instalment-based payments fuel consumer demand by making it easier for consumers to buy more. See also CONSUMERISM, HIRE PURCHASE and CREDIT.

integrated marketing see MARKETING SPECIALIZATIONS.

intentions particularly buying intentions, can be both extrapolated by an intentions life cycle study (that people buy different things at different times in their lives) and also by direct market research in which respondents are asked about their intention to buy something and the timing of that intention. For example, at different stages of the life cycle consumers buy different financial products: at the earliest stage, children may have a personal savings account and perhaps a simple checking account; students start to have credit cards and various loan products; young adults start to buy mortgages, insurance pensions; adults at the peak of their earning power will buy investment products, bonds, stocks and shares as well as more advanced insurance and additional pensions; older people buy annuities and short term investment products that return cash, as well as medical insurance etc. Marketing to consumers can increasingly be focused on different intention stages. See also BUYING and CONSUMER MARKETING under MARKETING SPECIALIZATIONS.

interactive agency one typically offering Internet technology consulting, on-line advertising, interactive marketing, and e-business consulting. Interactive agencies rose to prominence during the first wave of the commercial Internet, which has become known as the dot.com boom. Initially they exploited the slowness of traditional marketing and advertising agencies to harness the marketing potential of the Internet. Most companies and businesses as well as institutions now have their own websites. Later, the traditional agencies absorbed interactive marketing into their own portfolio of services. This, combined with the e-commerce market crash, led to the demise of many of the pioneering agencies. See also ADVERTISING.

interactive marketing see MARKETING SPECIALIZATIONS.

interactive television an advance on pre-programmed broadcast and cable television. It moves television from being a passive experience to an active one, in which the broadcaster and the audience can interact in ways that were not possible before. Interactive television is two-way rather than one-way: it enables Internet access via a television receiver, on-line television shopping, the ability to pause live television shows, sending and receiving e-mail, instant messaging, ordering videos on demand, playing video games on-line, conducting webcasts, video chats, participation in chat lines and also normal telephone calls. Currently this is delivered over cable and satellite via a set-top box, but the technology is in its very early stages. TV penetration is far greater worldwide than that of PCs; thus there is some possibility that the television could acquire all the functions of a PC, whilst remaining more familiar to the bulk of the population. Television will become a major interactive marketing channel rather than just a medium to broadcast advertising and entertainment.

interest an indicator of the potential customer's disposition towards the product or service. It is a prerequisite stage prior to eventual purchase. Without interest there is little possibility of advancing the purchasing cycle.

internal audit is part of the MARKETING AUDIT and examines the internal strengths and weaknesses of an organization. This is linked closely to the identification of the organization's principal competencies. See also MARKETING PLANNING.

internal marketing see MARKETING SPECIALIZATIONS.

international marketing see MARKETING SPECIALIZATIONS.

INTERNET, AND ITS IMPACT ON MARKETING

Internet the network of networks, linking by protocol component networks that are two-way, interactive, point-to-point, and electronically enabled. Often referred to as the Information Superhighway, the Internet was initially developed as ARPANET in the 1970s as a technique for maintaining communications networks in the event of a nuclear attack on the US. It is underpinned by a technique called *packet switching* that enables data to be broken up, distributed down multiple networks and reassembled in a single place. The Internet was made available first to high-ranking academics and then to educational establishments. With the development of the World Wide Web and easy-to-use browser technology the Internet was fully commercialized in the mid-1990s. Since then its growth has been explosive across the world. It continues to develop today and it has had a dramatic impact on marketing and commerce.

The World Wide Web and the Internet brought many benefits that are in the process of extending the marketing and communications technique. It has enabled marketing, previously dominated by the technique of 'pushing messages and products at customers', to become much more interactive with target customers, as the Internet provides instantaneous and high-speed interactivity. Additionally, customers have greater choice and greater control over how they engage and interact with sellers and merchants. Beyond that, it enables marketers to customize products, messages and services to small audiences of common interest, and, usually, with the complicity and permission of the customer. The Internet also enables a much lower cost marketing channel to sell directly to customers, often allowing the complete elimination of expensive channels. Smaller enterprises have benefited, because the Internet gives them global reach and wide search facilities at much lower cost than traditional international marketing. Marketers can have instant dialogue with each other and their customers. They have a whole new range of communications media: webcasting, multi-directional e-mail communications, websites. There are also new channels that combine with older ones through which to market to customers: Interactive TV, on-line shopping. wider database access and search facilities have also improved market research techniques and speed of intelligence gathering.

The Internet has also brought a whole new, but radically different, dimension for marketing's most classic discipline: advertising. The target audience is younger on the Internet (it was becoming difficult to appeal to the 15-30 group through traditional advertising). Advertising can be tailored to each site, and can be quickly changed and updated without major cost. Information transmission and follow-up from adverts to customers can be instantaneous. Advertisers can give away clever screensavers to promote their brand. Advertising can be better linked to an entertainment experience and it can run globally around the world clock.

Another two derivatives of the Internet (which is public) that have impacted marketing are: extranets and intranets. An **extranet** is a company's secure site that can be accessed with a password and which can be used by third parties, often for commercial transactions. The extranet provides a link with the company customers, partners and suppliers and enables a 'community of interest' to be formed. An **intranet** belongs to an organization, and is designed to be accessible only by the organization's members, employees, or others with authorization. An intranet's website looks and acts just like other websites, but has a firewall surrounding it to fend off unauthorized users. Intranets are used to share information. Secure intranets are much less expensive to build and manage than private, proprietary-standard networks. The development of intranets within companies has brought many new dimensions to internal communications. See also INTERACTIVE MARKETING, WORLD WIDE WEB.

interview see MARKET RESEARCH.

investor relations a part of the public relations function dealing specifically with communications to the financial community, particularly equity analysts, researchers and investors. It is a form of marketing that seeks to influence those investors to recommend or buy the stock of a company and to comment favourably on it to other potential investors. See also PUBLIC RELATIONS.

invisible trade the exporting and importing of services, as distinct from physically visible goods. This is increasingly important as greater percentages of the world's gross national products come from trade in services. In the advanced economies, services now constitute a greater part of the total economy than manufactured goods. Consequently, in the past decade the marketing of services has also gained in strength and sophistication. See also EXPORTING, INTERNATIONAL MARKETING under MARKETING SPECIALIZATIONS.

invisible Web the portion of the Web not accessible through Web search engines.

issue life the total amount of time that a publication may be looked at, which often goes beyond the next edition. See also MEDIA.

Javascript a scripting language developed by Netscape used to create interactive websites, which are an important tool in overall marketing and image development.

jingle a short and memorable piece of music or song that accompanies an advert. Jingles began life in radio advertising and in the earlier days of television. Jingles are now considered too old-fashioned for broadcast advertising and have been largely replaced by full songs and scores. They continue to be popular for short adverts (for example Direct Line's 'car horn') and radio advertising.

Jobs, Steve (1955–) Apple Computer. A pioneer of consumer technology marketing, particularly the personal computer, Jobs was a co-founder of the legendary Apple Computer in 1976. Apple started as an innovative company with a central idea: that they would make PCs accessible to all, to improve creativity and productivity. Jobs, from the outset, understood marketing's role and, with Chiat/Day, created the seminal 1984 ad and promoted the idea of Apple as a cool and casual company for the new generation, fixing the image of Silicon Valley. Following disputes over the future direction of Apple, Jobs left in 1985 to create new companies, including the successful Pixar Animation Studios. Jobs returned to a failing Apple in 1996 and directed a turnaround marketing effort that led to the advanced design and ergonomic new iMac computer. He employed advertising heavily (again via Chiat/Day), to project Apple's spirit, with the new campaign 'Think different'.

junk mail unsolicited promotional and advertising material that is received through normal physical postal services. See also E-MAIL SPAM, E-MAIL MARKETING and DIRECT MARKETING under MARKETING SPECIALIZATIONS.

juxtaposition is an advertising term, when competitors' posters deliberately appear next to one another. See also ADVERTISING.

key account one of the more important customers to a supplier, usually meriting a dedicated key account manager to ensure customer satisfaction. There is a range of reasons as to what makes an account 'key', the main one being the volume of revenues generated by the account. Certain companies offer preferential terms to their key accounts and dedicate entire service teams directly to them.

key code a code that is placed on direct mail shots so that responses can be analysed quickly. See also DIRECT MARKETING under MARKETING SPECIALIZATIONS.

keyword a word used in a performing an Internet search.

keyword density the number of keywords expressed as a percentage of indexable text words.

keyword marketing an on-line technique of putting the desired message in front of people who are searching using particular keywords and key phrases. The advantage of keyword marketing is the potential to reach the right people at the right time.

keyword research the search for keywords related to your website, and the analysis of which ones yield the highest return on investment. See also INTERNET.

knocking copy anything that attacks a competitor overtly whether in the press, in advertising or in company literature. See also COMPARATIVE ADVERTISING under ADVERTISING TERMINOLOGY and COMPETITION.

Kotler, Philip (1931–) one of the foremost thinkers on the profession and the techniques of marketing in the modern age. A professor of marketing at the Kellog Graduate School of Management, Northwestern University, his many books include the much-referred-to *Marketing Management: Analysis, Planning, Implementation, and Control*. Kotler's works have also charted the inexorable march of marketing into not-for-profit organizations as well as in the more traditional commercial sector.

Kroc, Ray (1902–1984) McDonalds Corp. A consumer marketing genius who fundamentally altered the eating habits of America and the world as the brain behind the expansion of McDonalds. The company became a global icon of fast food consumerism and a quintessentially American approach to eating. He successfully promoted, advertised and championed the McDonalds winning formula of quality, value, cleanliness and convenience within a global branded franchise. A former salesman of milk-shake mixers, Kroc was so impressed in 1954 by the original McDonalds in San Bernardino, California that he made a franchise deal. By 1961, when he bought out the McDonald brothers, he was operating hundreds of McDonalds retail franchises. Kroc instituted food preparations, service, teamwork, standardized menus and franchisee training schools. He also targeted the expanding U.S. suburban market, employed teens and seniors, offered popular premiums, founded Ronald McDonald House and remained committed to heavy advertising and promotional support of the McDonalds brand.

Krone, Helmut (1925–1997) Creative Director, Doyle Dane Bernbach Agency. An outstanding art director, he was also involved in the legendary Volkswagen campaign. Krone pursued perfection in all his work. He introduced a new minimalist approach that revolutionized advertising's look and appeal. See also ADVERTISING (Volkswagen campaign).

label a visible composition of all written, printed or graphic display on the container or box around an article. A label is usually composed of principal and secondary display panels – those most likely to be seen by the consumer in a retail outlet. It will have the identity of the product and will also include a description of contents, such as weights, composition and ingredients. Additional information will include the name of manufacturer and place of manufacture. Good labelling is often taken for granted but is a hugely important part of marketing.

launch the introduction of something new into the marketplace. Launches are the staple of new campaigns and can involve new products and services, concepts, public relations stunts, promotional materials and advertising campaigns. See also MARKETING COMMUNICATIONS and ADVERTISING.

Lawrence, Mary Wells (1928–) Wells, Rich, Greene. The first woman in advertising to attain superstar status. She also became the world's highest-paid female executive. Born in Ohio, Mary Wells Lawrence generated Hollywood-scale media buzz for years. Her glamour, lifestyle, taste and advertising legend status stemmed from her achievements during the 1960s and 1970s at McCann-Erickson, Doyle Dane Bernbach and Interpublic's Jack Tinker & Partners. Her TV breakthroughs for Alka-Seltzer and Braniff Airways led to the April 1966 creation of Wells, Rich, Greene. Mary Wells Lawrence took WRG public and added to their portfolio with the highly successful 'I love New York' and Benson & Hedges 100s cigarette campaigns.

layout the draft of a finished advert. See also ADVERTISING.

lead time the time between the concept and the completion of an advertisement. See also ADVERTISING.

leapfrogging the practice of overtaking competition through bypassing a whole generation of technology developments and 'leapfrogging' to the next stage. For example, it is often suggested that developing economies such as China and Eastern Europe will 'leapfrog' past a whole generation of fixed line communications and go straight for the more advanced mobile communications, thereby avoiding the cost of laying millions of miles of communications cable and supporting infrastructure. Other successful examples of technological leapfrogging are the development of semiconductor industry in South Korea, consumer electronics and photography in Japan, Dutch micro-lithography, and the technological development of missiles and artificial satellites in China. In its 10th Five-Year Plan for National Economic and Social Development (2001-2005), the Chinese central authority announced that China would adopt a leapfrogging tactic for its technological development.

leasing the acquisition of fixed assets without incurring capital expenditure. Leasing is a popular method of obtaining large capital goods items such as ships and aeroplanes, and among consumers increasing numbers of cars are bought through leasing arrangements.

licensing a commercial contract whereby the licensor gives something of value to the licensee in exchange for certain performances and payments. It may involve the transfer of intellectual property, designs, rights to produce a patented product or use a patented production process, manufacturing processes or expertise, technical assistance including the supply of essential materials, components, industrial plant and machinery, marketing or commercial assistance, rights to use a trademark or brand. Typically, the owner of the product or intellectual property (the licensor) permits the a licensee in a foreign country to make use of the intellectual property or technology in exchange for access to the local market and a share of the profits from sales. Often the licensee will set up production facilities in the market and sell the product locally; the licensor may or may not give exclusive rights to the licensee, and will receive a royalty payment for sales over a defined time period. Often the licensor will provide training and support for the licensee. This is a frequently used method of technology transfer from wealthy countries to less advanced countries. There are several types of licence agreement, such as the joint venture or the **franchise**. Licensing is also a tried and tested, relatively low-risk, way of entering foreign markets.

There are many mutual advantages in licensing. For the licensor the most tried and tested reason is that it is a relatively low-risk, low-cost, fairly fast and uncomplicated way of entering foreign markets that may otherwise be either closed or very difficult to enter. It is a ready-made set of technologies, products or know-how for the licensor. There may be a government commitment to a certain market that facilitates the transfer of technology, particularly military technology. There may be a need to find a new market for a product that is declining in a more advanced market. New products can be introduced to many countries quickly because of low investment requirements. It can provide all the usual benefits of overseas production without major investment. It can be a source of competitive advantage, giving the licensor greater market access and return on investment.

There are disadvantages, however. Licensing usually does not generate high revenues from royalty payments. There is some risk that the licensee may eventually become the licensor's competitor in the foreign market. The licensee may not have the sales and distribution capability to fully exploit the product. There are potential risks that the product quality may deteriorate if the licensee has lower quality control standards. There could be government restrictions or conditions on payment of royalties to the licensor or on the supply of components. Policing and controlling a license agreement is notoriously difficult no matter how well the original contract is specified. See also INTERNATIONAL MARKETING under MARKETING SPECIALIZATIONS, COMPETITIVE ADVANTAGE and EXPORTING.

life cycles see PRODUCT LIFE CYCLE and FAMILY LIFE CYCLE.

lifestyle the consumer's pattern and mode of living that is reflected in their consumer behaviour. It is manifest in the consumers' homes, interests, tastes, leisure pursuits, opinions and use of time at home, at work, at play, on holiday and in pastimes, hobbies and sports. See also GEODEMOGRAPHICS, CONSUMER MARKETING under MARKETING SPECIALIZATIONS.

line extension the practice of extending a successful brand to other closely related products or services. For example, Nike's brand has recently been extended to golf clubs and golf balls. Virgin's brand was extended to mobile telephone services and trains. Nivea hand lotion was extended to suntan lotion, etc. See also BRAND.

line filling the practice of filling the entire range out with products to ensure that there are no gaps in the market left for the competitors to fill. Many computer companies have attempted to line-fill their entire range from PC to supercomputers. Microsoft is continuously developing its line of software for new platforms, such as personal digital assistants and television set-top boxes, as well as every type of server and PC. See also PRODUCT.

linking strategy a method of connecting various websites. It exploits one of the Web's fundamental strengths, that is the ability for any public document to connect to any other public document. For example, deep linking (linking to a web page other than a site's home page) has started to cause some controversies in recent times as the Web has become more commercialized. Proponents of deep linking contend that the ability to link freely is central to the philosophy behind the public Internet. However, the legality of deep linking has been called into question in several lawsuits involving well-known corporations. Opponents of deep links, typically large corporations, argue that deep linking unfairly eliminates the ability of the home page to contribute to brand building and advertising functions.

Other forms of link are: inbound link, which is a link from a site outside of a site, outbound link, which is a link to a site outside of a site, and reciprocal links, which are outbound links exchanged for inbound links. See also INTERNET MARKETING.

link popularity a measure of the quantity and quality of sites that link to your site.

linkrot the disappearance of Web pages previously accessible at a particular URL, caused by movement or deletion of the pages.

link text the text contained in (and sometimes near) a hyperlink.

list broker an aggregator who collates and sells names and addresses for direct mailing purposes to other companies. This has now expanded from just household addresses to also include e-mail addresses. See also DIRECT MARKETING and E-MAIL MARKETING under MARKETING SPECIALIZATIONS.

list price the price at which it is suggested that an item should be sold to the end-buyer or consumer. Also known as the **Manufacturer's Suggested Retail Price** (MSRP). The list price acts as a baseline from which various sales and discount promotions can be measured (x % off list price, for example).

localization for marketers this can have two meanings. First, it can mean the process by which globally launched campaigns, products and services can be customized and made relevant to the local market. In some cases this could be as simple as translation into the local language; otherwise it could mean a complete redesign of the global product or service to meet the needs and customs of the local market. Secondly, it can mean marketing exclusively to local markets, with in-depth knowledge of the local market's demographics, tastes, wants and needs. This latter type of marketing often acts as a counterpoint to the globalizing trends in marketing that have been dominant in the past 20 years. Most global companies are now more highly sensitized to localization than they used to be. An example is CNN, a global broadcasting network that has also started to develop local language news reporting.

log file a file that records the activity on a Web server.

logo (see also BRAND and TRADEMARK) a sign, a letter, or a symbol, or a combination of all of these, that represents and illustrates a company's approved trademark. A logo is often a trigger of memory for the company's total brand.

long domain name a domain name that is longer than the original 26 characters, up to a theoretical limit of 67 characters (including the extension, such as .com).

loss leader a product which is sold for very little profit or a negative profit in the hopes of improving business and leading to the sale of more expensive products which would more than make up for the negative product sale. This pricing strategy is used to bring people into retail stores and can also help to clear out items that are not selling well. It works well for retailers who are selling items which are not unique and where there is little brand or store loyalty, such as consumer electronics or domestic appliances. In many instances, consumers are searching for the best price. If the price that a retailer pays for a stereo is £200, the retailer will want to make a profit while covering overhead expenses, and so the retail price would be £ 250. One store may advertise the stereo for £200 or even less to draw in customers. Once customers are in the store, salespeople would try to point them to higher-priced stereos or sell them accessories or other items to make up for the low cost of the stereo. See also CONSUMER MARKETING under MARKETING SPECIALIZATIONS and PRICING.

low-involvement product in contrast to a HIGH-INVOLVMENT PRODUCT, a product which does not demand any research, deliberation or thought in selection and purchase. It also carries little risk if the wrong purchasing decision is made, as these are usually low-cost and consumable items. See also IMPULSE BUYING.

loyalty faithfulness to a brand or company and the making of repeat purchases. See also BRAND LOYALTY.

loyalty card a card used by the consumer to gain loyalty points that can be used for a variety of purchases, usually controlled by the supplier. Loyalty cards have become a prerequisite of both retailing and services marketing. Most major food retailers or airlines have some sort of loyalty card scheme to encourage repeat purchase and to retain customer loyalty.

loyalty points points earned by a purchase in a company's loyalty programme. Points can then be redeemed for free or discounted merchandise or travel. Some programmes offer more points per purchase once a threshold has been reached.

loyalty scheme a programme to entice consumers to be frequent purchasers. Typically discounts and other benefits are given, depending upon the total amount or quantity purchased. A loyalty scheme is used when there is not very much differentiation between various brands. Travel companies are some of the biggest users of the loyalty scheme with frequent flier points, free upgrades, free hotel nights and suite upgrades.

McCann, Harrison King (1880-1962), H.K. McCann Co. and McCann-Erickson. McCann introduced the 'total marketing' agency concept in 1912. This has led to the marketing services conglomerates that we know today. Enthusiastic about motivational research studies, he took advertising beyond its creative focus and introduced public relations, research library, sales promotion and production survey services. The U.S. ordered Standard Oil Co.'s breakup soon after McCann became its ad manager in 1911, so he formed H.K. McCann the next year to provide ad continuity, and opened overseas offices. In 1930, the Depression led him to merge with Albert Erickson's smaller 17-year-old agency.

McGraw, James H. sr. (1860-1948) McGraw-Hill Publishing Co. McGraw was a pioneer in the creation of publications for market niches. While selling space as a college student, McGraw saw a need for specialized publications to serve the machinery, equipment and systems fields, which were undergoing spectacular growth at the time. In 1885, McGraw borrowed money to acquire an electrical industry publication. His prospering McGraw Publishing Co. then acquired Hill Publishing to create McGraw-Hill. When McGraw retired in 1936 as chairman, McGraw-Hill had 24 national trade publications, plus *Business Week* and McGraw-Hill Book Co., the largest technical book company. Known for high editorial and advertising standards, McGraw became the first to publish circulation figures and was known as the dean of industrial publishing.

McLuhan, Marshall Herbert, (1911–1980), Canadian visionary, polemicist and educator on the power of mass media. In media, he studied both its overriding effects on society and its character as an extension of the senses of the individual. He offered critiques of the fragmentation, commercialization and mechanization of being caused by the mass media phenomenon of the 20th century. His major works are: *The Mechanical Bride* (1951) on mass media and popular culture, The *Gutenberg Galaxy* (1962) and *Understanding Media* (1964) in which he proposed a media-centred view of history. In this work, McLuhan divided history into four phases characterized by prevailing media of communication: Phase I – orality; Phase II – emergence of the phonetic alphabet and the scribal tradition; Phase III – the Gutenberg publishing revolution; Phase IV – the electronic age. Communication media, for him, constituted a pervasive environment that saturates us with a whole series of perceptions of which we are largely unaware. Environments are invisible to their inhabitants and it takes a shock to discover and understand them. Well known for his semi-poetic and gnomic writing style, he is better known for his one-liners than his overall work: 'The medium is the message' (perhaps his most often quoted phrase), 'art is anything you can get away with,' 'electric light is pure information.' McLuhan predicted the future global role of media in creating the 'Global Village'.

Madison Avenue the generic name for the advertising industry in the US after the 1920s. Originally the location of the entire New York advertising indusry, its name is synonymous with an industry and its culture in the same way that Wall Street is synonymous with the finance industry. See also ADVERTISING.

magazine a physical print publication that appeals to a specific lifestyle or specific interests of its readers. The range of magazines has increased dramatically in the past 20 years as computer aided publishing and printing has reduced costs, from very narrow specific interest magazines (eg, *The Embalmer's Weekly*) to mass audience magazines (the *Radio Times*). Magazines are major sellers of advertising space and can often deliver a tailored audience for very specific products or a mass audience for products and services seeking a wider audience. See also MEDIA, ADVERTISING.

mail shot material sent out to potential customers as part of a direct mail campaign. See also DIRECT MARKETING under MARKETING SPECIALIZATIONS.

manual submission a way of adding a URL to a search engine individually by hand.

manufacturer brand any brand that carries the name of the original manufacturer (e.g. Johnson and Johnson, Hoover, Ford, Microsoft, Hewlett-Packard, IBM). See also BRAND.

market an identifiable grouping of likeminded, potential customers, with similar needs and wants, with a defined location, lifestyle or income type, or industry category, who are likely to buy products and services to satisfy those needs and wants and who have the means and inclination to do so. The defining characteristic is an *exchange* between a buyer and a seller. The exchange is made possible by the exchange of money for goods and services and is made more efficient by the two-way flow of information and communications between the sellers and the buyers. Originally, a market meant the physical location where sellers and buyers came together to exchange products for money or for other products. As the definition evolved, sellers became known as an industry, the buyers as a market. Market can also be used as a term of aggregate demand for a product or service. Just as the sellers and providers have multiple segments based upon the division of labour and expertise, so the market has spawned multiple segments and classifications, including geographical markets, industry markets, channel markets, psychographic markets, gender markets, lifestyle markets, customer function markets, mass markets, niche markets, capital markets, business markets, product markets, service markets. See also CONSUMERISM and MARKETING.

market attractiveness an assessment based upon the following elements: the overall size of the target market; the market growth rate; competitive intensity with the defined market; the cost of entering and of serving that market and its profit potential. The determination of market attractiveness is an early part of market strategy and planning.

market demand the total demand for a specific product or service over a defined time period as demanded or likely to be demanded by total number of customers (existing and potential) in a defined geographical area.

Key determinants of market demand are: market size, value, profitability and growth rate. There are three types of market demand: historical, current and future. The first is manifestly the easier to determine, the latter the hardest. The determination of market demand is one of the more difficult tasks confronting the marketer charged with launching a new product or service. The history of marketing campaigns is littered with cases of companies that either over- and underestimated market demand. A key variable is the extent to which marketing programmes – elements of the **marketing mix** – can manifestly alter normal market demand. Although all markets are susceptible to stimulation, the main determinant of market demand is the condition of the economy. See also ANSOFF MATRIX.

Current market demand is measured by taking the total number of buyers in a defined market and multiplying by the average quantity or value of the average amount purchased by each buyer. This is different from total market size, which also measures potential purchase and focuses on the total available or discretionary budget. The most difficult part of the calculation is to determine the number of buyers in any given market segment. Often this is broken down into defined geographical territories or market segments and demand is estimated for each cluster. This will also involve identifying competitors and estimating their sales volumes. This is also a good way of working out the relative market share and relative growth rate for the company in question.

Future market demand is altogether more difficult to estimate, particularly in today's world where very few markets show a level of stability and predictability that permit extrapolation of future demand based upon historical demand. Forecasts are often composed of an aggregate vision of macro-economic forecasts (such as inflation, GNP, interest rates, employment, investment, saving, spending and government economic policy), industry-specific forecasts (industry analysts' forecasts of the future or, in some cases, what customer research tells the company about customers' future buying intentions), and company-specific sales forecasts, including those of competitors that are externally reported.

Scenarios for future demand are being increasingly used to give a range of potential market demand projections, rather than just one, as history has shown that a completely repeatable, accurate market demand forecast is impossible.

A market demand forecast is a calculation of expected market demand.

There are three elements of market demand forecasts:

1. the economy, including a review of Politics, Economics, Social, Technological (PEST);

2. market research, which is designed to acquire information on specific markets and estimate total demand for a product;

3. an evaluation of market demand for both the firm and competitor products that are regarded as substitutes. See also DEMAND.

market dynamics changes that occur within the market, but external to a company, which influence its decision-making and impact upon its performance.

market growth rate the rate, commonly expressed as a percentage per annum, at which a market is increasing in size relative to the previous year. This is often unreliable, because markets are seldom static and often change in form and the basis of measurement is constantly changing. See also MARKET DEMAND.

MARKETING

Marketing in its modern form began at the turn of the 20th century. As a business discipline, it is seen to have passed through three phases: the *era of production* in which marketing was constrained only by limitation on production (up to the 1930s); the *era of sales* in which the marketing pushed whatever the company produced (up to the 1950s) and finally the *era of the customer* in which the customer was placed at the centre of all marketing activities.

The fundamental change in the definition and purpose of marketing in the later 20th century is that, as a business discipline, it has developed far beyond the simple facilitation of commercial exchanges and transactions between the producer to the consumers. Initially, marketing was very much focused on the producer's interest – of getting the right products to the customer at the right time, at the right price in the right place. The underlying assumption of early marketers was that the producers controlled the market. Management, functions, roles and processes aligned around this model of producer-centric marketing management. This is no longer a valid assumption in the Information Age of the 21st century.

So what is marketing in the early 21st century? A successful or accepted new model, one that takes account of the dynamism (and often irrationality) of global markets, capricious and unpredictable customers that defy classic analysis, purchasing patterns and market forecasts, the rise of services and intangibles, the fragmentation and new combinations of markets beyond the old industrial classifications, the increasing power of customers and the new tools and techniques of interactive marketing, has not yet come into being on a grand scale or started to translate into company marketing organizations and processes.

There are so many definitions and all-encompassing 'definitive' pronouncements about what marketing is (I counted at least 50 in compiling this dictionary) that it would be valueless to add yet another to the pile. It is, however, worth drawing attention to the different interpretations of the practice of marketing and the functions and skills that actually constitute it. In the 21st century markets have become more complex and more global, and so has marketing as a professional discipline. As a newer profession it lacks universal clarity, classification and delineation of role. Different companies and organizations tend to define marketing after their own fashion.

Some companies continue to confuse marketing with selling; some even see marketing as a subset of sales! Others, more correctly, see selling as a subset of marketing. There are a few, more practically, who see selling and marketing as separate management disciplines. In some countries, such as the US, there is a tendency to separate marketing and communications professionals: public relations, speechwriting and internal communications are often separated out from marketing, which is more focused on taking products and services direct to customers. Other companies adopt an integrated approach in which all communications, sales, direct and indirect marketing are managed holistically. The e-commerce, or 'dot.com' companies, at the other extreme, were criticized for being all marketing and no substance.

There is another strong argument that marketing is everyone's role, not just that of a marketing department ('marketing is too important to be left to the marketing department', said David Packard, the co-founder of Hewlett-Packard). A modern view is that those who bear the title of marketing managers are really expert consultants and integrators who galvanize and inspire the entire organization towards a market-centric, or customer-centric, frame of mind, approach and mode of operation. They apply their individual expertise to certain aspects of marketing. See also INTRODUCTION.

marketing audit a systematic evaluation of a company's existing marketing environment, objectives, strategies, programmes, and organization with a view to determining effectiveness and improvement areas. All aspects of the audit should be done relative to competitors and perceived best practice in the industry. The components of a systematic marketing audit are:

marketing environment audit which covers the external macroeconomic environments (demographic, social, political, technological, cultural) as well as microeconomic (customers, competitors, dealers, distributors, suppliers and internal factors) that form the dynamic context within which a full evaluation of the company's marketing programmes and functions can be

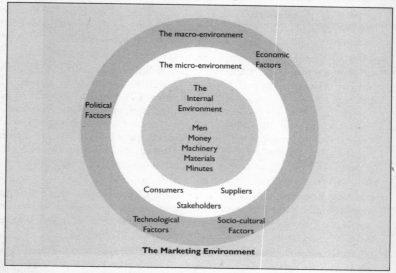

Reproduced courtesy of marketingteacher.com

undertaken. The dimensions of the marketing environment to be analysed in the first part of the audit are illustrated overleaf:

marketing strategy audit is an examination of the company's mission and the role of the marketing objectives and strategy to achieve this. Particularly important in this part of the audit is the alignment of the marketing objectives and strategy with the business objectives and strategy. The key marketing components are market segmentation and articulation of desired positioning within those segments;

marketing functional audit examines how marketing is organized, its skills and how it works within the organization. Organizationally, the audit asks if the marketing functions are designed to meet the strategic objectives and if the marketing resources are deployed in the optimum way. The skills, effectiveness and impact of the marketing team are also evaluated. Also, this part of the audit looks at how marketing operates with other company departments, such as sales, production, purchasing, R&D. It would then evaluate the objectives of each of the functional areas: product, service or solutions marketing; distribution and channel marketing; promotional marketing, such as communications, advertising, new media, publicity and sales promotions. All functions of selling would also be examined, whether a direct or an indirect sales forces: objective, size, scale, coverage, skills, organization within territory, management, productivity measures, compensation schemes, morale, processes for setting targets;

marketing systems audit is an examination of marketing intelligence, planning, budgeting, measurement and processes. Again, it is important that these are aligned to and supportive of the overall business strategy and plan;

marketing productivity audit this is partly a measure of the cost effectiveness of marketing and also a analysis of the profitability of the company's main marketing channels and its various segments.

marketing budget the substance that can make the overall marketing and sales plan translate into high-impact programmes and results in the external market. As marketing and sales are variable budget costs, it is financially prudent to forecast, plan and control them. Good budget forecasting and control processes are vital in uncertain and dynamic markets. Although an essential financial discipline, it is problematic in marketing given the difficulty in determining both likely demand and the likely cost of achieving a given sales target. Marketing and sales information inputs to the budgeting process could be: sales performance, revenues, market share and costs of distribution channels.

marketing concept a business orientation or philosophy that holds that organizational success is dependent upon the efficient identification of the needs and wants of target markets and customers and the effective satisfaction of them. See also CONCEPT TESTING.

marketing ethics although these have been (hitherto) uneasy bedfellows, ethics and marketing are increasingly coming together. Waves of business scandals and malpractice have shown the damage that can be caused to the plan contains information about your company and its products and services, marketing objectives and strategies, as well as how to measure the success of marketing activities. The plan describes all the marketing activities that will be executed over a specified time period.

A marketing plan will also describe a company's interpretation of its addressable market, include any background information and research results used to select the target markets and to define the marketing programmes. The marketing plan will indicate the overall investment required to achieve the planned marketing activities as well as the measurements used to determine return on investment.

Most often, a marketing plan is a component of a **business plan**. A business plan states the way in which a company intends to be operated, what its main goals are, how much money it will take to achieve the goals and what activities will be performed and what investments will be made to achieve the goals. Marketing is an integral activity in a business plan. Marketing plans can be presented in isolation, but should always support and be closely linked to a company's business objectives.

Basic elements of a marketing plan

A marketing plan should begin with an **Executive Summary**. This part of the marketing plan will introduce the proposition and explain the major features and recommendations of the plan to executives.

1. Introduction: briefly describe the nature of your business and the products or services you offer.

- As well as a high-level description of the context and objectives of the plan, the introduction should also contain a description of business activities including revenues and customers and current market position. Accomplishments and successes to date should also be mentioned.

- For new markets or new market entry, the introduction should also describe the experience, training and competencies that would enable the company to achieve the objectives as set out.

2. Vision, Mission Statement and Objectives

- Mission statements should focus on the longer-range, more enduring purpose and meaning of what the marketing plan is trying to achieve (for example, ' Our success is making our customers successful' or ' To educate, entertain and enlighten').

- Company objectives are more specific and action-orientated: such as 'we will deliver consultancy services in the UK to the top 100 companies and will seek billable revenues of at least £20 m from each' or ' We will deliver a balanced range of broadcasting services to the population of the UK through two terrestrial channels'.

3. Team description

- It is important to describe the organizational resources and structure of the team who will deliver the plan.

- Describe the skills and capabilities of the management involved in the execution of the marketing plan.

- Close with a brief statement of the main marketing objectives and strategies contained in the plan.

Current market conditions

In the **Current Situation** section of the marketing plan, one should provide information about market trends and dynamics as well as the target market and competitive environment.

Market trends and dynamics

This section should highlight those macroeconomic trends and forces that will directly affect the target market that the plan will address. For example, relaxation of import duties may cause an influx of foreign goods that will increase competition in a national marketplace; or, new developments in technology may render a current product range liable to obsolescence; or, a rise in unemployment will diminish purchasing power for goods and services in a given marketplace; or, a decline in interest rates combined with easy availability of credit will cause the market for certain goods and services to rise; or, government regulation and intervention, for example through price regulation, could cause changed in market dynamics.

Target market description

Critical to success in marketing any product is aiming all marketing efforts programmes precisely at a **target market.** Planning your marketing strategy without knowing the target market and target customers is to court disaster. Therefore all good marketing planning should be preceded by very detailed **market segmentation.**

- It is important to describe the size of the target market. This should be specific and include statistics about the size of your target market. Also included will be information on whether the size of your target marketing is *growing, shrinking, or staying the same.* Causes for change should be indicated and explained.

The description of the target market ought to contain the following elements:

Example of target consumer segment:

- *Characteristics* of the customers in the target segment, such as age, income level, sex, race, number of children, marital status, location, disposable income etc.
- *Habits and patterns* that the target customers exhibit. For example, the target audience may tend to purchase in a certain way, may have some shared values, may have certain preferences and dislikes.
- *Description of their wants, needs and desires* and how the product or service fulfils them.

Description of the target customers' *buying habits.* For example, how do they spend their disposable income? When do they buy? How much? How often? By what means?

When the marketing plan is addressing multiple market segments, it is important to identify the primary market, which tends to be those customers who buy the products or services most often and who display the greatest brand loyalty or who can be served most profitably.

Competitive analysis and issues analysis

A deep understanding of competition, both existing and potential, will be necessary to a successful marketing plan. This section of the marketing plan should include a brief description of competitors together with a brief descriptions of external issues that are relevant to the market. Competitors will be described in detail in the competitor and issues analysis of the marketing plan.

A *competitive analysis* includes information about those competitors whose products and services compete in the target market. This section should also look to develop actions to counteract or defeat competitors in the given marketplace.

An *issues analysis* briefly lists key external issues (such as new legislation or the impact of a technological advancement) that present potential challenges or opportunities for your business.

SWOT analysis

SWOT stands for Strengths, Weaknesses, Opportunities and Threats and is critical to the marketing plan. Strengths and weaknesses are determined by internal elements, while external forces dictate opportunities and threats. *Opportunities* and *threats* (OTs) ought to be identified first in order to more quickly highlight the product *strengths* or *weaknesses*. For example, if it is discovered that a competitor is losing certain licensing rights to a product in the next year, this information could be used to quickly fill that gap in the market.

Strengths and weaknesses should focus upon the following:

1. company's philosophy or mission
2. product features, benefits or quality
3. product's competitive advantage (Is there a competitive advantage?)
4. distribution methods or distributor satisfaction
5. pricing structures. Is it priced much higher or lower than the competition?
6. target market's awareness of the product
7. target market's attitudes toward the product (or its category)
8. target market's brand loyalty
9. competition's activities (for example, new product launches, price changes, new companies, etc.)
10. overall market trends (shifts in needs, trends, behaviours, etc.)

Opportunities analysis could for example focus on the following questions:

- What problems do customers currently have with the product that could be addressed by improvement? These improvement areas may not be immediately obvious or explicitly stated.

- What steps does the buyer go through to purchase, use, and dispose of the product? This method might bring to light new product ideas (or just enhancements or packaging), services, or other value options.

- What are the customers' desires? These can often yield new opportunities: for example, customers who say that they would love to be able to communicate to anyone from anywhere in the world yields a huge range of opportunities for mobile device and service providers.

Other areas may also need to be addressed depending on the company, product or market.

Strengths can be defined as any available company resource that can be used to improve market share or financial performance. Weaknesses are any company resources that may cause you to lose a competitive advantage, position or financial state. There will be a strong correlation of threat (previously identified) and company weakness.

A threat can also be an opportunity, and strength can also be viewed as a weakness, all depending upon who is looking at it. For example, one may see your large selection of products as a strength, while customers may consider it confusing and difficult to find what they need.

STRENGTHS, WEAKNESSES, OPPORTUNITIES, and THREATS
TEMPLATE

External	Strengths	Weaknesses	Opportunities	Threats
1. Company/ product reputation				
2. Market share				
3. Product's ability to meet market needs				
4. Product's ability to meet market trends				
5. Value product brings to the market				
6. Product quality				
7. Customer service and support quality				
8. Quality/ effectiveness of past marketing				
9. Pricing				
10. Distribution				
11. Geographic location				

Internal	Strengths	Weaknesses	Opportunities	Threats
1. Operational leadership				
2. Financial strength				
3. Manufacturing capabilities				
4. Responsiveness of workforce				

The introductory analytical part of the marketing planning process should also include a list of assumptions that underpin the plan. This may, for example, include an assumption about the future market growth rate, or currency exchange, or price competition, or the inflation rate, or the actions of competitors.

Marketing strategies and objectives

A marketing objective is that which the marketer on behalf of the company management wishes to achieve; a marketing strategy is the plan and means to achieve the objective.

Marketing objectives should be:

- clear
- measurable, and
- timetabled.

Some examples of these types of marketing objectives are:

- Increase product sales in the target customer base by 30% in one year.
- Inform target audience about features and benefits of the product and its competitive advantages, leading to a 10% increase in sales in one year.
- Decrease or remove potential customers' resistance to buying our product, leading to a 20% increase in sales that are closed in six months or less.
- Increase market share in the target market by 5% in one year relative to the competitors.

There can be multiple objectives. It is important to ensure that these are mutually reinforcing and do not conflict with each other. Also, the various marketing plan components – the marketing strategy, budget, action programmes, controls and measures, people resources – must support the overall marketing objectives.

The marketing mix

Before considering the individual ingredients of the marketing mix, an overall positioning has to be established. Positioning is the perception that the target audience has of the products and services or of the company itself. Planning the positioning of the product or service must involve taking into consideration such issues as the **competition** and how their products are perceived, the needs and desires of your **target audience**, and the element of

personality and emotion that the product or service evokes in the minds of the audience.

In crowded markets it is very important to position the product or service appropriately. In order to be differentiated, the product or service has to have very clear positioning in the audience's minds.

First, it is necessary to develop a **general positioning** strategy. This means determining if the product or service should be targeted on a market niche, should be a low-cost-leader, or should be highly differentiated (see COMPETITIVE ADVANTAGE). The chosen path will then lead to specific messages that re-enforce the positioning. Think of the qualities of your product, its strengths and weaknesses, the opportunities you've uncovered, the pricing you've considered, and your target market to determine which broad position you will be taking.

Next, it is necessary to develop specific **positioning**. This could be based on a certain quality or benefit of your product or service (such as ease of use, durability, reliability, safety, convenience, delivery).

Answering the following questions can further sharpen the positioning:

1. What views do your audience already have and how can your product relate to them?

2. What are your target audience's needs and desires?

3. Is there a gap in the market that can be filled by the product and services and targeted positioning?

4. Are there certain core capabilities that underpin the chosen positioning?

5. What are the greatest benefits of the product and services and how can they be capitalized upon?

6. Is there a specific use or application that your product or service fits particularly well?

7. Can a positioning idea upstage the competitor's positioning?

8. Can the desired positioning be based on quality or pricing strategies?

9. Can the product or service be focused on new opportunities that have been uncovered by research?

Once the product or service's positioning has been decided upon, there are further points of refinement:

- The communications messages around the positioning need to be kept simple.
- The name of the product or service ought to reflect the positioning.
- The believability of the positioning should be tested.
- Will the positioning create impact in the minds of the target audience?
- How specific or how general is the positioning relative to the target audience?
- How clear and comprehensible is the positioning?
- What is the value of the desired market positioning?

The **marketing strategy** section of the plan has outlined the overall approach to achieve the marketing objectives. This section will contain the mix of programmes necessary to achieve the objectivess, classically known as the 4 Ps. See MARKETING MIX.

Product features and benefits

Products can be described in terms of their features and benefits. **Features** are product characteristics that deliver benefits; products are mainly purchased for their benefits. **Features** are product characteristics such as size, colour, capability, utility, functionality, design, hours of business, content, expertise etc. **Benefits** describe the value to the buyer of the product that they would not have in the absence of the product. Product features, being mainly tangible, are usually easier to describe than product benefits, which are often intangible. Emotional benefits run the gamut of human emotions and experience but basically allow the buyer to feel better in some way. For example, buying products made from recycled materials offers the buyer the sense of being environmentally responsible. Buying a package holiday can often make the buyer more fulfilled or relaxed. Other products and services focus on bringing the buyer financial reward, for example to:

- save money (a discount on a holiday package deal or an airfare);
- make money (savings plans or premium bonds);
- gain convenience and time (fast foods, supermarket shopping).

Identification of product or service benefits

It is necessary to articulate the product or service's benefits from the viewpoint of the buyer or customer rather than from the point of view of the supplier. To do this, it is important to have a continuous dialogue with target customers, either through regular surveys or by panels to get their views on the product's benefits. It is important also to start to profile the typical customer who has bought the products and services in the past. The profiling exercise will yield direct information on what customers value from the product and service features.

In conducting the dialogue with customers it is valuable to ask for:

- suggestions for improvement
- complaints and prospect inquiries
- their views on competitors' products and services.

A deeper understanding of the product features and benefits from the buyer's standpoint enables better

- description of the products and services in publications, marketing literature and in sales situation.
- articulation of how the product is differentiated from competitor products and services.

Product and service differentiation

Certain products and services may be either unique or virtually indistinguishable from competitors' products and services. Highly differentiated products and services require different marketing strategies from undifferentiated or commodity products and services. Differentiated products and services must be clearly set apart from the competitors' products and services in the minds of existing and potential customers. Having a thorough understanding of how the product and services' benefits compare to your competitors' will enable and inform competition based upon differentiation.

Strategies based upon product or service features

- One strategy could be the 'first to market' – for example the Sony Walkman – which confers the distinction of originality and foundation.

- Another strategy could be that of the Improver or Modifier. Instead of being the originator of totally new features, one could be known as an improver. This has tended to be the position of Microsoft's products.

- Another strategy is to combine or group or 'bundle' features, such as 'end to end' IT services, or building services: these would combine consultation, design, creation, building and maintenance. Combined financial services may be 'one-stop shops' that offer pensions, savings, lending, investing and insurance services.

See also PRODUCT MARKETING, SERVICES MARKETING.

Strategies based on pricing

Pricing the product or service is an integral element of marketing strategy. Central to pricing is to ensure that the target market is willing to pay the prices proposed and that they generate profit for the company. Without these factors, there will be little possibility of a successful outcome.

There are many approaches to pricing, some scientific, some not. **Price** is the selling price per unit customers pay for the product or service.

Price floors and ceilings

The cost of producing the product or service is the 'floor': prices must set prices above the floor in order to cover costs. Occasionally, for marketing purposes, such as rapid market entry or a price war against competitors, prices can be set at or below cost.

The 'ceiling' is the price at which customers are willing to pay for a perception of value from the product or service, based upon what the product or service is worth to them. This is sometimes described as 'what the market will bear.' Perceived value is created by an established reputation, marketing messages, packaging, sales environments and results delivered relative to customer needs. An obvious and important component of perceived value is the comparison customers and prospects make between the company and its competition.

Somewhere between the floor and the ceiling is probably the right price for your product or service; a price that allows the company to make a fair profit and that seems reasonable to customers. Consequently, once there is an understanding of the cost floor and the value price ceiling, an informed decision about how to price the product or service can be made.

In summary, if the customer doesn't perceive value worth paying for at a price that offers you a fair profit, then the marketing strategy and plan must be reworked.

See also BREAKEVEN ANALYSIS, PRICING.

There are several pricing strategies that can be followed once the fundamentals of costs floor, price ceilings and breakeven have been established.

Pricing for profit: cost-based pricing

- Establishing a high price to make high profits initially. This strategy is used to recover high research and development costs or to maximize profits before competitors enter the market. (Pharmaceutical companies often use this strategy when introducing new drugs or very innovative high-technology consumer goods.)

- Setting a low price on one or more products to make quick sales to support another product in development. (Some companies also employ this strategy when they need to increase cash flow.)

- Setting prices to meet a desired profit goal. For example, if the desired profit per unit is 20% and unit costs are £10 (taking into account your fixed and variable costs), then the price can be set at £12.

Pricing for profit: value-based pricing

How high can a price be before the product or service is priced out of the market?

To understand the customer's perception of the value of a product or service, the more subjective criteria such as customer preferences, product benefits, convenience, product quality, company image and alternative products offered by the competition have to be taken into consideration. The following questions are useful in establishing the market's appetite for value based pricing:

- How do customers describe what they get for their money?

- Do they save a great deal of money or time by purchasing the product or service?

- Do they gain a competitive advantage from using the product or service?

- Is it more convenient to use the offered service rather than try to do it themselves?

- What are the customer's choices?

- What does the competition charge?

With this information, one can begin to understand the maximum price the customer will pay for the benefit received. A few value-based pricing strategies are listed below that take into account the breakeven point, but are heavily weighted with subjective judgments rather than just empirical data:

- Price the same as competitors. This strategy is used when offering a commodity product, when prices are relatively well established or when there are no other means to set prices. The marketer's challenge then becomes to determine how to lower costs so you can produce a higher profit than your competitors.

- Establish a low price (compared to the competition) on a product in order to capture a large number of customers in that market. This strategy may also be used to achieve non-financial objectives such as product awareness, meeting the competition or establishing an image of being low-cost. It works if one can maintain profitability at the low price, or to maintain an acceptable level of sales should prices be raised later.

- If the product or service has a history, a uniqueness that is valuable to customers, then one may be able to charge a very high price relative to cost. Also, if the target market had high disposable income and the intention is to position the product as a 'prestige' product that confers status upon the buyer, an especially high price could be in order. (For example, Rolex and Cartier watches, Ferraris and Rolls-Royces.) This strategy of charging 'what customers are willing to pay' requires close attention to brand building and also to the customers' mindset. To go 'out of fashion' can lead to drastic losses and the entry of competitors.

Discounts

The pricing strategy within the marketing plan can also include discounts to customers to whom a business benefit is offered:

- Cash discounts can be offered to customers who pay promptly. This rewards those who help the company maintain a steady, positive cash flow and reduce credit-collection costs.

- Offering quantity discounts for large orders often makes economic sense when the cost-per-unit to sell or deliver a product declines as the quantity increases.

- Seasonal discounts given to buyers who purchase during a product's slow season reward customers who essentially assist a company in balancing its cash flow and in meeting production demands. For example a hotel that offers special packages for weekends of winter seasons – enables the hotel to smooth its cash flows over high and low seasons.

- Trade-in allowances for returned old products for either re-use or re-sell for a profit may benefit both a company and customers. An example would be part exchanged deals on used cars.

- Promotional allowances often make economic sense. For example, if a retail chain that includes the company's product in its ads, or in promotional activities sells a product, those activities amplify the producing company's marketing efforts. Price discounts may be offered to these retail chains.

Promotion plan

The promotion plan element within the marketing plan details the activities necessary to promote or create awareness of the product or service in the target marketplace. It is alternatively known as marketing communications. Promotion follows when all the analytical work has been done on the market, the market properly segmented, the customers targeted, the product and prices established for those markets. A promotion plan outlines the *promotional tools or tactics* to accomplish the marketing objectives laid out in the overall plan. To the new or inexperienced marketer, the promotion plan might be mistaken as the entire marketing plan because it outlines where the majority of the marketing *budget* will be spent. It is, however, just *one* component of the marketing plan – there are additional strategy and planning components described in a marketing plan.

The following components can be included in a promotion plan:

- Description of the promotional programme and tactics.
- Projected costs of the promotional programmes for the year.
- Explanation of how your promotion tactics will support marketing objectives.
- Measures of success for the promotional programmes.

Preparation of promotional tactical plan

Research: a good promotional plan relies heavily on research. It includes activities such as gaining insight into the target market and finding out what competitors in the target market are doing.

A *customer-centric approach*: all of the promotional activities need to be grounded in media areas that will directly touch the target customers. Therefore, all the promotional activities need to be directly linked to the customers, what they read, what they listen to, what they attend, where they meet etc.

Description of promotional tactics: the major component of the promotion plan is the description of the planned promotional tactics and how they are budgeted and the likely outcomes. The promotional plan is what brings the marketing activity to bear on sales activity: all sales promotions should dovetail with and support the selling strategies and the company image.

It is important not only to measure costs incurred against budget, but also to have specific objectives by which one can measure success or failure in each specific area of the promotional mix:

- Advertising
- Sales promotion
- Collateral materials, such a brochures and product descriptions
- Public relations
- Personal selling
- Direct marketing
- Interactive tools
- Trade shows and conferences
- Publishing articles and ideas
- Seminars. See also DISTRIBUTION.

Business presentation: a regular and often overlooked dimension of business image and promotion. There are many occasions when the individual or the company will be called upon to explain its business. These business presentations will be given to many diverse audiences including potential customers, bankers, suppliers, and investors. Each group requires different information about your business and it should be presented in a format appropriate to the situation.

Information provided in the detailed presentation will vary by audience. It is important to take into consideration the audience of the presentation.

Suppliers may want to know about the exposure their products will receive, your target market, and your ability to the supplier. The following questions should be covered in every business presentation:

- Who are you?
- What do you want to do?
- When do you want to do it?
- Why do you want to do it?
- Who do you want to do it for?
- How are you going to do it?
- What is your experience to do it?
- What do you need to do it?
- What will it cost to do it?
- How much will you make when you do it?

Creating a successful promotional strategy begins with knowing which aspects of the business to promote and why. It also involves knowing which promotional activities are most effective. Knowing these things helps identify promotional goals, an important element in developing a winning promotional campaign.

Promotional programmes in a national market could include the following execution actions:

- Advertise in the classified advertising section of your community newspaper.
- Advertise in the Yellow Pages.
- Advertise in retail stores.
- Approach your prospective customers over the phone.
- Approach your prospective customers in person.
- Approach your prospective customers through the mail.
- Be a guest speaker at seminars and presentations on your area of expertise.
- Be a guest speaker on radio shows.
- Build and maintain a customer mailing and contact list on database software.
- Build your image with well-designed letterhead and business cards.
- Design a brochure that best explains the benefits of your services.
- Design a mail order campaign.
- Design a point of purchase display for your product.
- Design a telemarketing campaign.
- Design an image-building logo for your company.
- Design and distribute a quarterly newsletter or an industry update announcement.
- Design and distribute company calendars, mugs, T-shirts, caps, pens, note pads, or other advertising specialties displaying your company name and logo.

- Design and distribute a free instructional manual related to your industry.
- Design bumper stickers or balloons with your company name, logo or slogan.
- Design T-shirts displaying your company name and logo.
- Explore cross-promotion with a non-competing company selling to your target market.
- Explore the costs of advertising in newspapers, magazines, on radio, television, billboards, bus shelters and benches.
- Explore ways to share your advertising costs using cooperative advertising.
- Follow up customer purchases with a thank-you letter.
- Follow up customer purchases with Christmas or birthday cards.
- Have your company profiled in a magazine or newspaper that is read by prospective customers.
- Hire an advertising agency or public relations firm.
- Hold a promotional contest.
- Hold a seminar on your service, product or industry.
- Include promotional material with your invoices.
- Look for prospective customers at trade shows related to your industry.
- Look for prospective customers in associations related to your industry.
- Look for prospective customers at seminars related to your industry.
- Look for prospective customers in magazines and newspapers related to your industry.
- Package your brochure, price lists and letter in a folder for your customers.
- Place a pavement sign outside your store or office.
- Place flyers on bulletin boards and car windshields.
- Place promotional notes on your envelopes, mailing labels.
- Place signs or paint logos on your company vehicle(s).
- Prepare a corporate video.
- Prepare a list of product features and benefits to help you plan your advertising and promotional campaigns.
- Prepare proposals offering solutions to your customers' needs.
- Provide free samples of your product or service.
- Provide public tours of your operation.
- Sponsor a charity event.
- Sponsor an amateur arts or sports team.
- Sponsor a cultural event through a community arts organization.

Distribution (Place) plan

The plan for how one sells and distributes the product or service makes the entire marketing plan a reality. It is necessary first to have a strategy for distribution: how available are the products and services to be? Will they be sold directly or indirectly? As with pricing, the places where the product is available directly reflect both the quality and 'status' of the product or service. Channels of distribution must match the image goals of your product or service. There are several key elements when planning a distribution strategy. For example, there must be alignment and consistency between the distribution channel and the customers' perception of your product and service. The distribution strategy must be closely linked to the optimum dynamics of the addressable market. Also, the product or service must get the attention it needs from the chosen channel: for example are the sales staff trained and knowledgeable about the products and services? Are retailers willing to give adequate and visible shelf-space? How many competing products does the distributor also carry?

Marketing strategy primarily involves making choices about which parts of the market to focus upon and how to compete within that target market. The strategy must be based upon a thorough analysis and the ways and means of addressing target markets and customers. The key decision upon which the entire marketing strategy can stand or fall is the **market segmentation:** which segments of the market are being targeted and how the marketing mix and the product/service offering is to be positioned for each segment. **Positioning**, which is the second core element of the marketing strategy, defines, in the consumer's mind, the comparisons between one capability, service, idea, product and those of the competitor. The task is identifying weaknesses in competing products and services and strengths in your own which can be reinforced so as to gain competitive edge.

Below is one comprehensive example of a range of approaches to market strategy in a competitive environment, The Strategy Clock:

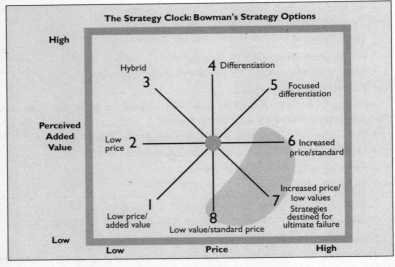

Reproduced courtesy of marketingteacher.com

This Strategy Clock is based upon the work of Cliff Bowman from 1996. See also PORTER, COMPETITIVE STRATEGIES. Bowman considers competitive advantages in relation to cost advantage or differentiation advantage. There are eight core strategic options:

Option one – low price/low added value

- This is most probably a segment-specific approach.

Option two – low price

- This approach could lead to a price war and low margins. The necessity is to be a 'cost leader' in the defined market place.

Option three – hybrid

- This a combination of low-cost based approach combined with a reinvestment in low price and associated differentiation, such as great value at lowest cost.

Option four – differentiation

(a) There can be a strategy of differentiation without an added price premium, based upon perceived added value by user, which often has the benefit of yielding market share increases, or

(b) There is the more likely strategy of differentiation to justify a price premium, in which there is perceived added value sufficient to bear price premium.

Option five – focused differentiation

- This is when there is perceived added value to a very narrowly defined market segment (luxury holidays for wealthy widows, Harley Davidson top-quality motor cycles for the over-50s American market with high disposable income) that warrant a premium price

Option six –increased price/standard

- This strategy involves continuously raising the bar in terms of quality and professional standards. Higher margins can be gained if one company is able to transcend competitors with lower standards and if competitors are losing market share.

Option seven – increased price/low values

- This type of strategy is only possible in the absence of free competition and is more characteristic of a very closed market with insurmountable entry barriers or else a monopoly situation

Option eight – low value/standard price

- Such a strategy is suicidal in marketing terms and will inevitably lead to loss of market share. This can only be justified in terms of a managed withdrawal of an under-performing or loss-making product from the market.

See also MARKET SEGMENTATION.

marketing process management responsible for particular segments, industry or customer groups, brands, products or services or specific marketing functions. Marketing managers are also responsible for the management of marketing staff, budgets and programmes. Marketing is a combination of expert functions, planning, processes and management. Occasionally, market managers are also responsible for revenues and profits. Philip Kotler provides useful shorthand for the key elements of textbook marketing management process:

$$R \longrightarrow STP \rightarrow MM \rightarrow I \rightarrow C$$

Where:

R = market research, which should be the start point of the marketing management process. Without a deep understanding of the marketplace and the customers within it, failure becomes more likely. While experience has shown that it is impossible to forecast with complete accuracy the behaviour of a market, it has also shown that failure to fully understand all the dimensions of a market and its dynamics can lead to disaster.

S = segmentation, which is the most important part of the marketing management process, because if the segments selected are the wrong ones, then all the marketing programmes that follow will be jeopardized. Segmentation eventually leads to accurate targeting. It must also take into account the organization's abilities and resources to address the chosen market segments.

T = targeting, which involves careful selection of customers within the selected segment(s), and emerges from the detailed segmentation

P = positioning, the place that the company wants to occupy in the minds of those target customers within the selected segments and, by extension, how it wishes to compete in that target market place.

MM = marketing mix, the combination of product/service, distribution, pricing and promotional elements designed to reach those customers within the target segment that re-enforces the desired positioning.

I = implementation, how all the various marketing mix programmes are executed with the customers in the target segments. This will be a combination of the marketing mix with other relevant parts of the company and the distribution channel. A key element in implementation is co-ordination with the producers (of products or services), the marketing team and the sales channels.

C = control, where the measurement and feedback on all that has been planned and implemented takes place. Results are audited and evaluated and improvements and corrections are made in the overall management chain. The original segmentation can be validated, rejected or adapted. It is most important that the feedback comes directly from the marketplace and is not a collection of internal opinions.

Arguably, marketing has now become more sophisticated than this neat division of labour and sequential approach to marketing tasks and functions. However, these are fundamentals that are rarely changed by fad or fashion and are as applicable to the new economy as the old economy.

MARKETING SPECIALIZATIONS

As marketing has grown and evolved as a business discipline, it has segmented into various specialized disciplines that have their own techniques, methods, development paths and careers. Some marketing specializations are more portable than others – for example, the functional specialists of public relations, advertising, communications, events marketing are more portable from company to company than a specialization in, say, fast-moving consumer goods branding. The following items are a range of the main specializations in marketing:

business-to-business marketing the marketing of products and services to other businesses or organizations rather than to individual consumers. It can also be known as industrial, commercial, trade, organizational or institutional marketing. This type of marketing requires a different set of techniques and analysis from consumer marketing. The main difference is that the buyer in the industrial market does not purchase for final consumption. Purchases in the business-to-business market are made for further processing, for adding value, or for incorporation into finished products. The target buyers are not end consumers, but those in the supply chain that reach the final consumer, such as manufacturers who make the products, internal users within companies, wholesalers who buy the products in bulk and distribute them, and retailers who merchandise and sell them to final consumers. This determines an entirely different type of segmentation, channel and pricing strategy from those engaged in consumer marketing.

The business-to-business market has different dynamics from the consumer market. It is characterized by larger purchasers, fewer buyers and by different types of demand: for example, derived, volatile and concentrated. Derived demand means that the demand for the product and services of another business is ultimately determined by demand from the final consumer. Volatile demand in business-to-business markets – as we often see in oil or aero engines – is much greater than volatility in consumer markets. Economists calculate that a 20% rise in consumer demand can cause an increase in industrial demand by up to 200%. For example, if demand for PCs or mobile phones rises by 20%, this can cause a current rise of 200% for microchips. Businesses-to-business markets are also more prone to concentrated demand than consumer markets – largely because many industries are more geographically concentrated than consumer industries. This tends to cluster industrial buyers in specific geographies.

Buyers in business-to-business markets tend to be expert buyers, knowledgeable in the product area and highly trained. Committees of experts make buying decisions. This, in turn, requires a more sophisticated form of personal selling and salesperson to address and negotiate with these types of buyers.

Also, in business-to-business marketing, there are different ways of obtaining the product apart from straightforward purchase – for example leasing is quite normal for industrial equipment. In some markets, without stable currencies, there is counter-trading, in which one form of good is exchanged for others in lieu of monetary purchase.

There are several ways of segmenting the business-to-business markets, the most common of which is to use the standard industrial classification code that divides industries into various generic markets. Another way is to segment the industrial market by type of manufacturing: capital equipment, batch, discrete and process manufacturing.

The key elements, approaches and techniques of business-to-business marketing are:

- A heavier emphasis on relationship marketing – an unremitting focus on retaining customers through building trust and commitment.

- A deployment of a key account manager for large customers who has excellent communications, problem-solving and negotiation skills.

- Additional services such as technical advice and technical specification are required in business-to-business marketing.

- Because the preparation and negotiation of competitive tenders to win new orders is at a premium, there must be experienced sales and sales support teams with the requisite skills in these areas.

- Prices are usually negotiated rather than set in advance, with a high emphasis on discounting and loss leaders.

- There is a high skill requirement for sophisticated personal selling,

- Promotion is focused on trade press, specialized advertising, exhibitions, trade shows and business press publicity rather than mass media outlets.

- Image building is usually focused on individual customers or small clusters of customers rather than to mass audiences. See also BUYING.

cause-related marketing a strategic positioning and marketing approach that links a company or brand to a relevant social cause, for mutual benefit of sponsor and sponsoree. The term was copyrighted by the American Express Corporation and it specifically refers to promotional programmes that link charitable contributions to sales of a specific good or service bought with a credit card. A certain percentage of the purchase price of a good or service is contributed to a defined charity. In a broader sense, the term has also come to mean the sponsorship of causes by major corporations, or groups of corporations, which enables the company to associate its brand with a worthy cause. As business ethics and corporate responsibility climb higher up the agendas of major companies, cause-related and not-for-profit marketing are taking on new dimensions of importance. See also CHARITY MARKETING.

charity (or not-for-profit) marketing is of rising importance for those charities trying to gain greater exposure for their cause and greater support for it. Charities are primarily using marketing not for profit, but for contribution. In recent years, organizations such a Médecins Sans Frontières, OXFAM and Save the Children have become increasingly assertive in their advertising and sponsorship-seeking efforts. Increasingly, charities seek out corporate sponsorships in order to improve their funding; corporations seek out charities to improve their reputation. See also CAUSE-RELATED MARKETING.

consumer marketing is characterized by selling goods directly to the consumer for personal consumption. In contrast to the business-to-business marketer, the consumer marketer must address a market of many buyers with very few decision-makers in the overall pattern of purchasing. The amounts are usually relatively small and there is little direct contact or communication between the producer and the end customer. Consumer goods are largely sold through retailers and intermediaries rather than directly, which makes pricing and channel management very important components of the consumer marketing mix. See also BUSINESS-TO-BUSINESS MARKETING FOR CONTRASTS, BUYING, CONSUMER BEHAVIOUR.

customized marketing is the means by which marketers can customize products and services for individual customers. This is specifically when a supplier creates a product or service for an individual customer that did not exist before. This can exist in both personal service markets as well as in business-to-business markets. See also RELATIONSHIP MARKETING, CUSTOMER and MASS CUSTOMIZATION.

database marketing is a form of targeted marketing that makes use of customer data captured through customer transactions and communications. This data may be used independently or in conjunction with outside data to guide targeted customer prospecting, customer retention, promotions and other marketing efforts. For example, a database may have a collection of available information on past and current customers together with future prospects, structured to allow for implementation of effective marketing strategies. Consumer goods and services companies as well as political parties and organizations use these widely for various campaigns.

Database marketing began in the mid-1980s as computers and software became quite sophisticated and economical. It was possible to store information about customers, and use the information to build lasting relationships with them. As a result, it was possible to increase sales and profits by:

- changing customer buying behaviour;
- promoting cross sales, repeat sales and upgrades;
- computing customer lifetime value and using it in strategy evaluation;
- creating referrals and customer loyalty.

Database marketing progressed in sophistication and applications to become one-to-one marketing. However, in practice and in reality very few companies ever achieved effective one-to-one marketing. They used models to create customer profiles, segmenting customers into profitability or preference groups, and developed a different strategy for each group. But, to devise a different marketing strategy for each person who would be treated as a 'market of one' was really beyond the capability of any but the most sophisticated marketers. The Internet transformed and evolved the pursuit of highly customized marketing even more. It took several years before most marketers realized the potential of the Internet, but when they did they saw that the Internet had created a huge and inexhaustible database marketing system with worldwide ubiquity and scope. Using the Internet, it is possible now to do things that were only dreamed about in the early database marketing days.

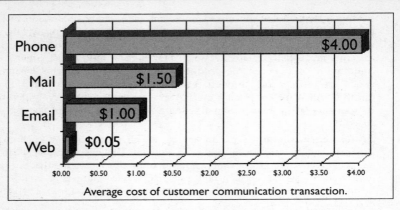

Average cost of customer communication transaction.

The range of database applications could support the following marketing programmes:

1. Focusing on new prospects;
2. Evaluating new prospects;
3. Cross-selling related products;
4. Launching new products to potential prospects;
5. Identifying new distribution channels;
6. Building customer loyalty;
7. Generating enquiries and follow-up sales;
8. Targeting niche markets.

Probably the greatest change in database marketing resulting from the commercialization of the Internet in the mid-1990s is in the area of customer service. Toll-free (1800 in the US, 0800 in the UK) numbers with customer service agents have advanced in the last fifteen years. Customer service agents began using computers to obtain the information asked for by customers from the database. They read the answers off the screen over the phone to the customers. Then they type into the customer database what happened and what was discussed during the call. It was a big advance on previous customer service, but customers started to complain that the service sounded wooden and robotic.

With the advent of the commercial Web, the approach to customer service is now about empowering the customer. Companies are giving customers web access to the same screens that the customer service agents see. Customers are now enabled to do their own searches and get their own answers. Customers can now get much more information over the Web than they could ever get from a live operator with a computer. Companies now put page after page of technical data, product specifications, descriptions, services, special offers and details on their websites with adequate indexing so that any customer or prospect can get all the information they want or need. This is valuable to the customer and the company for the following reasons:

- There is no long-distance call to pay for.
- There is no Customer Service Agent to pay for (an internet enquiry costs a bank only 10% of the processing cost for a customer service agent to handle the call 'live').
- The system is open for business 24 hours a day.
- The company can track what information people want and who wants it.
- Once the system is set up, the variable costs are almost nothing.

Unfortunately, despite the tremendous advantages of the Web, most companies have not fully exploited its promise and its power. For the Web to succeed it must be very value-added to customers. This will only happen when websites are designed and managed by marketers who understand the thinking of customers rather than technologists.

Some companies are using collaborative filtering with special software to make product suggestions to their customers both on the phone and on the Web. This software, linked to your customer database, starts to 'sense' and understand customer preferences based upon previous purchases and enquries. Amazon.com has excelled in this technique and is able to make book and CD recommendations whenever a returning customer comes to the website.

Many cataloguers are moving to put their entire catalogue on the Web, with photographs and descriptions of each product. Most companies that have done this have been disappointed with the response. A physical catalogue is still a better marketing tool than a digital catalogue on the Web in terms of portability, clarity of colour, and convenience. Where the Web wins is in its simplicity and speed of ordering the product, so long as the customers know what they want.

direct marketing is a technique rather than a marketing medium. It is a type of targeted marketing that uses several types of media (direct mail, printed material, telephone, fax, text message, e-mail) to effect a measurable customer response and, in some cases, a commercial transaction. The main purpose is to make a sale or to obtain a sales lead in a highly targeted but low-cost way. Direct marketing is an aspect of total marketing that is characterized by measurability and accountability, with heavy reliance on lists and data. The direct marketing explosion has been partly created by increasingly sophisticated database and database trading between companies who sell address and e-mail lists to each other. Additionally, the increase in the number of delivery services and high use of credit cards has also created greater channel range for the sale and delivery of goods directly. There are also some lifestyle components to this phenomenon: people increasingly have less time to shop and are equipped with computers and credit cards to make purchases from their homes. See also DATABASE MARKETING.

Based on a 2000 study in the U.S. (which is the most intensive exponent of direct marketing) the Direct Marketing Association's *U.S. Direct & Interactive Marketing Today* compared 'traditional' direct marketing with newer forms of direct marketing, generally called interactive marketing. Traditional direct methods continue to be the driving force of the advertising and marketing industries, generating $1.7 trillion in directly attributable sales for 2000, with a projected growth to $2.7 trillion in 2005.

Perhaps surprisingly, interactive direct marketing, while growing quickly, has not yet started to rival traditional marketing methods, and, in terms of usage, still lags behind virtually every other category of direct marketing (including, in order: direct mail, telemarketing, newspapers, magazines, television and radio) in both total expenditures as well as sales revenue attributable to direct marketing activities.

Traditional Direct Marketing

Value of direct marketing driven sales	$1.7 trillion
Value of traditional U.S. direct marketing expenditures in 2000	$191.6 (billions)
Projected growth of traditional direct marketing expenditures 2000-2005	9.6%%

Interactive Direct Marketing

Value of U.S. interactive direct marketing driven Sales	$136,412.7
Value of interactive U.S. direct marketing expenditures in 2000	$40,706.9 (millions)
Projected growth of interactive direct marketing expenditures 2000-2005	41.3%

Source: DIRECT MARKETING ASSOCIATION (North America)

Even though e-mail is much less expensive at an estimated 25 cents per mail sent compared to a traditional letter package at nearly $2.00 (according to Jupiter Communications) traditional direct marketing is projected to continue to outspend, outearn, and in general outpace interactive direct marketing until at least 2005.

Consumer research has shown that consumers are expressing distrust and irritation towards certain specific types of direct marketing. Personal privacy is a major element of these concerns. This trend could have a detrimental effect on the burgeoning direct marketing industry. The gradual buildup of negative attitude into consumer behaviour that rejects the approach could jeopardize the future of well-defined types of direct marketing communication. See also JUNK MAIL.

Moreover, there are an increasing number of initiatives being taken, not only by national and supranational authorities (such as the European Union) but also by consumers' organizations and direct marketing umbrella organizations to regulate the telemarketing business and to minimize irritation for the public. Public bodies tend to perceive direct marketing as a public nuisance that needs to be reduced and contained. The negative aspects of telemarketing, particularly intrusive cold calling and high-pressure selling, have come to the fore. This perception undermines this multifaceted marketing instrument that can be of service to both companies and customers in various ways.

direct response marketing is marketing directly to consumers, by mail, catalogue, or other home delivery, attempting to solicit orders by mail or a toll-free number. This can also include advertising through any medium designed to generate a direct, measurable response. See also DIRECT MARKETING and DATABASE MARKETING.

e-mail marketing is the use of e-mail to market goods and services. E-mail marketing content can be either general or customized. Frequency of transmission to targets can consist of fixed, frequent intervals or sporadic intervals, occurring only when there is something newsworthy to communicate, or else be based upon agreed permissions and registered interest from the receiver. Sophistication (and cost) can be very low or very high. E-mail can also be used to confirm orders of existing customers made through websites and to cross-sell to existing customers. E-mail is a new and convenient development of direct marketing.

Along with the marketing power of e-mail however, comes the abuse of e-mail, commonly known as spamming, which is unwanted and unsolicited e-mail. While some users fail to distinguish between permission marketing and e-mail spam, spamming is actually a major threat to legitimate e-mail marketers, as a glut of messages could make the entire e-mail medium less effective. It is the on-line equivalent of junk mail and is starting to be regarded as a public nuisance, but its global medium makes it much more difficult to regulate than junk mail which is delivered through national postal services and can be regulated by national consumer bodies. See also DATABASE MARKETING , INTERACTIVE MARKETING, E-MAIL SPAM AND DIRECT MARKETING.

enlightened marketing A marketing philosophy holding that a company's marketing should embody the five principles of **enlightened marketing**:

Consumer-oriented marketing A principle of enlightened marketing that holds that a company should view and organize its marketing activities from the consumers' point of view and place the customer at the centre of everything a company does.

Innovative marketing A principle of enlightened marketing that requires that a company seek real product and marketing improvements that are of benefit to mankind.

Value marketing A principle of enlightened marketing that holds that a company should put most of its resources into value-building marketing investments over the longer term.

Sense-of-mission marketing A principle of enlightened marketing that holds that a company should define its mission in broad social terms rather than narrow product or profit terms.

Societal marketing A principle of enlightened marketing that holds that a company should make marketing decisions by considering consumers' needs, the consumers' long-run interests together with society's long-run interests.

guerrilla marketing is a term coined by Jay Conrad Levinson in 1984 broadly meaning unconventional marketing in order to get maximum results from minimal resources. It is focused on gaining rapid attention and amplification through word of mouth. Guerrilla marketing is contrasted with traditional marketing, as guerrilla warfare is different from traditional warfare. It has come to represent low-budget marketing in which innovation, daring and wit are used to gain maximum exposure and attention using a targeted approach and concentrating both on new and unusual means of communication. Originally intended for small businesses who did not have access to vast corporate marketing resources, guerrilla marketing is now catching on in even the largest corporations who are seeking new ways to differentiate themselves in a noisy and cluttered market space. See also VIRAL MARKETING.

integrated marketing is based upon an integrated approach to marketing communications that influences transactions between an organization and its existing and potential customers, clients and consumers. Integrated marketing is more of a new marketing management approach than a new type of marketing. The primary focus of integrated marketing is to ensure that all communications, the brand positioning, propositions, reputation development, brand personality and messages, are delivered coherently and impactfully across every element of communication and are derived from a single brand positioning and message platform. This holistic approach to marketing communications includes well-managed co-ordination between advertising, public relations, new media, interactive marketing, internal communications, sales promotions, event and sponsorships. This is very necessary because of the simultaneous fragmentation and globalization of media channels and the growth of the Internet as a major communications channel. As clients became more sophisticated and media costs spiral, many companies feel a need to move away from mass advertising to a more targeted approach to selected media but where a similar message would repeat across all the channels.

Successful integrated marketing requires strong leadership, clear guidelines and policies, sophisticated media planning, a single marketing agency and a highly targeted approach to critical audiences as well as an avoidance of organizational silos and a strategic approach to communications. Creativity, as well as process integration, is required across all communications channels and programmes. Internal and external communications should also be integrated as employees are themselves the major representative and the major channel of communication to the customer. There should be little difference in the essence of messages to employees and messages to customers. See also INTERNAL MARKETING.

interactive marketing is usually conducted by a products or services company and is focused on serving customers using the Internet as the main two-way, direct marketing channel. Customers are showing an increased preference for dealing with suppliers interactively and remotely partly because it is convenient and saves time, particularly with problems of customer parking and crowding in city shopping areas. They also have the opportunity to gain a good deal of information and to look at alternatives in a low-pressure environment (i.e. their home) before buying. They can interact with the supplier and obtain advice. Interactive marketing has become most popular for banking where the customer can become his own transaction manager 24 hours a day, transferring funds between accounts, checking balances, paying bills, buying and selling shares and arranging other financial services without entering a bank's premises. Interactive marketing can also be used to create online, networked communities of interest around specific subjects. (See also PERMISSION BASED MARKETING).

Marketers using interactive techniques are increasingly able to customize their services to suit the customer as well as gather unprecedented information about the customer over a relatively low-cost channel. Specialist groups can be targeted and all interactions are only with the permission of the customer. New products and services can be tested far faster over the Internet. This helps with the development of customer relationships without the impediments of geographic separation. The main problem is the lack of personal contact that may limit the range of services to the transactional and the 'low touch' products. See also E-MAIL MARKETING, DIRECT MARKETING, DATABASE MARKETING, VIRAL MARKETING.

internal marketing is increasingly viewed as a vital part of the overall marketing mix. Previously confined to employees' internal communications, internal marketing is now seen to help in changing the behaviour and motivation of the organization. The rising importance of internal marketing is recognition that people are the main assets of most companies and that they are the main channel of customer communication and the service agents who deliver the final customer experience. It is very difficult to achieve excellence in customer marketing with demotivated employees. Many believe that there is an equation between satisfied internal customers and satisfied external customers.

Therefore, internal marketing has a role in galvanizing the organization as well as in overcoming any resistance to change. It informs and involves all staff in new initiatives and marketing strategies and can help to bring the brand to life at the level of individual behaviour. Internal marketing has similar processes and structures to external marketing. The main differences are that 'the market' is the staff and colleagues from within the organization.

In the diagram overleaf, Jobber (1995) describes a structure for the implementation of internal marketing. The process is straightforward.

- Set objectives for internal marketing: for example it may be to persuade employees of an intended course of action and to gain their consent and support.

- Tactics would include an internal application of the marketing mix, and could include staff forums, presentations, an intranet, away days, videos, webcasts, personal visits by company directors or newsletters.

- Evaluation would use an employees survey to determine the results of the internal marketing campaign.

The next stage in development in internal marketing is for marketing to be a force of integration within the organization: to link together business, financial, investment, human resources, marketing and marketing communication objectives against common, market or customer-centric objectives. For this purpose, internal marketing serves as an agent of change management. Key audiences should be identified and segmented. As with external customers, these internal constituencies will have their own buyer behaviour, or way of 'buying into' the changes the organization is trying to implement. The similarity in differing groups of internal customers allows segmentation. As Jobber (1995) explains, you can target three different segments, namely 'supporters, neutral,' and finally 'opposers.' Each group requires a slightly different internal marketing mix in order that internal marketing objectives can be achieved.

Internal marketing can also play a role in employee retention, which is more important than ever, given the high costs of recruiting and replacing a lost member of staff.

Internal Marketing (Jobber 1995)

international marketing combines multiple disciplines, but is mainly focused upon marketing goods and services across geographical boundaries, of entering foreign markets, or sustaining marketing and sales efforts within foreign countries and of co-ordinating marketing activities in multiple countries and regions. Each practitioner faces a hierarchy: global, international, regional, local and intriguing interplay between them. International marketing is one of the more problematic areas: striving for global, regional and local relevance and balance as well as economies of scale and brand. Segmentation is particularly difficult: are customers to be segmented on a country-by-country basis, or are they more appropriately grouped across geographic boundaries based upon their common needs and wants? Products – can they be standardized for international markets or do they need to be customized and adapted to each geographical market? The nature and methods of international marketing will also vary greatly depending on whether the company is addressing industrial or consumer products or services.

Often international marketing moves by degrees to become global marketing, by tracking the space of international expansion of the overall company and its activities: this can begin with small scale exporting and develop into full overseas acquisitions. Indeed, the task of the marketer relative to international expansion has become even more complex, because, as the level and scale of overseas expansion grows, the marketing becomes increasingly dependent upon a network of agents, alliances, collaborations, suppliers, sometimes joint venture partners, sometimes full acquisitions.

Once the company's international strategy and goals are formulated, the process of international marketing planning begins. As always, a good start point is to use dedicated market research to understand the geographical target. This is primarily a measure of market attractiveness: growth, size, GNP and general economic situation, strategic location, accessibility, experience in similar markets, social, legal, language and cultural understanding, risks of entering such as political volatility, friendliness of government (national or pan-regional) to business, business risk and competitive and currency risks.

The next stage is the evaluation of the costs of entry into these markets: investment, control, risk and return. Then the whole range of marketing planning begins in each country, with the appropriate level of marketing mix selected for each marketplace. Key decisions relate to adapting the right mix for the right country are: Product: can it be used in standard form or does it need to be customized? Distribution: what level of coverage and density, type of channel for the specific country and the distribution logistics? Prices: how are these to be determined for the local market and in what currency? Promotion: what is the most appropriate media channel and type of direct promotion in the given culture? It is also important for the marketing team to have a culturally diverse group with experience of international marketing rather than taking a team that have been successful in one geography and taking it to another.

Market entry

Market entry is a prelude to full establishment and penetration of the overseas market.

There are various ways in which a company can enter a foreign market: these can be divided into direct entry methods and indirect entry methods:

Direct entry methods

Formation of an International Division to control exports.

Establishment of foreign sales offices, sales force and branch offices.

Public trading agencies.

Investment in production and distribution facilities in foreign countries.

Joint ventures, particularly with companies with a strong presence in the target domestic market.

Creating a wholly-owned subsidiary located in the target overseas market.

Direct foreign acquisition of a local company in the target overseas market.

Indirect entry methods

Exporting directly to the target overseas market.

Use of export houses to market and sell product in the target market.

Franchising: create a franchise for a domestic local franchisee with local market knowledge and experience.

Licensing: for example licensing product rights to a local manufacturer or distributor.

Management contracts (whereby the contractee manufactures or assembles a product on behalf of the contractor).

Mail order or other forms of direct marketing from the domestic country to consumers in the target overseas market.

INTERNATIONAL MARKETING AND SALES STRUCTURES

There are several types of international marketing and sales structure:

1. The International Division of a company that handles: exporting, relationships with intermediaries and alliance partners, foreign currency operations, documentation and marketing programmes, foreign governments,

2. The International Product Division which handles the full panoply of non-standardized products and is filled with people knowledgeable of each market in which they operate and who are able to work directly with local sales forces to customize products to local markets.

3. The regional structure is a way of dividing the world into regions: typically North America, Asia Pacific and EMEAI. The concept is based on the view that transborder marketing and sales forces are not practically effective and that people of a particular culture and with local knowledge must carry out these operations within the country.

4. The functional organization that is set up around various international functions, such as capital markets, exploration and mining.

5. The matrix organization is an attempt to be more flexible and to combine geographical, expert functions with global management functions. The main draw back of this organizational form is factionalism over resource allocation and complexity of reporting and decision-making. See also EXPORTING.

location marketing is the use of marketing techniques to promote a specific place, such as a resort, a district, a city, a country or a region. This can be to attract tourists, inward investment or even to change the image of a location. Given that tourism is among the world's largest industries, this is a very important type of marketing.

macromarketing is an approach to the aggregate of all the producers and consumers within the population. Macromarketing tries to balance producer supply and consumer demand to produce a stable economy. Macromarketing differs from micromarketing in that micromarketing is looking at the economy from the consumer's perspective. See also MICROMARKETING.

mass marketing is a philosophy in which the seller views the market as a homogeneous whole, and, therefore, has only one marketing programme. A product of the Industrial Revolution, mass marketing implies the same product, the same price, the same promotion and the same distribution system for everyone. Mass marketing is declining as the dominant marketing technique in the advanced economies but is still healthy in the developing economies. Also referred to as **unsegmented marketing** or **undifferentiated marketing**. See also CONSUMER SOCIETY.

micromarketing is the study of marketing from the perspective of micromarkets or very narrowly segmented markets right down to individual customers in very small locations. These elements include the firm's suppliers, competitors, marketing intermediaries, customers and publics. See MICROSEGMENTATION.

micromarkets markets in which the volumes of demand are relatively small owing to the fragmentation or splintering of mass markets; markets in which there is great diversity in the needs and wants of customers. See MASS MARKETING.

microsegmentation the division of a market into smaller groups of customers on the basis of more narrowly defined needs and wants, after having already divided or segmented it on the basis of broadly defined needs and wants. See MARKET SEGMENTATION.

network/multilevel marketing is a form of direct selling in which distributors of a product attempt to sell to end-users and to others who will become themselves distributors. A network effect is created.

niche marketing is a marketing segmentation strategy designed to fill a specific or unserved need in a tightly defined part of the market. The entire company marketing efforts and resources are focused on serving one segment of the market. A concentrated marketing campaign will help to both gain deep knowledge of the specific niche and also ensure the product becomes more and more customized to meet the needs of the specific market. Niche marketing can be in the pursuit of higher profits or in an attempt to be the leader in a small market. Also known as **concentrated marketing** and **competitive advantage.**

non-profit marketing is marketing activities undertaken by organizations whose primary objectives are other than the traditional ones of profit, market share and return on investment. For example, this could be charities, organizations set up to promote certain ideas, educational institutions and purposes, religion, performing arts, cultural institutions such as museums and galleries, military services, government campaigns for health, good and humanitarian causes, political parties and the environment. The sources of funds and support for these types of organizations are rarely the beneficiaries of their work. The purposes of non-profit marketing are to bring in a source of revenue for the organization and also to create a positive climate of consent or appreciation for their work or cause. Sometimes called **non-business marketing**. See also CHARITY MARKETING.

permission marketing is a new school of marketing thinking popularized at the time of the e-commerce explosion; marketing whose central idea is that marketing of the future can only thrive by obtaining customer consent for direct marketing by discovering their natural affinities rather than hard selling. Coined and popularized by Seth Godin of Yahoo! in a book of the same name in 1999, permission marketing is the opposite of traditional 'interruption marketing', which is based on snatching the time and attention of customers who have not given their consent. Permission marketing is about building an ongoing relationship of increasing depth with customers, or to use Godin's own phrase in, 'turning strangers into friends, and friends into customers.' Permission marketing has been hailed as a way for marketers to succeed in a world increasingly cluttered with marketing messages and declining effectiveness of mass advertising. See also VIRAL MARKETING and RELATIONSHIP MARKETING.

relationship marketing (also known as one-to-one marketing) is the process of meeting customers' needs on a continuous and repeating basis by developing a long-term, one-to-one relationship with individual customers. It is, fundamentally, about marketing to customers, individually, one at a time. The purpose is to sell many services or products to the one customer rather than selling one service or product to many customers. It requires different mindset, different techniques. Relationship marketing is more prevalent in services businesses than in product businesses. The philosophy of relationship marketing recognizes that keeping existing customers happy, loyal and satisfied ensures repeat business (which is much cheaper than obtaining new customers). It is an approach that takes the long-term profit potential of an existing customer relationship into account. There is maximum emphasis on customer commitment, contact, keeping promises and building trust and human contact. Contact happens at multiple levels in the organization under a regime of customer account management.

Relationship marketing is distinguished from other types of marketing by a focus on customer outcomes and benefits rather than just selling product features. The relationship marketer must always take the long-term view of the customer relationship. It is an older style of marketing which got lost during the mass production age and which is being revived in the information age. In the past, salesmen or retail store staff accomplished much on an individual basis when confined to a physical local environment. Today, interactive technologies make it possible to perform similar functions on-line. The Web allows companies to track consumer preferences closely, both by asking the consumer directly and by auditing the consumer's actions as they surf the company website. This information can be used as a basis for providing a product or service that is customized to the consumer's preferences. With web technologies, a consumer's preferences can be polled during visits. The polled information can instantly be used to customize the product to meet the consumer's preferences, all in the same session. However, true relationship marketing cannot rely on these techniques alone and needs to be complemented with direct human interaction.

scientific marketing is marketing based on a systematic and fact-based approach that will help to maximize profits for a product or service. This discipline of marketing relies heavily on empirical data, trend forecasting and directly measurable results. It is where marketing meets mathematical modelling. Alternatively, scientific marketing can refer to the marketing of scientific innovation, research or services.

services marketing involves the marketing of something that is intangible and which is usually consumed at the point of delivery. Services can cover a wide range of offerings and be delivered by the same company or organization: professional services, customer services, medical services, entertainment services, personal care service, maintenance services. Services marketing has a different range of techniques and challenges from other forms of marketing. See also SERVICE MARKETS.

Key elements of services marketing:

1. People: in services businesses the delivered quality of many services depends on the quality of the people delivering it. See also INTERNAL MARKETING.

2. Physical evidence: given the intangible nature of services it is important to constantly illustrate the benefits with tangible evidence of success, for example customer reference sites where the application of the services have been successful.

3. Delivery processes: how the service is actually delivered can define the marketing programmes and the overall branding of the company.

The four core marketing management tasks for service marketers are:

1. Managing differentiation against competitors. Customers make fewer price comparisons with services than they do with product, but they do consider differentiation and unique qualities, particularly delivery and quality of the people delivering the service.

2. Managing the overall brand image. The customer's perception of the company is a critical factor when deciding to buy a service. Without a good reputation, it is impossible to have powerful service marketing programmes.

3. Managing the quality of service delivered to customers and setting their expectations. Customers view services as having variable and inconsistent quality. It is important to invest time in reducing the customer's uncertainty and only to promise what can be delivered, to avoid disappointment and loss of reputation and trustworthiness.

4. Managing communications: use clear, unambiguous messages to communicate the range, depth, quality and level of services. Messages should emphasize the benefits of the service rather than their technical details. Build on word of mouth communication from one satisfied customer to another.

social marketing is a concept advocated in the 1970s by Philip Kotler and Gerald Zaltman that applies commercial marketing principles to the propagation of ideas and behaviours that should bring about social benefit and change. Among the important concepts are: that marketing can influence action; that action is undertaken whenever target audiences believe that the benefits they receive will be greater than the costs they incur; that programmes to influence action will be more effective if they are based on an understanding of the target audience's own perceptions. Examples might be to change a society's eating and drinking habits to promote better health, or campaigns to encourage people to register to vote, or to promote energy conservation.

symbiotic marketing is a marketing method in which one manufacturer sells its finished product to another for resale under the second manufacturer's label, where that manufacturer already has access to the market through a well-established distribution system. It is a mutually beneficial and reinforcing relationship.

viral marketing is a new marketing phenomenon that facilitates and encourages people to pass along a marketing message, usually by word of mouth but also using interactive networks and forums. It depends on a high pass-along rate from person to person. If a large percentage of recipients forward something to a large number of friends, the overall growth can multiply very quickly. If the pass-along numbers get too low, the overall growth rapidly declines. At the height of the dot.com boom, it seemed that every Internet start-up had a viral component in its marketing strategy. However, relatively few marketing viruses achieve success on a scale similar to Hotmail, Microsoft's free e-mail service, which is widely cited as the first example of viral marketing. Its spread helped Microsoft to dominate Internet access. See also WORD OF MOUTH.

---

market leader the company in an industry with the largest market share relative to competitors. It usually leads other firms in price changes, new product introductions, distribution coverage, and promotion spending. To be market leader in a defined market space is generally the goal of all marketers.

market nicher a company that serves small segments of an industry that the other firms overlook or ignore. Being a 'niche player' is often a deliberate choice, based upon evaluation of target markets and an attempt to create competitive advantage. See also COMPETITIVE ADVANTAGE.

market positioning the technique by which marketers give their company, its product and services and capabilities, a distinctive position or image relative to competing products and services.

The key elements of a market positioning programme are:

1. market segmentation (see below);

2. targeting customers within the market segments;

3. well-defined and articulated differential advantage around products, services and propositions;

4. a coherent brand positioning strategy and integrated marketing plan to support it;

5. an overall strategy for maintaining the desired position relative to the competitors;

6. a message architecture, with messages tailored to different audiences within a given market. For example, there may be one set of positioning messages for the media that reports on a given market and another set for the actual customers who compose and define the market;

7. increasingly, an internal communications plan that encourages employees to 'live' the positioning in their day-to-day behaviour and in their interactions with clients;

8. a fully integrated set of communications programmes to execute the positioning. See also MARKETING STRATEGY, COMPETITION.

market penetration a strategy to encourage intensive growth of current products and services in current markets, measured primarily by relative market share. There are three general marketing methods to achieve greater market penetration:

- sell more to existing customers;
- win customers from competitors *or*
- win new customers for existing products and services.

Market penetration also informs on consumer demand and acceptability in a given market. See also ANSOFF MATRIX, COMPETITION and PRICING.

MARKET RESEARCH

A major discipline of marketing whose main function is intelligence gathering and analysis on a particular market, industry, geography, customer group, competitors or specific product or service area. Marketing campaigns are like war strategies: they are highly dependent upon good intelligence, before, during and after the event. In successful marketing campaigns, market research is vital to bringing a deeper understanding of the target market: its size, growth, segments, trends and dynamics, customer groupings, customer wants, needs and desires, competitors and their campaigns, demographics.

The main uses of market research are: to position a business or strategic programme; to assist in new product or service launches; to evaluate a product or service's strengths and weaknesses which will help determine how to improve a product or service; to determine consumer wants, needs and desires; to analyse competition. Research can also help to identify new market opportunities for a product or service. Market research can help test concepts to get initial market testing and evaluation. It can research responses to marketing programmes. Market research can identity and analyse consumer attitudes and intentions and feed these back to marketing managers to test viability of new launches.

Example: Market research and new product launches.

Before a marketing campaign for a new product begins, substantial research needs to be done. Secondary research is carried out to see if there is a similar type of product or service currently in existence or in the marketplace. If such a product or service does exist, then the market researcher scans all published information and data about it in order to determine its market position and the market potential for a rival product or service. If the market is forecast to be very large, the company may choose to launch the product and compete with existing companies that are currently in the market. If the market is not supposed to grow, the company may decide to reconsider or may launch something different.

Suppose a company wants to launch a new car. Secondary market reports and forecasts for cars may provide useful information, but primary research would be more applicable. Since consumers purchase cars based upon brand name, features as well as reputation, consumer wants and needs are extremely important. Interviews or focus groups may be conducted. Consumers may be interviewed to determine which features are of the most importance. They may also be shown sketches of different versions of interiors, exteriors or various features such as headlights or dashboard configurations to see which ones are preferred. Based upon these interviews and focus groups, the car manufacturer will know what features to include with the car based upon primary research.

While the product is being developed, primary research is again used to determine consumer reaction, or in the car example, which additional features or packages would be most popular.

Once the product is completed, marketing of the product begins. In many instances, a smaller, test market may be used to test consumer acceptance before the product is launched nationally. Again, primary market research plays an important role. A group of consumers may be asked to try the product and report their findings. Perhaps a new food product is being launched and interviewers will give consumers a taste of the new product and study their facial expressions and ask them questions about what they liked and didn't like about the food product. At this point, modifications may still be made before a national launch. Perhaps, the consumers did not like the colour of the product or maybe they did not like the smell. These are all changes that can be made before a national launch, whereas, if the product was not tested before a small group, the consumers who end up purchasing the product may never buy it again. The consumer-tasting panel can help make or break a new food product. When the product is launched nationally, consumer panels may still be used to bring about product awareness. In addition, the company will probably advertise the product heavily as well. Further research on product purchase data can then be gathered to see what areas of the country are good markets for the product. Areas where the products do not sell as well would need to be researched in order to determine why. If consumers are not aware of the product, they may not purchase it. Advertising would need to be increased in these markets to increase awareness and potential sales. Further research may show that a specific area is just not a good market for the new product.

The continued success of the product is dependent upon post-launch research. Primary research needs to be done to ensure the consumer's interests and tastes are met by the product. Potential enhancements for a new and improved version can be gained through customer panels, interviews and focus groups feedback as well as surveys of current users. Continuous research on the product and how it can be improved will always leave a good impression with the consumer, who will view the manufacturers as very customer-oriented and thereby bring product differentiation between their product and the similar product from a competitor. Competitor research also plays a crucial role in the continued success of a product. Research also needs to be done to find out the market share of the competitor, and why people are buying the competitors' products. If the company wants to increase market share, it may do additional primary research to study the buying habits of the consumers in order to determine how to get more customers. If the product is lacking a wanted feature, it can be added. All this can be determined by good research. The successful product will continuously use research to see how the product can be improved.

TECHNIQUES OF MARKET RESEARCH

There are many market research tools and techniques, which are listed below:

ACASI is audio computer-aided self-administered interviewing. These are self-administered surveys in which the respondent listens to the questions over headphones. Responses are usually registered using a computer-based questionnaire. If responses are recorded on paper it is known as audio SAQ.

anthropomorphic is a research technique in which participants describe a product, service or brand in terms of a human being with personality traits so that the participants' feelings about the object/brand can be determined.

applied research is any research that is used to answer a specific question, determine why something failed or succeeded, solve a specific, pragmatic problem, or to gain better understanding.

area samples are samples that include specific geographic areas as part of the sample design.

at-home testing is when a product sample is provided for participants to use at home. The reaction to the product is determined in a follow-up telephone survey, written survey or in a group session.

attitudinal scaling is used to understand a respondent's feelings or attitudes towards a certain area. In most instances, respondents are asked how they view or rank two different variables in relationship to each other. For example, how would someone view the price of a product relative to the perceived value that the product provides?

audit is the examination and verification of the sale of a product. A method for measuring sales in a store by counting beginning inventory, adding new shipments, and subtracting ending inventory. Also used to determine inventory lost to theft. See also MARKETING AUDIT.

back room is the room from which client personnel observe and listen to focus group proceedings through a two-way mirror. Also called the **observation room** or **viewing room.**

benchmark is a source against which one compares the area that is being researched. For example, one may compare the results of a study in one region to the results of the nation as a whole. See also BENCHMARKING.

bias in market research is the opposite of detached objectivity. There can be biased questions, biased responses or biased samples within market research. Biased questions occur when the questions are slanted in such a way as to elicit a particular response from the respondent. Biased questions can occur from the way the questions are phrased. Bias can also be introduced from an interviewer's facial or body expressions. A biased response occurs when the respondent says something that is not true. Biased responses can be made consciously or subconsciously. A biased sample occurs when the sample used is not representative of the population.

bipolar scale is a scale used for a range of responses with the extremes at opposite ends and more moderate responses in the middle. It forces the respondent to make some sort of choice rather than to stay neutral. An example of a bipolar scale would be the following choices:

1. Unacceptable;
2. somewhat unacceptable;
3. somewhat acceptable;
4. Very acceptable.

A four-point scale is useful if what is being measured does not have absolutes. Many researchers stay away from five-point scales because respondents frequently choose the middle (3) or average response if they do not have a strong leaning one way or another.

bivariate data is a data set where there are two sets of variables.

CAPI (computer-aided personal interviewing) is interviewer-administered surveying using a computer-based questionnaire.

CASI (computer-aided self-administered interviewing) is self-administered surveying using a computer-based questionnaire.

CATI (computer-aided telephone interviewing) is interviewer-administered telephone surveying using a computer-based questionnaire.

causation is the inference that a change in one variable is responsible for an observed change in another variable.

clarifying is a follow-up technique for getting complete responses to open-ended questions by asking respondents to explain general terms in their answers.

clinical focus groups are focus groups that explore subconscious motivation. Psychologists are frequently used as facilitators on these focus groups to interpret the buyer behaviour patterns.

closed-end question questions that ask the respondent to choose from a limited number of pre-listed answers.

cluster analysis is used when the sample is divided into different groups based upon various types of data or facts that are similar, or where there are very small differences. Cluster analysis is typically used for brand research or consumer segmentation. This would simplify the analysis process since large clusters rather than many small pieces of data only would need to be analysed. The differences within a particular cluster must be smaller than the differences between different clusters. Once the clusters or segments are identified, marketing themes can be identified for each specific segment or cluster.

cluster sampling the selecting of clusters of units in a population and then performing a census on each cluster. The selection of clusters could be based on some desired feature of the population or could be a random sample of clusters in the population.

conjoint analysis is a versatile market research technique that can provide valuable information for market segmentation, new product development, forecasting and pricing decisions. The technique is important in competitive positioning of new products and in new product development. It seeks to determine the relative importance and strength of various combinations of product attributes in the minds of target customers. The background research on conjoint analysis focuses on combinations rather than individual attributes of products and services. Respondents are asked to evaluate various combinations of attributes, and then asked to evaluate them overall. The objective is to find the right combination for the right target market. For example, the perfect combination for the British middle-class buyer of a Volvo may be safety and durability, rather than safety and style. In a real purchase situation, buyers examine and evaluate a range of features or attributes in making their final purchase choice. Conjoint analysis examines these evaluations and exchanges to determine what features are most valued by buyers. Once data is collected the researcher can conduct a number of 'choice simulations' to estimate market share for products with different attributes/features. This lets the researcher know which products or services will be successful before the product is introduced to the market.

Conjoint analysis helps to answer the following questions:

Which new products will be successful?

Which features or attributes of a product or service drive the purchase decision?

Do specific market segments exist for a product?

What advertising appeals will be most successful with these segments?

Will changes in product design increase consumer preference and sales?

What is the optimal price to charge consumers for a product or service? Can price be increased without a significant loss in sales?

conjoint association is a moderation technique in which participants are asked to choose between two hypothetical products or services, each of which has different attributes. The objective is to stimulate discussion about the various attributes in order to gain insight into the relative value of each.

consumer unit all related members of a particular household; a person living alone or sharing a household with others, who is financially independent; two or more persons living together who pool their incomes to make joint purchases.

co-op payment the payment provided to participants as an incentive to come to the focus groups or answer surveys. The amount varies dramatically, based on the difficulty of recruiting the participants. Also called the **honorarium** or **incentive**.

corporate marketing research department oversees and/or conducts research to support the firm's present or future marketing efforts, particularly overall positioning and market strategy.

cross-elasticity the extent to which products are substitutes for one another. Marketers use differentiation and quality to seek to minimize cross-elasticity and thus it could be seen as part of brand equity or marketing effectiveness.

cross-tabulation a table that shows the number of times a variable may occur. Cross-tabulation is the most popular of all multivariate and bivariate statistical procedures. It is used to show the link, or correlation, between variables and can be easily set up. This method of analysis is frequently used for analysing demographic data. An example would be the correlation between age and neighbourhood location.

customer satisfaction research research conducted to measure overall satisfaction with a product or service and satisfaction with specific elements of the product or service. Increasingly, many companies use this research as part of the compensation of their executives responsible for serving customers.

data for market research purposes, a collection of relevant information or informed observations. Collecting good and valid data is crucial to marketing since it drives strategic and tactical decisions. When gathering data, it is important to determine the source of the data as well as the context the data has come from. Not all sources of data are reliable, so it is necessary to understand how the data was gathered, where it was gathered from, what means and techniques were used and what was included in the data set in order to draw correct conclusions. Data is usually the raw and untreated facts and opinions that have been gathered through the data gathering process. Hard data is the scientific collection of the latter; soft data is more a collection of emotions and opinions around the same subject that have been collected anecdotally.

Also, in the context of market research there is primary and secondary data. Primary data is that which is collected directly from the target respondent group, for example by means of a structured interview or questionnaire. Secondary data is information that has been gathered for another purpose, neither directly by the user nor specifically for the user, often under conditions not known to the user. Secondary data, for example, may include Government reports, economic information, industry analyst information, trade associations reports. Banks, stockbrokers and market research reports are other potential sources of information. International secondary data can be collected in the home country or in the country to be researched. Non-governmental sources include consultants and international agencies.

There is also internal data that is specific to and generated by the organization, for example, sales statistics (by customer, by product), financial data such as profitability (by product/by customer), customer complaints, inventory levels or debtor information.

Secondary and internal data are useful background and context setting for primary research. With the tools available today, it can be gathered very quickly, and is much lower-cost than primary data collection.

data mining the process of gathering or locating pertinent information from a database. This is particularly key to customer marketing as it enables multiple combinations, for example customers who bought a certain type of car at a certain location in a certain time period. The key to data mining is to understand what data you are trying to collect and to go through all the combinations and variable data until you find that which is needed.

data processing the organization of data for the purpose of producing desired information, involving recording, classifying, sorting, summarizing, calculating, disseminating and storing data.

data protection a range of security measures used to protect valuable data. Gathered data on a database needs to be protected against hackers as well as software and network system failures. Many software packages exist which password-protect information and also provide data back-ups so that important information will not be lost.

density a measure that is computed by dividing the total population of a geographic unit by its land area measured in square miles or square kilometres.

depth interview a one-on-one interview that probes and elicits detailed answers to questions, often using nondirective techniques to uncover hidden motivations.

desk research another name for SECONDARY RESEARCH

diary panel a survey in which the same respondents keep a diary of what they watch, listen to, or buy, etc., over specified period of time.

direct computer interviewing where consumers are intercepted in a shopping mall or other central location and interviewed by a computer that asks questions and accepts responses.

double sampling collection of data through an inexpensive sampling technique for a sample larger than the final desired sample size. A subsample of this group is then selected and sampled, usually with a more expensive technique.

exhibit anything that is shown to respondents during an interview. Examples might be a print advertisement, a card listing income categories or a new package for familiar products. Also known as **external stimuli.**

expected value the mean of a probability distribution. It is the value of the probability distribution we would expect in the long run.

experiencing focus groups focus groups that enable a client to observe and listen to how consumers think and feel about products and services.

exploratory focus groups focus groups that aid in the precise definition of the problem, in pilot testing, or in generating hypotheses for testing or concepts for further research.

exploratory research preliminary research to clarify the exact nature of the problem to be solved.

external stimuli see EXHIBIT.

factor analysis used by researchers to make large sets of data more manageable by reducing the number of variables and by determining commonality between these variables. For example, if there is a questionnaire with 100 questions on how travellers choose which hotels they frequent, the answers can potentially be grouped together by similarity to bring the total answer set down to 20 or 30. There may be a category called service that would include things like speed and efficiency of checkins and checkouts, or how fast room service or housekeeping respond to inquiries. Another item that might be included in the service factor could be how friendly the staff is.

field research the gathering of survey data on location. Field research is a technique used in primary research.

focus group a method of studying behaviours or responses by having an organized group of participants discuss a given topic or product or idea. Focus groups are typically used in consumer research where it is necessary to obtain information about an individual's reactions, behaviours and usage patterns and to understand the reasoning behind these patterns or behaviours. It is a qualitative market research technique and needs a skilled moderator. A good size for a focus group is about 10 people. Typically, 3-4 focus groups would be run around a specific topic. The first focus group should provide a lot of insight. The next couple of focus groups should re-inforce the conclusions that have come out of the first focus group. After 3-4 focus groups, there is not as much valuable information that can be obtained and there are diminishing returns for the investment. Focus groups can be used in conjunction with interviews.

geocoding (or geographic encoding) the process whereby addresses are segmented by county, district, road, etc., in order to compare them with information about the demographics and psychographics of those geographies. Geocoding is integral to demographically enhanced mailing lists and cluster analysis. See also GEODEMOGRAPHICS.

geodemographic segmentation system a multivariate statistical classification technique for discovering whether the individuals of a population fall into different groups by making quantitative comparisons of multiple characteristics. The differences within any group should be less than the differences between groups. Often used for consumer segmentation and brand positioning. Often known as **cluster analysis**. See also ACORN, GEODEMOGRAPHICS.

global focus groups focus groups conducted using satellite video technology in which participants are located in different places, normally in different countries. Also called **video focus groups.**

grid a graphic provided to focus group participants in conceptual mapping and attitudinal scaling exercises.

group interview a qualitative research technique involving a discussion among eight to ten respondents, led by a moderator. Also called **focus groups, group discussions, panels,** and **group depth interviews.**

hedonic scale a scale for measuring general overall opinion of a product

honorarium see CO-OP PAYMENT.

host/hostess the individual responsible for greeting the focus participants as they arrive at the facility and for preparing the room. The responsibilities of a hostess include providing food for the participants and the client observers, screening respondents when they arrive, preparing name tags, etc.

incentive a fee that is paid to respondents of a questionnaire or a focus group or an interview. Incentives will protect against non-response rates for surveys or focus groups. Often, the people who choose not to respond are very different from the people who choose to respond, so increasing the response rate will allow for a less biased result.

intercept an interview method in which an interviewer stops people in an airport, shopping precinct or other public location and administers a research survey.

interviews in market research are the gathering of information by asking participants questions. Interviews are one of the most widely used techniques in **primary research**. Interviews can be used to gather both quantitative as well as qualitative information depending upon how open-ended the questions are. Interviews can be conducted in a variety of ways: in person, over the telephone, on-line or via the mail.

laddering a probing technique, used in one-on-one interviews and focus groups, designed to delve into the real reasons for participants' attitudes and behaviour toward the topic. It is generally considered to be an intensive technique. The moderator seeks the reason behind each answer until he or she arrives at a basic human need such as ego or status.

Lelly triads are also known as repertory grids. Used especially by advertising agencies to elicit consumer language for the products in question. Products (or whatever) are written or pictured on cards that are dealt three at a time. The respondent is invited to pick the odd one out and explain why it is odd. The language and key discriminators are noted. See also ADVERTISING.

lifestyle research research that attempts to explain behaviour by analysing people's attitudes, hobbies, activities and opinions. Often associated with psychographic research.

lifestyle selectivity selectivity based on lifestyle habits of segments of the population, e.g., hobbies, interests, ownership etc.

mapping the process by which a computer generates thematic maps that combine geography with demographic information and a company's sales data or other proprietary information.

Markov model sets out in matrix form the probability that the user of each brand in a category will switch next time to each other brand. Mathematically sound, and now measurable through retail scanners and point of sale systems.

metropolitan area used by the US Census Bureau to define an area where there is a concentration of people that can be used for statistical purposes. A MSA or Metropolitan Statistical Area is defined as a city or urbanized area with at least 50,000 inhabitants.

moderator the person who is the leader for a focus group or a discussion group. A moderator is necessary for open-ended discussions in order to keep the discussion on track and to make sure everything gets covered in the time allotted. Also known as a **facilitator.**

multidimensional scaling is a type of analysis used for making a perceptual or concept map. In multidimensional scaling (MDS), each statement or concept is represented by a single point. Things that are perceived to be similar to each other are grouped together. MDS is used as an alternative to factor analysis where the comparisons must be linear. MDS is frequently used to determine perception of how similar different brands are. MDS will allow for a visualization of product positioning. It helps answer the following questions:

- How should a product be positioned?
- How is the product positioned compared to our competitors?

multivariate statistics a method of looking at several groups of data where there are many different variables, then studying the relationship between these variables simultaneously. By grouping the variables or people, it would be much easier to identify factors for success. Product usage as well as the relationship between advertising and product purchasing can also be determined. Common types of multivariate analysis include: **factor analysis, multidimensional scaling, cluster analysis, conjoint analysis and regression analysis.**

mystery shoppers people employed to pose as consumers and shop at the competitors' and their own stores to compare prices, displays, merchandising and sales offers.

observational research the collection of data by observing behaviours or actions. Observational research is often used in focus groups where a two-way mirror allows people to view the reactions and behaviours of the respondents. Though observational research only provides information on current behaviour, it is nonetheless a very inexpensive and accurate way of providing behavioural data. This type of research is also extremely useful when it is difficult to persuade the respondents to verbalize their behaviours or thoughts. For example, a child's toy manufacturer may set up new toys in a play area and watch how the children play with the toys to determine which ones might be most successful.

observation room see BACK ROOM.

omnibus panel a study over time in which the sponsoring research company defines the audience to be surveyed and the intervals between studies. Numerous clients participate by submitting proprietary questions. Generally clients only receive results from their proprietary questions and general demographic questions.

on-air testing testing used to measure the impact of television and radio ads after they have begun to run on the air. See also ADVERTISING.

paired comparison a comparison between two different products or variables. Paired comparisons are frequently used to determine which product a consumer would prefer, for example Coke or Pepsi. Marketers can then use these comparisons to claim one product is superior to another in their marketing campaigns.

panel a survey where the respondents are interviewed repeatedly over a length of time. Also known as a **longitudinal study**. The term panel can also be used to describe the respondents in a group interview. See also FOCUS GROUP.

Pearson's Coefficient Correlation the most frequently used method to determine the strength of the relationship between two variables. The correlation coefficient is between -1 and 1; if there is a positive relationship, the coefficient is 1 and if there is a negative relationship the coefficient is -1. For example, if the statement that the taller an individual the more he would weigh were always true, the coefficient would be 1 since as the height increased, the weight would always increase. If the person would weigh less the older he became, it is a negative coefficient.

penetration analysis an analysis of how pervasive or widespread a particular product is in a given market. This is used to calculate market share or market penetration. See also MARKET PENETRATION.

perceptual mapping the 'mapping' of a product or service based upon its attributes. For example, a perceptual map of a luxury item would include how it was perceived on a number of attributes such as price, quality, reputation, and customer service and prestige. Mapping has a variety of marketing purposes including market segmentation, identifying whether or not a product has any weaknesses as well as consumer preferences and perceptions. Perceptual mapping can also be used to determine how a company is perceived against variable perception attributed to its target audience.

primary research original data collection or research direct from the target respondents. Primary research is different from secondary research in that secondary research uses data or research that has already been collected. Primary research includes qualitative and quantitative research and can include surveys, focus groups, questionnaires and interviews. Since primary research typically takes anywhere from weeks to months to gather and is very expensive, secondary sources are typically exhausted first before any primary research is conducted.

product positioning research research used to determine how competitive brands are perceived relative to each other on key dimensions.

product pricing research research used to measure consumer sensitivity to different prices for a product.

product prototype tests tests conducted to obtain the reactions of targeted customers to early working versions of new products.

professional respondent a participant who attends many sessions by volunteering for the recruitment lists of different facilities. Most moderators seek to eliminate professional respondents from groups, since they do not generally respond in the same objective way that fresh respondents do.

psychographics research that attempts to explain behaviour by analysing people's personality traits and values. Often associated with lifestyle research.

qualitative research research based upon subjective evaluations of behaviours, attitudes or events. Qualitative research techniques include **focus groups**. Qualitative research involves a much smaller sample of respondents and is often used to verify quantitative research techniques. For example, if buyer statistics show a certain age group favours a particular brand of car (quantitative research), qualitative research will indicate why people are buying this brand. This customer understanding can help to market this brand of automobile. For example, perhaps people buy this brand because it feels more luxurious and comfortable. A marketing campaign on the comfort and the luxury may help bring about further sales.

quantitative research research based upon hard data where there are definitive and absolute answers. Large groups of people can be surveyed and statistics and data can be gathered. Quantitative research is frequently used in conjunction with qualitative research to provide hard evidence. For example, if focus groups (qualitative research) show that consumers buy a certain brand of automobile because of all the safety features, the researcher may want to gather accident statistics to determine how safe the automobile is. If the statistics show owners of a certain type of automobile indeed have fewer accidents, then the safety record of the vehicle can be used in an advertising campaign.

questionnaire a set of questions that are used to draw conclusions and to collect data. Questionnaires can be used in both quantitative as well as qualitative research depending upon how open-ended the questions are.

questions the route to knowledge in the market research process. Two types of questions are used: open-ended questions and close-ended questions. Open-ended questions are used to determine attitudes or opinions. There is not a finite set of answers for open-ended questions. Close-ended questions require a finite set of answers such as a yes or no or a multiple choice. Close-ended questions are used to gather statistics and data that can then be used to monitor usage of a product for sales or forecasting purposes. Close-ended questions are also called **structured questions.**

quota a predetermined number of interviews or questionnaires that must be completed. The quota can be defined by the market researcher or by the company requesting the interviews.

regression analysis is used to study the relationship between several independent variables and a dependent variable. For example, two individuals can have the same amount in terms of disposable income, but one individual could have a family to support while another individual may not. These variable factors can affect how much money the individual would choose to spend on a new goods and services.

respondent the person being interviewed or surveyed. Also called **participant, unit, unit of analysis, subject** or **experimental unit.**

response bias an error that results from the tendency of people to answer a question falsely, through deliberate misrepresentation or unconscious falsification.

sample a portion of the population which is used to study behaviours, attitudes or events. Determining the proper sample size is crucial for delivering accurate research results.

sampling the method by which the sample is selected. There are two major types of sampling: probability and non-probability. Probability sampling is where every element of the population has an equal chance of being part of the sample. Common types of probability sampling include **random sampling, systematic sampling, stratified sampling** and **cluster sampling.** Random sampling is typically done by computer-generated random numbers. Phone calls can be made with a random number dialler. A random sample is based upon chance where each element has equal weighting. Random samples can be used for both quantitative and qualitative research.

Systematic sampling starts with a random number and then every nth number after that becomes part of the sample population. For example, if there is a total population of 100 and the researcher decided to look at 10% of the population, there would be a random number drawn, say 45. Then the researcher would choose every 10th number until you reach your sample size. So systematic sample would be: 45, 55, 65, 75, 85, 95, 05, 15, 25, and 35.

Stratified sampling is used to ensure the sample size is representative of the larger population. For example, in a population of 100, there are 60 men and 40 women. If 10 people are needed, then it is necessary to make sure that 6 are men and 4 are women in order to have the same ratio in the sample size. A random or systematic approach is then used to choose the 6 men and 4 women.

Cluster sampling is used when there are many people to be interviewed in order to save time and money. For example, if all chief purchasing officers in the Fortune 500 companies were to be interviewed, the researcher could group all the chief purchasing officers in each company into a cluster and treat each individual company as one single entity. Then companies would be chosen based upon a random or systematic approach and the researcher would then interview the purchasing officers within the selected companies. If the researcher interviewed all the purchasing officers within the company, it would be a single stage cluster sample. If the researcher broke down the list of purchasing officers within the selected company and used a random or systematic approach to interview a sub set of those individuals, this would be a two-stage sample.

Non-probability sampling is when certain elements of a population will have a greater chance of being selected than others. Respondents are chosen with some subjectivity because the interviewer feels they are representative of the population they are trying to survey. Types of non-probability sampling include: **quota sampling, convenience sampling, judgmental sampling, snowball design** as well as **self-selection**.

In quota sampling, a quota is determined by what the population at large is composed of. For example, someone may want to interview 100 shoppers. If 10% of the shopping population is determined to be male and elderly, the interviewer must then interview 10 elderly, male shoppers.

Convenience sampling is where an interviewer will talk to anyone at random who is willing to stop and be interviewed. This is sometimes mistaken as random sampling; however, it never provides a true random sample of the population since there will be a much higher probability of bias and skewed results. Convenience sampling is often used as a pre-test to a questionnaire to determine if the questions are understandable and produce the desired results.

Judgmental sampling occurs when the researcher uses his expert opinion to determine what would constitute a representative sample. Judgmental sampling is typically more biased. For example, if someone chooses to interview the shoppers in the in the middle of a workweek during the day, it is more likely that business people would not be well represented. However, sometimes it may be the intent of the interviewer to interview more housewives or retired people since they are the ones who may be doing the bulk of the shopping. In addition, if the sample size is very small and limited to a few people, a judgmental sample may deliver more representative results than a probability sample. In the shopping centre example, the interviewer may deliberately choose to question one businessperson, one student, one retiree, and one housewife. A random or probability sample of four people would most likely not produce a businessperson to be interviewed.

Snowball design is a type of judgmental sampling where the respondents are then asked to identify additional candidates to be interviewed. This method is very useful for identifying very specialized groups of people to be interviewed where it would otherwise take a great deal of research to identify these individuals.

Self-selection sampling occurs when the respondent makes the decision whether or not to participate in the survey

screening a preliminary set of questions that are asked to determine if the respondents are suitable for a particular study. Screening is done at the beginning of the entire interview process.

secondary data has been collected through a third party. This is different from primary data where the data is collected specifically for the research project. See also DATA.

secondary research (or **desk research**) uses information that has already been compiled and formatted. It is different from primary research, which is also known as original research. Analysis is frequently done with research that has been provided by a third party. This is also known as syndicated research. Other sources for secondary research include investment banks and associations or organizations. In research, it is important to assess the secondary information that exists before time and money is spent to conduct new research. Since primary research takes a much longer time to complete and is extremely expensive, decisions are often made to go with whatever secondary research is available in the interest of both time and money. A good secondary researcher will be able to suggest proxies or alternatives in lieu of performing primary research.

semantic differential a method of examining the strengths and weaknesses of a product or company versus the competition by having respondents rank it between dichotomous pairs of words or phrases that could be used to describe it; the mean of the responses is then plotted in a profile or image.

statistics compiles data to reach conclusions

survey a questionnaire that is used to gather information on attitudes or behaviours.

survey research is a research technique that uses questionnaires to gather data. See also PRIMARY RESEARCH. Types of survey research include: *Interpersonal*, when the questions are asked in person. This method allows the interviewer to study the reactions of the respondents more easily. Personal interviews generally allow for the greatest amount of flexibility and can also deliver a substantial amount of data. However, personal interviews are one of the most expensive ways to gather data. There are various interpersonal interview channels. Questions can be asked over the *telephone*. This method is used for shorter surveys that typically last about 10 minutes. However, there may be some issues with the accuracy of the data that is gathered via a telephone interview. Also it is difficult to observe body language and include group interaction over the telephone. *On-line* is when the questions are asked via an e-mail or a website survey. This method is very convenient as the respondent can fill out the questionnaire at his convenience. However, there may be some biases towards Internet-enabled households. Cost-wise, on-line surveys are the cheapest to administer and can deliver the best response rate. *Postal* surveys are answered via the mail. Mail surveys generally produce very good, non-biased results and are relatively inexpensive to administer. However, the amount of data that can be collected is not as good.

syndicated research is conducted by a third party based upon their definition as to who the survey respondents would be, as well as what questions are asked. The data, once collected, is sold to anyone who would be willing to pay the price. Successful syndicated research firms typically specialize in specific markets. The advantage of using syndicated research is that the research is perceived by the public to be more objective than research conducted by companies trying to market their own products. A secondary researcher will look at what syndicated research is available. See SECONDARY RESEARCH.

telephone focus groups are used in qualitative research, in which seven to ten people are connected in a telephone conference call and a trained moderator leads them through a discussion about a particular topic. Basically a focus group that is conducted via conference calling.

telephone research is survey research that is done over the phone. This can either be qualitative or quantitative, depending upon whether or not the questions asked are open-ended.

time series analysis data that is collected and reported in intervals of time. This is also called **exponential smoothing.**

top-of-mind awareness (TOMA) is used in brand research where a respondent is asked which brand names come immediately to mind, without any prompting or mention of specific brand names. Also known as **unaided recall** or **unaided awareness.**

touch-tone aided telephone interviewing (TATI) is interviewer-administered telephone surveying in which the respondent uses the touch-tone buttons of his or her phone to provide answers. Also known as **touchtone data entry (TDE).**

unstructured segmentation a process of segmenting a market using data and analysis when no prior ideas are held about the number of segments, what they are, or how and why they are different.

validation a process used to ensure the interview was done with the respondent as stated. The respondent's name and contact information are verified. The interview process itself must also fall under the parameters that have been set up for all the other interviews. Validation can be done via telephone, mail, in person or on-line.

---

market segmentation a fundamental technique of marketing strategy that was first defined by Wendell Smith in a groundbreaking article of 1956. It effectively signalled the end of the mass marketing age. Smith was concerned at the time to separate those companies that simply offered a range of product variety (to what was viewed as a homogeneous market) from those that designed tailored products (for multiple heterogeneous market segments). Its central idea was that there were different groupings of customers with wants and needs who required different products. What resulted was the division of a totally heterogeneous market into groups or sectors with relatively homogeneous needs and wants. Good marketing, from then until the present day, would rely on increasingly sophisticated segmentation of markets, gradually weakening the entire concept of mass marketing. The minutiae, the variety, the clustering of customers against various criteria needs became central to research for marketers.

Segmentation brought three distinct advantages: it made marketers think of the customer ahead of the product; in researching customers' needs at a granular level, it brought a better dialogue with customers and it opened up all sort of new segments of markets that were previously unexplored by the mass marketers hitherto looking to serve the producer interest. It also ushered in a new era of competition that did not always mean that the largest producer would dominate the market (because now a whole range of smaller competitors could be dominant in a number of segments) and made it unlikely that there would ever be the total domination of markets that had characterized the first half of the 20th century. The rise of the Internet, intelligent databases and various multimedia has made the task of the marketer easier in identifying, unifying and selling to market segments.

The first stage of segmentation is to establish criteria for segmenting the market, then to divide the heterogeneous market into relevant, clustered subgroups. One of the first limitations of segmentation is that if the market is subdivided into very small niches, it may not have enough customers to be profitable; or it may be too costly, requiring constant changes to the marketing mix to serve segments. Market segments should be measurable, and detailed information on customer characteristics should be obtainable cost-effectively so that the marketer can size the segment; information should be accessible so that the company can communicate effectively with the chosen segment using marketing methods; it should be substantial enough to consider for separate marketing activity and meaningful – having enough customers who have different preferences that can be addressed by marketing efforts.

Following that, the characteristics of these groups are identified and analysed. Once the market is subdivided into segments it is important to evaluate market segment attractiveness: for example, the structure, size and growth rate of the market segment; the company's reputation within that segment and its ability to serve that market; the intensity of competition within that market; the costs of adapting products and services for the segment. The marketer must find the potentially profitable segments and sort these out from the unprofitable ones.

From this relatively simple idea of segmenting according to customer needs and wants, now the staple of modern marketing, were spawned multiple segmentation techniques.

Some examples are:

Geographical segmentation the most classical form of segmentation, dividing the market into regions, countries, cities, states, provinces, suburbs or neighbourhoods. In the age of global markets geographical marketing is quite limited as a form of segmentation, but it enables predictable and transparent resource allocation and it is relatively easy to distinguish the profitable from the non-profitable territories.

Demographic segmentation is the most widely used segmentation technique for consumer products. There is much census data available on age, income, sex, gender, consumer preference, neighbourhood, ethnicity to help the marketer segment these groups in multiple ways.

Brand loyalty segmentation is based upon the loyalty that consumers have for one brand over another. This can be applied to services as well as products. This is often a reflection of lifestyle disposition.

Usage level segmentation clusters those groups who are light, medium or heavy users of a service or product.

Product segmentation defines the market by different types of customer who prefer different product attributes. See also CONJOINT ANALYSIS.

Benefit segmentation is the segmentation of customers who prefer a similar type of benefit. For example, some prefer high quality and luxury; others prefer low prices and simple functionality; others prefer the newest innovations; yet others buy for security, predictability and safety.

Lifestyle segmentation is the grouping of people around how they spend their disposable income on leisure and personal taste.

Market niche is when the broad industry is segmented into smaller and smaller segments until a niche of buyers with similar wants and needs that can be satisfied is identified.

Psychographics segmentation is a way of segmenting the market by cultural attitude and psychological type: for example the middle-of-the-road, the fashionable, the thrill seekers, the security seekers, the risk takers, the risk-averse, the aspirational, the image-conscious; the conspicuous consumers, the high achievers, the individualists, the reformers, the highly educated, the family-oriented, the self-actualizers; the strivers, the strugglers etc.

market share at a basic level this is the total sales of a product or service in a specified market expressed as a percentage of total sales by all entities offering a similar product or service. Originally developed for the consumer market for tangible product, this metric has proven both enduring and popular. The more precise way to calculate market share is sales as a percentage of the total in the defined target market over a given time period. Market share remains one of the classic, if flawed, measures, of market and marketing success. There is no generally accepted formula that links market share to profitability. It is difficult to apply to markets for services and intangibles.

mark-up the amount of the selling price of a product that is over and above its cost. A retailer, for example, will add a mark-up to the product to cover expenses associated with the selling of the product that would include showroom or shelf space as well as other expenses. This practice is regarded as a more outdated way of pricing than targeting pricing to what the market will bear. See also PRICING.

Maslow's hierarchy see HIERARCHY OF NEEDS.

mass customization a new technique of marketing in which goods and services are produced at scale but are sold at a reasonable price and are highly tailored to meet individual customer needs. Mass customization is different from mass production where production in quantity is the goal. Mass customization typically uses mass production techniques to complete part of the product, the rest of it then being customized based upon customer demand that will still keep costs down. Mass customized products include Ping brand golf clubs that can later be adjusted to an individual player. Ping uses a series of coloured dots to differentiate things like player height, stance and swing patterns. Other mass customized products include Levis jeans, which can now be custom-made for customers' individual dimensions without much extra cost. See also RELATIONSHIP/ONE-TO-ONE MARKETING.

MEDIA

media a range of nonpersonal communications channels that includes print media (newspapers, magazines, direct mail), broadcast media (radio, television), and display media (billboards, signs, posters, CD and DVD) and new interactive media (telephones, Internet, instant messaging, e-mail).

Marketers tend to speak of two classes of media channel:

Above-the-line (or 'mass') media that is:

The press and magazines, radio, television, outdoor or ambient and cinema.

These are for wide coverage and cannot have highly targeted audiences.

Below-the-line media that is:

1. direct mail
2. exhibitions, shows and events
3. point of sale materials and
4. sales literature.

Below-the-line media tend to have limited coverage and are intended for highly targeted audiences.

In recent years, there have been proliferations of types of media channel.

See also ADVERTISING.

Basic media characteristics of major media channels:

1. **Television**.

- Ability to build high awareness levels; the dominant media channel worldwide of the 20th century, particularly from the 1950s onwards.
- Large audiences. Although these are declining for single channel viewing, the BBC can still garner up to 20 million viewers for a single show.
- Visible demonstration of product in use (sound and vision).
- Compulsiveness: television has proven to be the most addictive of all media.
- Viewed at home in a relaxed manner, often at the centre of family social gathering.
- Commercial: with the onset of multiple channels, largely funded by advertising sales, public, non-commercial broadcasting funded by taxpayers is diminishing in influence. However, the downside is that the proliferation of advertising in television is irritating in its frequency and ubiquity.
- Transient medium.
- Not fully interactive: this has become the major criticism of television in the age of the Internet. Often, alternatives to television, such as entertainment delivered interactively over television or PC, is seen to be more attuned to the needs of the new generation. In the late 1990s, the sales of PCs worldwide actually started to outstrip television sets.

2. **Magazines and journals**

- Opportunity for quality print: printed material allows greater depth of content than the broadcast media or daily tabloids.
- Appropriate, non-sensationalist editorial environment (for example in contrast to daily newspapers that need sensational headlines).
- Allows careful targeting of audiences.
- Advertisements are expected by readers, and are often seen as an integral part of the magazine.
- Longer life span than newspapers: people tend to read magazines over a longer term than newspapers, often collecting them.

3. **National print press**

- Wide coverage of the population and large circulation volumes.
- Good flexibility in terms of media buy timing – space can be booked at short notice.
- Poor method of reaching the target audience, given that these publications rely on mass audiences. Some of the 'quality' newspapers, such as the *Financial Times* and *Wall St. Journal*, do make claims to an elite audience.
- Advertising content is often avoided by the readership.

4. **Print posters**

- These give an opportunity for colour reproduction.
- They present an opportunity to communicate a brief message.
- They can be used at point of sale or point of consumption.

5. **Cinema**

- An effective way of reaching a young audience, given that the dominant group of cinemagoers is in the 16-24 age range.
- High production cost for cinema advertising can be reduced by the adaptation of TV creative advertising transposed to the large screen.
- Segmentation possibilities – for example by age, taste and locale.
- Audiences tend to be smaller and highly localized.

6. **Radio**

- A medium that has established itself over the years as an 'intimate companion' with smaller audiences.
- Sound is very portable, and has taken on a whole new life in cars and portable radios.
- Segmentation possibilities – for example by timeslot, by locale, by age range and by lifestyle.
- Lack of visual demonstration can often be a hindrance in a world dominated by visual images.
- Transient medium: radio broadcasts are the least likely to be stored or taped by the audience.
- Small local audience size. Radio is in retreat as a national or international medium but has had a new lease of life over the past 30 years as a medium serving local audiences.

7. **Outdoor and transport advertising.**

- This medium has an ability to build high awareness levels, especially given traffic congestion and volumes.
- In highly congested areas a well-placed poster can have a huge audience.
- Relatively low costs.
- Campaigns are possible on billboards (the Wonderbra adverts in the UK are a recent example of this being done successfully).
- Segmentation possibilities – particularly around locale and traffic density.

8. **Satellite broadcasting**

- Ability to reach a large number of audience segments at different times of day and night around the world.
- Can reach a global audience.
- Ease and speed of access to medium.
- Control of message in different countries is a challenge.
- Measurement, in some cases is very difficult: satellite broadcasting has created so many channels that the broadcaster has no control of medium, with the majority of the audience having little channel loyalty and prone to continuous flicking of channels.

Media selection criteria

Marketers when using media for marketing purposes take the following areas into consideration:

- Costs of media buy
- Ability to communicate the message effectively
- Frequency of the medium (for example a single ad in a daily newspaper is unlikely to yield any result)
- Target market
- Flexibility (lead times)
- Temporal constraints
- International/national/regional audiences served by the medium
- Volume of business using the medium
- Past results of the medium
- Reputation of the medium.

MEDIA POWER

Media became an industry in the 20th century. Before that it had been a means of transmitting information. New technology and economies of scale enabled the media industry to become global. Media market leaders became more and more dominant and invested more, and this in turn attracted more readers, which attracted more advertising revenue, greater economies of scale, and more money to invest in attracting more readers. The 20th century also created a clear distinction between the quality and popular press which continues today. The vast majority of the national papers launched in the early 20th century were popular papers operating on the 'mass-market leads to more advertising revenue' model. However, the quality papers did not follow that business model. The quality papers (which all have quality websites) carry a large proportion of news and current affairs material and have not followed the human interest, tabloid headlines, sensationalist or prurient stories to attract mass audiences that the tabloids have in the search for readerships of millions. The 'quality' newspapers have created fewer media barons and empires: they operate on a quality, not quantity, principle. They deliver smaller readerships to advertisers, but their readerships are affluent elites with plenty of disposable income. Advertisers will pay more for access to those groups and thus the qualities do not require such large readerships. Quality newspapers tend to generate about 70% of their income from adverts, compared to 40% for the popular tabloids that make more through sales of their papers.

In the UK there was increased concentration of ownership of media after 1945. 1947-1989 saw the three biggest press groups increase their share of the market by more than 30% and by 1995 they sold three out of four national papers sold in Britain. Media groups now tend to be owned by institutional shareholders rather than individuals, which has limited the power of the individual media barons.

Newspapers also remained heavily dependent on advertising. In the 1950s and 1960s paper circulation fell while costs of production continued to rise. Then came the most significant development of the postwar period, which was the introduction of new technology to printing and publishing in the

1980s. This revolution involved the replacement of old ways of printing papers with new computerized processes. This allowed media barons like Rupert Murdoch to break the power of the print unions whose control of the printing process had given them great leverage and bargaining power. Photos are now transmitted digitally, stories are e-mailed from across the globe, and perhaps more importantly scoops are announced on websites by freelancers running their own fairly small on-line media agencies.

At the beginning of the 21st century, however, the majority of North American newspapers are local rather than national. There are around 1500 daily local newspapers in the US. Even the well-known qualities like *The Washington Post* and *The New York Times* don't really circulate outside the northeastern United States. Most Americans read a local daily paper, such as *LA Times, Boston Globe, Atlanta Constitution and Journal*. Virtually all the national and international news carried by local papers in the US is supplied by news agencies, especially *Associated Press* and *United Press International*. This leads to a lower level of diversity of reporting in the US and a higher fulfilment of demand for news being met by the broadcast media. Local titles such as *The New York Times* and *The Washington Post* have a national influence, if not a national readership, because they are the papers read by the politicians in Washington, many local papers follow their lead on stories, and because even the TV networks do so as well.

Overall, the 20th century was marked by the inexorable rise of media power. The great historian Carlyle predicted this in the 19th century when he coined the term 'fourth estate' to describe the rising power of the press and reporters. The 20th century began with only very few media channels, such as local newspapers, and ended with multiple channels of vastly increased range, scope and sophistication. The power of media and its rise created powerful media barons who have been able to influence the course of history. Media and power became closely intertwined. Media and political power, whether on a democratic or non-democratic basis, were inextricably linked. The following are a few examples of those who have extended the power and influence of media, sometime for good, and sometimes for nefarious, purposes:

Beaverbrook, 1st Baron (1879-1964) Canadian-born British newspaper proprietor and Conservative politician. Born William Maxwell Aitken in New Brunswick, his newspapers included the *Daily Express*, which became, under his rule, one of the bestselling newspapers in the world, as well as the *Sunday Express* and the *Evening Standard*. Hearst (qv) commented that Beaverbrook applied tabloid methods to broadsheets. Beaverbrook's papers notoriously reflected his own political agenda quite closely (notably on imperial Free Trade, in favour of Edward VIII during the abdication crisis). He boasted that his newspapers were run for influence, not for profit. He said that the modern press was 'a flaming sword that will cut through any political armour'. The journalist Malcolm Muggeridge claimed that, whenever Beaverbrook felt unease at the thought of dying, his editors would commission articles proving the existence of life after death. Beaverbrook would then read the articles and be relieved of his fears. Beaverbrook was a war reporter for the Canadian government in World War I, then served in the

British Cabinet, as Minister for Propaganda and Information. He was elevated to the peerage by Lloyd George. Lady Astor dismissed him as 'Lord Been-A-Crook'. During World War II, he served in Churchill's war cabinet as Minister of Aircraft Production during the Battle of Britain (1940), Minister of Supply (1941-42), Minister of War Production (1942) and Lord Privy Seal (1943-45). His newspaper group was dismembered after his death in 1964.

Goebbels, Josef (1897-1945) German Nazi politician. As Hitler's Minister for Enlightenment and Propaganda (1933-45), Goebbels devised many propaganda campaigns, most notably for the glorification of Hitler and the Nazi regime and, most sinisterly, against the Jews. Propaganda was one of the more powerful aspects of the Nazi regime and Goebbels was its controlling hand and instigator. He made use of every technique of mass psychology to build a base of support for the Nazi regime. Goebbels is sometimes described as a marketing genius, though he himself conceded that his techniques derived in large part from the mass propaganda techniques developed in the USSR. His maxims include: 'Never lose sight of the fundamental principle of all propaganda, the constant repetition of the most effective arguments' and 'the more the movement grows, the more we must exploit technology'. See also RIEFENSTAHL.

Graham, Katherine (1917-2001) American newspaper proprietor. Following the suicide of her husband in 1963 she took control of the *Washington Post*, and was publisher of the paper 1969-79. She gave full backing to her editor Benjamin Bradlee's decision to publish the so-called 'Pentagon Papers', the Pentagon's own 'secret history' of the Vietnam War, in defiance of both legal advice and the US government, and gave full support to the journalists Woodward and Bernstein during their 1972 investigation of the Watergate scandal, support which led to the exposure and fall of Richard Nixon. Her reign at the *Washington Post* proved the power of media to unseat even the most powerful man in the world.

Hearst, William Randolph (1863-1951) founder of the Hearst Corporation. Hearst was born on April 29, 1863, in San Francisco, California, as the only child of George Hearst, a self-made multimillionaire miner and rancher. In 1887, at 23 he inherited the *San Francisco Examiner* which his father, George Hearst, accepted as payment for a gambling debt. Trained initially as a newspaper reporter and influenced by Joseph Pulitzer, Hearst revolutionized popular journalism and newsprint. He was, along with Joseph Pulitzer, viewed as the pioneer of 'yellow journalism'. Much of what we take for granted nowadays as classic tabloid journalism was pioneered by Hearst: 'mass appeal' editorial content; interconnected newspaper chains; top writers as 'star' journalists (he employed Mark Twain, Jack London and Stephen Crane); bold banner headlines, lavish illustrations such as halftone newsprint photos; colour comic strips; the use of latest technology applied to journalism as well as heavy promotion and marketing of the newspaper itself (see his editorial guidelines below). At the pinnacle of his power, he owned 28 major newspapers and 18 magazines, along with several radio stations and film companies. His worldwide publishing empire eventually would include 32 major city papers; 13 magazines; King Features Syndicate; radio and TV stations; Metrotone News; and movie and book companies. Hearst turned his newspapers into a combination of investigative reporting and sensationalism. Hearst was a member of the United States House of Representatives (1903-07). In the 1920s Hearst built a castle on a 240,000 acre ranch at San Simeon, California. The Great Depression weakened his financial position and by 1940 he had lost personal control of his vast communications empire. He became a pro-Nazi in the 1930s and a staunch anti-Communist in the 1940s. He is generally regarded to be the basis for the character of Charles Foster Kane in Orson Welles' legendary film, *Citizen Kane* (1941), which he tried to have banned.

Hearst Newspapers Editorial Guidelines (1933)

1. Make a paper for the nicest kind of people of the great middle class. Don't print a lot of dull stuff that people are supposed to like and don't.

2. Omit things that will offend nice people. Avoid coarseness and a low tone. The most sensational news can be told if told properly.

3. Make your headlines clear and concise statements of interesting acts. They should answer the question: What is the news? Don't allow copyreaders to write headlines that are too smart or clever to be intelligible.

4. The front page is your forum. Put important items and personal news about well-known people there. Sometimes condense a big story to go on the first page rather than run it longer inside the paper.

5. Nothing is more wearisome than mere words. Have our people tell stories briefly and pointedly. Let people get the facts easily. Don't make them work at it.

6. Please instruct copyreaders to rewrite long sentences into several short ones. And please try to educate the reporters to write short sentences in the first place.

7. Photographs of interesting events with explanatory diagrams are valuable. Make every picture worth its space.

8. If you cannot show conclusively your own paper's superiority, you may be sure the public will never discover it.

Malone, John (1941–) American entrepreneur, known as the 'Godfather of Cable Television'. A former researcher with AT&T and then a management consultant, Malone is noted for the development of cable television as well as 'interactive TV', the holy grail of media investment speculation just before the Internet boom. His company, TCI, grew rapidly throughout the 1980s. He invested heavily in programming services. TCI was merged into AT&T, which made Malone a personal fortune. In 1990 Malone became chairman of Liberty Media, which he continues to lead today.

Maxwell, Robert (1923-91) British media owner, publisher and Labour politician. Born Robert Hoch in Slovakia, he founded Pergamon Press in 1949 and was chairman of Mirror Group Newspapers Ltd (1984-91). A ruthless entrepreneur, he funded his expansion in the media in the 1970s and 1980s largely through financial leverage, and as was later discovered, by legerdemain. In the UK, he became Rupert Murdoch's main newspaper rival in the tabloid market. Maxwell's death by drowning is generally believed to have been the result of suicide as his financial liabilities were about to be exposed. After his death, it was revealed that he had stolen large sums of money from his employees' pension funds, and his once highly influential publishing empire was broken up.

Murdoch, Rupert (1931–) creator of News Corporation, formed in 1980 from diverse companies, the world's largest media-entertainment-communications empire, which controls both media content and distribution. News Corp is the world's only truly global media empire. Murdoch was born in Australia into a newspaper-owning family. In the 1950s he inherited his first paper, the *Adelaide News*, from his father, Melbourne publisher Sir Keith Murdoch. He made continuous acquisitions across the planet. In the 1960s, it was Sydney (the *Mirror*), London (the *News of the World* and the *Sun*); in the 1970s, New York (the *New York Post*); in the 1980s, Hollywood (20th Century Fox and Fox TV) and again London (acquiring *The Times* and *Sunday Times*) and satellite television in the UK, called BSkyB; in the 1990s, Asia (Star Television). News Corp holdings now include a lion's share of the newspaper industry in Australia, about one-third of British newspapers and BSkyB, through which pay-per-view was introduced to the UK in 1996. In the U.S. News Corp owns film and TV interests, newspapers, book publishers (HarperCollins), sports teams, and several other companies such as TV Guide. Recently, News Corp has moved into interactive media with LineOne.

Northcliffe, Viscount (1865-1922) British newspaper proprietor. Born Alfred Harmsworth in Dublin, he founded the *Daily Mail* (1896), the *Daily Mirror* (1903), and bought *The Times* in 1908. His brother, Viscount Rothermere (born Harold Harmsworth) joined him and proved to gifted in garnering advertising revenue, which came to be the dominant revenue source of newspapers. Their Amalgamated Press (including *Comic Cuts*, famously labelled as 'Amusing Without Being Vulgar') became one of the world's largest media empires of its time, with a specific marketing slant towards the new reading public of literate working men and (especially) women. Northcliffe's papers were initially regarded with contempt by the British establishment. Lord Cecil's view on the *Daily Mail* was typical of the upper class reactions of the time: 'a newspaper for office boys written by office boys'. However, Northcliffe's genius for flattering and understanding his essentially educated working class and lower middle-class readership, resulted in massive sales. His advice to his journalists was always 'Explain, Simplify, Clarify', and his shrewd assessment of the newspaper business remains perfectly valid today: 'News is what somebody somewhere wants to suppress, all the rest is advertising'.

Pulitzer, Joseph (1847-1911) Hungarian-born American newspaper proprietor. His *New York World* was notably aggressive in its campaigns, perhaps most notably for organized labour, and for war against Spain in the 1890s. He founded the annual Pulitzer Prizes in 1917, which award excellence in American journalism, literature, drama and music.

Rothermere, Viscount see NORTHCLIFFE.

Turner, Ted (1938–). A pioneer of global media and a strong believer in the acquisition of content, after rebuilding his late father's outdoor advertising business in Atlanta, Turner acquired a failing independent TV station in 1970, successfully upgraded its programming and bought Major League Baseball's Atlanta Braves franchise. Recognizing cable TV's potential, he rented satellite transmission time to transform WTBS into the US's first cable superstation. He next created the all-news, all-day Cable News Network (CNN) and TNT cable network. CNN, despite widespread predictions of disaster, became a global 24-hour all-news cable channel and soon proved its worth with minute-by-minute coverage of such events as the space shuttle *Challenger* disaster in 1986 and the Persian Gulf War in 1991. Turner bought Hanna-Barbera's cartoon studio and MGM's film library, created the Cartoon Network and, in 1995, following a failure to buy CBS, merged his media company with Time Warner to create a $17 billion conglomerate. He is also widely known for his philanthropy.

---

media analysis a study of the effectiveness of various media in reaching the intended audience.

media broker an agency that buys bulk media space from media owners then sells it on in parcels to clients.

media buying a function within an advertising agency that buys time and space for advertising from television, radio and print media owners. Buying television media time is the most complex of the media buying skills. It is normal now for advertisers to bundle together their media buying requests in order to improve their purchasing power with media owners.

media buying service where a company other than an ad agency purchases media time and space.

media impact the qualitative value of an exposure through a given medium.

media kit a resource created by a publisher to help prospective ad buyers evaluate advertising opportunities.

media plan an outline of the objectives of an advertising campaign, the target audience, and the specific media vehicles that will be used to reach that audience. Media schedule is the formal listing of which adverts are to appear where.

media planning the systematic selection of the most appropriate media to deliver messages to target audiences.

media schedule an agreed publication schedule for running advertisements or television commercials between the advertising agency and the advertiser.

merchandizing a range of advanced selling and display techniques designed to increase the sale of goods in retail outlets. See also CONSUMER MARKETING under MARKETING SPECIALIZATIONS.

message that which conveys from the transmitter to the receiver the underlying theme, vision or idea. Lead and supporting messages are what support a brand positioning of a company and any of its collateral material. Messages can be conveyed through all types of media in different ways. See also ADVERTISING and COMMUNICATIONS.

metasearch engine a search engine that displays results from multiple search engines.

Metcalfe's Law Named after Bob Metcalfe, the inventor of the Ethernet computer-networking technology, this states that the value of a network grows in proportion to the square of the number of users. Once a network achieves a certain size, it becomes almost irresistibly attractive. Metcalfe reasoned that 1000 people on a network could have roughly one million different conversations, so the value of a network grows in proportion to the square of the number of users. This is an important law for marketers, because as far as potential consumers are concerned, given the choice of joining a large existing network with many users or a new one with few users, they will almost always decide that the bigger one is far more valuable. The result is often explosive, accelerating growth once a network establishes dominance. This law is most demonstrably felt in the world's two great interactive networks – the Internet and the global telephone network.

me-too a product modelled consciously on a successful competitor: the type of product that appears on a market with no differentiating features from already-existing products.

middleman an intermediary. A middleman can be someone who is between the producer or manufacturer and the retailer or consumer. See DISTRIBUTION.

milking a marketing pricing approach of charging high prices when a product is first launched and spending heavily on advertising and sales promotion to obtain sales. Progressively, prices are lowered as the product moves into the later stages of its life cycle. The profitable cream is therefore skimmed off in stages until sales can only be sustained at lower prices. Also known as **skimming.** See also PRICING.

minutage the number of minutes allowed per hour for television advertising. The amount allowed varies from country to country. See also ADVERTISING.

missionary selling one of the more important aspects to getting good sales is to have a highly effective sales force. Missionary selling involves educating those who will be responsible for end-user sales and bringing about an attitude of mind and technique that will lead to higher sales. See also SALES.

mission statement a brief description, no longer than a few sentences, that explains an organization or company's reason for existence. The mission statement should explain what the company hopes to achieve in the future. It should discuss its values and its work ethic. A mission statement should be evaluated every few years to reflect current changes. Though a company's reason for existing may not change, the methods of achieving its goals may change with the times and the mission statement should be modified to reflect these changes. See also MARKET PLANNING.

moderator someone entrusted by the on-line administrator to help discussions within a forum to stay productive and within the guidelines or objective. Good moderators are essential for good forums. Basic moderator duties include deleting or modifying inappropriate posts, educating newcomers about forum guidelines, and possibly deleting accounts of repeat offenders.

Additionally, moderators may be experts in their field who can help minimize unanswered questions. Most moderator openings are volunteer positions, although there may be substantial indirect rewards.

monopoly a non-competitive market situation in which there is only one seller. Monopolies are often state-owned.

monopsony a market situation in which there is only one buyer.

motivational research Ernst Dichter founded the Institute of Motivational Research in New York in 1946. Using psychology to try to sell a product, motivational research is heavily used to promote particular lifestyles or a certain quality of life. Studies are done to determine the motivation or the reason behind why someone would want to purchase a product. The message which under pins motivational research is that the purchase of a given product will greatly improve your lifestyle and your overall position in society. See also MARKET RESEARCH.

mousetrapping the use of browser tricks in an effort to keep a visitor captive at a site, often by disabling the 'Back' button or generating repeated pop-up windows. Mousetrapping is one of the most extreme marketing tactics on the Web. The goal is to extract maximum value from one-time visits, typically by bombarding visitors with a never-ending supply of traffic-exchange banners and pay-per-click links. Mousetrapping comes in many varieties. The mildest form of mousetrapping involves disabling the 'Back' button. More aggressive forms of mousetrapping include disabling of key browser features and continuous loading of pop-up ads.

Murphy, James E. (1936–). Chief Marketing Officer, Accenture; founder, Chairman and CEO of Murphy & Co. A pioneer of professional services marketing and branding and a trained journalist, Murphy, throughout his career, was a strong advocate of an integrated approach to marketing communications and brand management. Murphy held senior communications roles at several major corporations, including Owens Corning, Beatrice and Merrill Lynch and then was chairman and CEO of the public relations company Burson-Marsteller, in the Americas. He became involved with Accenture (then Andersen Consulting) in 1987 when Burson-Marsteller was asked to help the former parent company of Accenture establish a consulting arm. He became head of marketing and communications of Accenture in 1993 where he brought to bear many of the techniques of integrated marketing management that he had garnered throughout his career. His greatest triumph was the launch of the new Accenture brand name in January 2001, one of the most extensive and most rapid name changes ever undertaken, which within a year established it as one of the best known in the business market for professional services.

narrowcasting a term used in reference to cable television in the U.S., where cable TV stations, with specialised interests such as sports, news, weather, movies, etc, allow advertisers great selectivity; that is, advertisers can narrowcast their messages rather than broadcast them.

Nast, Condé (1873-1942) Condé Nast Publications. A pioneer in upmarket fashion magazines. Growing up poor in St. Louis, Nast joined *Collier's Weekly* in 1898 and there developed his idea that a market existed for magazines catering to the tastes of the affluent and fashionable. He put his ideas to the test in 1909 by purchasing *Vogue*, then a struggling New York society weekly. Editor Edna Woolman Chase and Nast turned it into an influential, stylized, photo-fashion monthly for women that attracted leading advertisers. After buying *Vanity Fair* and *House & Garden* he created Condé Nast Publications in 1922. Nast lost his fortune in the 1929 stock market crash but was able to create *Glamour* in 1939 to further extend his publishing vision.

navigation the facilitation of movement from one web page to another.

negotiation the art of two sides going back and forth with their demands until some sort of compromise is reached where both sides are happy with the outcome. Usually no one will get everything that is desired. The key is to focus on the points that are the most important and arrive at a situation of mutual benefit. This is key in **personal selling**.

netiquette short for network etiquette, the code of conduct regarding acceptable on-line behaviour. The term is commonly used in reference to popular forms of on-line communication, including e-mail, forums and chat. While some netiquette issues are technical in nature, all fundamentally concern how people relate to each other in cyberspace. Once the technical nuances are grasped and abstract concepts are understood, on-line etiquette is not much different from off-line etiquette. Violating the code of conduct for a community (e.g. using spam) may get you banned from the community. What does netiquette have to do with marketing? It is essential to have a good understanding of acceptable ways to communicate with potential customers. Netiquette is an early definition of the new culture of cyberspace.

network effect the phenomenon whereby a service grows in value as more people use it. For example, services that operate over networks such as fax, e-mail, text messaging and mobile voice communication rise in value the more people are connected users. This phenomenon is spread early in the growth period through word of mouth, and then later the market expands exponentially as the consumer believes that 'everyone' is linked to the network. See also METCALFE'S LAW.

new product development and launch one of the most hazardous areas of marketing, where reputations can be won and lost instantly. No one has yet devised a fail-safe marketing technique to make new product launches successful. At best, the marketer can reduce the likelihood of failure. Most new product launches fail because they misinterpret or ignore some vital part of the market they are targeting. These misinterpretations can range from an over-optimistic assessment of market demand, overpricing, making the product or service too complex for current demand, or by mistiming market demand (many excellent products are simply launched before the market demand is of sufficient volume to ensure success). See also PRODUCT LIFE CYCLE.

newspapers one of the oldest information and advertising media of all, currently being re-invented electronically on the Internet. Newspapers are local, regional, national, international or electronic. Their main revenue comes from advertising. It is always difficult for advertisers to distinguish between what a newspaper's core readership is and its published circulation figures, which makes targeting difficult. See also MEDIA and ADVERTISING.

Nielsen, A.C. sr. (1898-1980) A.C. Nielsen Co. A guru of market research, Nielsen created the concept of market share in 1923. This occurred when pioneering market researcher Nielsen's new company began checking food and drugstore shelves to tally product movement. His sales audits answered client questions about their marketing efforts, and as TV arrived Nielsen adapted his audit to deliver 'the Nielsens,' those influential audience totals for programmes and commercials. AC Nielsen Co is his market research company, founded in 1923 in the USA, that has become the market researcher of choice for the provision of consumer data on consumables, drugs, mass merchandise and alcoholic beverages. A.C. Nielsen Co. became the world's largest marketing research organization. It conducted retail and consumer audits and benchmarking services around the world. Nielsen's research continues to influence decisions related to campaigns, media schedules, sales promotion programmes, distribution patterns, entertainment and event production. Many consumer products frequently use Nielsen data and packaging companies to determine which product lines would be the most successful for each location. It regularly publishes the Nielsen Index, which describes shopping patterns. The Dutch company VNU NV acquired AC Nielsen Co in 2001.

noise in communications terms, any influence external to the sender or receiver that distorts the message in the communication process.

observation collecting information by watching behaviours or actions. It is the oldest marketing research technique of all. See also MARKET RESEARCH under MARKETING SPECIALIZATIONS.

odd pricing pricing a product so it ends in an odd amount such as £ 9.99 or £9.95 instead of £10. Consumer psychologists claim a product will sell better since consumers will have the perception that the odd-priced product is a much better value than the one selling at the even price. See also PRICING.

offerings (market) products or services that are designed to meet a particular segment need. Consulting services have a multitude of market offerings in many industries that are designed to meet the needs of their client companies. See also MARKET SEGMENTATION.

Ogilvy, David (1911-1999), co-founder of Ogilvy and Mather, Ogilvy emphasized fact-based advertising. His agency created powerful ads distinguished by graceful, sensible copy and respect for the consumer's intelligence. His major campaigns were for Hathaway shirts, Shell Oil, Sears, KLM, American Express, International Paper, IBM, Schweppes tonic, Rolls-Royce and Pepperidge Farm. Ogilvy pioneered a fee system, as opposed to commissions, which changed the economics of the advertising industry.

one-stop shopping shopping in a single place without having to go to any other locations. It has come to mean a service provider who provides a range of integrated services that were previously provided by specialist individual providers.

opinion leader someone or some company that can influence or sway public sentiment on an issue. Opinion leaders are often the targets of marketing campaigns.

opinion poll a survey that is conducted to find out public sentiment on different issues usually dealing with politics or policy. Gallup is an organization known for its opinion polls. See also MARKET RESEARCH and GALLUP, GEORGE.

opt-in e-mail e-mail that is explicitly requested by the on-line recipient. This forms the foundation stone of PERMISSION-BASED MARKETING.

opt-out 1. a type of program on-line that assumes inclusion unless stated otherwise or 2. the action of removing oneself from an opt-out program. The term opt-out is often used in relation to ad tracking programs. By default, ad-tracking programs track everyone. In response to growing privacy concerns, some major advertising networks have offered individuals the option to be removed from tracking.

outsourcing employing an outside company to perform functions previously done inside the company. For example, payroll, security, catering, cleaning, building maintenance, janitorial services, accounting, customer fulfilment, and information systems are functions that are frequently outsourced since costs can be quite high and they can be done more efficiently by specialized companies. Economies of scale can be achieved by using a large company with existing equipment and expert personnel that specializes in specific functions. Increasingly, companies are starting to outsource their critical business processes and functions, such as customer care and acquisition, their supply and logistics operations, and often their training and human resource functions. Outsourcing has become a major market in its own right, and is starting to segment into various areas of expertise.

over-the-counter (OTC) used in different markets to mean different things: goods selected by individual customers which are weighed, packed and priced (as required) by staff prior to being passed to the customer for payment at that point, or subsequently at a cash point; or in pharmaceutical products markets in which medicines and drugs can be sold by a pharmacy direct to customers, without a doctor's prescription; or any good or service available for direct sale without modification or specific work, especially where an element of such work might be expected.

Ovitz, Michael, (1946–) Creative Artists Agency. One of the most powerful dealmakers in Hollywood with his innovative talent company, Ovitz personally changed film industry dynamics in 1990 by brokering huge studio mergers for Japan's Matsushita and Sony. Then, in September 1991, he rocked the advertising world by signing Coca-Cola, ostensibly for marketing and media aid.

own brand/label a brand or label that is produced internally. This is now frequent in retail stores, where the store's own brands compete with other brands in the same store. See also BRANDING.

packaging an extremely important aspect of marketing, particularly consumer marketing and retailing. Packaging serves a number of purposes: it protects the product; it fits well with the manufacturing process that creates the original product (for example, the package has to be the right size to receive the product from the production line); it makes the product highly attractive to customers; it makes the product easy to use or to consume; it meets legal requirements (for example on material, on waste disposal, on consumer information); and, occasionally, can add value to the customer experience of the brand. The most visible form of packaging for marketing purposes is the consumer package. These packages must give high visibility to the brand name. They must have an appropriate size relative to the product contained within. The package must be highly attractive in order to command the consumers' attention. This attractiveness may come as a result of colour, originality or distinctiveness of design or quality of materials used in the package. An impression of good quality is always important even if the product is low price.

Packard, Vance (1914-1996) Author of the best-seller *The Hidden Persuaders* in 1957. His book played to a public perception that the advertising industry was able to persuade defenceless consumers to buy unneeded goods and services by devious means. Packard explained that ad agencies used psychiatry, motivational research and related social sciences to create subliminal selling patterns. See also ADVERTISING.

pagejacking the theft of a page from the original website and publication of a copy at another site. Pagejacking does not mean taking over a page on the original site. In fact, the original site can be completely unaware that the theft has occurred. Pagejackers siphon off traffic indirectly though the search engines.

page view a request to load a single HTML page. This is important to the revenue stream of a website. If a site earns much of its revenue from advertising, then page views are important because of their contribution to ad inventory. If a site only earns revenue on sales, then page views are not a key metric.

paired comparisons see MARKET RESEARCH.

panel see MARKET RESEARCH.

Pareto Principle named after the 19th-century economist, Wilfredo Pareto, and also known as the 80-20 rule, simply put this means that 20% becomes responsible for 80%. 20% of the costs are using 80% of the resources. 20% of the customers are responsible for 80% of the revenues. Eventually effectiveness will go down due to diminishing returns. By using the Pareto principle, marketers can learn how to use their resources more effectively to bring about maximum results.

pass-along rate the percentage of people who pass on a message or file. Pass-along rates are a measure of **word-of-mouth marketing**. Objects typically passed include e-mail messages, Web pages and multimedia files. Content typically passed includes humour and entertainment, late-breaking news, and shopping specials.

payment threshold the minimum accumulated commission an affiliate must earn to trigger payment from an affiliate programme at a specified time interval.

pay per click an on-line advertising payment model in which payment is based solely on qualifying click-throughs. In a PPC agreement, the advertiser only pays for qualifying clicks to the destination site based on a prearranged per-click rate. See also ADVERTISING.

pay per click search engine a search engine where results are ranked according to the bid amount, and advertisers are charged when a searcher clicks on the search listing.

pay per lead an on-line advertising payment model in which payment is based solely based on qualifying leads. In a pay per lead agreement, the advertiser only pays for leads generated at their destination site. No payment is made for visitors who don't sign up.

pay per sale an on-line advertising payment model in which payment is based solely based on qualifying sales. In a pay per sale agreement, the advertiser only pays for sales generated by the destination site based on an agreed commission rate.

penetration strategy see MARKET STRATEGY.

perception what someone believes to be true. Successful marketing of a product is based upon the perception the consumer has as to how good the product is. See also BRAND and PERCEPTUAL MAPPING.

perceptual mapping see MARKET RESEARCH.

personal selling see SALES.

piggybacking a low-cost market entry tactic in which manufacturers of products arrange for manufacturers of complementary, non-competing products to represent their products in another country or region.

pilot a test of a limited number of users to test the feasibility or acceptance of a product. Pilot testing is a crucial stage before any major project launch.

pitch/pitching attempts to sell a concept, idea or product. Marketing managers and salespeople will 'pitch' a product. See also SALES.

PIMS (profit impact of market strategy) a database that started in the 1970s, a coming together of an internal research programme at General Electric and the Market Sciences Institute at Harvard Business School. PIMS has a database of over 4000 participating companies, with each business profiled on 200+ factors over a five-year time horizon. This enables the profitability of actions taken in the market and relative market share to be assessed. For marketers, the most common use of the PIMS database has been the regression model, which has nearly 40 variables grouped into seven categories:

PIMS: Profit Impact of Marketing Strategies

- attractiveness of the business environment
- strength of competitive position
- differentiation of competitive position
- effective use of investment
- discretionary budget allocations
- characteristics of the owning corporations
- current change in position variables.

point of purchase the location where the item is purchased, such as an in-store display.

point of sale the location where the item is sold, such as at an in-store check-out counter.

pop-up window an ad that displays in a new browser window. Pop-up windows come in many different shapes and sizes, typically in a scaled-down browser window with only the Close, Minimize and Maximize commands. There is a strong resentment by some Web surfers towards pop-up ads. Marketers often do not realize the ill-will generated by pop-ups because it is easier to click the 'close' button than send an e-mail to complain. What can often be seen is an above-average click-through rate, although some of this can come from 'false positives,' unintentional clicks when the pop-up gets in the way of the desired target. Advertisers can get a better picture of the effectiveness of pop-up advertising by paying attention to conversion rates and return on investment (ROI).

portal a site featuring a suite of commonly used services, serving as a starting point and frequent gateway to the Web (Web portal) or a niche topic (vertical portal). It is a cornerstone of on-line marketing.

Porter, Michael C. Roland Christensen Professor of Business Administration at Harvard Business School (HBS). An influential business guru in the field of how firms compete in industries and how they gain competitive advantage. Porter joined the HBS faculty in 1973 after earning his doctorate in business economics at Harvard, and he soon became one of the School's youngest tenured professors. A prolific scholar, he has written 16 books and more than 75 articles. His 1980 seminal work, *Competitive Strategy: Techniques for Analyzing Industries and Competitors*, has been translated into 19 languages and is considered the pioneering treatise on corporate competition and strategy. He has also worked on the competitive advantage of nations and why some cities, states, or nations can be more competitive or prosperous than others (*The Competitive Advantage of Nations*, 1990). He has also written on how competitive thinking can be applied to social problems. His various models have become cornerstones of market strategy and analysis. In his own words, he has defined his groundbreaking work: 'From the start, my goal was to integrate what we knew about the economics of markets and industrial organization and what we knew about companies and business strategy. These two fields had never really intersected before. In addition to scholars, I wanted to reach practitioners, offering them a systematic framework for developing an overall strategy for competing in an industry.' Porter has served as an adviser to several governments, including the US (Reagan administration), Canada, India, Ireland, New Zealand, Portugal, the United Kingdom, and the seven nations of Central America. He has also worked with leaders in Catalonia, Scotland, Connecticut, Mississippi, and other states and provinces. See also COMPETITIVE ADVANTAGE, see also FIVE FORCES MODEL.

positioning the way in which a company or organization is perceived relative to competitors in its marketplaces by existing and potential customers. Positioning, therefore, indicates how a company or organization wishes to compete in its marketplaces. Positioning is one of the most important elements of strategic marketing. If it is not right for the company, or its products and services, then many of the marketing executions that flow from the positioning idea will be ineffective. Positioning is closely related to **brand equity** and **market segmentation**, as all good positioning must be related to external market realities and dynamics. It is most dangerous to claim a market position for a brand which the company or organization cannot or can no longer deliver against. Also, the overall position should be relevant and compelling to a sufficient mass of potential buyers to make investment in the overall brand positioning worthwhile. Also the market must value the specific positioning of an attribute. See also MARKETING.

Theoretical models of positioning: Michael Porter has suggested three types of positioning strategy: cost leader, product differentiation and niche player.

He argued that successful firms must be superior in at least one of these positions and cannot be average, or dominant, in all three positions.

While Porter's framework remains valid and relevant, in marketing terms it has been further developed. Others (such as Treacy and Wiersema) have developed a framework of value disciplines:

Product leadership (for example Gucci or Sony),

Operational excellence (for example IKEA, Dell or McDonalds) and Customer intimacy (for example Virgin Atlantic Airlines, or Disney).

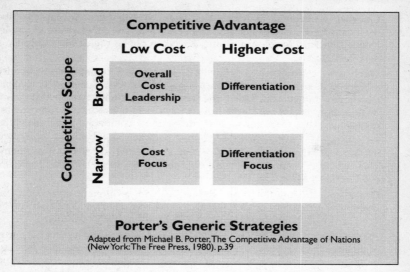

Porter's Generic Strategies

Adapted from Michael B. Porter, The Competitive Advantage of Nations
(New York: The Free Press, 1980). p.39

Trout & Ries defined positioning in terms of its outcome – how it leads to perceptions in the mind of the customers, either existing or prospective.

Philip Kotler has produced a detailed taxonomy of specific types of positioning:

Attribute positioning, in which the company, organization, product or service promotes a prominent attribute or feature (e.g. the world's best selling car, England's oldest hotel, the most expensive perfume).

Benefit positioning is a more typical type of positioning that focuses on the benefit derived from the product or service (e.g. the fastest overnight parcel delivery, the cleanest clothes after washing, the most reliable power tools, the greatest number of software applications that run on the device).

User/application positioning in which a product or service is positioned for a definite application or use (e.g. a first-time buyer's mortgage, golf clubs designed for low handicap golfers, the best clothes for resisting heavy rain and inclement weather).

User group positioning in which a company, organization, product or service aligns and creates affinities with a specific user group (e.g. The Gap for fashion-conscious youth, Volvo with safety-conscious drivers who also value durability, Disney with families, Saga with senior citizens).

Competitor positioning in which a company defines itself relative to its main competitors. Frequently companies that are challenging the market leader or dominant brand use this type of positioning (in the early days Apple did this, by implication, with IBM in which Apple promised freedom and creativity with its PC; Pepsi is constantly inviting customers to compare its drinks with those of Coca-Cola; Virgin Airlines constantly positions itself against British Airways). See also COMPARATIVE ADVERTISING. This type of positioning often defines the market in terms of the top two or three brands.

Category positioning in which a company or organization may describe itself as a leader in a category, rather than a specific product (for example, Hewlett Packard in colour printing, Kodak in photographic film, Coca-Cola in soft drinks).

Quality/price positioning in which a product or service promotes its quality relative to its pricing (for example McDonald's burgers being the best value for money rather than being the best burgers, Stella Artois beer being 'reassuringly expensive', Best Buy being the best products at the lowest prices).

Re-positioning is the set of marketing activities that changes the target market and buyers' perceptions of a given product, service or a company. This can cover a number of types of repositioning (see D. Jobber, *Principles and Practice of Marketing* 1995.):

Image repositioning the same product but with a different perception (for example the Marlboro cigarette being moved from a woman's cigarette in the 1950s to a rugged, macho man's cigarette from the 1960s onwards).

Product repositioning in which a product is adapted to either meet the needs of its target market more closely (Microsoft's various versions of Windows) or to increase the size of the market (e.g. Lucozade being adapted and repositioned from a single bottled drink that people took when they were poorly, to being an energy inducing drink for sports and other active people in various forms and flavours).

Intangible repositioning in which a different market segment is targeted with the same product (for example taking Disney theme parks to the very different markets of Japan and Europe).

Tangible repositioning target markets and product/service are changed (see for example the evolution of Nokia from a wood products company to a mobile phone and services company).

Value positioning Luxury goods and services that command a high price premium but which confer status on the user (Ferrari, Mercedes, Rolls-Royce, Gucci, Mont Blanc, Berlutti shoes).

Brands of equal quality and features to luxury brands but at lower cost (e.g. Audi vs. Mercedes, or BMW; Handspring vs. Palm Pilot personal digital assistants, Virgin Upper Class seat and service versus BA and American Airlines business class seat and service).

Wholesale, factory outlet and discount stores can provide leading brands for less than other stores. Also, various Internet websites can provide lower prices than traditional or branded retail outlets. This is usually based upon bulk purchasing and retailing techniques. In this case the outlet – either physical or virtual – is the leading brand rather than the individual products that it sells (Wal-Mart, Toys 'R' Us, Best Buy, Matalan, Amazon.com).

There is now a range of 'no-frills' product and service providers that offer a basic service or product at much lower price than competitors by eliminating some service features (e.g. IKEA requires the customers to assemble purchased furniture from flat packs; South West airlines, Easy Jet and Ryan Air have introduced very low-cost air travel by eliminating certain service features such as food onboard and preassigned seats, using direct booking

product petrification a term used to describe the small but persistent demand by loyal customers for a declining product.

product portfolio the mix of products manufactured or distributed by a company.

product positioning strategy marketing decisions and actions intended to create a particular place for a product in the market and in the minds of consumers. This strategy may attempt to differentiate a marketing offer from a competitor's or make it appear similar.

product position map a tool used in comparing consumer perception of the differences between products or brands. Consumers are asked to mark the particular location of a product or brand on a two-dimensional 'map', where the axes of the map are attributes felt by consumers to be important. See PERCEPTUAL MAPPING.

product recall the advertised request by a company that a product be returned to it by those who have already purchased it, often deemed desirable when a product proves to be unsafe or unreliable.

product testing exposing consumers to a new product, in final or prototype form, so that they might compare it to their usual brand and rate it. The results of product testing will indicate to the company whether further evaluation of the product in test markets is desirable.

---

psychographics a general term to describe and measure the psychological and behavioural characteristics of consumers. See also MARKET SEGMENTATION.

PUBLIC RELATIONS a practice that is less than 100 years old. In 1988, the governing body of the Public Relations Society of America formally adopted a definition of public relations which has become most accepted and widely used: *Public relations helps an organization and its public adapt mutually to each other.*

Public relations, as a practice and as a profession, has its critics in a new world of pseudo-events created for an ulterior purpose, of infomercials, of fictitious letter-writing campaigns, of manufactured celebrities and political 'spin doctoring' which have disoriented people and created suspicion over what is fact and what is not. Politicians and their parties are seen to be in the grip of public relations, which has greatly increased the sense of distrust that the public has of politicians.

The earliest definitions of public relations emphasized the roles of press agency and publicity, since these were major elements from which modern public relations grew. As it developed, public relations developed into a near-scientific discipline, with a strong need for research prior to initiating actions, as well as careful planning and thorough evaluation or measurement of results. Public relations became a continuing, systematic process instead of a one-time or single activity. It became an essential function of business management and public administration. Public relations defined itself through multiple audiences.

The essential elements of public relations are:

- Anticipating, analysing and interpreting public opinion, attitudes, and issues that might impact, for good or ill, the operations and plans of the organization.

- Counselling management at all levels in the organization with regard to policy decisions, courses of action, and communications, taking into account their public ramifications and the organization's social or citizenship responsibilities.

- Research: determining attitudes and behaviours of the public and their causes in order to plan, implement and measure activities to influence or change these attitudes and behaviours.

- Media relations: working with communications media in seeking publicity or responding to their interest in an organization.

- Publicity: disseminating planned messages through selected media without payment to further an organization's interest.

- Employee/member relations: responding to concerns and informing and motivating an organization's employees or members and their families.

- Community relations: continuing, planned and active participation within a community to maintain and enhance its environment to the benefit of both an organization and the community.

- Public affairs: developing effective involvement in public policy, and helping an organization adapt to public expectations.

- Government affairs: communication directly with legislatures and regulatory agencies on behalf of an organization.

- Issues management: identifying and addressing issues of public concern in which an organization is, or should be, concerned.

- Investor relations: creating and maintaining investor confidence and building positive relationships with the financial community.

- Industry relations: communicating with other firms in the industry and with trade associations.

- Fundraising: demonstrating the need for this, and encouraging an organization's members, friends, supporters and others to voluntarily contribute to support it.

- Special events and public participation: stimulating an interest in a person, product or organization by means of activities designed to enable an organization to listen to and interact with public.

- Marketing communications: a combination of activities designed to sell a product, service or idea, including advertising, collateral materials, publicity, promotion, packaging, point-of-sale display, trade shows and special events.

- Crisis management: public relations help to protect the present position when an organization is under attack.

As it develops public relations is also taking on multimedia dimensions, making greater use of the web to disseminate and control messages. For example, corporate websites display testimonials from satisfied customers, announce new products, services and prices as well as responding to events. This ability to self-publish on the web has diminished the need to have journalist write copy.

COMPARISON OF PUBLIC RELATIONS AND ADVERTISING:

Advertising

Space or time in the mass media is paid for by the user.

The advertiser shapes the central message and it is under their control.

The message transmitter controls the timing of the message.

Tends to use the mass media.

One-way communication – using the mass media is not interactive and does not enable direct and immediate feedback from the target audience.

Message sponsor is identified.

The intention of most messages is to inform, persuade, or remind about a product or service or company or organization.

The public may view the message as 'commercial' because the public recognizes advertising as an attempt to persuade or, in some cases, 'manipulate' them.

Is a very powerful tool for creating image.

Message is usually reductive and writing style is usually persuasive, can be very creative, often taking a conversational tone.

Public Relations

Coverage in mass media, such as the press, is not paid for.

The interpretation of the message is in the hands of the media.

The timing of the message is in the hands of those who control the media.

Tends to use more focused forms of communication, such as speaking engagements, community involvement, team or programme sponsorships, lobbying, lecture tours, publicity stunts.)

Two-say communication – public relations venues and communications channels usually allow direct and immediate feedback between the message transmitter and the target audience.

Message sponsor is not overtly identified.

The intention of public relations efforts is often to create good will, to keep the company in the minds of the public, or to build or to sustain a reputation.

The public often sees public relations messages that have been covered by the media as "news" and therefore, regard it as more neutral or believable.

Can also create image, but not as powerfully as advertising.

Writing style relies heavily on journalism talents – any persuasion is artfully inserted in the fact-based content such as press releases.

See also Edward BERNAYS

pyramid selling an illegal selling programme in which the person at the top makes the most money. For every person recruited to sell items, the person recruiting them receives some portion of the revenues every recruit sells. For the recruited individual to make money, he must then recruit others to sell the product. As more and more people are recruited each subsequent level gets wider and wider leading to a pyramid structure in terms of how revenues are distributed.

qualitative research see MARKET RESEARCH.

quantitative research see MARKET RESEARCH.

quantity discount a mark-down in price which is given to someone who purchases volumes of same item. Generally, the more someone buys, the greater the discount. This is because the cost of selling a single unit is greatly decreased since no additional marketing needs to be done to sell the additional units.

questionnaire see MARKET RESEARCH.

quota see MARKET RESEARCH.

R

random sample see MARKET RESEARCH.

rate card a document detailing prices for various ad placement options.

recall a one-dimensional measure of the effectiveness of an ad campaign in print and broadcast media. Recall is how much people remember a specific advertising campaign after the campaign has ended. Recall figures can be improved substantially by vast spending. Recall, however, is one-dimensional because it does not measure whether or not the target audience has developed any preference for the brand advertised.

recruitment advertising see ADVERTISING.

reference group a baseline group used for marketing or research purposes. All other groups are then compared to the reference group. Also known as a **control group**.

regional market a population in a particular area having characteristics that are distinguishable from other areas. A region can either be part of a nation state or a cluster of nation states (for example western Europe).

registered design a design that is licensed, so that only the person who owns the licence can use the design. See also TRADEMARK.

relaunch a new presentation to the marketplace of a product, service, organization or individual that was previously known to the marketplace. A product can be relaunched if the first launch was not as successful as hoped since a launch of a product will typically be highly advertised.

reliability the length of time that a product will last before it breaks down or needs repairs.

repositioning a dramatic change in how something is presented to the external marketplace. A product may be repositioned to sell to a different audience. See also POSITIONING.

research brief a short paper where data and statistics are used to explain things. Typically research briefs are not very in-depth but only give an overall view or impression of things. See MARKET RESEARCH.

retailer cooperative a voluntary contractual marketing system led by a group of retailers.

retailing activities involved in selling goods or services directly to final consumers for their personal, non-business use. Retailers are powerful intermediaries that purchase goods from wholesalers, or in some cases, directly from producers. See also DISTRIBUTION and CONSUMER MARKETING under MARKETING SPECIALIZATIONS.

retail mix the mix of variables, including location, merchandise, communications, price, services, physical attributes and personnel, which form the overall strategic marketing components of retailing.

return days the number of days in which an affiliate can still earn commission on a conversion (sale or lead) by a referred visitor.

reverse engineering originally a term used in computer science where a system is analysed to understand how its parts fit into the whole. This is the opposite of forward engineering, where individual parts are used to make a system. It can now mean stripping down a competitor product to see how it is made then, searching out improvements.

rich media a multimedia format that offers an enhanced experience relative to older, mainstream formats. New formats are regularly being introduced and old formats become part of the mainstream (or disappear altogether). Standard graphic formats such as JPEG and GIF would not be considered rich media. Some popular formats commonly considered rich media include Macromedia Flash and Shockwave, along with various audio and video formats. See also MEDIA.

Riefenstahl, Leni (1902–) German photographer and film director. A highly controversial figure, whose involvement in the Nazi regime is still actively debated, she is particularly remembered for two films, *Olympia* (1938), a dazzling portrayal of the 1936 Olympics (notable also for showing Hitler's anger at the black US athlete Jesse Owen's gold medal-winning performance), and *The Triumph of the Will* (1934), her film about the Nazi party rally at Nuremberg, which glorifies Hitler. In the film, one of the shrewdest blends of documentary and propaganda ever made, Riefenstahl emphasizes the emotional over the rational: Hitler is not a political figure but has godlike qualities of leadership. The rally is a spectacle designed to appeal to the subjugation of the individual to that of the serried ranks of the national consciousness. Riefenstahl subsequently described the film as a blight on her life ('it casts such a shadow over my life that death will be a blessed relief'), but its influence has been long-lasting. Riefenstahl later became a distinguished documentary filmmaker, making films of African tribes and underwater photography. See also GOEBBELS.

roll-out a phrase for the implementation of a service or product launch. Generally, a region or portion of the population is chosen so there can be more control over the supply and demand of the product or service.

Rubicam, Raymond (1892-1978) Young & Rubicam. An N.W. Ayer & Son copywriter in Philadelphia, Rubicam demonstrated leadership, teaching and supervisory gifts. His Squibb, Rolls-Royce and Steinway work fuelled Ayer's success. In 1923, denied a partnership, he and his colleague, John Orr Young, opened Young & Rubicam. Y&R embodied a 'creative revolution' by focusing on creative excellence. With radio's arrival, Y&R produced popular shows with Jack Benny and Arthur Godfrey. Rubicam resigned George Washington Hill's $3 million Pall Mall cigarettes account rather than replace a creative team. He instituted Y&R research, a trust fund, profit-sharing and bonuses, and was recognized as 'advertising's statesman.'

run-of-network an on-line ad-buying option in which ad placements may appear on any pages on sites within an ad network. Run-of-network buys are similar to run-of-site buys, except the ads appear on many sites instead of an individual site. See also ADVERTISING and MEDIA.

run-of-paper an ad-buying option where ads can appear anywhere in a given publication. See also ADVERTISING and MEDIA.

run-of-site an ad-buying Internet option in which ad placements may appear on any pages of the target site, with advertisers generally giving up authority over placement in return for low rates and broad reach. Ads may be placed randomly in unsold, less valuable portions of the target site. Run-of-site is similar to run-of-network, except the ads appear on an individual site instead of many sites.

S

sales meaning direct personal selling, continue to be of huge importance in the economy of the 21st century, particularly in the sale of services and in business-to-business marketing. However, many companies are now debating the extent to which they balance their selling functions between direct and indirect sales. While transactional and commodity sales are mainly done through indirect sales channels, larger, more complex sales are done through direct sales channels. Personal selling, combining the cost and training of a salesman, together with his relative lack of coverage and high compensation plans, make direct selling the most expensive way to sell, but in some ways the most valuable. On average 80% of sales calls are made by a direct sales force, but 20% of sales are made by indirect sales. Also, the cost of an individual sales call has risen gradually. Consequently, it is important to get the most out of sales calls and this has caused greater professionalization in the selection and training of salesmen.

The role of sales relative to marketing has long been a thorny issue. My own personal view is that sales is actually a type marketing done at the level of individuals or groups of customers: it is not separate from marketing, and it is neither superior nor inferior to it.

sales analysis a control measure that analyses sales orders by region, product, customer, market over a given period.

sales branch the supplier's office established to facilitate sales in a specific territory.

sales calling part of sales management: the number of times that a salesperson will call a customer over a given time period, either by a direct visit or by telephone. This requires a prioritization of the importance of customers, as well as good pre-planning and effective execution of the sales call. Sales calling can also be divided into calling on existing customers and calling on new prospects.

sales concept the orientation of an organization that emphasizes aggressive selling to achieve company objectives. This orientation is often seen to be at odds with the marketing concept, because companies that have this orientation often resort to pressure selling and manipulative sales techniques to win business and recruit salesmen with that profile, who are very short term and transactional results-orientated, often to the detriment of long-term relationships with customers.

sales contest a form of motivational incentive aimed at members of a company's sales force. These are competitions designed to boost sales and lift performance by offering awards or prizes to top achievers in a sales team in a given period. They also encourage competition between salespeople. Most companies with field sales forces offer an all-expenses-paid holiday for salespeople reaching defined quotas; it is a major incentive to salespeople not to miss the holiday.

sales forecast an estimation of the projected volume of sales, measured in either money or units, for a future planning period. Sales forecasting is usually done on the basis of past trends, sales force estimations, surveys of consumer buying intentions, managerial judgement, or quantitative models.

sales force the generic name given to the direct sales channel of a company. Their territories and their targets define sales forces. Sales forces can be combinations of types of salespeople: for example, account managers, who manage existing customer accounts and who are looking to constantly expand sales in that account; new account salespeople, whose main focus is winning new accounts and beating the competitors; sales support, who are experts in product or service and who act as auxiliaries to the sales force but do not carry a commission-based sales quota; telesales, for transactional sales that do not require a direct sales force. This is also known as the sales force mix.

sales force composite a simple sales forecasting method that estimates future demand for a product or service by aggregating what each member of the sales force expects to be able to sell in his or her territory.

sales kit a collection of sales materials, such as manuals, brochures, calendars, posters, adverts etc. prepared to explain a particular product or service promotion to retailers or other customers.

sales lead an individual, organization, or business that might be a likely prospect for the company's product or service. A lead may, with further qualification, become a prospect, prior to becoming a full customer.

sales literature printed material for external use, usually prepared by marketing, consisting of brochures, catalogues, price lists, presentations, videos to be used to assist the selling process.

sales management management of salespeople, involving balancing objective and target setting, allocation of sales territory, performance management, overseeing sales calling patterns, accompanying salesmen on major calls, overseeing sales budgets, selection and coaching of salespeople, keeping salespeople motivated, setting and allocating compensation targets and sharing success. The eternal law seems always to apply: that successful individual salespeople do not tend to make good sales mangers.

sales planning a detailed assessment of the current situation in a sales region, the setting of objectives, the formulation of strategies and tactics, and the establishment of control and evaluation procedures. This may also involve account planning, which is a detailed strategy and plan to enhance sales to individual customers.

sales potential an organization's expected sales of a product or service in a given market for a specified period and against installed competition; the share of the total market that a company can expect to attain in a given time.

sales presentation the salesperson's demonstration or display of a product, service, and concept to a prospective buyer in order to make a sale. This can either be done formally as a set-piece presentation or informally.

sales promotion where marketing and sales co-exist and work together most intensely. The sales promotion is a direct inducement, either by offering added value or a direct incentive to the indirect sales channel (such as retailers and resellers), the direct sales force itself, or from the salesforce to the consumers. The promotions are usually a range of tactical marketing techniques, within a larger strategic marketing framework, that incentivize the sale of products and services in order to achieve specific sales and marketing objectives. These wider objectives might be:

- to add appeal to the product brand and enhance its image;
- to encourage trial or repeat purchase;
- to defend the product from competition;
- to encourage customer loyalty and repeat purchase;
- to increase sales and market penetration;
- to identify and attract new customers;
- to educate customers regarding product improvements or new product introductions;
- to bring more customers into retail stores;
- to stabilize inventories or to obtain more and better retail shelf space and displays.

There are various types and mixes of sales promotion which could include trade shows, exhibitions, point-of-sale retail displays, personality endorsements (such as book signings), attractive packaging, sponsorships, special offers, customer demonstrations with giveaways, contests and games, gifts, free products, extra products, rebates and price discounts, buy-one-get-one-free combinations, straightforward cash incentives (such as 'cash back' on new mortgages and credit cards), loyalty points or stamps, free services, savings schemes, buy-back guarantees, low-interest financing of the sale and trade-in allowances on the old product. Sales promotions need to be legal; some, such as pyramid selling, are not.

sales quotas volume targets set for salespeople stating the amount they should sell and how sales should be divided among the company's products and services.

sales ratio a marketing control measure used to determine whether the cost of selling in a given period was excessive. Total expenditure on sales is expressed as a percentage of total sales revenue for the same period. The Promotion-to-Sales Ratio is another marketing control measure used to determine whether the amount spent on sales promotion was excessive. Total expenditure on sales promotion in a given period is expressed as a percentage of total sales revenue for the same period.

sales report a salesperson's detailed record of sales calls and results for a given period. Typically, a sales report will include information such as the sales volume per product or service line, the number of existing and new accounts called upon, and the expenses incurred in making the calls.

sales technique the methods that a salesman uses from initial contact with a prospect through to closing the sale and often including long-term account management. Sales technique has attracted an enormous body of literature, which testifies to the continuing importance of personal selling in the economy. The time-honoured fundamentals of good selling technique are:

being able to build rapport and relationships with customers and prospects; ability to qualify sales situations and customers very early; persuasion skills, especially in the advancement of proposition and presentation; sensitive and rational objection handling; good call planning and execution; advanced customer listening skills; being able to understand situations from the customers' point of view; negotiation skills, particularly taking the customer to a place where he feels that he has benefited from the sale; good time management and organization; being personable and easy to do business with, and very importantly, the ability to close a sale and win the order.

sales territory a way of structuring the sales force so that it can achieve the overall sales objectives. It is also the allocated area for which a salesman is responsible. Sales territories tend to be allocated by sales managers and do not necessarily accord with market segments as defined by marketers. Most sales managers favour managing sales territories on a geographical basis, rather than more abstruse market segments, but some also do it on the basic of customer accounts or by product or service types. Territorial salesmen analyse their territory, work out their sales schedules and customer calling patterns and frequencies. They tend to represent all of the company's products and services to customers in that territory.

sales volume an organization's total sales, in terms of units or revenue, for a specified period. Sales volume (by sales region or territory, industry, customer type, etc) is commonly used as an aid in determining the effectiveness of the selling effort.

Other popular sales terms

ABC a popular sales acronym for Always Be Closing.

canvas to look for potential new customers for a product or service. Canvassing is typically done in person rather than over the phone or via other channels.

churn the percentage of customers who have no product loyalty and who will switch to a competing product.

clincher an additional inducement offered to a potential buyer by a salesperson in order to close a sale. Inducements might include price discounts, rebates, extended credit, reduced delivery charges, etc.

closing skill the ability of a salesperson to obtain the buyer's commitment to the purchase.

closing techniques methods employed by a salesperson when asking for an order and aimed at obtaining a favourable response from a buyer.

commission money paid to the salesperson after the successful completion of a sale. Commissions are typically predetermined and can be a percentage of sales or the number of units sold.

draw money paid to a salesperson before the sale is actually completed. The draw is then applied towards the commissions earned from future sales. Draws are used for salespeople where income is based entirely upon a commission. Draws can be either recoverable or non-recoverable. Recoverable draws occur when the salesperson is required to reimburse the company if the commission targets are not met; non-recoverable draws cannot be recovered if the targets are not met.

elephant a potential customer who would bring in a good amount of revenue if successfully converted to a customer. See also WHALE.

farmer someone who is responsible for increasing sales from current accounts. In sales, the farmer will 'grow' sales as in agriculture the farmer will grow crops.

funnel a sales pipeline management system to distinguish 'leads' from 'prospects' from 'qualified prospects' from 'potential customers'.

goal a monetary amount or number of units which should be sold in a specified period of time.

hunter someone who is responsible for locating and bringing in new sales (often contrasted with the farmer).

inbound inquiry an unsolicited question about the product placed by a potential customer.

ISO Independent Sales Organization, or a sales force which is not part of the company that produces the products to be sold.

lead a potential customer who has been identified as being interested in a product or service. Leads will typically be converted into actual sales.

lock-out revenue money generated from a customer who perceives it would be too much trouble to switch to a competing product.

personal selling a two-way, interactive form of selling which is usually conducted face to face, but which can also include telephone selling. It is a tried and tested form of oral persuasion and negotiation involving the seller and the potential buyer. The seller attempts to build interest and rapport, while also informing, then persuading the potential buyer to purchase products and services. The customer is able to demand greater and more detailed information, then to negotiate. Personal selling enables the formation of a personal relationship between buyer and seller, which brings another dimension to the product and service. Although this type of exchange is highly effective and informative, it is declining as a way of selling commodity goods and transactional services. In the first instance it is an expensive way of selling. The salesperson usually earns a commission, raising the overall cost of sale. Potential customers may not always react well or trust the individual salesperson and be wary of his individual persuasion techniques. Additionally, personal selling has a very limited range of coverage. Internet-based selling, which provides the customers with information without the inducement pressure of an individual salesman, has done much to move simple products and services such an insurance, that were previously the domain of personal salespeople, to indirect selling over phone and internet. The future of personal selling appears to be moving toward high-value products and services.

prospect a potential customer.

qualified prospect a potential customer who has been subjected to various probability criteria related to eventual sales.

quota a number of units or revenue which must be generated by a salesperson. See also GOAL.

referral recommendation by a current user of a product of another potential customer. Referrals are the most effective form of advertising since the recommendation is based upon personal experience.

SLA Service Level Agreement. An agreement between the buyer and seller that the seller will guarantee a specified level of service for the product.

USP Unique Selling Proposition; that which differentiates one product or service from that of the competitor.

WIIFM What's In It For Me; a salesperson should always tell the customer what benefits he would personally get from the product.

weight-out a decrease in the weight or package size of a product while retaining the same price. This will give the illusion that the price of the product has not changed, even though there is less product in the new package. This will also help to maintain the company's margin on the product since smaller packaging will make up for increased production costs.

whale someone who will have a huge influence on sales if successfully brought in as a customer. See also ELEPHANT.

sample see MARKET RESEARCH.

sampling see MARKET RESEARCH.

screening the examination of a population based upon certain criteria to determine the suitability of an individual for a product or service. Screening in market research will help determine the most suitable individuals for interviews or product tests.

search engine a program on the World Wide Web that indexes documents, then attempts to match documents relevant to a user's search requests. Web search engines attempt to index a large portion of pages on the World Wide Web. There is also some confusion about the difference between a search engine and a search destination. A search engine powers the search process and provides results for a search destination. A search destination can use its own engine, a third-party engine, or a combination. Knowing the difference between an engine and a destination is important when submitting URLs; a destination using its own engine can accept direct submissions, while a destination using external engines may or may not provide a submission option.

search engine optimization the process of choosing targeted keyword phrases related to a site, and ensuring that the site places well when those keyword phrases are part of a Web search. Optimization involves making pages readable to search engines and emphasizing key topics related to your content. Basic optimization may involve nothing more than ensuring that a site does not unnecessarily become part of the invisible Web (the portion of the Web not accessible through Web search engines). Advanced optimization may include significant research into every element of page design, site structure, and off-the-page criteria.

search engine spam excessive manipulation to influence search engine rankings, often for pages of little or no relevant content.

search engine submission the act of supplying a URL to a search engine in an attempt to make a search engine aware of a site or page.

search spy a perpetually refreshing page that provides a real-time view of actual Web searches.

secondary data see MARKET RESEARCH.

sellers' market a market where there are more people interested in buying a product and where demand outstrips supply. The seller is almost guaranteed to be able to sell the product at any price.

selling-in the process of educating the sales force and distributors to sell a new product as part of the preparation for its market launch. This process involves presentations, the development of sales kits, briefings on the target market and competition, and outlining the organization's plans to create consumer demand.

service markets are the fastest growing in the developed world. Two-thirds of the GNP of the advanced economies is derived from service industries.

Service markets are characterized by their heterogeneity: services can range from plastic surgery to travel reservations to hotels to outsourcing information technology services to leading a major law suit conducted on behalf of a major corporation. Services are also integral to products; there is a huge service sector dedicated to the care and maintenance of tangible products and physical assets such as janitorial functions, cleaning, storage, maintenance. There are multiple services – business services – that happen within organizations that are not run as external businesses. There is a growing range of services that are moved from inside a company to be handled by external contractors – outsourcing services. The worldwide expansion of leasing, franchising and rentals business – from cars to aircraft to domestic appliances to fast food and personal care outlets – has added further growth. Deregulation of state-owned monopolies, utilities and capital markets, most of which are service providers, caused a huge explosion in the competitive services market. Also, we are also seeing the early stages of globalization in services businesses, some enabled by the World Wide Web, which were once thought to be intensely local activities.

Service marketing is now a major discipline in the overall marketing range of techniques and is radically different from product marketing. It came late to the marketing table, long after consumer goods, and a generation after industrial marketing. Professional services marketing was the latest entrant, following a period of restrictions, some self-imposed, upon the marketing of professional expertise. From the early 1980s onwards restrictions on advertising accountancy, legal, medical, optometry, architectural services were removed. Also, the entire field of services marketing has been broadened by the needs of the non-profit services, such as charities and public services and of franchises, which are burgeoning worldwide.

Some areas of the services growth that have affected marketing are: the World Wide Web, which enables interactive marketing of services to customers; customer care centres; the greater involvement of customers in self service (such as personal banking and investment) and the massively increased ability to gather, store and use customer information.

In essence a service is a benefit that one party brings to another that is neither tangible nor separable, neither standardized nor storable. These characteristics determine the various mixes and approaches to marketing as well as setting new, non-traditional challenges. Service marketers are particularly challenged to make a service differentiated, often by linking it to tangible evidence of its outcome, to manage fluctuations in demand and to ensure good service delivery quality.

The following are characteristics of services:

intangibility services disappear at the point of consumption and they cannot be possessed. Often the results are intangible, or at least not visible. Therefore, for services marketing the normal tools of promotion are not usable to create an abiding memory of the service brand: patenting is impossible and quality of delivery is variable because delivered mainly by people.

inseparability the production and the consumption of a service are usually simultaneous and inseparable (e.g. entertainment). Services are often sold before they are produced (e.g. travel). People usually deliver services, therefore direct selling and delivery is the only channel that can be used.

heterogeneity because people largely deliver services, it is impossible to standardize them; there are multiple variances in the type and the delivery of service. Marketers can often turn this to their advantage, as there is always a price premium for customization.

perishability services cannot be stored and displayed permanently. This is a major problem for service providers who cannot get full utilization (e.g. in professional services) of their services or spaces (e.g. aircraft seats, hotel rooms, theatre seats) that they are selling. Marketing of these services, therefore, needs to constantly cope with permanence of supply, but with huge variations in demand.

ownership unlike products, services do not result in a transfer of property ownership. See also SERVICES MARKETING.

service delivery involves the customer directly on many occasions: ordering a meal, using electronic banking, specifying a hairstyle, loading and unpacking groceries through a check-out, showing potential buyers around a house for sale, helping diagnose a medical problem. In these cases, human interaction and demonstrable expertise is paramount. In other cases, technology can be used to enhance customer service: travel booking, investment analysis, and security services. Services delivery has become a subtle interplay of technology and human interaction.

service distribution services are mainly delivered by people but in key locations, such as banks, aeroplanes, salons, travel agencies, restaurants, hotels, law offices, and hospitals. Services can be delivered remotely, such as broadcast entertainment, distance learning, financial and information services. Another way of distributing services is through a network of franchisees who have a common brand and who are trained in the same level of service delivery.

service encounter a moment of direct interaction between the service provider and the customer in which service delivery is put to the test. The customer's experience of this encounter can determine the brand reputation of the service provider for a considerable time after the encounter is past.

service environment the overall environment within which a service is delivered. This combines design, access, physical, emotional and atmospheric dimensions.

service guarantees are much more difficult to design and manage than unconditional product guarantees, but are becoming more prevalent as the industry expands. Holiday companies will often provide compensation for poor hotel rooms; airlines for delays; freight companies for lost packages. Service charters to customers are commonplace. The inability to offer unconditional guarantees in most of the service business has led to a higher emphasis on customer complaint handling and follow-up.

service marketing see MARKETING.

service pricing has as many forms as there are services: pricing of services is usually a combination of expertise, time taken, and speed of delivery. Price forms are also very different, for example, entertainment services are usually priced through admission tickets with all kinds of variables; personal care services are priced based upon skill levels and time; estate agents take commission based on sale value; buses, taxis, trains and planes take fares based upon length of travel; professional services charge fees based upon expertise by the hour or day; financial services charge interest based upon amount of debt or services; governments charge taxes for services, locally and nationally; employees are paid salaries, wages and bonuses for their labour and skill level.

service process very problematic particularly because of the difficulties of constantly keeping supply and demand in balance and the variability of service quality.

service promotion see SERVICE MARKETING under MARKETING.

service quality probably the single most important factor in any service business. The company's personnel are critical to this – much more, for example, than in a product company. Customers have rising expectations of quality service delivery and can easily take their business elsewhere. Service companies have to be committed to their employees and, effectively, market to them. Marketers in service companies must be constantly working on improving service delivery programmes and quality and identifying gaps in perceived quality by customers.

share of voice a measure of the total number of mentions that a company gets in its target media relative to its main competitor. It is a measure of awareness and image in the media rather than in the mind of target audiences.

shelf life literally, the length of time that something can stay on a store shelf. The length of time varies by product and is dictated by whether or not something will spoil or will no longer be of interest to the consumer. Perishables have a short shelf life whereas canned goods have a much longer shelf life. Generally, it has come to mean anything for which time can run out in the market place.

shopping cart on-line software that is used to make a site's product catalogue available for on-line ordering, whereby visitors may select, view, add/delete, and purchase merchandise.

shopping mall a large indoor or outdoor collection of many individual stores with common areas for restaurants and parking.

shrinkage the loss of merchandise by a retailer, usually due to theft, but sometimes due to other reasons.

silent commerce the use of microprocessors, sensors and tags to make everyday objects intelligent and interactive. When combined with continuous Internet connectivity, silent commerce provides for the collection of data and for the delivery of services through everyday objects. This type of commerce is 'silent' because objects communicate and commerce takes place without human interaction. Silent commerce is one aspect of the emerging world of untethered, unbounded, ubiquitous computing.

simulated test marketing a forecasting method that gathers data for predicting a product's likely market performance by marketing it in artificial (for example a computer model of a market) rather than real life test situations. See also CONCEPT TESTING.

simulation a test in a virtual environment to determine if something would be successful in reality. Simulations are often used when testing in a real environment would be too expensive or dangerous. Conditions are set up to mimic reality as closely as possible.

skimming see PRICING and MILKING.

skyscraper ad an on-line ad significantly taller than the 120x240 vertical banner.

Sloan, Alfred (1875-1966), General Motors. A pivotal figure, not just in the history of American business but also in the development of marketing. He joined General Motors in 1916 having sold his car anti-friction bearings business to them. He became president of GM in 1923 and was elected Chairman of the Board in 1937. He continued as Chief Executive Officer until 1946 and retired in 1956. His revolutionary 'standard procedures' concept, which is a market-oriented way of defining management effectiveness, is credited with enabling GM to overtake the hitherto dominant Henry Ford car company. Sloan's experiences, theories and personal customer-based research inspired a new approach to marketing strategy. It also led to the separate Chevrolet, Buick, Oldsmobile and Cadillac lines aimed at different consumer wallets and tastes. Through his customer-oriented management philosophy, Sloan's GM became a symbol of U.S. industrial leadership. He understood that the automobile industry's salvation depended on changing consumers' attitudes. While Ford viewed the car as a low-cost form of transportation, Sloan at GM changed the perception of a car into a symbol of attainment, one that could induce consumers to continually upgrade. To that end, Sloan introduced the concept of *planned obsolescence* through constant changes to the overall product, many of them simple changes to design, colour and model. To some extent Sloan pioneered an early approach to market segmentation, new channels of distribution and brand management: providing 'a car for every purse and purpose'. GM encouraged consumers to trade up as their circumstances improved, and provided dealers and customers with the credit tools for doing so. The car became a manifestation of conspicuous consumption. Sloan's market-centric approach triumphed over Ford's producer-centric approach. GM sales overtook Ford's in 1927 and since then, Ford's sales have never been greater than those of GM. Sloan showed decisively that increased sales were not necessarily dependent upon ever-lower prices or product improvements but on more intangible factors like status, range of choice, artificial needs and superficial change. He published *My Years with General Motors* in 1963.

slogan a phrase (from the gaelic for 'war cry') used to advertise or market a product that is short, compelling and memorable. A successful slogan will immediately cause the consumer to make the association between the slogan and the product. For example, BMW's slogan is 'The Ultimate Driving Machine.' See also ADVERTISING.

soft sell a method of selling merchandise where the technique is very low-pressure and undemanding. The soft sell approach is seen as more amenable to modern customers, making them more receptive to purchasing than the hard sell approach, which tests have shown makes consumers feel uncomfortable and that they must purchase the item. See also HARD SELL and SALES.

Sorrell, Martin (1945–) WPP Group. At Saatchi & Saatchi (1975-1986), Sorrell, as Finance Director, was the architect of the agency's massive acquisitions. He joined WPP in 1986. There he began to acquire below-the-line advertising-related companies and in 1987 made a $566-million hostile takeover of J. Walter Thompson Co. Sorrell followed this in 1989 with another dramatic hostile $825-million buy of Ogilvy & Mather. Today, WPP is one of the world's larger marketing service/advertising groups with more than 40 companies in 83 nations.

spam see E-MAIL SPAM.

splash page a branded, usually graphic-intensive, page that appears before the home page of a Website. Some splash pages automatically refresh to the home page upon completion; others require the visitors to click on an entrance button or text link. While some marketers believe that splash pages are a necessary part of the brand experience, users may not view them in the same light. It is worth noting that very few of the most highly trafficked destinations on the Web use splash pages.

sponsorship a major component of marketing communications, brand building and image development, sponsorship supports a cause or beneficiary both for altruistic reasons and for reasons that help the company gaining favourable attention through association. Sponsorship has three main advantages for the sponsor: (1) it provides them with media coverage; (2) it can have an internal benefit in terms of helping to improve employee morale;

(3) It can assist in business relationships if the company personnel bring clients and customers to whatever is being sponsored. Marketing sponsorship is prevalent in sports, the arts, charities, good causes and public institutions.

standard industrial classification originally a method used by the US government's Occupational Safety and Health Administration (OSHA) to assign a four-digit number to classify all establishments in the US by category: Agriculture, Mining, Construction, Manufacturing, Transportation, Wholesale and Retail Trade, Financial Services, and Public Administration etc. This classification system is also known as the SIC code and was last updated in 1987. It has since been replaced by the North American Industrial Classification System (NAICS) in 1997 in order to more accurately reflect the changes in the North American economy to include 350 new industries such as high technology categories dealing with computers, the Internet or wireless applications as well as things like Health Maintenance Organizations. The NAICS was updated in 2002. In 1999, the statistical agencies of the US, Canada and Mexico agreed upon a multi-phased approach to develop a new classification system for products to complement the industrial system. The North American Product Classification System (NAPCS) is currently under development.

statistics numerical data items that represent a population. Statistics are used to determine how attractive a market is, its growth, how successful a business is, how many items are sold and produced, what types of consumers buy things as well as point out what needs to be improved.

stickiness the amount of time that visitors spend on a website over a given time period Stickiness is often measured in the average minutes per month visitors spend at a site or network. Sometimes stickiness is measured in terms of page views. Stickiness has increasingly become a measure of the attractiveness and attention-holding nature of a website.

store a retail place where merchandise is offered for sale.

store design the overall layout of retail store displays. Proper lighting, space, atmospherics and store design will make shopping a pleasurable experience for the consumer and will help to sell more products. Generally, the displays in the front of the store should be interesting enough to bring people into the store. Grocery retailers tend to put fresh produce at the front of the store to give the idea that everything is fresh and natural. Basics are always at the back so that people have to walk through the store to get to them.

storyboard a series of drawings or pictures used to represent an outline of a commercial or advertisement. This is a technique borrowed from animation film studios (Disney are experts in it) that spread to marketing.

structured interview a formal interview with specific questions which have been predetermined. Used in primary research. See MARKET RESEARCH.

subliminal advertising advertising in such a way so the consumer is not consciously aware that a product is being advertised. This is illegal. See ADVERTISING.

supermarket a medium-sized store that sells groceries and packaged goods, usually in an urban setting.

superstore a large store which sells everything from groceries to packaged goods to clothing, usually outside an urban setting.

survey See MARKET RESEARCH.

survey research See MARKET RESEARCH.

SWOT analysis see under MARKETING.

syndicated research See MARKET RESEARCH.

tachistoscope an instrument that projects images on a screen in rapid succession in order to test memory recall.

target audience a group who have been identified as potential receivers of information or messages about a product or service or idea.

target market a particular audience or segment that have been identified as likely customers of a product or service.

teaser an advert designed to build up interest that does not reveal the product or brand that it is advertising. It sets up the next advert and stimulates customer curiosity. Additionally, a teaser can be some gift, given, usually at no charge, to convince the user to purchase the item for future use. See also ADVERTISING.

tele-marketing selling a product or service over the telephone. Typically, a computer randomly generates phone numbers from an address database; the individual trying to sell the product has a script to use.

telephone research See MARKET RESEARCH.

tele-shopping television home shopping. While extremely popular as a channel in the US, it failed to take off in other countries. However, the advent of interactive television holds out much promise for the television as a major two-way marketing channel.

television rating a system that measures how widely watched different television programmes are by viewers.

testimonial credential for a product or service based upon successful usage. Many products use customer testimonials on product or service success in order to market and sell the product to others.

test marketing testing a product prior to launch with a small representative group. Frequently, new products are released to a test market in order to determine market potential. Feedback is gathered and the product can be improved before it is rolled out to a larger market or audience. Samples of a proposed new product are tried out in areas that are supposed to be representative of the market as a whole. The key advantage of test marketing is that it is possible to evaluate a new product or service without launching nationally and incurring a large amount of expenditure on both promotional elements and sales training. Generally, test marketing is practised in consumer markets rather than industrial markets.

Objectives of the test marketing should be clear. Representative areas should be chosen so that when the findings are extrapolated to the whole sales area, the results are indicative of likely activity and market share. There are some limitations on test marketing; in particular, it can alert competitors to the new product or service and allow them to respond. Even if the test is successful and the test area is thought to be representative, there is no way of knowing for certain that the test area is representative of the full target market. If special plant and equipment needs to be commissioned to produce the new product, the fixed costs may make it uneconomic to launch on a limited scale and having carried out exploratory research, it may be better to launch to the full market.

text ad an advertisement using text-based hyperlinks. Their graphical-based counterparts, although common in e-mail, have superseded text-based ads on the Web. Affiliate marketing is one area where text ads have flourished. However, many mainstream advertisers are only beginning to discover the power of text. While lacking some of the advantages of graphical ads, text-based ads have some powerful advantages of their own. They download almost instantly and are not affected by ad-blocking software. See also ADVERTISING.

text link exchanges a network where participating sites display text ads in exchange for credits that are converted (using a predetermined exchange rate) into ads to be displayed on other sites.

three orders model developed in 1973 by Michael Ray as a work of synthesis of previous hierarchical models such as the Hierarchy of Effects, the Dissonance Hierarchy (which examined advertising as a method to counteract cognitive dissonance (conation-affect-cognition)) and The Low Involvement Hierarchy, which focused on the significant effect of repetition in advertising (cognition-conative-affect). Ray's model states that all three hierarchies can co-exist in a single multi-dimensional model. Different hierarchies would dominate in different situations and depending on different circumstances.

Using the different labels: Cognition (for learning and understanding of the product or service; C); Behaviour (or action/choice of purchase; B) and Attitude (the emotional response to the product; A). Ray formulated the three types of hierarchy into a single model that was related to different hierarchies for different types of purchase.

The Learning Hierarchy was characteristic of products in which the consumer was highly involved in the purchase and had to choose between numerous alternative products. In order to make a final, appropriate and satisfying choice and purchase the consumer must to enter into a 'learning' or cognition process (C) then develop an emotional response to the product through the learning (A) and then move to a purchase (B).

The Dissonance-Attribution Hierarchy was the reverse of the learning model. Here the decision is made without learning and occurs first (B), then is followed by the formation of reinforcing attitude (A). Cognition (C) occurs last, and only selectively in order to legitimize the choice and the behaviour. Ray describes this hierarchy as relevant to high-involvement purchases where nearly indistinguishable alternative products are present.

Finally, The Low Involvement Hierarchy is relevant to low-involvement products with minimal differences among alternative products. Cognition (C) takes place first, chiefly by means of frequent repetition of a message, followed by choice (B), and finally the formulation of an attitude (A) about the product.

Michael Ray
1973

	Learning	Dissonance	Low Involvement
Order	C-A-B	B-A-C	C_B_A
Involvment	yes	yes	no
Alternative	different	not different	not different

See also HIERARCHY OF EFFECTS, AIDA, DAGMAR, PURCHASING, MARKETING COMMUNICATIONS, ADVERTISING.

threshold model a buyer behaviour model based on the idea that consumers have a point or threshold beyond which they will not venture. See also BUYER.

title tag a HTML tag used to define the text in the top line of a Web browser, also used by many search engines as the title of search listings.

toll-free number a telephone number that does not cost anything to the person dialling the number. Most customer service lines have toll-free numbers.

top 10 the top ten search engine results for a particular search term on the World Wide Web. The majority of browsers never get beyond the top ten search results.

tracking study a quantitative technique for measuring advertising effectiveness, usually in the minds of the target audience. Tracking measures are primarily awareness and perception of brand as promoted by an advertising campaign. One of the primary measures is the respondents' ability to recall the advertising that promoted the brand, and their interpretation of the messages or points in the advertising campaign. Ultimately, the advertiser is attempting to create preference for the brand in the minds of the target audience – so preference and consideration relative to competing brands is also measured. See also ADVERTISING.

trade discount a reduced price that is given to members of a specific industry or practitioner group.

trade-in allowance the amount of money that represents the value of an item given in exchange for another item. This is popular for used car sales.

trade journal a magazine that focuses on a specific topic or industry. Trade journals are a method by which someone can keep up with the current events and issues in their industry. The trade associations whose members consist of the practitioners in a particular industry sponsor many magazines. See also MEDIA.

trademark gives a company the exclusive use of a name on a defined set of products and services in either a specific or a general category. For example, Kodak is owned as a general trademark by Eastman Kodak and cannot be used by another company. Other trademarks are restricted to specific categories and have exclusive right only in that category. This is important in brand management. See also BRAND.

trade show a major fair, display or event where the goods and services represented by a specific industry, topic or interest group are displayed and discussed. See also EXHIBITION.

traffic a measurement of how many individuals frequent a particular area or website. Internet traffic measures how often individuals frequent the Internet.

trial the testing of a product for usability and attractiveness to users.

trial offer an offer of the use of a product, for a short period of time, so that the user can decide whether or not to keep the product. The idea behind a trial offer is to let the consumer experience or use the product with little risk attached. Often, consumers will not want to sign up for a standard length of time unless the product is something that proves to be useful. See also CONSUMER MARKETING.

trick banner an Internet ad that attempts to trick people into clicking, often by imitating an operating system message, such as 'You have mail'. Trick banners seek to overcome 'banner blindness' and 'banner baggage' by disguising the fact that they are advertising devices. Typically, no mention is made of the advertiser, just an imitation of an operating system or popular application. While it is common for trick banners to attract a higher-than-average click-through rate (CTR), the quality of the clicks may be somewhat suspect, as visitors are likely to hit the 'Back' button once they realize what has happened. Aside from CTR, there is the issue of visitor satisfaction. Visitors may feel ill will towards a site that tricked them, and may decide not to return. A trick click-through is sometimes called a trick-through. See also BANNER ADVERTISING

two-tier affiliate programme a structure whereby affiliates earn commissions on their conversions as well as conversions of webmasters whom they refer to the programme.

umbrella marketing an advertising campaign that focuses on a family of brands, or a multi-product group.

under-delivery means fewer impressions, visitors, or conversions than contracted for a specified period of time, typically a 30-day period.

undifferentiated market a market thought to have little market segment differences or variation and which can be treated as a mass market with a singular marketing mix. See MASS MARKET.

unique selling proposition see under SALES.

unique visitor an individual who has visited a Website (or network) at least once in a fixed time frame, typically a 30-day period. Most measurements of unique visitors are estimates. Sites often calculate unique visitors based on the IP address information found in the log files, and sometimes through cookies.

unit pricing the price of a single item.

upmarket describes a product, good, etc. which is seen as more expensive or wealthy and having better quality. See also DOWNMARKET.

URL Universal Resource Locator, the location of a resource on the Internet, including the protocol, the domain name (or IP address), and additional path information (folder/file). URLs are often important to marketers in that they are part of the phrase 'Add URL', the process of submitting a site or page to another site, usually a search engine or directory. See also INTERNET.

users a vital group within the overall purchasing process who may initiate the buying process and help define purchase. See also BUYING.

utility the ability of a product or service to satisfy the customer's wants or needs.

value in simplest terms, the benefit that a good or a service provides, as perceived and measured by the beholder. What one customer finds of value can be different from what another finds of value. Good marketing will sell a product based upon its perceived value to a target markets.

value added the additional benefit that the product or service provides over and above its component parts. When there is little to differentiate one product or service from another, products and services that are perceived to have strong value added will generally fare better than those that don't. The value added is often achieved through providing additional services around a core service or a product. For instance, a car dealer may have the value-added service of picking up the vehicle at someone's house whenever it needs maintenance or repairs and returning it as well as providing them with a replacement car for the duration of the repair at no extra charge.

value-added reseller (VAR) an intermediary that buys basic products from producers, adds value by modifying or expanding the products, and then resells them to final customers.

value analysis a study on how much value a product or service is providing.

value chain originally, a description of the process of manufacture from a raw product to which various values are added (extra parts or processes) resulting in finished product to sell. More generally, it describes the relationships between an organization's value activities from input to output, modelling all of the value-adding activities in the chain. It can now be extended to any process, not just physical manufacture. As companies rid the supply chain of excess inventory, they must coordinate supply, production and distribution to exactly match output with demand. For example, a company's entire supply chain can benefit from improved performance through effective use of value chain analysis to impact cycle time, quality (including predictability) and innovation within the equipment, component, materials and service providers.

vertical banner a web banner ad measuring 120 pixels wide by 240 pixels tall.

vertical integration this occurs when a company expands its production capabilities to cover the spectrum of the product manufacturing process. It is also where a company merges with or takes over other companies in the same supply chain. So, if a wine maker takes over his supplier who makes wine bottles, that counts as vertical integration. A car company expanding into car tyre manufacturing is another example, or a furniture maker buying up forests and pulp mills.

vertical market a market with a distribution channel structure in which producers, wholesalers, and retailers act as a unified system; either one channel member owns the others, or has contracts with them, or has so much power that they all cooperate.

There are three major types of vertical market system (VMS).

Corporate VMS: a VMS combining successive stages of production and distribution under single ownership.

Administered VMS: a VMS that coordinates successive stages of production and distribution, not through common ownership, but through the size and power of one of the parties.

Contractual VMS: a VMS in which independent firms at different levels of production and distribution join together through contracts to obtain more economies or sales than they could achieve alone.

There are three types of Contractual VMS.

Wholesaler-Sponsored Voluntary Chain: one in which wholesalers organize a voluntary chain of independent retailers to help them compete with large corporate chain organizations.

Retailer Cooperative: one in which retailers organize a new jointly-owned business to carry on wholesaling and possibly production.

Franchise organization: one in which a channel member, called a franchiser, links several stages in the production distribution process. These are yet again of three types:

- Manufacturer-sponsored retailer franchise system;
- Manufacturer-sponsored wholesaler franchise system; and
- Service-firm sponsored franchise system.

virtual environment an event or situation that is not physically attended but simulated to give the illusion of physical attendance. Companies hold virtual meetings such as video- or webcasts, to extend reach and cut time and transportation costs. Virtual meetings have also become an important marketing medium both within the company and external to it. For example, investors and analysts are regularly informed about a company's progress by means of virtual meetings; employees regularly receive communications updates through webcasts.

vision generally, a perception, foresight or strategy for future events or direction. The relationship of vision to marketing is multi-dimensional. Marketing is usually one of the elements that can make a vision happen in reality; there can be visions of future markets or combinations that create new market demand that the current providers cannot currently see. Also, the vision itself can be marketed. This is particularly seen in 'internal' marketing where, for example, the Chief Executive will attempt to propagate his or her vision to employees and to stakeholders. Alternatively, the marketing arms of many political parties will market the vision of the leaders or the party to potential voters.

voiceover a technique used in advertising and the entertainment industry where a narrator's voice is added to an existing video, animation, advert, movie or television clip. As with radio, this voice is heard but not seen.

volunteer directory a Web directory staffed primarily by unpaid volunteer editors.

Wanamaker, John (1838-1922) Advertising's highest standards at the beginning of the 20th century were embodied by John Wanamaker, whose Philadelphia and New York department stores pioneered fixed prices and money-back guarantees with honest, consistent ad support. A religious man who refused to advertise on Sundays, he hired John E. Powers in 1880 as the first full-time (and highly paid) department store copywriter. Their stormy personal relationship succeeded on the professional level because Powers staunchly upheld Wanamaker's marketing philosophy. Wanamaker also reformed the U.S. postal system while serving as Postmaster General (1889-93) in the administration of President Benjamin Harrison and was president of the YMCA from 1870-83. Wanamaker is also remembered in the advertising business for turning a phrase still talked about today: 'Half my advertising is wasted; I just don't know which half.'

warranty is a guarantee that is given by the seller that the product is free of defects. If the product breaks down or if it has defects, the provider of the warranty promises to fix or replace the product free of charge, or at a reduced cost, for a designated period of time. Warranties are usually provided for more expensive items and typically last for at least a year, depending upon the value of the item purchased. The consumer can also purchase extended warranties for an additional period of time. Such service guarantees are now a vital component of product marketing and it is unlikely that customers would ever buy major goods from a retailer without a warranty.

wealth the abundance of materials, money or property, which has to be understood by the marketer, particularly those targets who own most of it. Wealth and, importantly, perception of wealth, is a prime conditioner of behaviour. For example, if the population of the UK believe that their wealth is increasing because their property prices are rising, even although their liquid assets or their disposable income has not increased, they tend to consume more.

Weaver, Sylvester L. 'Pat' (1908–) NBC. A media visionary, Weaver initiated the 'magazine format' at NBC-TV, which altered TV's content and buying patterns. His 1949-56 tenure as president and chairman led to 'Today' and 'The Tonight Show' as well as heavily promoted, star-studded specials. His bold concept of selling time in a network-controlled magazine format to a variety of advertisers was unpopular with major agencies, which would rather create and control clients' programming. But the concept revolutionized the TV industry. After his CBS Radio, Young & Rubicam, American Tobacco and NBC-TV years, Weaver served as McCann-Erickson chairman and went on to head a pioneering subscription TV venture.

web browser a software application that allows for the browsing of the World Wide Web.

webcast an increasingly important technique of having a virtual meeting on the Internet. Participants log on to a site where they can view the presentation and listen to the speakers. Webcasts can include sound and images or both. Questions can be asked via a chat room to give a greater degree of interaction. Whilst the picture quality of the transmission remains lower than television broadcasting, the cost is also much lower and is accessible to anyone with access to the web. Webcasting also has the advantage of interaction, whereas broadcasting is a one-way communications medium.

web design the selection and coordination of available components to create the layout and structure of a Web page.

web directory an organized, categorized listing of websites. The terms 'web directory' and 'search engine' are often used interchangeably. Web directories are organized website listings put together by human reviewers, whereas search engine listings are put together by automated systems and lack a navigable structure. Much of the confusion stems from the various hybrid models that have developed over time, as search engines have incorporated directory features to assist with issues such as categorization and site quality. There are advantages and drawbacks to using a web directory as opposed to a search engine. One vehicle may be better suited to certain types of searches than the other. Directories place an emphasis on linking to site home pages and try to minimize deep linking. This makes directories more useful for finding sites instead of individual pages.

web ring a means for navigating a group of related websites primarily by going forward and backward.

website a location on the World Wide Web where specific information is grouped together in a collection of pages. There is a main page where the user will be able to click on different links to the remaining pages in the collection. The website is among the foremost new marketing instruments of the late 20th century. It has multiple possibilities that are only just being discovered and developed. Many have software to enable commercial transactions and credit authorization. Off-line advertising – such as posters – are intended to drive greater traffic to the website. It is now unusual for a commercial organization not to have a website. Major institutions and organizations – NASA, the Library of Congress, the British Monarchy, the FBI, the CIA, the Vatican, governments, charities, tourist organizations – all have websites. Many celebrities, such as actors, authors, musicians, and models, have their own personal websites.

website traffic the total amount of visitors that a website receives over a given time period. This metric was initially viewed as the most important way of determining the success of a particular website or e-commerce business. Currently, the measurement of success has shifted back to the more traditional one of profitability. Website traffic is only partly a determinant of profitability, but it is no longer a major independent metric. It is nowadays typically combined with a visitor conversion metric to determine actual sales.

website usability a measure of how effectively visitors are able to use a website. Usability is important in the marketing of the website and the services that it provides: 80% of website visitors abandon commercial websites before they make a purchase. Nielsen's Law of the Internet is that 'users spend most of their time on other people's websites'. It is vital in an age of low tolerance to delay and short attention spans to keep a website 'sticky', to encourage multiple 'click-through' and create high 'conversion rates'. Ease of use is a prerequisite to all of these.

wheel of retailing concept a concept of retailing devised by Philip Kotler which states that new types of retailers complete a full wheel: usually beginning as low-margin, low-price, low-status operations but later evolving into higher-priced, higher-service operations, eventually becoming like the conventional retailers they replaced.

white goods usually utility and kitchen goods such as washing machines, dishwashers, and refrigerators. Their name is taken from their white metallic casing covers.

wholesaler a merchant who sells large quantities for retail purposes only and does not sell to the general public. See also BUYER, BUSINESS-TO-BUSINESS MARKETING, DISTRIBUTION.

word of mouth the oldest and, some would argue, the most effective way of gaining awareness. It is simply when someone finds out about something – a product, an event, a service, a place, a work – through someone else. Word of mouth is an effective method of advertising since the recommendations are coming from someone familiar – possibly who has had good experiences – and therefore gains a greater element of trust. The origins of the phrase are certainly direct and verbal (hence the title), but nowadays word of mouth can also include e-mail, chat lines, text messages as well as the telephone. The Internet itself has been described as a continuous conversation. See also VIRAL MARKETING and PERMISSION MARKETING.

WORLD WIDE WEB

The Internet and the World Wide Web have revolutionized not only the computer and communications, but also marketing as a technique. It covers so many of the areas that marketing in practice covered in a physical media: a worldwide broadcasting capability, a mechanism for information dissemination, and a medium for collaboration and interaction between individuals and their computers globally.

Commercialization of the Internet was enabled by the creation of the World Wide Web by Tim Berners-Lee in CERN (Switzerland) in 1990. The early version of the World Wide Web included a basic browser, along with an information server and a library implementing the essential functions for developers to build their own software. This was released in 1991 to the high-energy physics community via the CERN program library, so that a whole range of universities and research laboratories could start to use it. A little later it was made generally available via the Internet, especially to the community of people working on hypertext systems. By the beginning of 1993 there were around 50 known information servers. At this stage, there were essentially only two kinds of browser. One was the original development version, very sophisticated but only available on NeXT machines. The other was the 'line-mode' browser, which was easy to instal and run on any platform but limited in power and user-friendliness. It was clear that the small team at CERN could not do all the work needed to develop the system further, so Tim Berners-Lee launched a plea via the Internet for other developers to join in. This led to creation of browsers. For example, early in 1993, the National Center for Supercomputing Applications (NCSA) at the University of Illinois released a first version of their Mosaic browser. The existence of reliable user-friendly browsers on these popular computers had an immediate impact on the spread of web to a global community. The rest, is recent history.

Tim Berners-Lee, inventor of the World Wide Web.

Wunderman, Lester (1920–)Wunderman. A major direct-marketing force during the last half of the 20th century, Wunderman was a link to the work of direct-marketing pioneers Victor Schwab, Harry Scherman and Maxwell Sackheim. Hired as a copywriter by Sackheim at Maxwell Sackheim & Co. in 1947, Wunderman blossomed as a marketing strategist. Recognizing that many 'mail order' accounts were ripe for growth through broader marketing efforts, he introduced his 'direct marketing' concept. He established Wunderman, Ricotta & Kline in 1958 (acquired by Young & Rubicam in 1973) and, with his vast multimedia agency, often co-branded, direct-selling 'breakthrough' campaigns, built Columbia Record Club and American Express' travel and entertainment credit card businesses.

Y

Yahoo a portal located at yahoo.com. Yahoo was one of the more successful pioneers of the initial period of the commercialized Internet.

yellow journalism the forerunner of what we know today as sensationalist journalism. Developed at the turn of the 20th century in the US, the phrase was originally used to describe the journalism of Joseph Pulitzer, but became synonymous with the newspapers of William Randolph Hearst. At this time, when newspapers were the main source of news in America, it was common practice for a newspaper to report the editor's interpretation of the news rather than objective facts. If the information reported was inaccurate or biased, the public had little means of verification. Newspapers wielded much political power and, in order to increase circulation, the publishers of these papers often exploited their powerful position by sponsoring a flamboyant approach to news reporting that became known as 'yellow journalism.' Hearst, for example, is often accused of having started the Spanish-American War of 1898 by inflaming opinion using this type of approach. See also HEARST.

yuppie (Young Urban Professional) a term used in the 1980s and 1990s to describe someone who had a good education and made a high income in a professional service organization and tended to live in a city. Yuppies were characterized by conspicuous consumption, unabashed materialism, the acquisition of wealth, a hunger for luxury goods and designer clothing. For many the Yuppie epitomized the changing values and economic climates of the 1980s and later became a much derided lifestyle.

zapping an Internet term for either deleting or getting rid of something.

zero-based budgeting a method of budgeting in which past sales and previous expenditure levels are ignored. The company formulates its profit goals, determines the actions that will be required to achieve its goals, and estimates the expenditures that will be necessary to carry out the actions.

zone pricing a term devised by Philp Kotler for a geographic pricing strategy in which the company sets up two or more zones; all customers within a zone pay the same total price, and this price is higher in the more distant zones.

SOME NOTABLE SLOGANS

SLOGANS PROMOTING PRODUCTS AND SERVICES

Access takes the waiting out of wanting
Access credit card, UK, c. 1973

Access – your flexible friend
Access credit card, UK, 1981

I like Aeroplane Jelly ... Aeroplane Jelly for me,
I like it for dinner, I like it for tea
Originally sung by five year old Joy King, it began in 1938 and was in use in the 1980s

That'll do nicely, Sir!
Television advertisement for American Express card, UK, late 1970s onwards

Don't leave home without it
American Express card, USA, 1981

Apple - The Power to be Your best
Apple Corporation, USA, 1986

You too can have a body like mine
Charles Atlas body-building courses

The greatest show on earth
Barnum and Bailey's circus, from 1881

Worth a guinea a box
Beechams pills, c.1940

That's a h**l of a way to run a railroad!
Slogan for the Boston and Maine Railroad, derived from a cartoon, c. 1932, showing two trains about to collide. A signalman comments: Tch-tch – what a way to run a railroad!

Bounty – The Taste of Paradise
Long-running slogan for Bounty chocolate bars

Alas! My poor brother
Caption to a picture of a sorrowful bull looking at a jar of Bovril meat extract, 1896

The two infallible powers. The Pope and Bovril
Bovril meat extract, late 1890s

I hear they want more
One apprehensive bull to another, 1903; Bovril meat extract

Bovril – prevents that sinking feeling
Bovril meat extract, 1920

Let the train take the strain
British Rail, 1970

Inter-City makes the going easy, and the coming back
British Rail, from 1972

This is the age of the train
British Rail, 1980

We're Getting There
British Rail, 1980's

It's good to talk
British Telecom, 1994

And all because the lady loves Milk Tray
Cadbury's Milk Tray chocolates, 1968 onwards

Everyone's a fruit and nut case
Cadbury's Fruit and Nut chocolate, 1964 onwards

Perfume worth 9 guineas an ounce
Camay soap, c.1956

You'll look a little lovelier each day
With fabulous pink Camay
Camay soap, c. 1960

Milk from contented cows
Carnation Milk, 1906

Is it true ... blondes have more fun?
Lady Clairol, c. 1965

It's the real thing
Coca-Cola, 1970

I'd like to buy the world a Coke
Coca-Cola, 1971

Things go better with Coke
Coca-Cola, 1963

Cool as a mountain stream
Consulate menthol cigarettes

If we don't have the lowest fare, we probably don't fly there
Continental Airlines, USA

Don't just book it – Thomas Cook it
Thomas Cook Travel Agents

Thank Crunchie it's Friday
Crunchie chocolate bars

Trust Dettol to protect your family's health
Dettol antiseptic/disinfectant, 1978

Kills all known germs
Domestos bleach, 1959

I'm only here for the beer
Double Diamond beer

Drinka Pinta Milka Day
British Milk Marketing Board, 1958

Go to work on an egg
British Egg Marketing Board

Happiness is egg-shaped
British Egg Marketing Board

You can rely on the lion
British Egg Marketing Board

The Esso sign means happy motoring
Advertising jingle for Esso, UK, 1950s

Put a tiger in your tank
Esso, USA, 1964

You only fit double glazing once, so fit the best
Everest Double Glazing, UK

Now hands that do dishes can be soft as your face
Jingle for Fairy washing up liquid

Say it with flowers
Advertisement for the Society of American florists, late 1920s

High o'er the fence leaps Sunny Jim
'Force' is the food that raises him
Force breakfast cereal, 1903

They're g-r-r-r-eat!
Long-running slogan for Kellogg's Frosties cereal

Desperation, Pacification, Expectation, Acclamation, Realization
Fry's Chocolate, UK, post First World War, on advertisements featuring the 'five boys'

The greatest motion picture ever made
Promotional slogan for the film Gone with the Wind, 1939

Guinness is good for you
Guinness, c.1930s

My goodness, my Guinness
Guinness, c.1930s

Pure Genius
Guinness, 1994

Don't be vague – ask for Haig
Haig whisky, c. 1936

Happiness is a cigar called Hamlet
Hamlet cigars, UK

Does she ... or doesn't she?
Harmony hairspray 1980s

If you want to get ahead, get a hat
UK Hat Council, 1965

Heineken refreshes the parts other beers cannot reach
Heineken lager, 1975 onwards

Beanz means Heinz
Heinz baked beans

Make today a Heinz Souperday
Heinz soups, 1968

Let Hertz put *you* in the driver's seat
Hertz car rental, 1962

It beats as it sweeps as it cleans
Advertising slogan for Hoover vacuum cleaners, 1919

Horlicks guards against night starvation
Horlicks milk drink

It's fingerlickin' good
Kentucky Fried Chicken Co., USA 1950s

You press the button, and we'll do the rest
Kodak cameras and film

Never knowingly undersold
John Lewis stores, c. 1920

The mint with the hole
Life-Savers, USA, 1920; Rowntree's Polo mints, U.K. from 1947

Lucozade refreshes you through the ups and downs of the day
Beecham Foods c.1978

Nine out of ten screen stars use Lux toilet soap
Lux soap, USA, late 1920s

Out of the strong came forth sweetness
Lyle's Golden Syrup; from the Bible, Judges 14:14

Test drive a Mackintosh
Apple Corporation, USA, 1984

Chocolates with the less fattening centres
Maltesers chocolates, UK, 1965

A Mars a day helps you work, rest and play
Mars bars, from 1960

The right one
Martini, UK, 1970

Any time, any place, anywhere
Martini, UK, 1970s

For Mash Get Smash
Smash instant mashed potato

Good to the last drop
Remark made by Theodore Roosevelt, 1907, about Maxwell House coffee; later used as an advertising slogan

Murray Mints! Murray Mints!
Too-good-to-hurry-Mints
Advertising jingle for Murray Mints, UK from late 1950s

Naughty but nice
Slogan promoting the sale of cream cakes

All human life is there
Slogan promoting the News of the World

Mean! Moody! Magnificent!
Promotional slogan for the film The Outlaw, 1943

We are the Ovaltineys
Happy girls and boys
Advertisement for Ovaltine

Oxo is British – Made in Britain – By a British Company – with British Capital and British Labour
Early advertising slogan for Oxo, UK

Oxo gives a meal man-appeal
Oxo, 1958

Ask the man who owns one
Packard, USA, 1902

Keep that schoolgirl complexion
Palmolive soap, 1917

Since when I have used no other
Pears' Soap, 1884

He won't be happy till he gets it
Pears' Soap

Top breeders recommend it
Pedigree Chum dog food, UK 1964

The tea you can really taste
Brooke Bond PG Tips

P-p-p-pick up a Penguin
Penguin chocolate biscuits

You'll wonder where the yellow went
When you brush your teeth with Pepsodent
Advertising jingle for Pepsodent toothpaste, USA, 1950s

Persil washes whiter – and it shows
Long-running Persil soap powder slogan

Everything you hear is true
Pioneer hi-fi equipment, 1970s

Player's please
John Player and Sons cigarettes

What is home without Plumtree's Potted Meat? Incompleat [sic]
Early 1900s

Someone, somewhere wants a letter from you
Post Office campaign, 1960s

Snap! Crackle! Pop!
Kellogg's Rice Crispies, USA, c.1928

It's a lot less bovver with a hover
Qualcast Lawnmowers, UK

Don't forget the fruit gums, Mum
Rowntree's Fruit Gums, 1958 onwards

Have a break, have a Kit-Kat
Rowntree's Kit-Kat chocolate bars, from c. 1955

They laughed when I sat down at the piano. But when I started to play!
Advertisement for US School of Music, 1920s

Sch...you know who
Schweppes mineral drinks, 1960s

Some day all watches will be made this way
Slogan used by Seiko for its first quartz watches, late 1960s

Man invented time – Seiko perfected it
Seiko watches, 1980s

Complete satisfaction or your money cheerfully refunded
Selfridge's department store

The customer is always right
Selfridge's department store

You can be sure of Shell
Shell UK, c. 1931

Senior Service satisfy
Senior Service cigarettes

Every picture tells a story
Advertisement for Sloane's Backache and Kidney Pills, showing someone bending over in pain

Can *you* tell Stork from butter?
Stork margarine

You're never alone with a Strand
Strand cigarettes

Tell 'em about the honey, Mummy
Kellogg's Sugar Puffs

Tetley make tea-bags make tea
Tetley's tea

Top people take the Times
Slogan promoting The Times newspaper, 1957

Which twin has the Toni?
Toni home perms, USA, 1951

Treats. Melt in your mouth, not in your hand
Treats chocolates

Tunes help you breathe more easily
Tunes throat lozenges

Virginia is for lovers
Tourist board slogan, Virginia, USA

You've come a long way baby
Virginia Slims cigarettes

Think small
Volkswagen, USA, from c. 1959

Stop me and buy one
Wall's ice-cream, 1922

They came as a boon and a blessing to men,
The Pickwick, the Owl, and the Waverley Pen
Waverley pens

Where's the beef?
Wendy's Hamburgers

Breakfast of champions
Wheaties cereal, USA, 1950

Eight out of ten cats prefer Whiskas
Whiskas catfood, 1970s

We're with the Woolwich
Woolwich Equitable Building Society, UK, from late 1970s

Nothing over sixpence
Woolworth stores, UK, from 1909

Let your fingers do the walking
Yellow Pages, from American Telephone and Telegraph Company, 1960s

SLOGANS PROMOTING POLITICAL PARTIES AND SOCIAL CHANGE

One man, one vote
Campaign run by Major John Cartwright (1740-1824) against plural voting

No taxation without representation
In use before the American War of Independence, 1775-1783

Liberté! Egalité! Fraternité!
Liberty! Equality! Brotherhood!
French Revolution, 1793

Ulster will fight, and Ulster will be right
Ulster Volunteers opposed to Irish Home Rule, 1913–1914, from a letter by Lord Randolph Churchill, 1886

Votes for Women
Suffragette Movement, 1905, in Emmeline Pankhurst, My Own Story (1914)

Are we downhearted? No!
World War I, based on remark of Joseph Chamberlain

Your King and Country need you
World War I

Kraft durch Freude
Strength through joy
German Labour Front, 1933

Ein Reich, Ein Volk, Ein Führer
One realm, one people, one leader
Nazi Party, 1934

Dig for victory
Ministry of Agriculture, 1939

Is your journey really necessary?
World War II

Careless talk costs lives
British Ministry of Information, World War II

A bayonet is a weapon with a worker at each end
Pacifist movement, 1940

Coughs and sneezes spread diseases
Ministry of Health, c. 1942

No names, no pack drill
Used frequently in both World Wars

With thumb in bum and mind in neutral
US Navy catchphrase, 1940s

Fair shares for all
Labour Party; devised by Douglas Jay, 1946

The family that prays together stays together
Devised by Al Scalpone for the Roman Catholic Family Rosary Crusade, 1947

I like Ike
US button badge, first used in 1947, to support Eisenhower

Keep Britain tidy
British government, 1950s

Ban the bomb
Current from 1953 onwards

Better red than dead
British nuclear disarmament movement; 'Better dead than red' was also in common use

Life's better with the Conservatives
Conservative Party, 1959

Make love, not war
Common in the mid-1960s

Flower Power
Hippy slogan, 1960s

Let's go with Labour
Labour Party, 1964

In your heart you know he's right
Goldwater Presidential campaign, 1964

Don't ask a man to drink and drive
Road safety campaign, 1964

Thirteen Wasted Years
Unofficial Labour Party slogan prior to 1964 General Election

Prosperity With a Purpose
Conservative Party, 1964

Let's Go With Labour For The New Britain
Labour Party, 1964

Think For Yourself – Vote Liberal
Liberal Party, 1964

Black is beautiful
US civil rights movement, 1966

I'm backing Britain
Slogan, 1968; campaign to support UK economy after devaluation of sterling

Would you buy a used car from this man?
Campaign slogan directed against Richard Nixon, 1968

Power to the People
Black Panther movement, 1969

Out of the closets and into the streets
Gay Liberation movement, USA c. 1969

Burn Your Bra
Attributed, erroneously, to feminist movement, USA, 1970s

It smells like you're kissing an old ashtray
Health Education Council anti-smoking campaign, c. 1970

Of the Conservatives
Yesterday's men (they failed before!)
Labour party, 1970

What a Life!
Liberal Party, 1970

A Better Tomorrow
Conservative Party, 1970

Now Britain's Strong – Let's Make It Great To Live In
Labour Party, 1970

Clunk, Click, every trip
Road safety campaign promoting the use of seat belts, 1971

Dull it isn't
Recruiting advertisement for the Metropolitan Police, 1972

England Expects – Scotland's Oil
Scottish National Party, 1973

Let Us Work Together
Labour Party, 1974

Change the Face of Britain
Liberal Party election manifesto, 1974

Putting Britain First
Conservative Party, 1974

Scotland a Nation Once Again
Scottish National Party, 1977

Labour isn't working
Conservative Party, 1978

Lavorare meno – Lavorare tutti
Work less – work for everybody
From a collection of slogans used by students and workers during the 70s demonstrations

Be all you can be
Scottish Health Education Council, 1980s

Choose Life, Not Drugs
Scottish Health Education Council, 1980s

Britain is Great Again, Don't Let Labour Wreck It
Conservative Party, 1987

Don't Die of Ignorance
Department of Health AIDS campaign, 1987

Meet the Challenge, Make the Change
Labour Party, 1989

Green Policies in a Nutshell
Green Party, 1992

Independence in Europe: Make It Happen Now
Scottish National Party, 1992

Changing Britain for Good
Liberal Democrat Party, 1992

It's Time to Get Britain Working Again
Labour Party, 1992

The Best Future for Britain
Conservative Party, 1992

Good Health is Good Business
Health and Safety Executive, 1993